Capital Failure

Capital Failure

Rebuilding Trust in Financial Services

Edited by Nicholas Morris and David Vines

OXFORD
UNIVERSITY PRESS

OXFORD

UNIVERSITY PRESS

Great Clarendon Street, Oxford, OX2 6DP,
United Kingdom

Oxford University Press is a department of the University of Oxford.
It furthers the University's objective of excellence in research, scholarship,
and education by publishing worldwide. Oxford is a registered trade mark of
Oxford University Press in the UK and in certain other countries

First published 2014
First published in paperback 2016

Published in the United States of America by Oxford University Press
198 Madison Avenue, New York, NY 10016, United States of America

British Library Cataloguing in Publication Data

Data available

Library of Congress Cataloging in Publication Data

Data available

ISBN 978–0–19–871222–0 (Hbk.)
ISBN 978–0–19–878808–9 (Pbk.)

Foreword

Public trust in financial services matters. Without it, families are disinclined to put aside savings to meet their long-term needs for fear of being ripped off; entrepreneurs are less likely to take the financial risks that are necessary to create wealth and jobs; businesses think twice before investing in plant and equipment to meet future demand. For the UK economy, where financial services are one of the country's few areas of global competitive advantage, a loss of reputation and trust must be especially damaging.

The UK banking sector has suffered in recent years what the Parliamentary Commission on Banking Standards has described as 'a collapse of trust on an industrial scale'. Fixing the consequences is a matter of national importance. And this timely book puts forward a number of ideas about how to go about the task. Changes in regulation, it argues, will not be enough to win back public confidence. Other mechanisms will be necessary to secure more trustworthy behaviour both by institutions and by individuals in the financial services sector.

It's true that banking collapses such as the one experienced in recent years always shake the public's confidence in anything to do with finance. After such a shock, as J. K. Galbraith wrote in *The Great Crash 1929*, 'Money is handled with a narrow, suspicious eye. The man who handles it is assumed to be dishonest until he proves himself otherwise. Audits are penetrating and meticulous. Commercial morality is enormously improved.'

But even by past standards, the collapse in public confidence in finance since the bank failures of 2007–8 has been spectacular. There are obvious reasons. The banking crisis was the most serious of its kind in the UK for a century or more, bringing with it the country's first public bank run for 150 years. Banks have been found guilty of mis-selling a variety of financial products to the public, and in very large numbers. Bankers have received huge rewards, which too often appeared unrelated to the value of the work done and which were not surrendered when the collapse came: they had effectively privatised their profits and socialised their losses, as the government stepped in to halt the failures. Taxpayers, who suffered the economic consequences of a credit collapse, were outraged by the continued payment of large bonuses, and felt that too few of those responsible for what happened had been held to account in an appropriate manner.

And there has seemed no end to the stories of inexcusable behaviour. News in 2012 of the systematic abuse of interest rate instruments—the Libor scandal—was for many people the last straw. Bankers could no longer argue, in words that came to haunt Bob Diamond (then chief executive of Barclays), that the time for 'remorse' was over. From then on, they were in the dock.

They were not alone. It's true that other financial service sectors came through the crisis more or less unscathed. But it is not just the banks that have been mis-selling financial products in recent years: pension providers, life insurers, and others have been tarred with the same brush, and have played a part in undermining public trust.

A common theme is the sense that too many companies in the financial services sector gradually lost their sense of business purpose in the decades leading up to the crash. The long-term interests of their customers seemed to give way to those of their shareholders—or at least to those of them who insisted on quarter after quarter of rising earnings per share. Retail bank branches were set aggressive sales targets; credit decisions were made by computers; people who had presented themselves as trusted financial advisors turned out to be nothing more than high-pressure salesmen.

In his review of Barclays' business practices, Sir Anthony Salz wrote—in words that could apply to other financial service businesses—that 'the overriding purpose of Barclays in the lead-up to the crisis was expressed in terms of increases in revenues and profits', and the result was a culture that favoured transactions over relationships, and the short term over sustainability. It also tended to depersonalise links with customers and with society more broadly.

Banks came to express their business objectives in a single number—the targeted return on equity, invariably set at a level that could only be achieved by high leverage, high risk, and—too often—aggressive treatment of their customers.

Then came the collapse—followed by necessary changes at the top and widespread restructuring of many big financial firms, together with radical changes in regulation both at a national and international level. But two points are already clear. One is that trust can only be restored when it has been earned—and that is going to take years. Business cultures take a long time both to develop and to change: a whole generation of employees has grown accustomed to business practices that now seem unacceptable.

The second point is that although regulation is a necessary part of the rebuilding process, it is by no means sufficient in itself. Reliance on ever more complex rulebooks and larger compliance departments can come at the expense of personal responsibility and judgement. After a time, the question can all too easily become whether a proposed action is legal, rather than whether it is the right thing to do and in the client's best interests. You don't earn trust simply by following the rules.

So what other steps will be necessary to restore confidence in the financial services sector over the long term? Part of the answer lies in the way that firms are led. Business leaders in the financial services sector will have to show both by their own actions and by the way they recruit, promote, and reward their employees that their firms' long-term goals are absolutely aligned with their customers' interests.

But again, this may not be enough to change behaviour across an industry that has hundreds of thousands of employees, engaged in very different types of activity and dealing in a wide range of often complex products.

A supermarket knows that a customer will have an immediate view on the quality of a purchase, and will shop elsewhere if not satisfied. A financial service provider is usually not dealing with repeat customers in the same way, and the shortcomings of a product may not become apparent for years. Because there are real asymmetries of information between the seller and the buyer, the market discipline in financial services is much less intense than it is in the supermarket sector.

Moreover, these are often businesses where employees have more loyalty to the team that they are working with than to the institution as a whole, and may well move as a group from one firm to another. This makes it difficult to persuade people to change their behaviour by arguing 'that's not the way we do business round here'. In the run-up to the crash, as one witness told the Banking Commission, 'The ideas of loyalty and long-term service to one employer and its culture were discarded. Teams of specialists were bought and sold like slaves or football stars'.

So if improved regulation and better leadership are not enough to restore public trust in financial services, what else might make a difference?

That is the question posed in this book, which focuses on other ways of securing more trustworthy behaviour in the financial services sector. Building on the recommendations of the Banking Commission, it explores a number of relevant ideas: how to instil a sense of professional responsibility in a sector which sometimes seems to have lost its moral compass; how to define obligations both at an institutional and a personal level; how to hold people to account in an appropriate manner. And it underscores the need for reforms in governance and legal and regulatory arrangements to help address these issues.

One question posed both by the book and by the Banking Commission is about whether the competence and behaviour of individuals working within the system could be influenced by standard-setting professional bodies of one kind or another. The Commission spent some time debating whether banking could indeed be described as a profession, and concluded that compared with past times 'Banking now encompasses a much wider range of activities, has fewer features of a professional identity, and lacks a credible set of professional bodies.' But it also agreed that an effort to raise levels of competence and behaviour across the industry would be a worthwhile part of the effort to restore public trust.

In response, a number of banks have asked me to design a new institution to help achieve these goals. It will be a voluntary body with no statutory powers, and it will aim to cover all institutions doing banking in the UK. Although it will be funded by the banks, its governance structure must ensure its independence of them, and it will not be an advocate for the industry.

There are obvious challenges. One is the risk of double jeopardy—that wrongdoers could find themselves in trouble both with a professional body and with the statutory regulator. Unlike the General Medical Council, which can strike off misbehaving doctors, a voluntary body for bankers would not be able to discipline individuals by removing their licence to operate. Another issue is the sheer range of different activities that are undertaken by banks. It would be hard to come up with a set of relevant requirements that applied to everyone.

But efforts to raise standards across the sector are worth making. Only a minority of the million or more people who work in financial services around the UK were involved in the activities that have brought it into disrepute. The great majority have a strong interest in achieving a status that would be recognised by their clients and in their community, and would help to frame their business conduct. Financial services may not be a profession, but participants need to be professional.

What is required is a three-pronged programme of change that will over time lead to a more robust and resilient system, and one that places the needs of the client firmly at its heart.

The first stems from the kind of leadership that by its every action makes it plain that the priorities of the business are clear, consistent, and aligned with its values.

Leadership must set a clear and measurable purpose for the business, over and above the need to increase quarterly earnings and to grow bigger. Management must make it clear to all employees what they are in business to achieve, and must push to one side any obstacles that might get in the way of this objective.

The second prong is an approach to compliance that again is clear and consistent, and one in which it is not acceptable to agree to an action just because it is legal. It must also leave space within defined limits for individual employees to exercise responsible judgement, and when appropriate to turn away from business that cannot be reconciled with the firm's stated values.

And finally, there are the ideas put forward in this book: the need to develop a culture where individual employees can take a professional pride both in their work and in the company that they work for, and are prepared and empowered to place that pride above other considerations. Achieving that will take training and different financial incentives. People will have to be paid for the way they do business, and not just for the revenues that they generate.

All of this is going to take time. But the crisis of the past few years presents both the opportunity and the requirement for change. A healthy economy requires a trusted financial services sector, and this book helps to set out the pathway.

Richard Lambert*

---

* Sir Richard Lambert served as editor of the Financial Times from 1991 to 2001, was a member of the Monetary Policy Committee of the Bank of England from 2003 to 2006, and Director General of the CBI from 2006 to 2011. In September 2013 he was asked asked to create an independent body to promote high standards of competence and behaviour across the UK banking industry, after the series of scandals that had rocked the industry.

Preface

In the aftermath of the Global Financial Crisis, many books sought to describe and understand how the 'Great Moderation' could have been derailed so suddenly and so badly. These books discussed important technical questions about finance, including the search for yield, leverage, the interconnectedness between financial institutions. But at the same time many people said something rather different: "we don't seem to be able to trust anyone any more", and "there is a sense of moral outrage about what has happened".

It appeared important to understand the way in which the financial system depends on trust, and on the ethical principles which underpin that trust. It became clear that the standard tools of economic analysis—based on an assumption that all behaviour is selfish—are insufficient to evaluate these crucial questions. What we needed was an interdisciplinary approach, providing insights from philosophy, law, and history, as well as inputs from practitioners in the industry. It seems that these insights are necessary, if the practical reforms in finance are to succeed. Otherwise selfish individuals are likely to arbitrage away any reforms which are introduced.

Our wish for such this interdisciplinary approach coincided with the early development of the Balliol Interdisciplinary Institute (BII), the brainchild of Andrew Graham, then Master of Balliol. We are glad to acknowledge both the support of Andrew and of the BII itself. Under the auspices of the BII we held several series of seminars in Oxford, and would like to express our gratitude to those who talked at these seminars, and those who attended them and provided important insights. In addition to the authors of this book we would particularly like to thank Xuehua Bai, Wilfred Beckerman, Paul Davies (a different Paul Davies from the one who is an author), John Franks, Les Hannah, Bob May, Nick Monck, Jon Moynihan, Jaya Patten, and John Vickers.

Finally, we would like to thank Andrew Schuller for encouragement and advice on the development of the book structure, and Sue Jaffer and Natalie Gold for continuous support throughout the project.

Nicholas Morris
David Vines
September 2013

Contents

Contents

List of Figures and Tables

Figures

Table

Notes on Contributors

John Armour is the Hogan Lovells Professor of Law and Finance at Oxford University. He was previously a University Senior Lecturer in Law and Fellow of Trinity Hall at Cambridge University. John studied law (MA, BCL) at the University of Oxford before completing his LLM at Yale Law School and taking up his first post at the University of Nottingham. He has held visiting posts at various institutions including the University of Bologna, Columbia Law School, the University of Frankfurt, the Max Planck Institute for Comparative Private Law, Hamburg, the University of Pennsylvania Law School and the University of Western Ontario. John has published widely in the fields of company law, corporate finance, and corporate insolvency. His main research interest lies in the integration of legal and economic analysis, with particular emphasis on the impact on the real economy of changes in the law governing company law, corporate insolvency, and financial regulation. He has been involved in policy-related projects commissioned by the Department of Trade and Industry, the Financial Services Authority, the Insolvency Service, and the Jersey Economic Development Department.

Dan Awrey is an Associate Professor of Law and Finance at Oxford University, where he is also a Fellow of Linacre College. Before entering academia, Dan served as legal counsel to a global investment management firm and, prior to that, as an associate practising corporate finance and securities law with a major Canadian law firm. Dan's teaching and research interests reside primarily in the area of financial regulation and, more specifically, the financial markets, institutions, and instruments which together comprise the shadow banking system. He holds degrees from Queen's University (BA, LLB), the University of Toronto (LLM), and Oxford University (DPhil).

Justin O'Brien is an Australian Research Council Future Fellow and Professor of Law and Director of the Centre for Law, Markets, and Regulation at the University of New South Wales. He has a PhD, MPhil, and MA from Queen's University, Belfast, and a BA (Hons) from the University of Newcastle, UK. Professor O'Brien has held appointments at Queen's University, Belfast, Charles Sturt University, and Queensland University of Technology. He has been affiliated to the Center for the Study of Law and Society at the University of California, Berkeley and the University of Glasgow, where he was Visiting Professor of Financial Regulation and Policy. From 2009–12 he was Adjunct Professor at the Australian National University division of the Centre for Applied Philosophy and Public Ethics. He is currently a Visiting Network Fellow at the Edmond J. Safra Center of Ethics at Harvard University and a Visiting Professor at University College, Dublin. Professor O'Brien is a specialist in the dynamics of financial regulation, with particular reference to capital market governance. He has written extensively on the intersection between regulatory form and ethical considerations.

Boudewijn de Bruin is Professor of Financial Ethics at the University of Groningen, the Netherlands. He studied musical composition at the conservatoire at Enschede for a year, then mathematics and philosophy at Amsterdam, Berkeley, and Harvard. He was awarded a PhD by the Institute for Logic, Language, and Computation (Amsterdam) for a thesis on game theory and epistemic logic, which was also awarded a prize by Praemium Erasmianum. De Bruin has published widely in journals such as *Law and Philosophy, Journal of Political Philosophy, Journal of Business Ethics*, and *Business and Professional Ethics Journal*, and is the author of *Explaining Games: The Epistemic Programme in Game Theory* (Springer, 2010) and *a book on ethics in finance forthcoming from* (Cambridge University Press in 2014. De Bruin directs a large collaborative research programme on Trusting Banks with Cambridge University and several international partners from the banking industry. He has been a consultant to financial services firms, including Achmea, Atradius, and ING Group, as well as the Netherlands Institute of Chartered Accountants, and has taught in numerous executive education programmes.

Richard Davies is Britain Economics Editor at *The Economist*. Before journalism he worked at the Bank of England, the UK Competition Commission, and in private-sector consultancy. While at the Bank of England he was a lead author of the Financial Stability Report, covering the stability of the UK banking sector. His published economic research is on financial economics ranging from economic history to contemporary empirical studies. Richard studied economics at Brasenose College, Oxford and the London School of Economics; he previously held an economics lectureship at Lincoln College.

Joshua Getzler is a Professor of Law and Legal History at Oxford University. His first degrees in law and history were taken at the Australian National University in Canberra, and his doctorate in Oxford, as a member of Balliol and Nuffield Colleges. He has taught and researched at the Australian National University, the Hebrew University, Tel Aviv University, the University of Chicago, and most recently at the University of Pennsylvania as Bok Visiting International Professor of Law in 2012. He is a Conjoint Professor of Law at the University of New South Wales. Joshua's legal research is on the duties of investment agents in financial markets, on the legal and economic structure of debt and equity, on the tortious and contractual liability of entities, and on theories of co-ownership and fiduciary duty. In his historical research he works on the relationships of public finance and private banking and investment, and the evolution of property, trust, corporate and charitable forms, chiefly in the eighteenth and early nineteenth centuries.

Natalie Gold is a Senior Research Fellow at Kings College London. She studied philosophy, politics, and economics and has an MPhil and a DPhil in Economics from the University of Oxford. After postdoctoral fellowships at the University of Konstanz and Duke University, she was appointed as Lecturer in Mind, Reason, and Decision in the Philosophy Department at the University of Edinburgh. She moved to King's College London with a European Research Council Starting Grant, for the project 'Self-Control and the Person: An Interdisciplinary Account'. Her research is on behavioural decision making and moral psychology. She has worked on topics including framing, moral judgements and decisions, cooperation and coordination, and self-control.

Jeffrey N. Gordon is Richard Paul Richman Professor of Law, Co-Director of the Richman Center for Business, Law, and Public Policy, and Co-Director of the Ira M. Millstein Center for Global Markets and Corporate Ownership. Professor Gordon teaches and writes extensively on corporate governance, mergers and acquisitions, comparative corporate governance, and, more recently, the regulation of finance institutions. He graduated from Yale and Harvard Law School, clerked for a federal appeals court judge, practised at a New York law firm, and worked in the General Counsel's office of the US Treasury. He began his academic career at NYU in 1982 and moved to Columbia in 1988. While at the Treasury, he worked on the Chrysler Corporation loan guarantee programme and financial regulation.

Sue Jaffer is an economic consultant who has worked extensively in the areas of utility and infrastructure regulation and investment planning, health, and finance. Sue has a BCom (Hons) and an MA in Economics from the University of Melbourne. Sue worked at the Institute for Fiscal Studies before moving into consulting work with NERA and London Economics and subsequently with Tasman Economics and ACIL Allen. Sue has advised governments, aid agencies, regulators, and utility businesses across a range of sectors, in the UK, Australia, and South East Asia.

David Kershaw is a Professor of Law at the London School of Economics. He joined the LSE in 2006. Before joining the LSE he was a Lecturer in Law at the University of Warwick from 2003–6. He is admitted to the New York Bar and is a qualified UK solicitor. Prior to his academic career, he qualified as a Solicitor at Herbert Smith, London and practised corporate law in the Mergers & Acquisitions Group of Shearman & Sterling in New York and London. He holds an LLM and a doctorate from the Harvard Law School and an LLB from the University of Warwick. He has published widely in the fields of corporate law, takeover law, and accounting regulation. His most recent book, *Company Law in Context*, was published by Oxford University Press in 2012.

Susana Knaudt is a financial supervision and regulation practitioner. She was involved in financial sector reform in Bolivia and worked at the World Bank on the financial sector in Central Asia and Latin America. Susana has worked as an instructor for banking supervisors in developing countries. She holds a BSc in Economics from the London School of Economics and an MPP from Harvard University.

Seumas Miller is a Professorial Research Fellow at the Centre for Applied Philosophy and Public Ethics (an Australian Research Council Special Research Centre) at

Charles Sturt University (Canberra) and the 3TU Centre for Ethics and Technology at Delft University of Technology (The Hague). He is the Foundation Director of the Centre for Applied Philosophy and Public Ethics, and was Head of Humanities and Social Sciences at Charles Sturt University from 1994 to 1999. He is the author of *Investigative Ethics* (with I. Gordon) (Blackwell, 2014), *Moral Foundations of Social Institutions* (Cambridge University Press, 2010), *Corruption and Anti-Corruption* (with P. Roberts and E. Spence) (Prentice Hall, 2005), and *Social Action* (Cambridge University Press, 2001).

Nicholas Morris is Academic Visitor and Senior Research Associate at Balliol College, Oxford. He is an economist with thirty-five years of wide-ranging experience: in the finance, water, energy, transport, telecoms, and health sectors; in infrastructure provision; and in the design of regulatory structures. He was a co-founder and then Chief Executive of London Economics for a period of fourteen years, and, prior to that, was Deputy Director of the Institute for Fiscal Studies. Nicholas has an MA in Engineering and Economics and an MPhil in Economics from Balliol College, Oxford. He has been a visiting Professor of City University, a Governor of the charity Research into Ageing, and a Fellow of Melbourne University, and is a Guest Professor at the China Executive Leadership Academy, Pudong. In the 1980s Nicholas was involved in UK privatisation and the establishment of utility regulation; in the 1990s he worked on European, emerging, and developing-country issues related to the establishment of new markets and regulatory systems. During the last fifteen years he has worked extensively in Australia, South East Asia, and China, advising governments, regulators, and companies. He is currently advising the Indonesian government on infrastructure development.

Onora O'Neill combines writing on political philosophy and ethics with a range of public activities. She comes from Northern Ireland and has worked mainly in Britain and the US. She was Principal of Newnham College, Cambridge from 1992–2006, President of the British Academy from 2005–9, chaired the Nuffield Foundation from 1998–2010, has been a crossbench member of the House of Lords since 2000 (Baroness O'Neill of Bengarve). She currently chairs the UK's Equality and Human Rights Commission and is on the board of the Medical Research Council. She lectures and writes on justice and ethics, accountability and trust, justice and borders, as well as on the future of universities, the quality of legislation, and the ethics of communication, including media ethics.

Thomas Noe is the Ernest Butten Professor of Management Studies at the Saïd Business School. Prior to joining the Saïd Business School, Thomas held the A. B. Freeman Chair in Finance at Tulane University. He is a professorial fellow at Balliol College, and a research associate at the Oxford-Man Institute and the Centre for Corporate Reputation at Oxford University, and the European Institute for Corporate Governance. He is an expert on corporate finance and corporate governance, and his research appears in journals such as the *American Economic Review, Journal of Finance, Journal of Financial Economics, Review of Economic Studies*, and *Review of Financial Studies*. Currently, he is a co-editor of the *Journal of Economics and Management*

Strategy. He has served on numerous panels, programme committees, and editorial boards, including the board of the *Review of Financial Studies*. He has visited academic and research institutions on five continents, including the Federal Reserve Bank, Hong Kong University of Science and Technology, Massachusetts Institute of Technology, University of Auckland, Universidad de Chile, Universidad los Andes, and the University of Queensland.

Avner Offer is Chichele Professor Emeritus of Economic History and a Fellow of All Souls College at the University of Oxford. He has worked on land tenure, the economics of war, consumption and well-being, myopia and obesity. He is currently investigating the Nobel Prize in Economics as part of a study of the transition from social democracy to market liberalism.

Edward Sawbridge is a finance industry practitioner. He holds an MA in Literae Humaniores from Balliol College, Oxford. He is a Fellow of the Institute of Chartered Accountants in England and Wales, and the Royal Society of Arts. Edward worked for over thirty years mostly for American and French investment banks in the City of London.

David Vines is a Professor of Economics and a Fellow of Balliol College, at Oxford University. He obtained a BA in Economics from Melbourne University, and an MA and PhD in Economics from the University of Cambridge. David's research is on international macroeconomics and on global governance. His early work was with James Meade in Cambridge on the construction of inflation-targeting regimes. Between 1994 and 2000 he was the Director of an ESRC Research Programme on Global Economic Institutions, and from 2008 to 2012 he was the Research Director of a European Union Framework Seven Research Programme, PEGGED, on the Politics and Economics of Global Governance: the European Dimension. He is currently working on international cooperation on macroeconomic policies, designed to ensure that the recovery from the global financial crisis is sustained. Fifteen years ago he organized an interdisciplinary seminar on integrity with the philosopher Alan Montefiore, the proceedings of which were published as A. Montefiore and D. Vines, *Integrity in the Public and the Private Domains* (Routledge, 1999).

H. Peyton Young is the James Meade Professor of Economics at Nuffield College, Oxford University, and a James Martin Fellow of the Institute for New Economic Thinking at the Oxford Martin School. He is also a Research Principal at the Office of Financial Research, United States Department of the Treasury. He is a Fellow of the British Academy and of the Econometric Society, and is Past President of the Game Theory Society. He was previously the Scott and Barbara Black Professor of Economics at Johns Hopkins University, and a Senior Fellow and Co-Director of the Center on Social and Economic Dynamics at the Brookings Institution. Peyton holds a PhD in mathematics from the University of Michigan. He has written widely on cooperative and non-cooperative game theory, the evolution of social norms, the diffusion of innovations, and most recently the application of game-theoretic ideas to finance.

Part I
What Went Wrong?

1

Why Trustworthiness Is Important

*Sue Jaffer, Nicholas Morris, and David Vines**

1.1 Beyond Self-Interest: The Restoration of Trustworthiness

Until the recent deregulation of the financial services industry, those who worked in finance were guided by a sense of duty. They had a fiduciary relationship with their clients which brought with it an expectation that they would put their clients' interests first. But in the past thirty years this obligation has been superseded by a quest for sales and the pursuit of high personal pay-offs. Many of those working in finance turned from caring about the interests of their clients to single-minded pursuit of their own interests. This has led to a general breakdown of trust within the financial system. It is easy to exaggerate the degree to which financial sector employees ever really subscribed to an ideal of fiduciary duty. But such an ideal did exist.

This book focuses on methods of restoring a sense of obligation to others as a means of rebuilding trustworthiness in the financial services industry. The authors do not see trustworthiness as likely to re-emerge in a world where those in finance act in a selfish manner. There is, however, a standard view that trust can emerge even with selfish behaviour. Under that account, trust develops as a result of repeated interactions over time; the desire for future profitable trades can create a constraint on cheating even amongst those who are selfish. But as Adam Smith made clear in his *Theory of Moral Sentiments*, this repeated-games idea leads to a shallow and unreliable form of trust, compared to the form which emerges from a sense of obligation to others. The authors of this book see a need for a stronger form of trust in

* We are grateful to Natalie Gold, Avner Offer, and Onora O'Neill for many helpful comments on this chapter, and also to two anonymous reviewers for a large number of valuable suggestions.

financial services, built on a sense of obligation to clients, similar to what was once present.

The authors also see increased professionalism as a way of increasing trustworthiness. A professional is someone who *professes*, that is, someone who affirms allegiance to a set of beliefs. It is essential that financial institutions, and those who work within them, move away from the 'greed is good' philosophy that has underpinned much of the financial industry since the time of deregulation. Instead the industry needs to move towards norms of behaviour which include a sense of obligation to clients and a greater sense of professionalism.

Many have already called for a restoration of trust in the financial system,[1] and have argued that this would require a change in the obligations perceived by the industry and in the norms of behaviour within the industry. Recently Mark Carney, the incoming Governor of the Bank of England, discussed the 'fundamental loss of trust' which has occurred in the global banking system (Carney 2013), describing how big banks lost their way when they became more concerned about generating profits than with helping their clients. The Archbishop of Canterbury, Justin Welby, has called for the banking system to return to 'a broad sense of promoting the wellbeing' of those whom it serves, and argued for what he calls a change in culture (Welby 2013). Yet neither Carney nor Welby, nor others, describe in any detail how the required changes could be brought about. The authors of this book provide a number of proposals as to what might be done.

The authors form an interdisciplinary group: philosophers, historians, lawyers, economists, and financial practitioners. Our aim is to provide a historical account of why trust broke down and then to provide a philosophically engaged account of what a restoration of trustworthiness would require. Building on this, we aim to illustrate the kinds of actions which would be necessary for the rebuilding of trust.

This introductory chapter lays out the argument of the book and shows how the chapters contribute to this argument. First, we describe why trust is needed in finance. Second, we set out what went wrong in the financial services industry. Much has been written on the causes of the financial crisis; we focus on why what happened led to a breakdown of trust. Third, we explain the need to develop a stronger form of trustworthiness than one based on self-interest, one in which those who are trusted possess a sense of obligation towards those who are trusting them, or those whose trust they seek. And then we put forward a number of ways in which financial activity might be framed to encourage such trustworthiness. The overall aim is to explore how

---

[1] See for example Springford (2011) and Flint (2013).

the tasks of financial activity might be adjusted in such a way that the necessary obligations and norms are made clearer, encouraging professionalism to emerge.

The authors of the book explore this framing, both at the level of the individual, and at the level of the firms and institutions in which individuals work. They also examine how law and regulation might play a role in framing and in enforcing a set of obligations which firms owe to their clients. They see this framing as helping professionalism and trustworthiness to emerge again.

At each stage in this introductory discussion we refer to the chapters in which these ideas are discussed in more detail. The aim of both this Introduction and of the chapters which follow is to demonstrate the importance of trust in the financial sector, the role which enhanced trustworthiness might play, and the practical actions which might contribute to the rebuilding of trustworthiness.

1.2 Why Trust is Needed

1.2.1 An Economists' View

Until five years ago we lived in the Great Moderation. Economic policymakers were advised by neoclassical economists who believed that a lightly regulated financial system would work well, even if the individuals in it were selfish. The argument relied on economists' views that the activity of selfish individuals could give rise to good market outcomes.

Those who subscribed to this economic tradition looked to Adam Smith in support of their views. Smith famously described the effects of self-interested motivations:

> It is not from the benevolence of the butcher, the brewer, or the baker, that we expect our dinner, but from their regard to their own interest. We address ourselves not to their humanity but to their self-love, and never talk to them of our necessities but of their advantages. (*The Wealth of Nations*, Book IV, chapter 2, para. 2)

In Smith's view these self-interested motivations could—in some circumstances—give rise to good outcomes:

> Every individual...neither intends to promote the public interest, nor knows how much he is promoting it...he intends only his own security; and by directing that industry in such a manner as its produce may be of the greatest value, he intends only his own gain, and he is in this, as in many other cases, led by an invisible hand to promote an end which was no part of his intention. (*The Wealth of Nations*, Book IV, chapter 2, para. 9)

For Smith, this assumption about motivations seemed a reasonable one, in relation to people's business activities. If people acted according to these motivations in their business transactions, then this might well lead to good economic outcomes.

Economists have subsequently taken these ideas much further, by assuming that individuals are not only self-interested, as assumed by Smith, but actually selfish. In Chapter 6 of this book Natalie Gold discusses briefly how this change in view came about. During the twentieth century, economists used this stronger assumption to give a precise meaning to Smith's 'invisible hand'. They showed that a well-functioning competitive market can give rise to efficient outcomes—in which no person can be made better off without some other person being made worse off—even if all economic actors merely pursue selfish interests. In such well-functioning markets, consumers of any product will buy it to the point at which the value of the last amount that they buy just equals the price which they pay. And in a well-functioning competitive market, the suppliers of any product will sell an amount just up to the point at which the cost of making it is just equal to the price which they get from selling it. The result is efficient—the value given to a good by those who consume it being just equal to its cost of production. Neither too little of it nor too much of it is produced.

Known as the first theorem of Welfare Economics, this powerful argument is how many twentieth-century economists characterised Adam's Smith insight about the 'invisible hand', put forward in his *Wealth of Nations*. For Smith, writing in the 1770s, this idea had been important as a means of resisting international protection so as to promote freer trade with the American colonies. For contemporary economists, the theorem has underpinned their claim that markets should be deregulated to enable them to serve the general interest. Economists have been happy to take the view that economic actors are selfish, because they are able to use the theorem to show that selfish individuals can promote good outcomes of this kind.

From the 1970s onwards, the economists' ideal of efficient markets being inhabited by selfish players was applied to the provision of finance in the UK, in the US, and in other advanced western economies. Previously financial markets had been heavily regulated—a consequence of the Great Depression. That had led to credit rationing and an inability of households to borrow. But in the second half of the twentieth century, three important developments greatly increased the proportion of the population who utilised financial services: the spread of access to banking which made it possible for many more individual citizens to both save and borrow; an increasing demand by citizens to own their own homes, accompanied by an increasing need for loans with which to purchase housing; and the political encouragement of personal pensions which required a place for people to put their savings.

Gradually policymakers turned against financial repression and regulation, towards the view that financial markets should be opened up to foster competition and innovation. Financial deregulation began in the UK in 1971 with 'Competition and Credit Control' and accelerated with the 'Big Bang' of the 1980s. And as time went on, those making policy during the 'Great Moderation' of the 1990s further liberalised the financial system, which moved towards a loosely regulated system driven by the pursuit of private financial incentives.

Economists also applied this idea at the level of firms and agents within the financial system. The idea that monetary incentives are important goes back to Adam Smith and before. But ever since the advent of modern contract theory, monetary incentives have been thought to be an effective way to motivate employees and to increase productivity, in the presence of uncertainty and asymmetric information. Providing these incentives for employees would, it was thought, increase the profitability of firms, particularly when it was hard to determine how hard employees were actually working. Modern contract theory has had a major impact on how financial companies actually structure their compensation. Bonuses tied to performance (sometimes paid in the form of options or shares) were regarded as producing good outcomes, a development that was inspired and justified by academic work on the principal-agent problem (Shiller 2012).

Trust is important to the workings of the financial system. There is a large body of literature on this subject, which examines both the importance of trust for the financial services industry, and the components of trust.[2] The consequences for savers accrue long after the decision to save has been made, and so financial services involve a continuing relationship between the purchaser and the provider. Put another way, the purchaser of services enters into a principal-agent relationship with the provider which continues over a long period of time. Thus when we purchase a financial asset we expose ourselves to the risk that the promise of returns on that asset will not be fulfilled or that the asset itself will lose much of its value at some time in the future. The purchaser needs to trust the provider that, in due course, a good return will be received.

Untrustworthy behaviour damages the financial services industry (Aghion et al. 2010). If the industry is not trusted, then clients will choose to engage less. They may invest less in their pension funds, for example, fearing that the industry may manage these in a way which reduces their return. Or they may simply save less or purchase fewer of the products provided by the financial services industry if they are uncertain whether they can trust financial

---

[2] See for example, Mayer (2008), James (2009), Tomasic and Akinbami (2011), Pinotti (2012), and Moran (2013).

providers. This will damage both the industry and the economy, by reducing the availability of capital for productive purposes.

The proponents of a loosely regulated financial system, one inhabited by profit-maximising firms whose employees are selfish, have argued that the necessary trustworthiness could be sustained even if individuals have purely selfish motivations. The pursuit of selfish ends may—it has been argued—lead to reliable fulfilment of promises if there are repeated interactions between borrowers and lenders—'repeated games'—in which there are reputations for good behaviour and punishments for those who do not keep promises. Even without repeated interactions, a selfish provider of finance may still wish to be a person trusted to repay loans, because of the reputational advantages which this brings. Cheating may make it difficult to go on earning a reward as a financial provider.

In Chapter 2 we discuss the ways in which trust broke down in the financial system, in the run-up to the Global Financial Crisis. As we shall see, much of this breakdown appears to have happened because of the self-interestedness and selfish motivations of those who worked in in the financial system. It appears difficult to sustain trust in such a world.

1.2.2 An Alternative View

There is an alternative tradition of thought, also going back to Adam Smith, which argues that although individuals may be self-interested, they also have concerns for the welfare of others. This is the view put forward in Smith's earlier book *The Theory of Moral Sentiments*.

Readers of *The Wealth of Nations* would have known Smith's *Moral Sentiments*. In that earlier book, Smith talks about a person's 'own interest', an idea which is not synonymous with selfishness, because of the social context in which individuals live and the norms to which they would have been expected to adhere. A well-socialised person is engaged with his or her community. He or she can be self-interested and ambitious for his or her own well-being. But this does not imply pure selfishness—the pursuit of one's own aims without regard for one's obligations to others. Self-interest, for Smith, involves what he calls prudence—having regard for one's own affairs within the wider context of social obligations. The chief concern that arises is the way in which these obligations impinge on the pursuit of the individual's goals and objectives. Avner Offer discusses Smith's views on this question in Chapter 7 of this book.

Adam Smith saw clearly the importance of trust to the financial system. He wrote:

> When the people of any particular country has such confidence in the fortune, probity, and prudence of a particular banker, as to believe he is always ready to pay upon demand such of his promissory notes as are likely to be at any time

presented to him; those notes come to have the same currency as gold and silver money, from the confidence that such money can at any time be had for them. (*The Wealth of Nations*, Book II, Chapter 2, para. 28)

But he did not believe that trust would emerge from the reputations which are earned in repeated games. He believed, as this quotation makes clear, that trustworthiness would need to depend on the prudence of those providing finance—which would depend on something beyond selfishness.

This is the position we adopt in this book. We seek to describe the way in which obligations beyond selfishness can be brought to bear on those who work in the financial system.

1.3 How Trustworthiness was Eroded

1.3.1 Recent History

In Chapter 2, Sue Jaffer, Nicholas Morris, Edward Sawbridge, and David Vines document what went wrong as the financial industry was deregulated. They describe the way in which, until the early 1980s, the financial industry in the UK was based largely on relationships and moral suasion, which served to promote honesty and reliability. Financial institutions saw their role as helping their clients to make money. Then the financial system changed in response to political and economic realities. On the supply side, the industry consolidated into large 'financial supermarkets' able to deal with millions of additional customers. On the demand side, increased longevity led to the need for enhanced savings. Greater home ownership in both the UK and US led to a need for mortgage finance. The resultant commoditisation of financial services led to a weakening of relationships and of the conditions conducive to honesty and reliability.

With the change in the institutional structure of the industry came an eventual dominance of the 'sales' over the 'relationships' people within universal banks. This created conflicts between different employees within the banks and placed strain on the honesty with which products and services were marketed. Financial institutions were transformed into organisations whose purpose was to look for people from whom they could make money, in contrast to ones who saw their purpose as helping their clients to make money.

It was thought that deregulation would bring increased returns to customers through the provision of more innovative products and the better management of risk, and that the costs of intermediation would be kept at efficient levels. Instead, as described in Chapter 2, uncertainty and asymmetric information led to circumstances in which those who worked for financial institutions behaved in an untrustworthy manner.

At the core of the problem was excessive risk taking. Finance is uncertain: not only are many financial products highly risky, but the risk is also dispersed among multiple players. This may enable diversification of risks. But often it will also make knowledge more difficult to obtain, making the risks larger. In addition, the principal-agent relationship in the financial services industry is also one with a particularly severe form of asymmetric information. Because financial products are complex there is also an asymmetry of expertise. Financial services products are only imperfectly understood by those who consume them. Consumers are not able to acquire and assimilate information in the way which is possible when purchasing tangible products, particularly because financial products contain promises about delivering returns far into the future. As a result, consumers find it hard to identify and counter dishonest behaviour. The presence of both uncertainty and asymmetric information led to great temptations for those who possessed knowledge or expertise to behave dishonestly.

The complexity of products also enabled financial firms to set high fees, to charge high prices, and thereby to extract large rents. Chapter 2 outlines the way that financial firms often masquerade as cost-effective suppliers of financial services, but in fact extract monopoly profits from their clients. They are able to do this because the inscrutable nature of financial products means that few consumers are able to understand what they are being sold and whether it represents good value. When consumers seek help from advisors or delegate responsibility to trustees, fund managers, or asset managers,[3] these agents may also overcharge or have insufficient expertise to protect their clients.

Conflicts of interest also arose because of the complex nature of financial institutions. These organisations have rules and institutional cultures which induce behaviour of particular kinds. These rules may constrain the ability of individuals to act in their own interest, but nevertheless some individuals may still act so as to promote their own interests, by creating risks, or by not monitoring existing risks, or by charging high rents (and in the limit stealing assets) at the expense of other parts of the organisation.

The outcome was that the expectations of investors and of investment funds were not delivered. The deregulated financial system also led to instability of the economic system, with the economy as a whole becoming vulnerable to crisis. In effect, the entire financial system became untrustworthy.

---

[3] Collectively termed 'managers' in the remainder of this chapter.

1.3.2 Incentives, Self-Interest, and Failures of Trust

In Chapter 3, Tom Noe and H. Peyton Young provide a detailed argument as to how trustworthiness was eroded by incentives. They focus in detail on the implications of two features of financial services noted above: the presence of uncertainty and the effects of asymmetric information. The fundamental problem they identify is that selfish managers can easily set up arrangements that yield high returns for clients and themselves in the short run, while imposing severe risks which take years to materialise.

Noe and Young discuss how it is that the tying of bonuses to performance—remuneration structures which became commonplace in banks and other financial institutions—causes such problems to arise. These practices were originally justified by academic work on the principal-agent problem described above, which argued that performance bonuses would better align the interests of managers and shareholders. Noe and Young describe three reasons for failure, all of which are concerned with 'moral hazard', i.e. with circumstances in which a party to a contract—the agent—has incentives to take risks because the costs that eventuate are almost entirely imposed on the principal. These three features mean that the trustworthiness of financial institutions is likely to unravel if those working for the institutions are selfish.

First of all, new financial products make it easy for a manager to create the appearance of superior performance over long periods of time, even though he or she may instead be merely creating the risk of large losses in the future (often described as tail risks). Noe and Young show how a manager can use derivatives to increase investors' normal rewards, and his own reward, at the same time as creating tail risks for the investor. They show that it is easy for managers to do this by purchasing a derivative which regularly pays out a fee, in exchange for the occasional right to seize the entire asset—the 'tail risk' feature of such derivatives. Compensation schemes with bonuses usually have the feature that in the periods when the client makes a good return, the manager gets a good bonus. However, when the asset is seized by the person who issued the derivative, the investor loses everything, but the fund manager merely fails to get his or her bonus. It obviously benefits the fund manager to seek out such tail risks! And performance contracts would guard against such untrustworthy behaviour only if they enforced very large losses on managers in bad times—for example, bankruptcy or imprisonment—but managers do not often accept that possibility. Since such a set-up will normally yield good returns for the investor, it will take many years before investors can determine with any degree of confidence whether a fund manager who is generating good returns is actually trustworthy, or is instead acting in a dishonest way by inserting tail risks. Of course, this is made more difficult if the manager actually believes that he is acting in a trustworthy manner, but is unwittingly relying on tail risks to deliver the promised returns.

Second, Noe and Young point out that the complexity of new products and the size of modern financial institutions make it difficult and costly for investors to monitor their risky investments directly. They make it clear that a selfish manager cannot be made to do this for them by means of bonuses in his or her compensation scheme. This is again because, as in the previous case, such bonus schemes do not contain sufficiently large penalties in the event of a catastrophe. It may be true that if managers undertake monitoring on behalf of their clients, they will reduce the probability of such a catastrophe. But managers will face nothing worse than a no-bonus outcome if a catastrophe occurs. And there is only a low probability of this happening even if they do not carry out the necessary monitoring. As a result, they must be paid a very high bonus if they are to find it worthwhile to incur the cost of monitoring risk, merely in order to slightly reduce the (small) probability of earning no bonus. Unless this is done they will find it more attractive to act dishonestly and merely pretend to monitor, knowing that things will go well most of the time. It is apparent that performance contracts would induce managers to undertake monitoring only if they enforced very large losses on managers in bad times. But this does not happen. As a result, Noe and Young conclude that managers will not be sufficiently incentivised to monitor risks. Since the probability of catastrophe is low, it will take many years before investors discover that such monitoring is not in fact happening.

Finally, Noe and Young point out that financial markets are so complex that it is hard to determine whether managers are simply stealing assets. It may be that hidden add-on charges act as a way of implementing such theft (Gabaix and Laibson 2006). Noe and Young discuss whether bonuses might be an effective way to deter straightforward theft when monitoring is difficult, but they show that it is unlikely to work. Such a bonus system would certainly be inefficient, since in order to have any chance of working, it would need to expose both the financial institution and those working for it to the prospect of a large loss if there was too much theft. However, that would expose the financial institution to a risk of loss occurring not just because of theft but also because of bad external circumstances. Furthermore, Noe and Young suggest that those working for the financial institution could always work out how to steal the assets before such a threat of loss was likely to be implemented. As a result, they infer that relying on incentives to induce selfish managers to refrain from stealing assets is likely to be a hopeless task.

Overall, Noe and Young conclude that selfish individuals are unlikely to act in trustworthy ways within the financial system. They thus offer a rather simple explanation of why the bad outcomes described in Chapter 2 actually occurred, and argue that some other way must be found to induce trustworthy behaviour.

1.3.3 The Influence of Previous Crises

In Chapter 4 Richard Davies provides a historical background to this breakdown in trust, by examining the banking crises of 1792, 1825, 1857, 1907, and 1929 in Britain and the US. These crises bear a striking similarity to what happened recently. They all put in jeopardy the financial system at the time, and each was a systemic event. Following each crisis, reforms were introduced which led to transformative changes in the way in which the financial system operated. But these reforms also led to changes in the incentives faced by those working in the financial sector, changes which have had real significance for the underlying level of trust in the system. Four important things stand out.

First, each crisis involved what Walter Bagehot called 'blind capital' and what modern regulators call a 'search for yield'. This involved the systematic underestimation of risks by all financial market participants, including banks. In each case the pursuit of risk led to boom and bust—in Columbian debt in 1825, in American railroads in 1857, in flawed trust companies in 1907, and in the run-up to the 1929 crash.

Second, repeated cycles of crisis and reform served to gradually drive a wedge between the economic interests of banks' managers and owners, and their creditors. This is something which happened over a very long period of time. Before 1825, banks in England and Wales were owner-managed, so that if a bank failure wiped out depositors, it wiped out owners too. Various reforms, which Davies describes, have weakened these links, limiting the downside risk that banks' owners and managers face. As Noe and Young show in Chapter 3, loosening the link between depositor safety and owners' returns makes it much less likely that trustworthy outcomes emerge. It is now not rational for banks to take full account of downside risks, since these can be imposed on clients.

Third, there has been a repeated tendency to increase safety net support as a response to crisis. This happened in 1792 with Alexander Hamilton's bailouts, and it happened with the establishment of deposit insurance in 1933. The urge to support banks and depositors is understandable, but it changes incentives. Before American banks learned that they could lean on the Federal Reserve, banks voluntarily chose to hold much higher capital levels even though they were not required to do so by regulators. Furthermore, they were likely to bail one another out, and expected to have to do this, which led to further caution. In addition, before deposit insurance existed, depositors had a stronger reason to monitor the risky activity of their banks. The gradual build-up of state safety nets—creating an expectation of bailout at a time of crisis—both increased the economic incentives to take risks and lowered the incentive to monitor risks.

Finally, the crisis of 1825 in England and Wales and of 1929–33 in America left regulators dissatisfied with atomistic and undiversified banking environments, and led to laws that promoted consolidation and merger. The emergence of systemic institutions has actually been a consequence of previous regulatory activity. Such institutions, many of which have become too big to fail, have further increased incentives to take risks and diminished incentives to monitor them.

All four of these things have reduced the likelihood of a trustworthy outcome in the financial system. All four emphasise the need to search for a stronger form of trust and trustworthiness.

1.3.4 The Impact of Regulation and Governance on Trustworthiness

The regulatory and governance system for financial services has also eroded trustworthiness. In Chapter 5, Sue Jaffer, Susana Knaudt, and Nicholas Morris explore how regulation of the financial sector evolved in the UK, with a particular focus on how reliance on trust and relationships changed. They explore the nature of regulation's failures, including the ways in which regulation itself contributed to the erosion of trust.

Regulation contributed towards a neglect of the interest of clients. Misplaced faith in efficient markets (the 'invisible hand') led to a 'light touch' form of regulation. This failed both to identify the huge risks which were accumulating and to implement restrictions which would protect customers from the kind of poor outcomes which did in fact eventuate. Regulation did not focus adequately on the trustworthiness of the financial service providers. Furthermore, regulation did not encourage financial service providers to ensure trustworthiness themselves, in the mistaken belief that trustworthy outcomes would emerge from financial markets in which players were self-interested. There was very little focus on what was necessary to build strong trust, namely for financial service providers to have an explicit concern with the interests of clients.[4] In important cases, the presence of regulatory rules actually contributed towards the abrogation of responsibility for the necessary monitoring and decisions, by distracting management attention. One such example was Northern Rock, where management focused on meeting Basel II requirements but failed to identify the risks inherent in its financing structure.

---

[4] We discuss below the features necessary for trustworthiness and for strong trust.

In addition, regulation failed to secure the provision of the kind of information required by customers to allow them to assess the trust-worthiness of financial service providers. Indeed, the emphasis placed on disclosure often created a proliferation of data ill-suited to the needs of users. As a result, the kind of intelligent accountability advocated by O'Neill in Chapter 8, one which would support strong trustworthiness, did not emerge.

Jaffer, Knaudt, and Morris identify the reasons why reform of regulation will be difficult. The selfish behaviour which led to the decline in trust-worthiness of the financial sector encouraged players to block regulatory reform and to evade the reforms being put in place. Enhanced regulation, particularly the ring-fencing of essential banking services as proposed by the Vickers Commission in the UK and by Dodd-Frank in the US, is essential to limit the extent of moral hazard facing those making the decisions on risk. However, it is unlikely to be sufficient because merely limiting the size of the risks to be borne by taxpayers does not of itself engender strong trustworthiness, and so will only partly limit the kinds of outcomes described by Noe and Young. Jaffer, Knaudt, and Morris argue that the issues that remain demonstrate the need for additional mechanisms to improve trustworthiness.

1.4 Trust and Accountability

1.4.1 Motivations, Weak Trust, and Strong Trust

How can a form of trustworthiness emerge which is stronger than that solely based on self-interest?

When we trust someone to do something we place ourselves in a position in which the outcome for us depends on what that other person chooses to do. As Natalie Gold says in Chapter 6, trust can be thought of as a three-part relation: A trusts B in relation to X, where X can include both claims about the world and commitments to perform particular acts. It is important for A that B fulfil the trust, i.e. that B is trustworthy.

Trustworthiness requires reliability, but it requires more than this. As Gold makes clear, we do not say that we trust someone to do X simply because they do it from habit. Reliability can be used to describe a mechanical system such as a washing machine, but that is not enough for this purpose. Trustworthiness is a feature of actions which require conscious choice: for a person to be trustworthy it is necessary that the person making a promise intends to keep that promise and that, when the time comes, the promise is kept in a reliable manner. This statement is not something that can be said of a washing machine. Trustworthiness requires conscious choices to be made rather than merely being the outcome of a reliable process.[5]

Gold analyses in detail the relationship between motivation and trustworthiness. A person can be trustworthy even if he or she is motivated by self-interest. This is the basis of the economists' view of trust, described above. Even if concerned only with his or her own well-being, a person can be someone who is competent enough to be able to keep promises, who intends to keep these promises, and does in fact do so in a reliable way, merely because of the advantages which come from being such a person. But trustworthiness can also arise for other deeper reasons, beyond those concerned with an individual's own well-being, as a result of motivations that are concerned with the outcomes for other people or with following correct procedures, i.e. 'other-regarding' motivations.

In fact, people have many motivations. Adam Smith opened his *Theory of Moral Sentiments* as follows:

> How selfish soever man may be supposed, there are evidently some principles in his nature, which interest him in the fortune of others, and render their happiness necessary to him, though he derives nothing from it except the pleasure of seeing it.

Gold cites much evidence concerning this mixture of motivations. She distinguishes three different ways in which trustworthiness can arise for reasons beyond those concerned with an individual's own well-being, as a result of such 'other-regarding' motivations. The first comes from the existence of pro-social motivations, where individuals are concerned to bring about outcomes which are good for other persons. The most common of these motivations is altruism. A more limited form of pro-social motivation is a concern by individuals for the outcomes for members of the group to which they belong, as she puts it, a concern for 'our' well-being. A person may act in a trustworthy manner, even if to do so goes against his or her own outcomes, narrowly conceived, because he or she cares about outcomes for other people in this way.

Second, individuals may have procedural motivations, such as professionalism or a wish to see fair outcomes, motivations which require that a task is performed well according to accepted standards. These are not concerned with the outcomes for other people so much as the way in which a task is carried out. A person may act in a trustworthy manner, even if to do so goes

---

[5] For recent work on trust and trustworthiness see Hawley (2012), Ben-Ner and Halldorsson (2010), Charness, Du, and Yang (2011), Frazier et al. (2010), and the papers referred to by Natalie Gold in Chapter 6.

against his or her own interests, narrowly conceived, because he or she is unwilling to act in a particular manner.

Finally, trustworthiness can emerge as a result of motivations which pay attention to the outcomes for other people, even though the person concerned may in fact be self-interested. A wish to be held in high regard by others may lead to trustworthy behaviour, even if the person is ultimately concerned only with his or her own outcomes. In Chapter 7, Offer argues that in *The Theory of Moral Sentiments*, Adam Smith's understanding of human motivation takes this form: the approbation of others is central to a person's self-interest. Such a view of motivation is very different from the economists' conception of self-interest. Offer stresses that the 'impartial spectator' which Smith introduces in his *Theory of Moral Sentiments* brings other-regarding motivations to bear when choices are made, but argues that these motivations arise precisely because of the high value placed by individuals on the approbation of others. As a result, Smith's model of the 'impartial spectator' is driven not by our sympathy for other people, but by their sympathy for us.

Offer goes on to argue that approbation needs to be authenticated, and that in Smith's own model authentication relies on innate virtue, something which Offer views as unrealistic. He sets out an alternative model of 'regard', which makes use of signalling as part of the authentication process. Offer claims that the modern versions of Smith's 'invisible hand' put forward in rational choice theory, and in neo-liberalism, are radical departures from the ethical legacy of Enlightenment and utilitarian economics, and that they are inconsistent with Adam Smith's own position. Writers other than Offer have also argued that a person may pay attention to the outcomes for other people, even though the person concerned may in fact be self-interested. Brennan and Hamlin argue that people have motivations of this kind because they value esteem, rather than valuing approbation of the kind which Offer discusses (Brennan and Hamlin 1995, 2000). The overall point is that motivations of this kind can lead to trustworthy behaviour. A person may act in a trustworthy manner, even if to do so goes against his or her own interests, narrowly conceived, because he or she values the approbation or esteem of others.

It is clear that motivations have an effect on trustworthiness. Selfish individuals may display levels of competence and a willingness to keep promises, and may do this reliably, merely because they wish to have a reputation for doing these things. They may value the advantage which having such a reputation brings. But individuals possessing other-regarding motivations also possess additional reasons for being trustworthy.

As a result of this discussion, Gold introduces two terms: weak trust and strong trust. Weak trust and weak trustworthiness can emerge even if the motivations of the person being trusted are self-interested. But strong trust and strong trustworthiness emerge only if there are other-regarding motivations.

There are two different ways in which one can justify an appeal to non-selfish motivations, so that strong trustworthiness can emerge. Given that individuals do, in fact, possess a variety of motivations, more trustworthy outcomes will emerge the more individuals 'frame' a problem as one within which other-regarding motivations are relevant. Such framing involves statements such as 'This is not an issue on which only my own concerns matter'. One view is that good policy will encourage individuals to frame problems in such a manner when the potential effects on other individuals are large, in order to produce better outcomes (Thaler and Sunstein 2008). Parallel to this, good policy will attempt to select people with these motivations for such tasks.[6] Although he is not explicit, we can probably associate the comments of Mark Carney about finance, noted above, with such views. Philosophers would call this a 'consequentialist' justification of why policy should use other-regarding motivations to lead to better outcomes.

There is an alternative non-consequentialist view. Some people believe that there are obligations to others, and moral requirements concerning the way in which we treat others, but that the reasons why we have these obligations are not based on their consequences. This view holds that these obligations should guide behaviour, independently of the outcomes for others which actually emerge. Some people will frame problems in other-regarding ways because they believe that they are morally obliged to do so. The cultivation of non-selfish motivations may well assist in the pursuit of these moral obligations. Someone who takes this second view might think that it is the task of policymakers and other people of influence to make clear such obligations. The fact of doing this may, of itself, lead to a change of behaviour by some people, and thus to the emergence of strong trust. Archbishop Welby appears to take this view in his comments about finance which we cited earlier.[7]

Both lines of argument are important. They both lead to the conclusion that we should use policy to support and encourage non-selfish motivations, which is the thrust of this book. But they will each be appealing to different types of people and to different mechanisms. By appealing to both we may get a broader coalition in favour of the policy proposals which are made below.

In what follows, these proposals will be presented mainly in a consequentialist manner. One reason for proceeding this way is that it is easy to agree that there would be an improvement if the outcomes which bankers produced

---

[6] This is the view of Brennan and Hamlin (1995, 2000).

[7] He writes as follows: 'What does that mean in a world of business and competition? It means that companies should be communities of common interest which serve the common good. For that to happen there needs to be a store of value in them: a sense of what is right that is independent of our individual achievement; compassionate in its acceptance of us [i.e. of other members of the community]; [and] empowering in its interaction with us ... '.

were better. There may, in addition, be moral duties for bankers, but it is hard to reach consensus on a common moral framework, or on the correct under-pinnings for moral duties. (Archbishop Welby appeals to a Christian ethical framework, to which he is committed, but others are not committed in this way.) Saying that there are good consequentialist reasons for encouraging trustworthy behaviour doesn't preclude the possibility that there are other reasons as well. People who are motivated by moral considerations can be influenced if the implications of moral imperatives are emphasised.

1.4.2 Strong Trust and Intelligent Accountability

We are seeking a strong form of trustworthiness. In Chapter 8, O'Neill high-lights the role of accountability in ensuring trustworthiness, and the impor-tance of using intelligent frameworks of accountability. These arguments run counter to a popular claim that accountability can actually be used as a sub-stitute for trustworthiness, instead of supporting trustworthiness.

O'Neill describes how many observers have argued that relations of trust are actually no longer possible in the modern world, and that they therefore need to be replaced. Their view is that relations of trust arise only from face-to-face relationships, pre-eminently through relations of mutual goodwill. Since individuals now work in large and complex institutions such trusting rela-tions seem very difficult to achieve. O'Neill describes how these observers see formalised structures of accountability as an alternative, one which is neces-sary since trustworthiness cannot be relied upon.

O'Neill argues that this view of trust is a mistaken, unintelligent, one. And she argues that the accountability 'remedy' has also taken an unintelligent form. It has led to a managerial approach to accountability which sets stand-ards for performance—targets—and then measures success through 'tick box' approaches to the meeting of these targets. Accountability has become an extension of managerial process rather than requiring an accountability of managers for what they do. Much can go wrong with this form of account-ability, with chosen performance indicators providing simplistic and mislead-ing proxies (such as the length of hospital waiting lists) and even well-chosen indicators having the potential to create perverse incentives. As O'Neill argues, ticking boxes cannot substitute for informed judgement of performance. For this reason, where tick box recording is introduced into systems of account-ability, other more intelligent ways of securing good performance and holding people to account typically have to be maintained in the background. She concludes that if we actually wish to persist with this approach to accountabil-ity, there is no reason to assume that it could replace trust. On the contrary, if not ultimately based on relations of trust, managerial accountability will, she believes, spiral into an infinite regress of deferred accountability.

Consequently, O'Neill seeks intelligent conceptions of both trust and accountability, which would go hand in hand. She sees the placing of trust as being based on a judgement concerned with either the claims about the world or the commitments to action which are made. Trust in others' claims is well placed if their words are, or turn out to be, true of the world. Trust in others' commitments is well placed if they act in due course to shape the world in a way which is true to their word or to their implied commitments. Individuals, or the institutions for which they work, are trustworthy if trust in their claims or commitments is well placed.

An intelligent system of securing accountability would support rather than supersede the placing of trust. Intelligent structures of accountability should provide good evidence as to whether it is likely that the claims about the world made by the person, or by an institution, seeking to be trusted are true, and that their commitments are likely to be fulfilled. An intelligent system of accountability would support the intelligent placement of trust.

O'Neill discusses what is required to implement these approaches to intelligent trust and to intelligent accountability. She argues that the placing of trust should be based on judgement, which requires judgement of available evidence about track record. Trust is redundant where complete evidence or proof exists, so that trust must 'run ahead' of proof. As we cannot do without trust, controlling the level of risk by placing it intelligently matters.

There is a connection here with what we have been saying above about strong trust. Those with other-regarding motivations are, we have argued, more likely to act in a trustworthy manner. Those placing trust will need to seek evidence about the extent to which motivations are other-regarding, and in what ways.

O'Neill further suggests that an intelligent system of accountability comprises a definition of 'required actions' and a statement of the things that are necessary to ensure that claims about the world and commitments to action actually come about. These result in a set of obligations or duties of the individuals and institutions who are to be trusted. Intelligent accountability would, she argues, impose an obligation on the individual or organisation to render an account of (non-)performance of this primary obligation. 'Accountability is unintelligent if it is undertaken in ways that suppress or omit an intelligent account of what ought to be done. Managerial accountability, with its focus on proxy indicators of performance, is an unintelligent form of accountability because it does exactly this.' Intelligent forms of accountability also require informed and independent judgement on the adequacy of performance, and the communication of accessible evidence on performance by those responsible for the holding to account, if there is to be an intelligent placing of trust.

O'Neill argues that well-structured professions and institutions can provide cultural support for meeting obligations, in a way that managerial forms of accountability do not. But she notes that genuine professional integrity grows out of strong institutional structures. These include institutional and financial separation, robust systems for dealing with conflicts of interest, serious remedies for failure, and support for professional culture. Thus O'Neill counsels that only with robust forms of professional accountability will it be possible to secure the delivery of obligations without stultifying controls or proliferating legal sanctions.

1.4.3 Using Framing to Ensure Strong Trust in the Financial System

As described above, financial services involve a continuing relationship between the purchaser and the provider, i.e. the purchaser of services enters into a principal-agent relationship with the provider which continues over a long period of time. The consumer needs to trust the supplier that, in due course, a good return will be received. Some form of trust relationship is necessarily involved.

The arguments put forward by Noe and Young that we described above deal a blow to the idea that trustworthy behaviour can be sustained by weak trust. The problem is that, in the presence of uncertainty, it becomes difficult to determine whether the actor is behaving dishonestly. It is difficult to detect managers who are creating tail risks, and it is difficult to catch those who are not monitoring risks, or who are stealing. In these circumstances, strong trust is important; those placing trust need to be able to rely on other-regarding motivations since dishonest behaviour is unlikely to be apprehended.

In addition, circumstances change, particularly over the long period of time typically involved in the provision of financial services. Robustness is an important property when there are long time frames. Natalie Gold imagines two parties who are trying to broker an agreement for mutual benefit. 'If they can only rely on each other's weak trustworthiness, then they need to construct a contract containing clauses to cover every possible eventuality. If they are motivated by strong trust, then an incomplete contract may suffice. Since most contracts are by necessity incomplete, in the absence of strong trust contractors would often have to fall back on costly legal processes.'

Connections between motivations and trustworthiness in the operation of the economy have been considered in many contexts, not only in the financial sector. (See, for example, Frey 1998; Le Grand 2003; and Besley 2007.) That agents have a multiplicity of motivations leads to the question: when do different agents use the other-regarding motivations that might lead to strongly trustworthy behaviour? We can say that this depends on how the problem is framed, i.e. on what it is that the agent thinks is relevant to the problem under consideration. It is not that the agent can choose his or her own motivation, which would of course be rather strange, but that a policy-maker can alter the environment in ways that can affect an agent's motivation. In what follows, we discuss different ways in which problems might be framed, so as to bring other-regarding motivations to bear on these problems, and so make circumstances of strong trust more likely.

1.4.4 Using Legal and Regulatory Systems to Influence Framing

Adjustments to legal and regulatory frameworks could provide a way of influencing the extent to which issues are framed, and so influence the extent to which strong trustworthiness can be restored in finance. Chapters 9 to 11 consider the extent to which this could be done.

In Chapter 9, Joshua Getzler discusses how fiduciary obligations impose duties of loyalty and care to clients. He describes recent circumstances during the Great Moderation as ones in which asset managers took high fees but, by the time that the crisis had come, had moved their clients' wealth into assets which crashed in value. He argues that the law needs to provide a satisfactory response to such behaviour, and that the remedies available in contract law are inadequate. In particular, the law needs to impose a set of duties on asset managers which give rise to a satisfactory response in the face of the problems of uncertainty, asymmetric information and expertise, and conflicts of interest, which we have been describing above. These necessary additional duties would create something very similar to the fiduciary law we already have, but which we no longer use. Getzler describes how fiduciary duties are often attenuated or eliminated by implicit or explicit agreements that leave financial intermediaries with too much unmonitored power over their beneficiaries, and which open up incentives for incompetent or predatory performance. To fully unlock the potential of fiduciary law it is important not only to clarify the nature of fiduciary duties and remedies, but also to rein in the trend by which fiduciary duties are cut back by contract.

The financial crisis has exposed the difficulty of drawing a line between those clients who are owed fiduciary obligations by financial institutions, and those who are not. It has been the practice to cut back fiduciary duties by contract when dealing with 'sophisticated' investors, investors who are required—in the absence of these duties—to instead exercise the caution of 'buyer beware' or *caveat emptor*.

In Chapter 10, Justin O'Brien argues that it is essential to challenge the norms governing the financial industry, and to place ethical judgement above narrow legal permissibility and technical compliance. O'Brien begins by exploring the ethical foundation of the current market conduct and disclosure regime, which was initially established at the time of the New Deal in

America. He argues that there has been a progressive erosion of that compact, and that, in the aftermath of the Global Financial Crisis, powerful lobbying by the industry has been carried out with the aim of preventing such a compact being re-established.

O'Brien finds that the gatekeepers of market integrity, the legal and audit communities, have contributed to the decline in ethical behaviour through their elevation of technicalities above substantive ethical considerations. He uses two Australian examples of malpractice to demonstrate the need for change in professional behaviour: the marketing and sale of complex financial products, and the gradual but pronounced deterioration in the quality of audit work. The first of these examples concerns a landmark ruling, *Wingecarribee Shire Council v Lehman Brothers Australia*, in which the Australian Federal Court found that the investment bank had engaged in deceptive and misleading practice in individual transactions, in relation to investors who were not sufficiently sophisticated to understand the way in which they were being treated. The case, he argues, removes the legal basis for persisting with different regulatory requirements for sophisticated and retail customers, and more generally demonstrates significant failings in regulatory policy settings both in Australia and in the United States.

O'Brien expresses concern that Codes of Conduct can be used perversely, to protect the power of the industry. He suggests that extending responsibility and accountability requires regulation to integrate normative objectives and to move beyond concern for efficiency, in three distinct ways. First, he argues that regulators should actively consider the *permissibility* of products (i.e. whether a particular product can be sold and if so to whom and on what basis). Second, he argues that *responsibility* should become an object of regulation (which would require a consideration of who carries the risk when an investment sours and on what terms). Finally, he believes that regulators should examine the question of *legitimacy* (which would require regulators to consider whether a product serves a legitimate purpose). As result he suggests the need for a regulatory framework which is mutually reinforcing at the corporate, professional, and regulatory levels, with reciprocal obligations on each institutional actor to maintain the integrity of the governance arrangements and a common understanding of the ethical problem.

In Chapter 11, John Armour and Jeffrey Gordon explore the systemic harms imposed by the maximisation of shareholder value. They note that the generally accepted framework for analysing corporate law and governance implies that those running a corporation should seek to maximise the value of shareholders' claims, as measured by the stock price. However, for share price maximisation to enhance social welfare, a range of mechanisms—contracts, liability rules, and regulation—need to ensure that the costs which a firm's activities impose on other parties are internalised into that firm's profit function.

The extent to which traditional private law mechanisms—in particular, the law of tort—fail to internalise 'economic' or indirect harms has been under-appreciated. The activities of certain sorts of firms can cause economic losses to large numbers of parties through indirect and diffuse causal channels. In addition, the shareholder value norm creates incentives for firms to under-mine the efficacy of liability and regulatory mechanisms. Finally, the costs to other firms will not be fully reflected in the share price of the individual firm selecting the project. Hence, share price maximisation can in the pres-ence of systemic externalities lead to reduced returns to investors on their overall portfolio. These are harms which will be caused by a sole focus on the maximisation of shareholder value, in addition to those discussed by Noe and Young.

Armour and Gordon argue for an 'internal' or corporate governance solu-tion which would directly affect the pay-offs to parties controlling the firm, as opposed to regulatory intervention. In particular, they argue for a recon-sideration of 'old-fashioned' liability rules being imposed on directors and officers of banks. Negligence liability, appropriately structured, is likely to make managers more appreciative of the harm which they cause to others and so to behave in a more risk-averse fashion. Such liability would clearly change the way in which problems are framed—it would provide financial incentives to pay attention to the well-being of others. Here we can see that the internalisation of externalities by legal enforcement could lead financial service providers to pay attention to outcomes for others.

1.4.5 Framing at the Individual Level

We describe in Chapter 2 how those in the financial services industry have been able to supply products in a way which increases their remuneration, at the expense of a reduction in the well-being of their clients and of the wider society. A selfish financial-sector employee will exploit the opportu-nity to supply products in this way. With no interest in the well-being of others, such employees will attempt to do this as much as possible, within the limits provided by the risk of being detected, or by law or regulation. However, a financial services employee who frames the supply of these products in a way which values the wider good may decline to behave like this, even if he would benefit personally from doing so. If different indi-viduals have different frames, then part of the job of institutional design is to seek individuals who would frame the supply of these products in an other-regarding manner. These individuals should be selected for the roles in which important choices are made about the creation of tail risks, about the extent to which risks are monitored, and about the way in which fees are set.

In Chapter 12, Boudewijn de Bruin discusses how the values which individuals hold will help to frame choices and so influence the choices that are made, if motivations are not entirely selfish. Values lie behind the pro-social motivations described above: values such as a concern for equality or for fairness. The extent to which these values are important will have an effect on the way in which the individual behaves. Thus the value of fairness may lead to a choice not to act in an untrustworthy manner, not because trustworthiness itself is a value, but because untrustworthy behaviour would conflict with a motivation driven by the value of fairness. Many of the proposals put forward in this and later chapters seek to increase individuals' awareness of such values and how they underpin daily actions and decisions.

Individuals will have many complex values which influence pro-social motivations and so affect decisions about whether to act in an untrustworthy manner or not. De Bruin lists six values beyond those of equality or fairness: integrity, objectivity, competence, confidentiality, professionalism, and diligence. Some of these values do not merely concern outcomes for other people: some of them are procedural values—objectivity or confidentiality—and give rise to what Gold describes as procedural motivations. Others—like professionalism—may be partly attributable to ensuring the esteem or regard of others (although it is possible to value being professional for its own sake, and not just because it leads to being esteemed by others). Many of the chapters below discuss the influence of these values on the choices made by individuals in the financial sector, given the goals which they have. Of course, these values may conflict with each other in certain circumstances, making the subject a difficult one. But, nevertheless, these values will cause an individual to frame the problem in ways which show concern beyond his or her own interests.

1.4.6 Framing at the Institutional Level

We have focused so far on individual agents, who have complex motivational structures which include self-interested elements but also include elements which are concerned with the welfare of others. Importantly, these motivations are endogenous. Individual behaviour is determined by the interaction of the institutional setting in which individuals work with the motivational structure of these individuals. Different institutional structures will induce individuals to frame tasks in different ways.

The norms of behaviour within an institution or society more generally will constrain the way in which individuals frame their tasks. For example, it may become a norm to refrain from selling payment protection insurance to clients who cannot benefit from it, or a norm to refrain from disguising products having a possibility of catastrophic failure in a way which makes them appear to be high-yielding products, or a norm not to strip too much capital out of a firm which is taken over. Such norms of behaviour may ensure that individuals adopt other-regarding motivations with regard to particular problems.

The development of norms to which most people will adhere is a crucial part of encouraging ethical behaviour. In Chapter 13, Dan Awrey and Dave Kershaw explore whether cultural and ethical norms can be employed to restrain opportunism and socially excessive risk taking within the financial services industry. The authors note how these constraints are too often ineffective—crowded out by other countervailing influences. Their chapter explores how law and regulation might be utilised to influence norm formation at both the individual and organisational levels in favour of a more trustworthy culture. More specifically, it explores the potential efficacy of legal (e.g. fiduciary duties), governance (e.g. ethics committees), and regulatory (e.g. process-based regulation) strategies as mechanisms for introducing a norm of 'other-regarding' behaviour into the decision-making processes of financial services firms.

As de Bruin describes in Chapter 12, such norms of behaviour could be incorporated into codes of conduct, codes which similarly influence motivations. It is important that the norms of behaviour and codes of conduct make reference to the values described above. Otherwise these norms and codes may begin to appear merely as arbitrary lists of proscribed actions. De Bruin describes how, in a complex world, norms of behaviour and codes of conduct may be obtained not only from a value of fairness but also from a much wider range of values, such as those listed above. Such codes are likely to be contentious, especially if the values to which they appeal are in conflict with each other. Nonetheless, the process of developing such norms and codes of conduct in finance is part of the task of professionalising the industry. Achieving this outcome will require strong management action and systematic education of employees.

De Bruin also explores the scope for what he calls 'ethics management' in banking. He argues that if ethical issues in finance have limited moral intensity in comparison to other industries, banks will often fail to recognise an ethical issue, form a judgement, adopt a moral intention, or engage in ethical behaviour. The primary task of ethics management in banking is to develop tools that help management and employees to recognise a wider set of obligations, to cause those who work in financial institutions to frame problems in a way which gives importance to these obligations, and to encourage individuals to act in a way which respects these obligations.

De Bruin discusses communication with external stakeholders (clients, government, NGOs, etc.) as ways of assisting with such changes. He suggests that the financial services industry would benefit from using a tool that is gaining popularity in political decision making: deliberative polls. He then turns to ways in which finance firms can communicate with their employees and gives an example of an ethics training programme inspired by O'Neill's views of trust (as discussed in O'Neill 2002, 2012). Finally, he considers codes of ethics, arguing that several codes may have relevance in finance and banking, but notes the difficulty of establishing a meaningful professional code for bankers.

Seumas Miller pursues this theme in Chapter 14. He discusses how the government in Australia has recently introduced legislation concerning the professional ethics of a particular group of employees of the financial industry, namely financial advisors. This legislation bans various forms of conflicted remuneration for financial advisors and attaches fiduciary-like duties to their roles. The envisaged professionalisation process straddles the four dimensions of what he calls an integrity system, namely underlying, widely accepted, moral beliefs and attitudes, and (building on top of this regulation) market incentives and reputational incentives. As well as functioning as a part of an external integrity system for financial advisors, the Australian legislation provides for a new set of internal obligations constitutive of the role of the financial planner. Thus it seeks to build integrity both from without and from within. The intention is to transform an occupation formerly comprised of sales personnel into a profession comprised of purveyors of high-quality, independent, financial advice.

1.5 Learning from Other Experiences

In Chapter 15, Avner Offer provides an analogy with what happened in finance by discussing the bad outcomes that have arisen in the American health system. Offer suggests that these bad outcomes have come about because of a decline in regard for the welfare of others: a shift from the fiduciary norm 'first do no harm' to the neo-liberal market norm of 'let the buyer beware' (*caveat emptor*). His example suggests that professionalism is not sufficient by itself to resist selfish market norms and how these selfish norms need to be rejected explicitly. It is often believed that the medical system supports trust in the professional, but in US it does not appear to do so. Offer documents a very significant amount of cheating and argues that this is the result of norms inherent in the US medical system. Even a well-defined professional system can fall apart in the absence of other-regarding motivations.

In Chapter 16 Sue Jaffer, Nicholas Morris, and David Vines discuss contrasting experiences of a positive kind. They provide examples from a number of industries of moves towards a strong form of trust, describing cases where norms have been developed that frame problems as ones in which firms pay attention to the needs of others. Often the motivation for such action is concern that companies may lose the esteem of their customers. For example, clothing retailers such as Gap and Nike introduced mechanisms to prevent the exploitation of child labour by their suppliers, in response to adverse public opinion. This initiative relied on the development of codes of practice, enforced by sanctions imposed by the main international purchasers of the goods. The system has succeeded because of the interest of major players in protecting their reputation, and hence brand value.

The development of sophisticated, internationally agreed controls over advertising content followed concern about adverse customer reactions to advertising seen as damaging to both the specific advertiser and the wider industry. Major issues covered by the self-regulation of advertising are deception and the protection of vulnerable groups such as children. The system has been successful in policing these matters using an industry-funded self-regulatory agency. Self-regulation is underpinned in the UK by cooperation and reinforcement by government agencies such as the UK Office of Fair Trading.

In other cases, professional associations have emerged which seek to protect members from the erosion of reputation and standards by unlicensed operators. This has worked well in the UK for both the legal and medical professions. The medical profession has developed an integrity infrastructure which seeks to ensure the competence of medical practitioners, and their willingness to act in a trustworthy manner, in a manner which contrasts with the US. As a result, the profession is mostly held in high regard in the UK, and medical practitioners are regarded as trustworthy in most surveys. Similarly, the legal profession also has an established enforcement system, which until 2007 was administered by the Law Society (for solicitors) and by the Bar Council (for barristers). This system worked well from the nineteenth century for over one hundred years, until the 1990s, when changes to industry structure led to the need for adjustment.

In some cases, the development of the type of intelligent accountability advocated by O'Neill emerged as a result of crisis. The Three Mile Island nuclear accident in 1979 exposed severe failings of risk management and lax safety procedures in the US nuclear industry and led to a damning Presidential Inquiry. The 1984 gas leaks from a Union Carbide plant in Bhopal, India (which killed thousands of people) damaged the credibility of the chemical industry worldwide. Both events led to decisions by industry leaders that a proactive approach to repairing reputation was necessary. In both cases, an improved self-regulatory system was created which has remained in place, and been strengthened, for thirty years. Both systems have clear forms of public accountability. These initiatives resulted from actions taken by industry leaders, motivated by a desire to improve reputation and to head off potentially damaging government intervention.

These examples show that trust-reinforcing mechanisms can be made to succeed, even in complex and global industries. This can be done by developing reputations, by developing standards, and by developing self-regulation. All of these steps can be important for the financial industry.

1.6 Restoring Trustworthiness

This book argues that it is important that reform of the financial sector makes use of motivations which go beyond the selfish-motivation assumption on which economic analysis is normally based. The chapters of the book suggest how other-regarding motivations might lead those in the financial sector to act in a more trustworthy manner. The task is to ensure that those who work within the financial sector become more strongly bound by professional standards of behaviour, as in these other professional sectors and as once happened in finance.

In Chapter 16, Sue Jaffer, Nicholas Morris, and David Vines set out four steps for developing trust-enhancing mechanisms: defining obligations and responsibilities, identifying the responsibilities of different players, establishing mechanisms for the encouragement of trustworthiness, and holding to account the players who are responsible. Before examining the application of these steps to the finance industry, the chapter considers first a number of case studies on the mechanisms that have been applied in other industries, which provide useful lessons for financial services.

The chapter recaps the key obstacles to trustworthiness that have been discussed above, and the regulatory responses that have emerged to date. It concludes that proposals such as the Vickers ring fence, the proposed reforms to remuneration, and tighter restrictions on the level of leverage are important in that they remove or reduce a number of adverse incentives. However they do little to strengthen trustworthiness by bringing other-regarding motivations into play. The chapter goes on to consider the extent to which current practice and recent proposals for reform make adequate provision for our four steps for improving trustworthiness, and builds on this discussion to recommend further actions that could be taken. However, the devil is in the detail and different parts of the financial system face different challenges. Accordingly the discussion focuses on just three types of financial service providers: retail banking service providers, asset managers, and product engineers. In each of these cases the chapter examines the extent to which current practice could be further developed in the ways suggested in this book.

References

Aghion, P. et al. (2010). 'Regulation and Distrust', *Quarterly Journal of Economics*, 125(3): 1015–49.

Ben-Ner, A. and Halldorsson, F. (2010). 'Trusting and Trustworthiness: What Are They, How to Measure Them, and What Affects Them', *Journal of Economic Psychology*, 31(1): 64–79.

Besley, T. (2007). *Principled Agents? The Political Economy of Good Government.* Oxford: Oxford University Press.

Brennan, G. and Hamlin, A. (1995). 'Economising on Virtue', *Constitutional Political Economy*, 6: 35–56.

Brennan, G. and Hamlin, A. (2000). *Democratic Devices and Desires.* Cambridge: Cambridge University Press.

Carney, M. (May 2013). 'Economic Recovery Depends on Banks Rebuilding Trust with Public', *Calgary Herald* [online newspaper], <http://www.calgaryherald.com/business/Economic+recovery+depends+banks+rebuilding+trust+with+public/8334840/story.html>, accessed 9 June 2013.

Charness, G., Du, N., and Yang, C. (2011). 'Trust and Trustworthiness Reputations in an Investment Game', *Games and Economic Behavior*, 72(2): 361–75.

Flint, D. (2013). 'Rebuilding Trust in Banking', *HSBC*, <http://www.hsbc.com/news-and-insight/2013/douglas-flint-rebuilding-trust-in-banking>, accessed 9 June 2013.

Frazier, M., Johnson, P., Gavin, M., Gooty, J., and Snow, D. B. (2010). 'Organizational Justice, Trust and Trustworthiness: A Multifoci Examination', *Group and Organization Management*, 35: 39–76.

Frey, B. (1998). *Not Just for the Money: An Economics Theory of Person Motivation.* Cheltenham, UK: Edward Elgar.

Gabaix, X. and Laibson, D. (2006). 'Shrouded Attributes, Consumer Myopia Information Suppression in Incomplete Markets', *Quarterly Journal of Economics*, 121(2): 505–40.

Hawley, K. (2012). *Trust: A Very Short Introduction.* Oxford: Oxford University Press.

James, E. (2009). 'In the Wake of the Financial Crisis: Rebuilding the Image of the Finance Industry Through Trust', *Journal of Financial Transformation*, 27: 37–41.

Le Grand, J. (2003). *Motivation, Agency, and Public Policy: Of Knights and Knaves, Pawns and Queens.* Oxford: Oxford University Press.

Mayer, C. (2008). 'Trust in Financial Markets', *European Financial Management*, 14(4): 617–32.

Mayer, C. (2013). *Firm Commitment.* Oxford: Oxford University Press.

Moran, M. (2013). 'Schumpeter's Nightmare? Legitimacy, Trust and Business in Britain', *British Academy Policy Centre Report*, <https://www.britac.ac.uk/policy/Business_Legitimacy.cfm>, accessed 9 June 2013.

O'Neill, O. (2002). *A Question of Trust.* Cambridge: Cambridge University Press.

O'Neill, O. (2012). 'A Point of View: Which Comes First—Trust or Trustworthiness?', broadcast on *BBC Radio 4*, 9 December 2012, <http://www.bbc.co.uk/news/magazine-20627410>, accessed 9 June 2013.

Pinotti, P. (2012). 'Trust, Regulation and Market Failures', *Review of Economics and Statistics*, 94(3): 650–8.

Shiller, R. (2012). *Finance and the Good Society*. Princeton: Princeton University Press.

Smith, A. (1759/1976). *The Theory of Moral Sentiments*. Oxford: Clarendon Press.

Smith, A. (1776/1976). *An Inquiry into the Nature and Causes of the Wealth of Nations*. Oxford: Clarendon Press.

Springford, J. (2011). 'A Confidence Crisis? Restoring Trust in Financial Services', London: Social Market Foundation, <http://www.smf.co.uk/research/financial-services/a-confidence-crisis-restoring-trust-in-financial-services/>, accessed 9 June 2013.

Thaler, R. and Sunstein, C. (2008). *Nudge: Improving Decisions about Health, Wealth, and Happiness*. London: Yale University Press.

Tomasic, R. and Akinbami, F. (2011). 'The Role of Trust in Maintaining the Resilience of Financial Markets', *Journal of Corporate Law Studies*, 11(2): 369–94.

Welby, J. (2013). 'How Do We Fix This Mess?', speech given on Monday 21 April, <http://www.archbishopofcanterbury.org/articles.php/5050/how-do-we-fix-this-mess-archbishop-justin-on-restoring-trust-and-confidence-after-the-crash>, accessed 9 June 2013.

2

How Changes to the Financial Services Industry Eroded Trust

*Sue Jaffer, Nicholas Morris, Edward Sawbridge, and David Vines** *

> When the capital development of a country becomes a by-product of the activities of a casino, the job is likely to be ill-done.
>
> John Maynard Keynes (1936)

> ...there are enormous risks in bringing together deep-pocketed investors who are not adequately conscious of prices and risks, and the highly motivated private financial sector.
>
> Raghuram G. Rajan (2010)[1]

2.1 Introduction

Financial Services in the City of London ('the City') has a long and distinguished history, including support for major corporations such as the East India Company; financing of the ships, armies, and infrastructure required for the Empire; the development of worldwide insurance through Lloyd's of London; and the creation of the London Stock Exchange. Two World Wars and their aftermath were successfully financed during the twentieth century.

The current activities of the City continue to underpin the UK economy, providing services to governments, companies, and individuals on a worldwide basis. Services include running the sterling payments mechanism; attracting and investing funds; organising markets for securities, companies,

* The authors would like to thank Leslie Hannah, Avner Offer, and Jaya Patten for their discussion of ideas and comments on this chapter.

[1] R. G. Rajan, *Fault Lines* (Princeton and Oxford: Princeton University Press, 2010), 132. © Princeton University Press.

derivatives and commodities; financing projects in the UK and worldwide; and providing financial and commercial services such as insurance, leasing, hedging, and advice. Insurance companies are important both in reducing risk and in investing on behalf of savers and general insurance customers (Clarke 2008). Banking is a specific subset of the activities of the City, usually divided into commercial (payments, borrowing, and lending by companies and individuals) and investment (trading activities, primary market activities, and mergers and acquisitions, which involve participation in risky activities in exchange for a return on capital).

In the decades following the Second World War, financial markets were strictly regulated and international movements of financial capital were limited. The financial sector was highly fragmented, with participants being vetted to ensure they were 'fit and proper' to carry out their functions. Individuals, firms, and partnerships that fell below the highest standards of integrity were dealt with by their peers, and in extreme cases were excluded from the markets and from society.

However, the last forty years have seen pressures for change which have had far-reaching effects on the financial services system. As described in the following section, financial services depend on trust. Yet 'Big Bang' and the resulting change to business models, and the financial innovation that followed in their wake, appear to have reduced the trustworthiness of the industry.

This chapter describes how the institutional arrangements for UK financial services changed, and how these changes reduced the trustworthiness of functionaries and firms. As discussed in Chapter 1, trustworthiness can be engendered through different motivations. Examining how these motivations have been affected is a necessary first step to determining how best to restore trustworthiness to financial services.

2.2 The Importance of Trustworthiness

The financial services industry is trust-intensive by virtue of the nature of the product. When buying financial products, customers are buying the expertise of the product provider and/or the agent advising them (Springford 2011). Service providers need to be trustworthy because consumers do not have access to the information or the expertise needed to assess products in the way possible when purchasing a more tangible product such as a mobile phone. Moreover, unlike simple one-off transactions, products often involve long time frames which make the value of the product difficult to assess over the short to medium term. Yet the implications for the customer are likely to be much more significant in terms of well-being.

These problems of *asymmetric information* have worsened as financial products have become increasingly complex. The deregulation of over-the-counter derivatives, for example, led to an explosion in trading volumes, a lack of transparent pricing, and burgeoning counter-party, operational, and market risks dispersed among multiple players. Many parties did not understand the risks they were taking and third-party assessments of risk, such as those made by the ratings agencies, proved to be unreliable.

Financial intermediation should allow the expertise of the intermediary to optimise returns, diversification, and liquidity for the investor. Thus intermediation has as its *raison d'être* the information asymmetry between advisor and customer, with investors relying on the expertise of the intermediaries. However, intermediation may also lead to conflicts of interest and dual capacity problems. Investors who employ intermediaries place their funds in the hands of managers whose interests may not be aligned with their own. Moreover, most transactions now involve a chain of relationships, which makes it increasingly difficult to ensure that the interests of the ultimate investor are protected (Kay 2012b).

Given the prevalence of information asymmetries and principal-agent relationships, savers rely on the professional ethics of those with market expertise. Within English law there is a well-developed concept of a fiduciary agent, whose duty is to act in the best interests of his client and who the client retains for the agent's knowledge and expertise. Honesty, loyalty, and prudence are the key elements of a fiduciary duty, and it requires the removal of any conflict of interest.

However, as the following discussion shows, recent pressures on and changes to the industry have undermined the fiduciary nature of relationships.

2.3 Relationships and Integrity in the City as it Was

At the time of the first Labour Government under Attlee, the financial services industry consisted of five main sectors: ordinary banks, which offered current and deposit accounts as well as short-term lending through overdrafts; commercial banks; investment (merchant) banks; insurance; and mutual associations, building and friendly societies. Each of these groups operated largely separately, with a limited appetite for risk.

At that time, financial services were based on close relationships both within the industry and between the industry and its clients.[2] Local bank

---

[2] The Bank of England led a 'club' of senior bankers who defined and enforced ethical standards, as well as solving problems, often in an informal manner (Kynaston 2002).

managers were conservative, pillars of the local community, and were careful to ensure that those to whom they lent money could repay their debts. They usually had many years of familiarity with local conditions and businesses. They were trusted advisors to whom families and local companies could turn for advice on business and facilities for depositing their money. Often they had worked in the same bank all their lives, had some professional qualifications, and were concerned that their customers—many of whom they regarded as friends—achieved their financial objectives.

The customer base they served was largely drawn from better-off individuals and commercial companies: most of the population at that time was 'unbanked'. It was quite difficult to get a mortgage or loan, which required interviews, references, and, possibly, waiting for the finance to be allocated. Although the local manager might offer limited advice, he or she didn't normally try to sell other financial products unless pressed. Remuneration was relatively low compared with other professional earnings, with little or no element of performance-related pay. Deposit-taking and lending activities were the dominant activity of banks, and there was little pressure to cross-sell other products. As a general rule, managers avoided conflicts of interest as a matter of personal integrity. Competition on loan and deposit rates was weak, and rationing (often at government behest) led to large unsatisfied demand for credit from creditworthy customers.

The banking community at the time operated largely by self-regulatory agreement, but with some legal underpinning. The only institutions who engaged in complex or risky transactions were the merchant/investment banks and other specialist brokers and traders. They too were careful as they were taking risks mostly with their own funds, given that they were structured as partnerships. Investment bankers depended very much on their reputation, which was developed through long-term relationships with clients and other counterparties within the City (Armstrong 2012).

Professional standards were maintained partly by the firms themselves and partly by the training and qualification of various types of functionary. Industry bodies, such as the Chartered Institute of Bankers in Scotland, established in 1875, maintained a variety of qualifications for bankers. The Bank of Scotland, for example, had a 'Superintendent of Branches' and employed inspectors who were responsible for control of the Bank's 256 branches and for ensuring that rules and procedures were strictly followed and clients were served well (Cameron 1995). Most banks had similar inspection regimes.

The reputation of banking was also protected by 'recognition' by the Bank of England. The Bank expected self-discipline and mutual support for members who got into difficulties. The prime focus of the lending banker or financier was to ensure that their capital was safe. The Bank, as lender of last resort, played a leadership role in this system. It was able to do so partly because it was held in high regard, partly because its actions were regarded as appropriate, and partly because it had some power to punish transgressors: for example, by withdrawing access to essential facilities or to government business. The regulatory structure, managed by the Bank of England, played an important part in ensuring that the banking system was a trustworthy one.

2.4 Pressures for Change

2.4.1 Increased Demand for Financial Services

Three important trends greatly increased the proportion of the population who consumed financial services: the democratisation of banking, the rise of the 'property-owning democracy', and the political encouragement of personal pensions.

The Turner Review highlighted how total mortgage debt in the UK increased from 50% to 80% of GDP between 1999 and 2007, fuelled by a steep increase in loans to lower-income households (FSA 2009). The implementation of Basel II, which created incentives for banks to carry mortgage debt, contributed to a steep rise in mortgages in 2004. There was also a push by US-based lenders to enter into the UK mortgage market, bringing aggressive sales practices to a largely unregulated market. The ability of the main UK lenders to finance the rapid expansion of debt was facilitated by the availability of large-scale interbank funding and the ease with which they could securitise and sell rapidly accumulating credit assets (FSA 2009).

In addition, increasing longevity required savings for retirement and care. Regulations, taxation, and falling investment yields led corporate pension providers to transfer the risks of pension provision from themselves to their employees. Contributions into pension schemes rose steeply from the 1970s, creating sizeable funds to be managed (Johnson 2012).

Another factor fuelling the growth of the financial sector in Britain was the growth of world financial surpluses that needed to be invested: from petrodollars to the Chinese surplus. New types of transactions, leveraged buyouts, and private equity all needed to be supported. Capital markets became internationalised, and companies from all over the world came to list securities on UK markets. Investors wanted exposure not just to UK and US markets but also to an ever-increasing array of emerging markets. Mergers and acquisition (M&A) activities increased, with productive firms increasingly using leveraged finance to finance new acquisitions. In a number of cases, the acquisitions proved to be ill-advised. In retrospect, they masked an underlying weakness in operations (Kay 2012b). In addition, the privatisation of government-owned infrastructure industries created a new group of shareholders who had not previously owned shares. There was also rapid growth in government-introduced tax-free savings plans, such as TESSAs, ISAs, and SIPPs.[3]

2.4.2 Consolidation and Increase in Size

Unsurprisingly, the combination of increased industry activity, supported by increased automation, and the growth in demand for financial services generated rapid growth in the size of the sector. Figure 2.1 illustrates how in the period from 1970 onward, banking assets as a share of GDP in the UK rose from around 100% to nearly 600%. Over the same period other sectors declined, notably manufacturing. In the US the size of the banking sector likewise increased. However, in contrast to the UK, the banking sector in the US maintained a stable proportion of a growing economy.

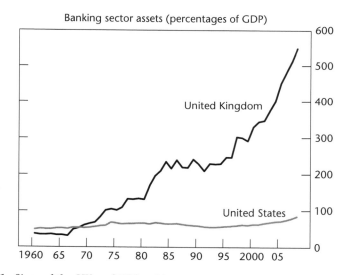

Figure 2.1. Sizes of the UK and US banking systems

Source: Sheppard (1971), Bank of England Federal Deposit Insurance Corporation, and ONS. Appeared in Davies et al. (2010). 'Evolution of the UK Banking System', *Quarterly Bulletin*, 50(4): 321–32

Growth in size was accompanied by consolidation. Figure 2.2 shows that the concentration of the UK banking industry was rapid, with the sixteen main banking groups which existed in the 1960s being consolidated into five by 2010.

---

[3] Tax-exempt special savings accounts, individual savings accounts, and self-invested personal pensions.

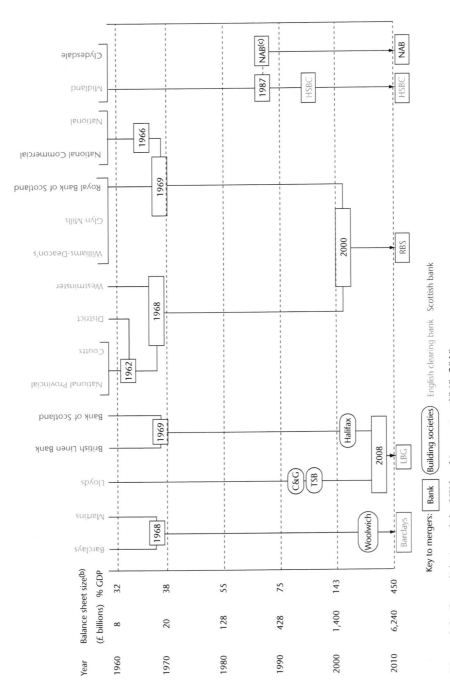

Figure 2.2. Consolidation of the UK banking sector, 1960–2010

Source: Bankers Magazine, Collins (1988), published accounts, and RBS Archives. Appeared in Davies et al. (2010). 'Evolution of the UK Banking System', *Quarterly Bulletin*, 50(4): 321–32

Consolidation was said to permit the British banking industry to compete internationally. However, as discussed below, the resulting banks became 'too big to fail', creating moral hazard problems and imposing externalities (Boone and Johnson 2010). The leaders of the banks aggressively pursued ever-higher returns, and acquisitions provided additional capital to underpin an increasingly wide range of activities. Banks acquired major institutions, such as building societies, which were less highly leveraged, in order to take advantage of their assets and customer base.[4] One effect of the amalgamation was that the banking sector took over activities previously carried out by building societies and trusts. Figure 2.3 charts the rapid growth of the banking sector, in a period when building societies and unit trusts hardly changed their share of GDP.

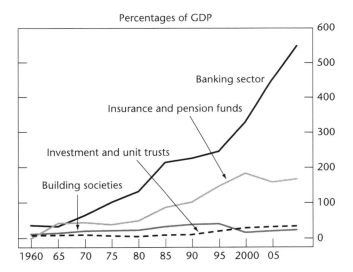

Figure 2.3. Assets of UK financial subsectors
Source: Sheppard (1971), Watson (2004), ONS and Bank calculations. Appeared in Davies et al. (2010). 'Evolution of the UK Banking System', *Quarterly Bulletin*, 50(4): 321–32

A similar consolidation occurred among the building societies themselves. As pressure on the building societies from the banking groups intensified, the over 700 building societies which existed in 1960 were reduced to under 100 by 1990. Demutualisation also led to many of the building societies carrying out wider banking activities, and to the takeover of some by the major banks.

---

[4] In the decade following 2000, two of the largest building societies (Halifax and Woolwich) were absorbed into the banking groups (Bank of Scotland and Barclays respectively).

2.4.3 Big Bang

In the 1980s the tide flowing in favour of deregulation swept away various rules and restrictions, altering the structure of financial markets in what became known as the 'Big Bang'. Fixed commission charges were abolished, as was the distinction between stock-jobbers and stockbrokers, and the Stock Exchange changed to electronic trading. The intellectual climate was united in its belief in efficient markets. Economists, business schools, and political rhetoric all emphasised the benefits for the economy of self-interest, guided by the 'invisible hand' of competitive markets. Financial innovation, and the growth in scale and complexity that it created, were accepted without question as making the system 'both more efficient and less risky' (Turner 2010).

After the Big Bang, previously separate financial organisations began to merge, and capital markets became dominated by global investment banks with large capital bases (Armstrong 2012). Firms that had previously been partnerships or operated under extended liability became large limited liability companies, creating incentives for greater risk taking (Haldane 2011). There was a wave of interest expressed by foreign-owned banks in establishing a presence in the City, often through acquisition.

The principal assets of the acquired businesses were their staff (particularly management and senior professionals). Moreover, there were many more banks seeking to acquire businesses than there were target businesses. Accordingly, the banks that could offer the most attractive remuneration packages (often US banks) ended up as the successful acquirers. Employees were no longer tied to firms through partnership structures and firm-specific skills (Armstrong 2012).

This internationalisation of investment banking accelerated two trends which Morrison and Wilhelm (2013) see as reducing trustworthy behaviour in banking. In the first instance, by weakening the nexus between an institution and any particular community it resulted in less attention being paid to conserving the social and reputational capital of the bank. In addition, the creation of 'star players' resulted in individual reputations that were not aligned with those of the institution itself.

The arrival of overseas banks was often accompanied by the formation of a 'markets division', managed by people who had begun their careers as traders. These individuals were often aggressive and abrasive, and came to dominate the boards and management committees of their firms. Their high levels of pay led to a compensating surge in the pay of other bank board members, which could only be justified by raising shareholder expectations of returns. These higher returns were achieved by increasing the levels of leverage and risk assumed by the bank and its shareholders (Haldane, Brennan, and

Madouros 2011). The foundations of a City which had been based on delivering a service were transformed into ones built on delivering high returns (both for financial firms and for managers) through the assumption of risk.

2.4.3.1 CHANGED BUSINESS MODELS

The major banking groups of today emerged from the amalgamation of three very different types of institutions, as illustrated in Figure 2.4.

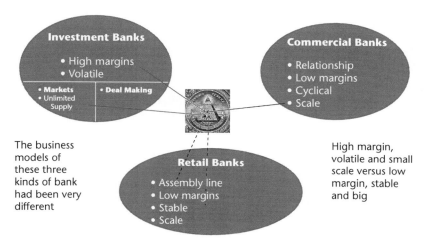

Figure 2.4. Changed business models

Prior to 1970, retail banks, such as Bank of Scotland, Midland Bank, Barclays, and National Westminster Bank, provided a stable but low-margin service, running current accounts, paying interest to savers and lending to borrowers through overdrafts and loans. Commercial banks, such as Standard Chartered and HSBC borrowed money in wholesale markets and lent to companies, financing major corporate investments both in the UK and worldwide. Their business depended on strong relationships with the corporate sector, but was highly competitive and hence also fairly low margin. Finally, the 'merchant' or investment banks, such as Goldman Sachs, Morgan Stanley in the US, Kleinwort Benson, and S&G Warburg took equity positions in major deals and infrastructure investments, facilitated mergers and acquisitions, and engaged in more speculative activity such as proprietary trading.

As markets permitted greater leverage, and risks became less transparent, investment bank activity became more profitable and grew rapidly. The amalgamations permitted the balance sheets of the retail and commercial parts of the business to be utilised to support the more risky activities of the investment banks. Moreover, consolidation was actively encouraged by successive governments in order to enhance the UK's position in global financial services markets.

The amalgamations reversed the separation of activities that had been imposed formally in the US by the Glass-Steagall Act and informally in the UK. One of the key benefits of the separation was to protect the payments system and deposit-taking activities, and hence the real economy, from banking crises. In doing so, separation limited the moral hazard problem which arose from the explicit guarantee of deposit-taking institutions and the implicit guarantee of financial bailouts for financial organisations whose failure would pose a major risk to the broader economy. Removal of the separation meant that the guarantees were extended more widely, to include the more risky financial activities conducted by investment banks.

Equally important were the changes in incentives and conduct that followed from the merger of businesses with very different assets and skills (Armstrong and Davis 2012). The skills of staff in investment banks were firm-specific, and tended to be learned 'on the job'. By contrast, the assets of retail banks were backed by collateral and involved clear property rights. Skills tended to be codified, with junior staff able to move between institutions easily. The merged banks created a wave of new assets, using the large capital base of the retail banks to increase the volume of proprietary trading. Instead of the partnership model of the investment banks, the merged firms were able to capitalise on limited liability, with senior executives able to move freely between them (Armstrong 2012).

Many have commented on the clash of the trading culture of investment banks with the more conservative and bureaucratic culture within retail banks, and the fact that the trading culture generally 'came out on top' of the merged banks (Kay 2010). Indeed, Wolf went so far as to suggest that the Independent Commission on Banking (ICB)'s recommendation of a ring fence should reduce the 'contamination' of retail banking by the short-term trading culture of investment banking (Wolf 2012). The consequences of these changes for the trustworthiness of the industry are discussed further below.

2.4.3.2 CHANGED SOURCES OF EARNINGS

Deregulation and amalgamation resulted in a change of business focus, reflecting changes in the main source of earnings for the major banking groups. In the 1960s banks mostly earned interest on loans, and fees for service and advice. In such a world, relationships and reputation were all-important.

In the period following deregulation, trading activities became progressively more dominant within the amalgamated banks, across an expanding and ever-changing spectrum of products (from asset-backed securities to weather derivatives). Size and reputation in a particular market brought increased client order flow, improving market information and trading performance. Market makers with large market shares were able to use their knowledge and skills to undertake profitable position taking and complex arbitraging (Turner 2010). The most important revenue streams became those derived from bank trading margins within particular markets, rather than from direct fees from clients, and the nature of client relationships changed. Clients became important as counterparts for the banks' proprietary trading and their contribution to the success of the banks' participation in a market, rather than as an entity whose prosperity the bank looked to increase.

Developments in information technology were also important. Much of the routine work undertaken by retail banks became computerised, leading to improved efficiency and the ability to exploit economies of scale. The growth of sophisticated risk models encouraged the development of a vast array of new financial products. Electronic trading led to the development of momentum trading and other entirely computer-originated strategies, further eroding relationships and opening the system up to increased risk of asset mispricing.

2.4.3.3 CHANGED TYPES OF PEOPLE

With this change in focus came changes in the type of people employed by the major banking groups. As market activities, risk taking, financial engineering, and innovation moved to the fore, a generation of the most numerate and highly educated graduates flocked to the banking sector. On the retail side, product sales staff became more important, and were often valued more for their marketing ability than for their knowledge of finance. The older relationship managers gradually retired and were not replaced, and back offices were pruned in search of higher profits. This was a generation who were still at or not even in school during the last serious economic crisis and who only knew the 'Great Moderation' economy.

As organisational complexity grew, it became less clear who was responsible for individual clients, for the bank's balance sheet, or for risk and control functions. Although ever-increasing amounts were spent on information systems, and regulatory compliance and risk divisions were maintained, compliance managers were often taken less seriously than the managers of highly profitable trading divisions. Information systems failed to keep up with businesses in a permanent state of flux. Reliable, timely, firm-wide information became increasingly impossible to acquire.

The growth of the financial sector coincided with a decline in the UK's traditional industries, such as manufacturing. At the time, it seemed that the growth of financial services would be the salvation of the UK economy, providing economic activity to replace that which was lost. Politicians welcomed the employment and taxation revenue collected from the banks. As global bankers, the UK had found a new niche, they believed, which could maintain the nation's living standards. The financial services industry encouraged this belief, by delivering ever-higher returns (and remuneration) in the period up to the Global Financial Crisis (GFC).

The industry's ability to deliver these returns was greatly enhanced by the rapid growth of credit derivatives and securitisation. Complex securitisation pooled assets, such as mortgages, and transformed risk/return characteristics, by tranching. The process also introduced new forms of balance-sheet transformation via structured investment vehicles, conduits, and mutual funds (Turner 2010). The associated trading in credit securities provided market liquidity, enabling the sale of assets despite contractually long credit security.

The resultant growth in credit derivatives was explosive, reaching some $1 trillion in value by April 2007 (and covering some $35 trillion in underlying value of assets). Some banking groups also set up captive monoline insurers to insure the securitised issuance of their own and others products.

2.5 Economic Outcomes and Trustworthiness

The institutional structure which had existed before the Big Bang had been one of close, trusting relationships between banks and their clients. Those relationships of trust had been underpinned by the regulatory framework established by the Bank of England. That framework was itself dependent on trust, in that supervision operated by means of close collaboration between key Bank of England figures and senior industry leaders.

The kind of institutional changes which we have been describing in this chapter would not have been accommodated by that earlier regulatory framework. In Chapter 5 we describe the move towards light-touch regulation that permitted these institutional changes. As we discuss in Chapter 5, that move was only possible because of a belief in the efficacy of liberalised markets to bring about good outcomes. Here we describe the changes in behaviour which flowed from the changes in institutional structure, and the move towards light-touch regulation. We further discuss the questions which these changes raised about the trustworthiness of the financial sector.

New business models accompanied the new institutional structure, and had important economic consequences. It was thought that the new structure would spur competition between banks, with customers benefiting from the provision of more and innovative products and from better management of risk. It was also thought that competition between banks would ensure that funds flowed to the most profitable projects/products, and that the costs of intermediation would be kept at efficient levels. What happened was very different, and called into question the trustworthiness of the financial sector.

We shall describe, in what follows, the outcomes of these changed governance relations.

2.5.1 Shareholder Value Maximisation

The changes described in the previous section were accompanied by changes in the structure of corporate governance. The economists' idea, described in Chapter 1, that monetary incentives should be used to motivate people and to increase productivity, was coupled with the idea that the firms for which people work should attempt to maximise the shareholder value of the firm. Economists argued that the ultimate measure of a company's success should be the extent to which it enriches shareholders. The argument was that—under certain well-specified conditions—firms which attempted to enrich shareholders would maximise their profits, by supplying the products which markets wanted. The monetary incentives for employees described in Chapter 1 were part of the governance arrangements which encouraged employees to carry out such shareholder value maximisation. Increasingly, directors were given a legislative duty to uphold the interests of shareholders. A range of governance arrangements were implemented to align the interests of managers with those of shareholders (Mayer 2013).

Stout and Mayer both argue that such governance structures produce bad outcomes, as exemplified by the performance of financial institutions during the GFC and subsequently (Stout 2012 and Mayer 2013). Rather than being the vulnerable party, the current arrangements have allowed shareholders to hold other stakeholders to ransom (including customers and creditors, and also some of the firms' employees). It is perhaps not surprising that the financial institutions that bore the greatest risks in the run-up to the GFC were those previously considered to have the best practice in corporate governance arrangements.

Mayer characterises the corporation as a 'commitment device', which allows the commitment of capital to projects in a manner that would be impossible for shareholders to do as individuals (Mayer 2013). Managers make commitments on behalf of the corporation to other stakeholders, who in turn make commitments to the corporation.

However, successive changes have served to weaken the strength of those commitments, including the move from partnerships to limited liability, the focus on short-term share price as the measure of shareholder value, and the focus on the market for corporate control. Focus on short-term share price means that managers have little choice but to pursue short-term gains even if they come at the expense of long-term outcomes. Failure to pursue short-term goals risks a hostile takeover from a competitor or from private equity in the UK or the US (unlike in most other jurisdictions where there are far greater protections against hostile takeovers). Likewise, the diversification of equity trading strategies has created new pressures on managers to maximise share price or face fierce scrutiny and aggressive short selling from hedge fund managers. The result is that the key decisions on corporate strategy are in effect being made by speculative shareholders, who have no long-term interest in the corporation.

Commitment of capital by shareholders has been lessened as a result of hostile takeovers, because these present an opportunity to withdraw capital for the shareholders of the target corporation. High dividend payouts (very often made even when additional capital is required for the business) have become another method of withdrawing committed capital. Yet only when capital is secure from the demands of shareholders and creditors can it be used in firm-specific investments (Stout 2012) and engender the trust needed for other stakeholders to make commitments to the firm (Mayer 2013).

Current governance arrangements have failed to deliver this commitment. Instead the market rewards those managers who are best able to transfer wealth from other stakeholders (whether from customers, creditors, or from those who rescue institutions when they fail). Shareholders paid managers to take high-risk strategies at the expense of creditors and taxpayers, and this is nowhere more evident than in the experience of the finance industry.

2.5.2 The Pursuit of Risk

Global interest rates were abnormally low between 2002 and 2005.[5] This created a search for yield by banks, both on behalf of their clients and in the interests of their own managers and shareholders.

A common way to increase yield is to increase the riskiness of lending. This was particularly prevalent in US mortgage lending, as well as in the UK and elsewhere in Europe. In the US, the fact that house prices were trending upwards enabled lenders, encouraged by government, to provide more

---

[5] This was an outcome which originated in the US, in response by the US Federal Reserve to a global savings–investment imbalance that was necessary, given the macroeconomic remit of the Federal Reserve, even if it helped to create the difficulties described below. We do not agree with Taylor (2011) that this was an inappropriate macroeconomic policy. See Adam and Vines (2009).

mortgages for poorer people—e.g. for subprime borrowers with poor credit histories—even though many of these people could not afford even the low rates of interest of the time. Many borrowers were snared by rock-bottom initial interest rates, but could not afford the rates to which the loan would reset unless they remortgaged with another special offer. Rising prices also facilitated the marketing of equity release products, encouraging existing borrowers to borrow additional sums for personal consumption against the increased value of their homes. Likewise in Ireland and in Spain, and to a lesser extent elsewhere in Europe, banks relied on rising house prices to underpin lending. In the UK and Europe, banks allowed very high loan-to-valuation ratios which exposed borrowers to the risk of negative equity.

A further way to increase yield was for banks to securitise loans, including mortgage loans (Tett 2009), dividing them into different risk tranches so that the yield of the sum of the parts was greater than the whole. Securitisation led banks to believe that they would increase profitability by turning over their balance sheet with greater velocity, by repackaging and selling on loans to investors, freeing them to make new loans and earn further fees. Because banks were planning to on-sell the assets, they paid less attention to the quality of the underlying assets. They suddenly found themselves forced to hold these underlying assets when investor demand weakened and subsequently evaporated as the GFC developed.

The risk assessment models of various banks suggested that the diversified portfolios contained risks which were not closely correlated. However, these models relied on data from the recent trouble-free years of the Great Moderation, during which risks, and the correlations between them, were unusually low. The findings of these models turned out to be highly misleading. Banks also sought to increase yield by increasing leverage; that is, by borrowing additional amounts in wholesale capital markets to fund additional lending, at a time when interest rates on borrowing were low.[6] However, this method of increasing return increased shareholder risk because the losses from both internally and externally funded lending have to be absorbed by equity.[7]

---

[6] A simple example helps understand this point. Suppose that if a bank invested $100 in mortgage-backed securities it would earn 3%. Suppose that, at the same time, the bank also borrowed $900, at an interest rate of 2.5% and also invested this, then the net earnings of the portfolio, after paying the interest on borrowing, would rise to $0.03 \times \$100 + (0.03 - 0.025) \times \$900 = \$7.50$. A leverage of 10 would have raised the return from 3% to 7.5%, even though the interest rate gap was only 0.5%.

[7] To see this, consider what would happen to the balance sheet of the bank described above, if the price of its mortgage-backed securities fell by 1%. This fall would reduce the value of these assets to $990. As a consequence, the value of the balance sheet liabilities must also fall to $990. But the value of the bank's borrowing remains unchanged at $900, and so the value of the capital—the other part of the balance-sheet liabilities—must fall by $10 to $90. Thus a 1% fall in the value of the assets in the portfolio would cause a 10% fall in the value of capital. A leverage ratio

The fact that the increase in leverage involved banks lending greater amounts to each other was also important. Additionally, bank treasuries had a propensity to hedge risk with derivatives while securing the greater part of the liquidity needed on a short-term basis (natural enough where assets are to be resold), exacerbating the effect of any squeeze on a bank's liquidity. The maximisation of leverage was subject to a constraint on their overall level of risk, typically measured by value-at-risk (VaR), but again they did this using over-optimistic data from the recent trouble-free years.

To avoid regulatory capital constraints, banks sold securities on to unregulated financial institutions—which were not required to hold any capital in support of this lending. They also held portfolios of diversified assets in off-balance-sheet 'special-purpose vehicles' (SPVs). The banks' capital requirements would have been pressed by regulators if they had continued to hold the lending on their own balance sheets, and the SPVs removed the need to sell them on to third parties.

Further, securitisation reduced incentives for good underwriting because the risks did not normally remain with the lender and were instead passed on to others. It is now well known that in the US many subprime mortgages came to be issued without the income of borrowers being properly documented—'low-doc' contracts—and with the borrower often having little or no income. Banks learned how to 'slice and dice' the resulting mortgage-backed securities into different tranches. Ratings agencies—also using models based on unreliable data from the trouble-free years of the Great Moderation—then obligingly declared the 'safer' part of this debt to be of AAA quality, i.e. to be extremely low risk. Banks obtained good prices for such debt, representing a clear case of moral hazard (Tett 2009; Lewis 2010).

Securitisation was accompanied by the growing use of insurance, often in the form of Credit Default Swaps (CDSs), which were designed to pay out in the event of a shortfall on the maturity of a security. CDSs were thought to safeguard the risks associated with securitisation. But the existence of CDSs exposed the system to speculation about the possibility of default which came to be self-perpetuating (Turner 2012b); and that speculation was not restricted to the underlying risk. The absence of any clearing mechanism also meant that unsettled contracts and counterparty risk between banks was grossed up far beyond the volume of underlying risk subject to the CDS. These three practices—expansion of risky loans, securitisation, and increased leverage—led to an accumulation of risk for clients of financial institutions

---

of 10 (i.e. a ratio of assets invested to capital of 10) has increased the proportionate variation in the value of capital by a factor of 10.

(Turner 2012a) and left those who had bought investments dependent on the continuing solvency of those institutions. The failure of financial institutions to understand that this was happening, and the failure of these institutions to protect their clients from these risks, had important implications for the trustworthiness of the financial system.

2.5.3 The Misallocation of Risk

Increases in risk were accompanied by a misallocation of risk and reward.

The charges levied by hedge funds were such that in good times the high returns were shared between the investor and the intermediary—with the intermediary receiving both a management fee and a reward for the return being supra-normal. Thus the typical charge for a hedge fund was a 'two plus twenty' fee structure, in which intermediaries obtained a fee equal to 2% of the funds under management plus 20% of any excess of return over a benchmark. Such a fee structure had the effect of generating high returns for both the investor and the intermediary in good times. But when a bad outcome occurs, the intermediary draws no 20% fee, but is not subject to loss. Such a 'non-linear' fee structure concentrates the losses on the investor, rather than the intermediary. It creates incentives for intermediaries to create risky products, and then allocates the risks to the investor. Similar principles can be seen at work in capital markets bonus pools.

The misallocation of risk was worsened by the creation of products which turned out to have an unexpectedly large possibility of catastrophic failure. Here the term 'unexpectedly large' refers to downside outcomes that are less likely to occur under symmetric distributions with thinner tails, such as the normal distribution. Such 'fat tail' products have the feature that they pay well in most years—yielding two plus twenty for a hedge fund—and only occasionally produce losses. These losses are borne by the investor, and can be very large. Incentives for the creation of products with tail risk of this kind are discussed by Noe and Young in Chapter 3.

The creation and pricing of risky products relied on mathematical models which turned out to be flawed. The report of the US Financial Crisis Inquiry Commission highlighted over-reliance on mathematical models as one of the problems contributing to the GFC (Financial Crisis Inquiry Commission 2011). Alan Greenspan has spoken of the 'vast and . . . virtually indecipherable complexity of a broad spectrum of financial products and markets that developed with the advent of sophisticated mathematical techniques to evaluate risk' (Greenspan 2010).

Many commentators have focused on the pricing models used for CDSs as a cause of the crisis (Murphy 2008; Hand 2011). However, the problem was wider than simple mispricing in the CDS market. In the late 1990s the collapse of Long Term Capital Management (LTCM) showed the dangers of over-reliance on models. LTCM used a model which suggested the risk spread on Soviet debt would revert to a more normal level. LTCM failed when this turned out to be incorrect (Lowenstein 2000). Very recently, in 2012, J.P. Morgan lost up to $9 billion from trading in derivatives, trading which was described by Jamie Dimon, CEO of J.P. Morgan as 'flawed, complex, poorly reviewed, poorly executed, and poorly monitored' (Silver-Greenberg and Craig 2012; Pollack 2012).

There were three clear defects in these models. First, as already noted, the models assumed that outcomes would be similar to those which had been observed during the previous period of the Great Moderation, when risks had been low. At the root of this difficulty lay an over-reliance on the efficiency of financial markets. The efficient market hypothesis assumes that the price of an asset is equal to the unbiased estimate of its underlying value (Kay 2012b). Thus the banks' models assumed that it is possible to make accurate forecasts of value. Furthermore, they assumed that, when liquidity is short, it would still be possible to liquidate risky assets without them suffering from a fall in price below true underlying value. But when the crisis came, large risk premia emerged for a wide range of assets or the market simply ceased to exist. The prices of these assets collapsed and the holders of these assets suffered large losses. The models underpriced risk, and those holding assets turned out to be bearing more risk than they had been led to believe would be the case.

Second, to aid tractability, many models assumed that shocks would follow a normal distribution or that prices were mean-reverting. Of course, tail risk can be difficult to identify in advance, so that some of these failures were due to mistakes—but again the result was that those who were sold these products bore a greater risk of bad outcomes than they had been led to believe. In addition, asymmetric knowledge between buyers and sellers enabled the sellers of products to hide behind models which they knew to be inappropriate, masquerading as being able to provide 'alpha' returns, even when they knew that bad outcomes were possible (Rajan 2010).

Operationally these models also posed a high degree of risk for banks in that they were developed in environments that favoured speed and flexibility over control and reliability. Those charged with reviewing their applicability and controlling their use rarely had sufficient levels of expertise in both financial mathematics (theory) and financial markets (practice).

Finally the models overemphasised the gains of diversification. It is clear that diversification of a single bank across uncorrelated assets reduces the probability of failure of that bank. But the banks all adopted similar diversification strategies, with disastrous consequences (Johnson 2012). In addition, banks became increasingly connected through interbank lending, such that the failure of one bank could lead to a failure to lend to other banks in the interbank markets. This seizing up of interbank lending risked the failure of other banks, even if they mainly held assets of good quality (Haldane and May 2011). 'A situation in which one percent of banks collapse each year is perhaps manageable, but certainly not a situation in which there is a one percent probability that all banks will collapse simultaneously' (Dewatripont, Rochet, and Tirole 2010).

The modelling errors described in this section—which were partly due to a lack of knowledge and partly due to a lack of ability and skill—led to a situation in which the returns for clients were very different from what had been promised. This has contributed to the untrustworthiness of the financial sector, and has led to questions about how to change this feature of the industry.

2.5.4 The Extraction of Rents

An increase in fees charged to customers went hand in hand with the misallocation of risk.

In retail banking, customers are generally not in a position to evaluate risky financial products. Such an asymmetry of information gives monopoly power to the sellers of these products. Furthermore, for many end-users of financial products, purchases are made only infrequently, returns only emerge gradually, and penalties may apply to early termination, so that customers are not able to switch providers in the same way as is possible for utilities such as electricity or telecommunications. Practice in the industry has tended to worsen the asymmetry problems faced by customers, with inconsistent and opaque terminology, unclear reporting, resistance to transparency, a proliferation of products, and a trend towards increasing complexity of the products offered (Sandler 2002). Indeed, the Sandler Review argued that the competitive process actually drives retail banking towards an outcome of increasing complexity and information asymmetry. The consequence of the asymmetry of information and of customer inertia was that banks and other financial institutions were able to extract rents through overpriced products.

Financial service providers were able to exploit customer inertia by competing strongly for first-time buyers and cross-subsidising from existing customers. Competition is particularly strong for first-time current accounts, since once they become captive they can be sold other products such as loans and credit cards (Springford 2011). However, one result of such competition has been an absence of charges for basic banking services. This has led to pressure to impose hidden fees and to incentives for mis-selling. It has also served to reinforce customer inertia, with the general sense of distrust leading customers to regard financial providers as 'all the same' and reducing their willingness to shop around.

On the wholesale side of banking, such monopoly power was facilitated by the increasing complexity of products. In the 1980s standard banking products were simple, mostly transparently priced, and easily understood, but came to be regarded by banks as having chronically low margins. Since then, securitisation, and financial engineering involving other forms of financial products, have led to a proliferation of opaque and high-priced products (Andrews 2012). The use of proprietary pricing models for these products means that it is not easy for investors to compare prices. In addition, investors are forced to unwind positions through the dealer from which they are purchased, meaning that the price they receive is entirely at the mercy of the dealer. And because new products are not transparent, they can be sold at a premium even if they are, in fact, little more than the packaging together of a few standard items. Banks and financial institutions concentrated their efforts on these higher-margin markets, persuading clients to purchase these items rather than more standardised products.

This quasi-monopoly environment allowed the charging of high fees, and rewards to shareholders and managers grew enormously. Recent studies have suggested that pay was significantly higher than justified by long-term performance (Cheng, Hong, and Scheinkman 2009), and that financial-sector employees earned large rents in the period from the mid 1990s, as measured by wages relative to similarly skilled employees in other sectors. Philippon and Reshef (2009) show that financial jobs were relatively skill-intensive, complex, and highly paid after the 1980s, but not before then. They attribute this increased demand for skills to financial deregulation and corporate activities linked to IPOs and credit risk. A further explanation of the increase in remuneration is suggested in submissions to the Parliamentary Commission on Banking Standards, which note that when investment banks shifted from being partnerships to limited companies this substantially reduced the risk to partners, but that there was no corresponding decrease in remuneration levels (Hermes 2011). As discussed earlier in the chapter, global competition for perceived global banking 'superstars' contributed to further escalation in remuneration.

There is nothing untrustworthy about seeking high profits (where there is no conflict of interest), including charging high prices. But questions about trustworthiness were raised by the fact that many of the risky products sold to wholesale clients turned out, *ex post*, to be worthless. A remuneration structure based on short-term performance with limited penalties for losses encouraged managers to take on risky positions and to develop risky, higher-yielding products of this kind, in order to inflate returns and hence bonuses. For example, the CEO of AIG amassed $280 million in personal remuneration for orchestrating the creation of $80 billion of CDS contracts over a five-year period. These instruments led to significant losses, leading to the need to rescue AIG (Dobos 2011).[8]

The Turner Review summarised what happened in wholesale banking as follows. 'It seems likely that some and perhaps much of the structuring and trading activity involved in the complex version of securitised credit, was not required to deliver credit intermediation efficiently. Instead, it achieved an economic rent extraction made possible by the opacity of margins, the asymmetry of information and knowledge between end users of financial services and producers, and the structure of principal/agent relationships between investors and companies and between companies and individual employees' (FSA 2009).

Moreover, such reward-seeking behaviour was not only concentrated on the wholesale side of banking. The consolidation of the industry imported performance-related pay into the retail side of the banking businesses. This created incentives to increase volume through the mis-selling of products (*Financial Times* Editorial 2012).

A deregulated financial sector which promised good rewards to those who invested in it now seems to have been untrustworthy because it combined three things. First, it used complexity and the exploitation of customer inertia to enable high prices to be earned for the products which were sold. Second, these products turned out to be much more risky than expected by customers, and in many cases worthless. And yet, third, those in the industry obtained high rewards for such activity.

To achieve a more trustworthy outcome for the retail sector, the Sandler Review recommended that a suite of simple and straightforward products be made available, with standardised features that would facilitate competition (Sandler 2002). These arguments have been echoed in the more recent Sergeant Review, which has called for a range of simple products to build trust and improve the engagement of customers with financial products (HM Treasury 2012). But to achieve a more trustworthy outcome in the wholesale sector appears to require much more than a restriction of the products which may be offered at the retail level. It requires action to deal with the misallocation of risks.

2.5.5 Conflicts of Interest between Financial Institutions and Clients

What has just been described—increasing riskiness, the misallocation of risks, and the extraction of rents—involved conflicts of interest between financial

---

[8] AIG's mispricing was not recognised as such until after the crash, but it should have been apparent (and was to some other players such as Goldman Sachs which began shorting AIG well before its collapse).

institutions and their clients. The change in the nature of banking which occurred was brought home to us two years ago in a conversation with a colleague from the financial industry. This colleague joined an investment bank at a time when, he said, the objective of the firm was to help its clients to make money and to earn good fees from doing so. But by the middle of the 1990s his firm had changed into an organisation whose purpose was to look for people from whom it could make money. Recently this remark was reinforced by much publicised criticism of Goldman Sachs along these lines by a senior departing executive (Smith 2012).

These conflicts followed from the asymmetry of information. That asymmetry not only enables the extraction of rents. It also makes a trusting outcome difficult to achieve. The standard example of this problem is the market for 'lemons'. The amount that a buyer is willing to pay depends on the quality of the good which is being offered. But the buyer does not know whether the good is good quality or whether it is a lemon. If the buyer purchases the product then the buyer bears a risk of overpayment because they cannot trust the quality of the good. This may mean that there will be disappointment, or it may mean that the market collapses (Gold, Chapter 6 in this book). Solutions to this problem in, for example, the market for used cars include the offering of warranties, and the use of external advisors, e.g. mechanics, to give advice. In the financial sector, this problem was less serious, in both the retail sector and the wholesale sector, when products were simple and more easily understood. Furthermore, it was the role of financial advisors to advise clients about the quality of the assets which they were purchasing. In giving this advice, the advisors owed a fiduciary duty to buyers, imposed explicitly to deal with the problems of asymmetric information.

However, the growth of integrated financial institutions has made the imposition of fiduciary duties more difficult to sustain. The financial services industry contains a range of individuals with a range of functions: brokers, introducing brokers, inter-dealer brokers, fund managers, investment advisors, and wealth managers. In the pre-Big-Bang City of London, these agents were largely independent. Financial advisors had the kind of responsibility to clients that an inspecting mechanic would have to a purchaser of a car. But the emergence of universal banks brought different individuals with a range of functions together inside the same institution. Given the potential for the extraction of economic rents, it is no surprise that the sense of obligation to customers disappeared, and that conflicts of interest emerged. This happened at both the retail level and at the wholesale level, and issues surrounding dual capacity were not addressed with as much vigour in the UK as in other jurisdictions.

At the retail level, customers were sold unsuitable products. It is true that fiduciary duties are owed to such customers by those who are acting as financial advisors. But integrated firms were able to disguise the fact that they were in fact acting as sellers and not as fiduciaries.

At the wholesale level, transactions were carried out on a different basis with customers who were labelled as sophisticated. Much fund management fell into this category, including pension funds and the fund management done for small local authorities. Contract law was used to explicitly override the fiduciary duties that would otherwise have applied to such customers, under arrangements that are now a source of widespread criticism and considerable litigation (O'Brien 2012). As discussed in Chapter 10, complex products were created and sold without regard to the risk of their failure or the fact that the bank or related parties (such as a hedge fund) may have had an interest in their failure. The Goldman Sachs Abacus case and the mis-selling of Lehman bonds to Australian local authorities are notable examples of what happened (O'Brien 2011). Deals which required a particular firm to act on both sides were regularly sanctioned, often by agents who were conflicted themselves.

The misalignment of incentives between financial institutions and their customers, and the resulting conflicts of interest, led to outcomes which violated the trust of those who believed that financial institutions could be relied upon to look after their interests. The disappearance of the independent advisory function led to the erosion of the fiduciary duties which would have helped to ensure a trustworthy outcome. Boards of banks failed to prevent this behaviour, at both the retail level and the wholesale level (Turner 2012a).

2.5.6 Institutional Failings in Fund Management

Severe conflicts of interest have emerged from the behaviour of actively managed funds, which have extracted large economic rents. Haldane has presented evidence that on average, actively managed portfolios underperform passive portfolios, largely because the former gather transaction costs and the latter do not. Over and above these costs, end-savers have to bear additional costs in the form of management fees which add to substandard portfolio performance (Haldane 2012). In addition, excessive trading has served to reduce the value of funds. Woolley estimates that for the typical member of an actively managed fund, excessive trading reduced the end-value of the fund by more than 25% (Woolley 2010). John Bogle (CEO and Founder of the Vanguard Group) estimated that in a period when the S&P 500 rose by 791% (1984 to 2002), the average equity fund in the US rose by 442% but the return to the average investor was just 66%. Fees, commissions, and excessive churn account for the remaining 336% (Bogle 2003). Wide bid–offer spreads are often used to fund a web of hidden complex sales and distribution incentives which in turn further undermines investor returns.

Furthermore, the prevalence of frequent performance reporting and relative performance assessment creates pressures for 'closet indexation' of funds—i.e. passively managed funds that masquerade as actively managed and thereby incur active management fees (Kay 2012b).

These problems arise partly because of the large numbers of intermediary layers between the investor and the market. At each stage, principals delegate to agents, who have more and better information and whose interests are rarely aligned with those of their clients. Such agents are able to extract economic rents through excessive fees and trading costs, at each stage of the chain (Woolley 2010).

Active fund management has come to seem untrustworthy. Active funds have been masqueraded as being able to deliver excess returns. However, they have been, in the aggregate, a means of extracting rents rather than passing on to clients the returns which were being earned from the assets held.

2.5.7 Short Termism in the Equity Market

Short termism in the equity market has amplified these problems, and has been widely criticised (Stout 2012). Emphasis by financial intermediaries and shareholders on short-term share value will harm long-term investors when it forces managers to focus on short-term outcomes rather than on the capabilities and performance of their company. Stout and others suggest that corporations need to be protected from the pressure to behave opportunistically in this way.[9]

The Kay Review of UK Equity Markets examined these concerns for the UK. 'Short-termism in business may be characterised both as a tendency to under-investment, whether in physical assets or in intangibles such as product development, employee skills and reputation with customers, and as hyperactive behaviour by executives whose corporate strategy focuses on restructuring, financial re-engineering or mergers and acquisitions at the expense of developing the fundamental operational capabilities of the business' (Kay 2012b). Kay described an outcome for equity markets in which pressures induce asset managers to seek short-term rewards, and in which, as a result, producers seeking to raise funds likewise need to focus on delivering short-term results at the expense of longer-term capabilities.

This is a prisoners' dilemma, i.e. it is an outcome which cannot be changed by the behaviour of any one player. To understand why this is so, Kay holds up as a benchmark an equity market which would deliver relationships based on trust and respect. Kay views trust as a behaviour which shows a

---

[9] Both Stout (2012) and Kay (2012b) invoke the story of Ulysses and the sirens as an example of a device used to combat short termism.

willingness to invest for the longer term. Respect is taken to mean a recognition, both by investing firms and by the financial intermediaries that provide them with capital, that savers seek the high returns which go with successful, longer-term investment.

Financial intermediaries are forced—by inter-institutional competition—to aim for short-term return. Longer-term relationships are difficult to sustain in the workings of anonymous markets, which enable participants to make short-term gains at each other's expense (Kay 2012b). Such competition encourages exit over voice, and precludes an engagement by the financial intermediaries with the longer-term interests of the firms in which they invest. Voice requires an analysis of firms' underlying fundamentals. The ability to carry out such analysis requires financial intermediaries to develop knowledge of a few companies in which their money is invested, and the investment of significant resources in that analysis. That is, acting in a trusting way is costly for intermediaries. It is at present under-rewarded in the equity market, since intermediaries who invest for the long term will not benefit if other investors demand that firms instead aim for short-term returns. The Sandler Review expressed concerns about the excessive focus on past performance and the short timescales used for performance assessment (Sandler 2002), and these concerns are repeated by Kay (2012b).

Producers who seek to raise funds face a similar structural problem. They can attempt to build their core competencies over the longer term, or they can aim for shorter-term rewards. An unwillingness by financial intermediaries to invest for the longer term leads to a focus by productive firms on delivering short-term rewards, activity which includes an overemphasis on financial engineering. It also leads to a governance structure which focuses on such short-term rewards.

Such an emphasis on relative short-term performance encourages herding, as asset managers want to avoid being seen to underperform relative to the average, and hence tend to follow what other asset managers do (Kay 2012b). Furthermore, such herding creates momentum, in which case it becomes rational for traders to respond by further adopting momentum strategies, thereby reinforcing momentum behaviour in the market (Woolley 2010). This can lead to asset price bubbles and to systemic instability, as happened in the run-up to the recent crisis and also during the dotcom boom of 1999–2000. The current disclosure regime does not solve this problem and the operation of a mark-to-market accounting system accentuates these difficulties.

These problems are driven by the effect of short termism on the remuneration of those who work in the financial sector. Remuneration structures involve annual performance fees for asset managers, with large bonuses based on short-term profits. These structures give rise to decisions which produce short-term returns, encouraging asset management behaviour that protects relative performance at the expense of underlying value.

The consequences identified by Kay are that equity markets fail to meet both the financing and governance needs of companies seeking to invest for the longer term and the expectations of savers seeking high returns from companies (Kay 2012a). The structure of the equity market as a whole makes it difficult to achieve a cooperative outcome which supports either trust or respect. More cooperative outcomes require a number of features, which we discuss later in the book.

2.5.8 Macroeconomic Collapse, Regulatory Failure, and Externalities

By 2007, the proportion of subprime mortgages not being regularly serviced had increased considerably in the US, and investors in mortgage-backed securities started to mistrust the quality of banks' lending policies. In the UK, banks like Northern Rock, which had relied on short-term wholesale funding for its mortgage lending, became short of liquidity. Uncertainty spread as to which banks were most exposed to mortgage losses, or to liquidity shortages, or exposed to another bank suffering from these problems. Banks ceased to trust the ability of other banks to repay their debt and were only willing to lend to each other at very short maturities, if at all (Miles 2011), forcing central banks to intermediate in the provision of daily liquidity.

There were fundamental failings in the regulatory framework which enabled this to happen. The details of these regulatory failings are discussed in Chapter 5; here we describe their macroeconomic implications.

The first failing involved the way in which capital requirements were regulated by the Basel Accords. The Basel I Accord—launched in the late 1980s—required that regulators enforce a minimum of total capital equal to 8% of banks' assets, with the assets weighted by coefficients designed to reflect their relative riskiness. But the risk weights adopted were arbitrary. The Basel II Accords—promulgated in 2004 after much negotiation—responded by allowing banks to use their own internal ratings and statistical models and experience to calculate lower levels of prudential capital where these processes had been reviewed and approved by their supervisor. The view embodied in Basel II—that it is appropriate for regulators to identify capital needs in this formula-based way—placed a great faith in the mathematical models underpinning the internal ratings-based (IRB) formulae. However, such faith was grossly misplaced in the light of the changes in the financial regime, and the failings of the models which we have identified above. Furthermore, the required calculations were embedded in a spectacularly obscure system. 'The outcome was a regulatory framework...far too complex to permit anyone external to the relationship between bank and supervisor to judge whether the supervisor [had] done its work properly' (Dewatripont, Rochet, and Tirole 2010). This was a framework perfectly designed for regulatory capture, and it became impossible to protect regulators from aggressive pressure from the regulated banks for yet looser regulation. Consequently, regulation failed to prevent banks from holding too little capital protection as they pursued risky returns. In the aggregate, banks were not holding sufficient capital against the risk that an outlying contingency would materialise, both at the individual level and at the systemic level.

More importantly, the Basel Accords failed to recognise the importance of liquidity. In the GFC, banks needed to be rescued because, regardless of their overall capital position, they had insufficient short-term liquidity to meet their immediate liabilities. The pre-Big-Bang system of financial regulation had required that banks hold very significant amounts of liquid assets—as discussed in Chapter 5. But these requirements were steadily eroded in favour of a concentration on capital. It is well known that Northern Rock determined that under the new Basel II rules, there was so much spare capital that it was appropriate for it to increase its dividend by 20% in July 2007. According to IRB-type calculations its capital requirement was only £1.52 billion. Three months later the bank collapsed because of a liquidity crisis, created by a massive withdrawal of wholesale funding and panic on the part of its depositors. When this happened the British authorities had to inject £23 billion into the bank. Similarly, in the US, a few days before bankruptcy Lehman Bros boasted a Tier 1 capital ratio of 11% when the regulatory requirement was for only 4% (Dewatripont, Rochet, and Tirole 2010). The whole system failed to identify new threats, with neither accord foreseeing the possibility of default on EU government debt.

Another failing was macroeconomic. When the financial crisis arrived in 2008, it turned out that the assets held by banks were not as diversified as they thought; the risks on these assets were highly correlated, for macroeconomic reasons. The regulatory system failed to identify the systemic consequences of this correlation, or to ensure that the financial system held enough capital to guard against the systemic risk.

It is open to question whether the financial services sector was ever capable of earning sufficient returns to enable it to hold the amounts of capital required to support the levels of risk being run. As capital is subject to constraints, less risk is as relevant as more capital. In sum, the regulatory framework mismanaged capital requirements, liquidity risk, and macro-prudential risk.

Prompted by government policy, securitisation had fuelled excessive credit creation, which created a massive bubble in asset prices. When the crisis came and asset values collapsed, the banks did two things—both of which had widespread significance. First, banks were forced to sell some of their assets because the resulting losses impacted their capital ratios. But that caused asset prices to fall further, leading to further write-downs on a mark-to-market basis. This required further sales and caused further falls in price: a 'fire-sale' outcome.[10] This fire sale was transmitted internationally, and a large shock in the financial sector led to a massive crisis *within* the financial system.

Another action that the banks took was to withdraw from lending to each other. With such 'network interconnectedness' a withdrawal from lending can lead to a domino effect in which the withdrawal of funding leads to the collapse of other institutions (Haldane and May 2011).

The collapse in banking was transmitted to the real economy in a brutal manner. The financial shock—which was initially small—was magnified so much that it caused, at least initially, a downturn in economic activity which was the greatest since the Great Depression and from which recovery is proving very difficult. The collapse in the balance sheet of the financial sector led to a radical increase in personal-sector savings, the effect of which was reinforced by a collapse in the value of the personal sector's holdings of housing wealth. The collapse in the balance-sheet value of the financial sector and the related poor economic outlook also made it difficult for the corporate sector to invest. These balance-sheet difficulties led to a major recession, even after an accommodating fiscal policy and the bailout of the banking system.

The costs of these bailouts and the consequences of the recession have been borne by taxpayers and by the wider community. The risks which banks pursued have thus imposed a massive externality on the remainder of the economy.

Further, the bailouts have led to the perception that banks can take on greater risk and/or misprice risk, safe in the knowledge that they will not be allowed to fail. Moreover, the subsidy provided by this implicit government guarantee itself serves to subsidise large, too-big-to-fail (TBTF) institutions. This is because the guarantee serves to reduce the cost of debt, but it is focused on large institutions to the exclusion of small and medium-sized financial firms.[11]

These macroeconomic outcomes served to make the financial system, and the regulatory framework in which it was contained, a system which could no longer be trusted. It failed to deliver the returns which had been promised. It did this for macroeconomic, economy-wide, reasons, as well as reasons driven by the behaviour of the individual firm and its employees.

---

[10] Krugman (2010) calls this a 'financial multiplier' process.
[11] Haldane has estimated the annual value of the implicit subsidy provided by the expectation of bailouts to be over £50 billion per annum for the top five banks in the UK (Haldane 2010).

2.6 Conclusion

Three trends greatly increased the reach of the financial sector within the UK economy: a greatly increased penetration of basic banking services, an increase in home ownership (supported by mortgages), and the increasing use of personal pensions rather than (or in addition to) reliance on state social security. Then the Big Bang brought about the consolidation of financial intermediaries, both in terms of mergers of banks and building societies, and importantly in terms of the amalgamation of different types of institutions which had previously operated separately (retail, commercial, and investment banks), creating financial behemoths that were too big to fail.

These amalgamations had important implications for the business models of the merged institutions, with trading activities, risk taking, and financial innovation taking on increased importance and contributing to greatly increased profitability for firms and much higher remuneration for staff.

The new business model had an implication for the trustworthiness of firms within the financial services industry. It was thought that deregulation would bring increased returns to customers, through the provision of more innovative products and the better management of risk, and that the costs of intermediation would be kept at efficient levels. We have described above how, instead, this led to excessive risk taking, extraction of rents, mispricing of risk, and more general conflicts of interest. As we have described, the outcome meant that the expectations of investors, and of investment funds, were not delivered. The new business model also led to an extraction of rents by fund managers as the equity market failed to meet the expectations of those who had invested.

The new business model also led to macroeconomic vulnerability, with the economy as a whole becoming vulnerable to crisis. In effect, the entire financial system became untrustworthy.

References

Adam, C. S. and Vines, D. (2009). 'Remaking Macroeconomic Policy after the Global Financial Crisis: A Balance-Sheet Approach', *Oxford Review of Economic Policy*, 25(4):507–52.

Andrews, P. (2012). 'Financial Regulation: Protecting Consumers from Poor Value?', *Agenda Advancing Economics in Business* (August): 1–6 [online journal] <http://www.oxera.com/Oxera/media/Oxera/downloads/Agenda/Financial-regulation-protecting-consumers.pdf?ext=.pdf>, accessed 19 December 2012.

Armstrong, A. (2012). 'Restoring Trust in Banking', *National Institute Economic Review*, 221 (July 2012): R4–R10 [online journal], <http://ner.sagepub.com/content/221/1/R4>, accessed 17 August 2012.

Armstrong, A., and Davis, E.P. (2012). 'Financial Structure: Lessons from the Crisis: Introduction', *National Institute Economic Review*, 221 (July 2012): R1–R3 [online journal], <http://intl-ner.sagepub.com/content/221/1/R1>, accessed 16 August 2012.

Bogle, J. (2003). 'The Emperor's New Mutual Funds', *The Wall Street Journal*, 8 July.

Boone, P. and Johnson, S. (2010). 'Will the Politics of Global Moral Hazard Sink Us Again?', in *The Future of Finance: The LSE Report*. London: London School of Economics and Political Science, 247–88.

Cameron, A. (1995). *The Bank of Scotland 1695–1995: A Very Singular Institution*. Edinburgh and London: Mainstream Publishing.

Cheng, I.-H., Hong, H., and Scheinkman, J. (2009). 'Yesterday's Heroes: Compensation and Creative Risk Taking', unpublished working paper, Princeton University, cited in H. Davies (2010). *The Financial Crisis: Who Is to Blame?* Cambridge, UK and Malden, MA: Polity Press.

Clarke, W. M. (2008). *How the City of London Works*. London: Sweet and Maxwell.

Collins, M. (1988). *Money and Banking in the UK: A History*. Beckenham: Croom Helm.

Davies, R. et al. (2010). 'Evolution of the UK Banking System', in the *Bank of England Quarterly Bulletin*, 50(4), Q4 [online journal], <http://www.bankofengland.co.uk/publications/Documents/quarterlybulletin/qb1004.pdf>, accessed 6 November 2012.

Dewatripont, M., Rochet, J.-C., and Tirole, J. (2010). *Balancing the Banks: Global Lessons from the Financial Crisis*, trans. K. Tribe. Princeton: Princeton University Press.

Dobos, N. (2011). 'Neoliberalism—Is This the End?', in N. Dobos, C. Barry, and T. Pogge (eds), *Global Financial Crisis: The Ethical Issues*. Houndsmills, Basingstoke and New York: Palgrave Macmillan, 63–81.

Financial Crisis Inquiry Commission (2011). *The Financial Crisis Inquiry Report*. Washington, DC: US Government Printing Office.

Financial Times Editorial (2012). 'Restoring Trust after Diamond', *The Financial Times*, 3 July.

Ford, J. (2008). 'A Greedy Giant Out of Control', *Prospect* (23 November) [online journal], <http://www.prospectmagazine.co.uk/2008/11/agreedygiantoutofcontrol/>, accessed 22 September 2011.

FSA (2009). *The Turner Review: A Regulatory Response to the Global Financial Crisis*.

Greenspan, A. (2010). 'The Crisis', *Brookings Papers on Economic Activity*, 41(1): 201–44.

Haldane, A. G. (2010). 'The $100 Billion Dollar Question', speech given at the Institute of Regulation and Risk, Hong Kong, 30 March 2010.

Haldane, A. G. (2011). 'Control Rights (and Wrongs)', Wincott Annual Memorial Lecture, 24 October.

Haldane, A. G. (2012). 'The Dangers of Haste: Short-Term Thinking Is Hurting the Recovery', *Prospect*, 198 (22 August) [online journal], <http://www.prospectmagazine.co.uk/economics/the-dangers-of-haste-andrew-haldane/#.UwtXrfl_uQc>, accessed 24 February 2014.

Haldane, A. G., Brennan, S., and Madouros, V. (2011). 'What Is the Contribution of the Financial Sector: Miracle or Mirage?', in *The Future of Finance: The LSE Report*. London: London School of Economics and Political Science, 87–120.

Haldane, A. G. and May, R. M. (2011). 'Systemic Risk in Banking', *Nature*, 469: 351–5.

Hand, D. (2011). 'Did Over-Reliance on Mathematical Models for Risk Assessment Create the Financial Crisis?', in M. Pitici (ed.), *The Best Writing on Mathematics 2011*. Princeton: Princeton University Press, 67–74.

Hermes Equity Ownership Services (2011). 'Submission from HSBC (SO18)', in Parliamentary Commission on Banking Standards, *Banking Standards: Written Evidence*. London: The Stationery Office Ltd, 161–5.

HM Treasury (2012). *Sergeant Review of Simple Financial Products: Interim report*, July, <https://www.gov.uk/government/uploads/system/uploads/attachment_data/file/191730/sergeant_review_simple_financial_products_interim_report.pdf>, accessed 17 August 2012.

Johnson, M. (2012). *Put the Saver First: Catalysing a Savings Culture*. London: Centre for Policy Studies.

Kay, J. A. (2010). 'Should We Have Narrow Banking?', in *The Future of Finance: The LSE Report*. London: London School of Economics and Political Science, 217–34.

Kay, J. A. (2012a). 'Finance Needs Stewards, Not Toll Collectors', *The Financial Times*, <http://www.ft.com/intl/cms/s/0/f61fe69a-d27b-11e1-8700-00144feabdc0.html#axzz224mTKTsg>, accessed 17 August 2012.

Kay, J. A. (2012b). *The Kay Review of UK Equity Markets and Long-Term Decision Making: Final Report*, available on the BIS website at <www.bis.gov.uk/kayreview>, accessed 30 July 2012.

Keynes, J. M. (1936). *General Theory of Employment, Interest and Money*. London: Macmillan.

Krugman, P. (2010). 'The International Financial Multiplier', available at <http://www.princeton.edu/~pkrugman/finmult.pdf>, accessed 30 July 2012.

Kynaston, D. (2002). *The City of London, Volume IV: A Club No More 1945–2000*. London: Pimlico.

Lewis, M. (2010). *The Big Short: Inside the Doomsday Machine*. New York: Norton.

Lowenstein, R. (2000). *When Genius Failed: The Rise and Fall of Long-Term Capital Management*. London: Random House.

Mayer, C. (2013). *Firm Commitment*. Oxford: Oxford University Press.

Miles, D. (2011). 'Monetary Policy and Financial Dislocation', speech given on 10 October, available at <http://www.bankofengland.co.uk/publications/Pages/news/2011/093.aspx>, accessed 30 July 2012.

Morrison, A. D. and Wilhelm, J. (2013). 'Trust Reputation and Law: The Evolution of Commitment in Investment Banking', unpublished mimeograph.

Murphy, A. (2008). 'An Analysis of the Financial Crisis of 2008: Causes and Solutions', Oakland University, Rochester, MI, December.

O'Brien, B. (2012). 'The Façade of Enforcement: Goldman Sachs, Negotiated Prosecution, and the Politics of Blame', in S. Will, S. Handelman, and D. C. Brotherton (eds), *How They Got Away With It: White Collar Criminals and the Financial Meltdown*. New York, Chichester: Columbia University Press, 219–39.

O'Brien, J. (2011). *The Price of Sophistication: Wholesale Investor Protection in the Aftermath of the Global Financial Crisis*, University of New South Wales.

Philippon, T. and Reshef, A. (2009). 'Wages and Human Capital in the US Financial Industry 1909–2006', *Wages and Human Capital in the U.S. Financial*

Industry: 1909–2006, National Bureau of Economic Research, Working Paper Series, Issue 14644.

Pollack, L. (2012). 'Two Billion Dollar "Hedge"', *The Financial Times*, 14 May.

Rajan, R. G. (2010). *Fault Lines*. Princeton and Oxford: Princeton University Press.

Sandler, R. (2002). *Medium and Long-Term Retail Savings in the UK: A Review*. London: HM Treasury.

Silver-Greenberg, J. and Craig, S. (2012). 'JPMorgan Trading Loss May Reach $9 Billion', *The New York Times*, 28 June.

Sheppard, D. K. (1971). *The Growth and Role of UK Financial Institutions, 1880–1962*. London: Methuen.

Smith, G. (2012). 'Why I Am Leaving Goldman Sachs', *New York Times*, 14 March.

Springford, J. (2011). 'Trust and Financial Market Failure', in J. Springford (ed.), *A Confidence Crisis? Restoring Trust in Financial Services*. London: The Social Market Foundation, 19–72.

Stout, L. (2012). *The Shareholder Value Myth*. San Fransisco: Berrett-Koehler Publishers.

Taylor, J. (2009). 'The Financial Crisis and the Policy Responses: An Empirical Analysis of What Went Wrong', NBER Working Paper No. 14631. Cambridge, MA: National Bureau of Economic Research.

Tett, G. (2009). *Fool's Gold: How Unrestrained Greed Corrupted a Dream, Shattered Global Markets and Unleashed a Catastrophe*. London: Little Brown.

Turner, A. (2010). 'What Do Banks Do? Why Do Credit Booms and Busts Occur and What Can Public Policy Do About It?', in *The Future of Finance: The LSE Report*. London: London School of Economics and Political Science, 5–86.

Turner, A. (2012a). 'Banking at the Crossroads: Where Do We Go From Here?', speech given at Bloomberg on 24 July.

Turner, A. (2012b). 'Securitisation, Shadow Banking and the Value of Financial Innovation', The Rostov Lecture on International Affairs, School of Advanced International Studies (SAIS), John Hopkins University.

Watson, K. (2004). 'The Financial Services Sector Since 1945', in R. Floud and P. Johnson (eds), *The Cambridge Economic History of Great Britain*, vol. III: *Structural Change and Growth, 1939–2000*. Cambridge: Cambridge University Press, 167–88.

Wolf, M. (2012). 'Seven Ways to Clean Up Our Banking "Cesspit"', *The Financial Times*, 12 July.

Woolley, P. (2010). 'Why Are Financial Markets So Inefficient and Exploitative—and a Suggested Remedy', in *The Future of Finance: The LSE Report*. London: London School of Economics and Political Science, 121–44.

3

The Limits to Compensation in the Financial Sector

Thomas Noe and H. Peyton Young

3.1 Background

It is widely believed that monetary incentives are an effective way to motivate employees' performance and thereby increase the profitability of the enterprises that employ them. Among economists this view has been in the ascendant since the advent of modern contract theory (Jensen and Meckling 1976; Hölmstrom 1979; Grossman and Hart 1983; Hart and Moore 1990). Moreover, this theory has had a major impact on how companies actually do structure their compensation. Bonuses tied to performance—usually paid in the form of options or shares—are now commonplace in the corporate world.

In this article we argue that such schemes in fact are not well-suited to inducing honest and trustworthy behaviour in the financial sector. Not only are compensation schemes ineffective at deterring 'cheats', they can also be gamed by people who are not delivering above-average performance. We argue that monetary incentives are ill-suited to resolving the agency issues surrounding three functions which are the key to efficient and stable financial markets:

- *Asset management:* Creating wealth through asset management
- *Risk management:* Vigilant monitoring of low-probability dire-consequence 'black swan' events
- *Asset trusteeship:* Protecting firm assets from diversion.

The specific reasons for the failure of incentive compensation vary. For fund management, the ability of managers to use financial engineering to manipulate the timing of returns makes performance-based compensation problematic. For risk management, the inherent infrequency of black swan events makes the relation between diligent risk management and firm performance very noisy, thus making incentive compensation for diligence very expensive. In the case of asset trusteeship, the ability of fiduciary agents to accelerate the maturity of asset pay-offs prevents principals from using the threat of future liquidation to discourage asset diversion. In each of these cases, the *transmutability* of financial assets—the ability of financial managers to use efficient financial markets to engineer the timing and volatility of cash flows—combined with the high sensitivity of financial asset values to low-probability but highly adverse 'black swan' events makes applying principal-agent contracting problematic.

3.2 Asset Management and Paying for Performance

The key problem that compensation contracts in the financial industry must tackle is tail risk. This term refers to small-probability events that have large adverse consequences. Such events are popularly known as 'black swans' (see Taleb 2005). The term suggests that such events occur naturally and are extremely unlikely. We claim, however, that standard compensation contracts in the financial sector often encourage people to *engineer* the swans; that is, they undertake investment strategies that have a certain probability of blowing up. Furthermore the probability of a blow-up can be quite sizable and still be rational from the standpoint of the agent (though not from the standpoint of the shareholders).

3.2.1 Swans: Natural and Engineered

Here is an illustrative example. A trader in an investment bank is promised a bonus equal to 20% of the amount by which his investments beat the market in a given year. Let's say that the market index is the S&P 500 and that the trader, Mr McCoy, controls $500 million in funds. McCoy's strategy is the following: he invests everything in the S&P 500, collecting dividends along the way. At some point he creates ('writes') a bundle of put options that he sells to third parties who wish to hedge against changes in market value. The options are designed so that the option holder gets all the shares in McCoy's fund if the S&P 500 price falls below a certain level by a specified nearby date, say at the end of the month. (Such an option is called an asset-or-nothing put and is a standard instrument in financial markets.) Prices in the futures market suggest that the chances of this event are about one in twenty.

This means that Mr McCoy can sell the options for about 0.05 times the current number of shares in his fund. He uses the proceeds to buy still more shares of the S&P 500 and waits until the end of the month while keeping his fingers crossed. The chances are 95% that the options are not called. In this case he can sit back and do nothing more until the end of the year. In other words, he can take on one big bet during the course of the year, and if it works out he will have 5% more shares of the S&P 500 than he did at the start. He has apparently beaten the market by 5%. If the market went up by 10% his fund is now worth $1.10 \times 1.05 = 1.155$; that is, it went up by 15.5%. If the market went down by 10% his fund is now worth $0.90 \times 1.05 = .945$; that is, it went down by only 5.5%. Whether the market goes up or down his bonus is 20% of the gain relative to the market, which comes to approximately 1% $\times$ \$500 million, or \$5 million per year. Of course this is the outcome provided that the black swan does not materialise (the options are not called). If it does his fund will be cleaned out and he will have to find employment elsewhere. But the probability of this outcome is small (5%), and it does not place him in legal jeopardy provided that he does not try to cover up what he is doing. After the fact he can always claim that the outcome was unfortunate and that in his judgement it had only a 'tiny' chance of occurring.

This example is merely illustrative and the specific numbers are unimportant. With his arsenal of derivatives, McCoy could have manufactured swans with different characteristics. For instance, he could have written options that had a 10% probability of being called. In this case he would have earned twice as much money in bonuses by taking on twice as much risk. From McCoy's point of view the optimally engineered swan would depend on his degree of risk aversion, his impatience to get the money, and so on.

The optimal-size swan also depends on another factor: the ability of the fund to attract more money. If a fund manager beats the market by a sizable amount year after year, people will think he is a genius and give him still more money to play with. This is true of fund managers and traders within large investment banks and it is also true of managers who operate their own hedge funds. One of the brilliant strokes of Bernard Madoff was to manufacture steady returns that were quite good but not so good that suspicions would be aroused. His returns were about 12% per year in good and bad markets, which in that era was about 8% over and above the rate available on safe assets such as Treasury bonds. Of course Madoff was a cheat: he achieved his apparently steady returns by cooking the books and paying off existing investors with funds received from new investors. McCoy's approach is more subtle: he is not cooking the books; he is just taking on risk. To produce apparent excess returns equal to 8% a year by this method, for example, it suffices to manufacture a black swan that shows up once a year with a probability of about 8%.

How long will it take before McCoy is 'discovered'? In expectation it will take about thirteen years. More generally, if p is the annual probability of the black swan materialising, it will take on average $1/p$ years for it to show up. But the deeper problem is that McCoy may not be 'discovered' even if the black swan does show up. The difficulty is that McCoy is doing nothing illegal: he is merely taking on risks in the hope of making profits. This is precisely what traders and investment managers are supposed to do. The preceding example might suggest that it is easy to spot strategies whose sole purpose is to game the bonus system, but this is not the case. First, there are many other investment strategies that have similar characteristics and look more normal. For example one could take leveraged positions in the foreign exchange markets, or in sovereign debt, or write credit default swaps, and duplicate the essential features of the above example. Moreover the investment manager may genuinely believe that he has a special talent for discerning arbitrage opportunities, and that his strategies really are going to make money, both for himself and the bank. In other words he may not be dishonest but simply delusional about his own investment ability.

Indeed it could be that he actually does have investment ability, and that his risky strategies will pay a handsome excess return on average. In this case the bank certainly would like to employ him. The difficulty is that there is no practical way of telling, within a reasonable length of time, whether or not he is the real McCoy. The problem arises from the fact that what distinguishes the real from the fake is the probability that the black swan will appear. However the probability of the black swan cannot be estimated without having a great deal of data.

Consider the following example. A hedge fund manager produces returns that are 8% over and above the market's returns and he does this for several years in a row. The investor asks himself how likely it is that the manager really has talent for spotting arbitrage opportunities, or is merely lucky in the bets he undertakes. His prior belief is 50:50 that the manager is truly talented. How many years of returns must he see in order to be 95% sure that the manager is talented? Let A be the event that the manager produces 8% excess returns for t periods in a row. Let B be the event that the manager is truly talented and that he can do this every year with probability one. (This is a somewhat extreme assumption but it illustrates our point with even greater force.) As we have seen, a manager with no talent (not B) can generate these returns for t years in a row with probability $1/(1.08)^t$. The investor's prior odds are 1:1 that the manager is talented versus not talented. Therefore, the posterior odds are $(1.08)^t : 1$. To be at least 95% sure that he is investing with a talented manager, the investor needs to see t years of returns where t satisfies

$$(1.08)^t = \frac{0.95}{0.05} \tag{1}$$

This means collecting about thirty-eight years of data!

In practice therefore it is virtually impossible to distinguish in a statistical sense between the really talented managers and those who are merely imitating the talented managers with high probability. However, it might still be the case that one can distinguish between them by designing their compensation in an appropriate way. Unfortunately this also turns out to be impossible in any practical sense. The arguments require a formal analysis that would take us too far afield here (Foster and Young 2010, 2012). We can illustrate the extent of the difficulty by focusing on an apparently plausible way to deal with the problem, namely deferred compensation. These schemes take various forms: the essential idea is to pay bonuses in a form that puts them at risk if future results are poor. One way to do this is to pay the bonus only after T years of returns have been observed, where T is typically three to five years. Another version is to pay the bonus in restricted stock which only vests after T years have elapsed. If the firm does badly in the interim, the value of the bonus goes down, which presumably acts as a deterrent for excessive risk taking. A third and more recent variant is to pay the bonuses in contingent convertible bonds ('cocos'). This is a financial instrument that pays interest like a bond, but that converts into common stock if the bank's capital falls below a target level. In other words if the bank gets into serious trouble, the coco holders are in the same boat as the common stockholders.

We shall make two simple points about such schemes. First, a deferral of three to five years does not amount to much of a deterrent. Consider McCoy again, and suppose that his bonus is computed on the basis of returns over a five-year period. If the annual probability of a black swan is 5%, the probability that no black swan materialises in five years is $0.95^5 = 0.77$. Meanwhile his excess returns have been compounding: he makes 5% above the market in every year that the black swan does not appear. After five years he has made $(1.05)^5 = 1.28$, which is a 28% higher return than the stock market. Hence at the end of five years his bonus will be 20% of 28%, which is 5.6%. Notice that this is actually larger than if he were paid a bonus in each year in which the black swan does not appear. (The latter is 20% of 5% = 1% for five years running, which comes to 5%.) Thus postponement for three to five years has relatively little effect on the incentive to take on risk; it merely forces the trader to wait longer for his money.

It is also instructive to look at the scheme whereby bankers are paid their bonuses in cocos, which has been proposed recently by some investment banks. The first point to observe is that the rate of interest on a coco bond must be larger than the risk-free rate because investors need to be compensated for the possibility that the bond will convert to equity when the bank gets into trouble (in which case the equity could turn out to be worthless). Suppose that the risk-free rate is zero and the probability of conversion is p

per annum. Assume for simplicity that conversion leads to a total loss. Then the appropriate interest rate on the cocos is $r = 1/(1 - p) - 1$, since this implies that the expected excess return is zero $((1 + r)(1 - p) - 1 = 0)$.

Suppose now that the managers of an investment bank are paid their bonuses in cocos, and suppose for the sake of argument that payment is 10% of the excess return. Their actions create the risk level p. Assuming they have no special investment talent, the excess return generated by taking on this risk is precisely r. At the end of a year the cocos are worth exactly 1 in expectation, because the extra interest offsets the probability of loss. Hence in expectation the bonuses are worth $0.10\,r$, which is increasing in r. In other words, under this scheme the managers are being paid to take on more risk. The difficulty is that the higher level of interest on the cocos offsets the increased risk; hence payment in cocos does nothing to alleviate the problem.

One can in fact establish a quite general impossibility result, which states that in the framework of limited liability there exists no compensation scheme that separates the talented risk takers from those who are merely lucky. Any scheme that rewards the former will also reward the latter to a significant extent. The only effective schemes are those that inflict severe personal penalties for bad performance (Foster and Young 2010).

3.3 Risk Management: Paying for Diligence

The preceding analysis shows that incentive compensation is likely to be ineffective for rewarding talented asset managers. Lack of talent is not an ethical fault per se. Fund managers claiming to be talented when they know that they are not is an ethical fault. However, such managers might simply overestimate their own ability. We now consider another agency problem that is clearly tied to moral fault: negligence in monitoring the firm's environment with the aim of detecting small-probability but large-magnitude risks, i.e. 'black swan' events. For example, before the financial crisis, academic research identified an increase in the systemic risk of mortgage-backed securities. To the researchers, this raised an issue of mispricing. A diligent risk manager might have been able to tease out the implications of this research for correlated default in response to large negative shocks, and thus saved the bank a lot of money.

Unfortunately, monitoring such risks is usually not terribly exciting work. Most of the time, even if the risk manager is not diligent, potential risks will never materialise. Militaries face a similar problem of monitoring for black swan events: watching the parapets for surprise attack by the enemy. Most the time, there is nothing very interesting to watch and most of the time, neglecting watch duties will not have any adverse consequences. However, when the enemy is actually approaching in the dead of night, neglecting watch duties can lead to the death or capture of the entire unit. Armies have developed simple, direct incentive mechanisms to motivate sentry diligence, for example:

> Any sentinel or look-out who is found drunk or sleeping upon his post, or leaves it before he is regularly relieved, shall be punished, if the offense is committed in time of war, by death. (Article 133, *US Uniform Code of Military Justice*)

The military solution to the problem of motivating sentry vigilance is simple and no doubt fairly effective. However, for it to work, negligence must be verifiable, i.e. third parties need to be able to verify whether the soldier is staring across the parapets or over the bar room table. Verification in the case of sentries seems straightforward. However, for financial professionals, third-party verification is much more problematic. Their tasks are complex and probably opaque even to well-informed outsiders. Making a verifiable distinction between an analyst diligently trying to ferret out financial threats and one simply going through the motions is difficult and perhaps impossible.

In addition, firms cannot impose the sort of penalties militaries impose. The worst penalty the firm can impose in an incentive contract is dismissal and forfeiture of incentive payments. When verification is costly or impossible and penalties are limited, a natural question is whether monetary incentives can substitute for punishment and monitoring.

We argue that, in these circumstances, it is very costly to use financial incentive contracts to motivate financial professionals to 'do their duty'. The contract's downside is limited, so upside rewards must do the heavy lifting. However, because the upside is fairly likely even when the agent is not diligent, the relation between upside rewards and diligence is very noisy. Thus, motivating diligence will require huge upside rewards: the rewards must be orders of magnitude greater than the risk manager's cost of effort. If a black swan event is sufficiently disastrous, the firm may be willing to pay this sort of compensation. Otherwise, it will simply take its chances, hoping that the black swan does not arrive. The result, in a world of amoral agents—i.e. agents who place no inherent value on diligence—is either that (a) some agents will receive compensation packages offering huge rewards with very low performance targets or (b) financial firms will skimp on watchmen, leading to an increased probability of disaster. To illustrate these ideas, we will first develop a very simple example which illustrates both the efficacy of monetary compensation for inducing some kinds of agent effort, and how costly and inefficient it can be for inducing agents to watch for and mitigate black swan events.

3.3.1 Black Swans and White Swans

First, consider the problem of motivating a scientist working in a research lab to produce a new invention, the 'white swan'. The scientist maximises his expected pay-offs which depend on how much effort he devotes to producing the swan and how he is compensated. If the scientist produces the white swan, the firm's value increases by £1 billion. If the scientist exerts high effort, the chance of producing the swan is 1%; if the scientist does not exert high effort, there is no chance of producing the white swan. High effort imposes a personal cost on the scientist with monetary value equal to £10,000. Whether the scientist is exerting high effort cannot be observed or verified by anyone but the scientist.

Note that, in the white swan case, high effort is a necessary but not sufficient condition for success. Thus, incentive compensation payments can be targeted precisely at effort. In fact, if the firm pays the scientist based on a simple bonus scheme—£1 million if and only if the scientist produces the white swan—the scientist will be willing to exert high effort. To see this, note that the gain from exerting high effort is earning the £1 million pound bonus whenever the scientist succeeds. With high effort, the scientist will succeed with probability 0.01. Thus, the expected gain from high effort 0.01 × £1 million = £10,000 which is exactly the cost of high effort to the scientist. Note also that the expected reward to the scientist for high effort exactly equals the cost of high effort, £10,000. The firm's gain from offering the incentive contract is simply the expected value of the invention given high effort, £1 billion × 0.01 = 10 million, less the cost of offering incentive compensation, £10,000. This is the best the firm could possibly do. Even if the firm could contract on the level of effort, the firm would have to pay the scientist a sufficient increment to induce him to sign the contract. That increment is the cost of high effort, £10,000, and exactly equals the expected value of the incentive payment.

Now let us turn to a problem which seems quite similar. The firm is a bank with a value of £1 billion. Its value will remain £1 billion so long as a black swan event does not occur. However, a black swan will lead to immediate collapse. If bank's risk manager is diligent, he can detect and avoid the black swan. However, if the risk manager is not diligent, in the rare situations in which a black swan event occurs, the bank's value collapses to £0. Diligence is costly to the risk manager, who would prefer tending his Facebook account to diligent risk management. Expressed in monetary terms, the cost of diligence to the risk manager is £10,000. The chance that diligence will be required to avoid collapse is 1%.

Note that in many ways this problem is similar to the scientist motivation problem discussed above: in both cases, the gain to the firm from the agent (i.e. the scientist or risk manager) exerting high effort is £10 million. In the white swan case, the gain is produced by a 1% chance of producing a £1 billion gain, and in the black swan case, it is produced by reducing the probability of a £1 billion loss by 1%. Moreover, the cost of high effort to the scientist equals the cost of diligence to the risk manager.

There is one difference between the two cases, a difference which will have dramatic consequences. In the white swan case, high effort is a necessary but not sufficient condition for success. In the black swan case, high effort is a sufficient but not necessary condition for success. This makes targeting rewards at effort very difficult. In the black swan case, there are only two possible outcomes: collapse and non-collapse. The least the risk manager can receive if a collapse occurs is £0. Paying him any more than this when the bank collapses will clearly not improve his incentives. Thus, the problem of incentive design reduces to how much to pay the risk manger when the bank does *not* collapse. Let's call this payment, p. If the risk manager is diligent he receives p 100% of the time and incurs the cost of high effort, £10,000. If the risk manager is not diligent, he will receives p 99% of the time but does not incur the cost of high effort. To induce diligence, the expected gain from diligence must exceed its cost; in other words, it must be the case that

$$1.0 \times p - 10,000 \geq 0.99 \times p + 0.01 \times 0 \qquad (2)$$

Thus, the incentive payment must at least equal £1 million. This is exactly the same incentive payment required in the white swan case. However, in the white swan case, the payment was only received when the invention is produced, which occurred with probability 0.01. In the black swan case, if the payment works to produce diligence, the bank will never collapse and thus the payment will be made with probability 1. Thus, the expected cost of the incentive payment is at least £1 million. In other words, the bank must pay the risk manager £1 million in order to induce the risk manager to absorb a £10,000 personal cost of diligence. Nice work if you can get it!

3.3.2 More Generally

The example given above is highly simplified and the simplifications might lead a reader to conjecture that the problem of motivating diligence through compensation is not nearly as hard as we assert. First, in the black swan case, the collapse can only occur if the risk manager is negligent. Thus, collapse is proof of negligence, in which case, tort liability for the risk manager might be an alternative incentive mechanism. There are, however, two problems with this argument. First, even if the parties know that negligence is the only possible cause of collapse, enforcing tort liability claims on the agent would require the bank to be able to *prove* to third parties that negligence and collapse are perfectly connected. Second, we can simply augment our analysis by positing a 0.10% chance of collapse even if the manager is diligent and thus break the perfect relation between collapse and negligence. Under this assumption, it is not possible to infer with a high degree of certainty that negligence was the cause of collapse. This modification only affects the level of managerial compensation by a small amount, but rules out enforcement through tort liability.

Another reasonable objection to the relevance of this example is risk aversion. If agents are risk-averse then they will be willing to exert significant effort in diligence to avoid large losses. It is indeed the case that, as risk aversion increases, the premium required to ensure diligence falls. It is certainly possible to posit levels of risk aversion at which the diligence premium is quite small. The relevant practical question, however, is whether the premium will be reduced to reasonable size when agents have 'typical' levels of risk aversion. Answering this question is not easy because instruments that measure risk aversion are plagued with problems of internal and external validity. Putting these questions aside, most of the literature that has attempted to measure the average risk aversion of human subjects using the simplest possible functional form for risk aversion—expected utility of wealth maximisation under constant relative risk aversion—estimates the relative risk aversion coefficient to be around two-thirds (see Harrison and Rutström 2008).

Using this estimate, and solving for the premium required to induce diligence in the example, yields an expected payment to the risk manager of approximately £330,000 which is still thirty-three times the cost of diligence to the agent. This is less than the cost under risk neutrality but it is still huge relative to the cost of effort. Firms might try to reduce compensation by screening agents for risk aversion but this would be rather difficult. The less risk-averse a potential risk manager is, the more attractive the strategy of accepting the risk management position and then being negligent. Thus, potential risk managers would have an incentive to hide their level of risk aversion. Because risk aversion is hard to measure even where there are no incentives to dissimulate, screening for risk aversion would be very difficult to put into practice. Moreover, even if firms could divine the risk aversion of potential employees, restricting hiring to the most risk-averse applicants might have an adverse effect on employee quality.

3.4 Paying for Honesty

Descending ever downward toward the depths of depravity, consider now the problem of using compensation to deter stealing, i.e. diversion of firm, client, or trust-fund assets. Consider the case of an amoral manager who is perhaps capable of superior performance but who is also able to divert corporate assets for his personal consumption. Examples are fairly easy to identify, e.g. Dennis Kozlowski, CEO of Tyco in 2002. When diversion cannot be verified or monitored by outsiders, is it possible to design contractual arrangements which deter diversion? At first glance, deterrence might seem impossible. However, contract theory demonstrates that contractual mechanisms do exist which can deter diversion even in this seeming hopeless situation. In the end, we will argue that such mechanisms will not be effective for financial firms. To understand why, we need to understand how these mechanisms work. Because the mechanisms are much more complex than simple cash flow sharing rules and because we aim for understanding rather than mathematical rigour, we will explain the mechanism through a fable and refer the reader to Clementi and Hopenhayn (2006) for a rigorous development.

3.4.1 Mother Goose: A Tale of Asset Hypothecation

Consider the problem of Jack, an entrepreneur endowed with a high net present value investment opportunity. Jack has the rather unusual ability to induce a particular goose, henceforth called 'Goose', to lay golden eggs. Jack can never be sure whether his magic will work. In fact, each week that Goose rooms with Jack, Goose has a 50% chance of laying a golden egg. Jack has one more magic ability—he can transform his golden egg into invisible strawberries which he can eat without being observed. Jack has an unlimited appetite for strawberries and in fact Jack desires to consume nothing but strawberries. Compensating for his two magic abilities, Jack has two handicaps. First, he is penniless, owning nothing, not even Goose. Second, Jack is amoral and, moreover, his morality deficit is known to all.

Craving strawberries, Jack conceives a plan. He will approach an investment banker, henceforth called 'Banker', to acquire funds with which to buy Goose. Jack proposes to Banker that, in exchange for financing, he will give Banker 50% of the proceeds from the sale of the golden eggs. Banker, however, is fairly shrewd, and rebuffs Jack, raising the objection that Jack will simply proclaim each week that a golden egg was not laid while transforming any egg that is actually laid into invisible strawberries. Jack, now crestfallen and about to leave Banker's office, remembers a paper he studied in graduate school on long-term contracting. Based on the paper, he proposes a new deal to Banker.

Under Jack's scheme, Banker will take Goose as collateral. In addition to funding the goose purchase, Banker will establish a bank account for Jack and moreover deposit a starting balance in the account. Each week, Jack will report whether the goose laid an egg. If Jack reports that Goose laid an egg, Jack will make a fixed payment to Banker and deposit the remaining funds from the sale of the egg into the bank account. If Jack reports that Goose did not lay an egg, Jack will make the same fixed payment to Banker out of the funds in the bank account. If the funds are not sufficient to make the payment, Jack will hand over all the funds remaining in the account to Banker. Banker will then draw lots: if Banker draws a long straw, he kills Goose; if he draws a short straw, he does not kill Goose and also tops up Jack's bank account, returning its balance to the starting level. If Jack ever refuses to make payments that he is able to make using the bank balance, Banker will seize the bank account and kill Goose. If Jack's bank balance becomes sufficiently large to discharge Jack's debt to the banker, Jack pays off Banker, the account is closed, and Banker exits.

Jack then solves a rather difficult mathematical problem of determining the required payment to Banker, the starting bank balance, and the ratio of short to long straws. He convinces Banker that under this scheme, even he, amoral Jack, will have an incentive not to divert the riches produced by Goose to personal consumption. Why? Because whenever Jack secretly transforms the eggs into strawberries, his bank balance falls because of the required payment to Banker. The reduced bank account lowers the life expectancy of Goose, Jack's only meal ticket. If Jack and Banker have their sums right, diversion will not be in Jack's selfish interest.

3.4.2 Moral of the Story

Our story illustrates both the power and the limitations of contracting to prevent diversion. On the one hand, even when agents are amoral and diversion is impossible to monitor or verify (and thus immune from legal sanction), contracts can prevent diversion. On the other hand, these sorts of contractual solutions are problematic for three reasons. First, they are not efficient. In our example, there is a positive probability that the banker will kill the goose that lays the golden eggs. Second, it is somewhat questionable whether this contract will be enforced. When the banker is about to draw the knife to Goose's neck, he realises that the scheme ensured that Jack was a victim of bad luck who never actually diverted funds and that killing the goose is pointless. One might argue that Jack could at this point propose to Banker that he simply restart the scheme, which would benefit both Jack and Banker. If a restart were allowed, amoral Jack would anticipate this from the start and thus he would have no incentive not to divert. However, even if we are willing to bear the inefficiency and can find a mechanism to enforce the contracted slaughter, there is a third difficulty. We need a goose: that is, we need a fixed asset with a return pattern that Jack cannot transform. This fixed tangible asset is the hostage required to coerce honest behaviour from an immoral agent. If Goose itself could be transformed, the problem of contractual control becomes hopeless. If, for example, Jack could dramatically accelerate Goose's current egg production at the cost of losing future production, Jack would simply speed up production, consume the eggs and let Banker seize the now worthless goose.

Even if compensation cannot play an important role when diversion of corporate wealth cannot be verified, perhaps compensation can play a role when opportunities for diversion are more limited. For example, consider the case where revenue is verifiable and thus not divertible but investment is not verifiable and thus divertible. Under this assumption, investors can see the revenue from the project they finance but not the investment that went into producing the revenue. An example might be a farmer who invests in seeds and fertiliser to produce a harvest. Investors in the farm can see the harvest and thus can verify its size and value but they cannot divine how much of the farmer's budget was actually invested in the harvest and how much was diverted to the farmer's personal consumption. Another example would be limited partners providing financing for a motion picture. The revenue from the picture might be fairly easy to verify based on box office receipts, but discriminating between expenditures which contributed to making the picture and expenditures which were simply personal perk consumption by the directors and producers might be very difficult. In these situations, reasonably effective compensation mechanisms can be designed (Noe 2009). However, while it seems quite plausible in the farm and movie examples that cash output is easier to measure than cash input, the input/output distinction makes little sense in a financial asset setting where managers transform one asset into another through trade and the assets traded do not differ to any appreciable degree with respect to tangibility, visibility, or verifiability.

In short, the defining characteristics of financial assets are mutability and intangibility. Financial asset managers are hired to manipulate the return structure of the assets they manage. Hence, forbidding asset transformation would defeat the very purpose of asset management. Manipulating the return structure requires little more than keystrokes entered on a computer terminal. Any control system so weak to allow diversion is not likely to be able to exercise control over the fine details of asset transformation. We conclude that paying unethical financial fiduciary agents is an even more hopeless task than paying them for vigilance or extraordinary performance.

3.5 Implications

We have argued that incentive contracts are ill-suited to resolving the agency problems in financial institutions. Since these institutions do function, albeit imperfectly, there must be some mechanisms at work that mitigate agency conflicts. Some of these mechanisms involve monitoring, which, like incentive compensation, acts to change the extrinsic rewards and costs associated with ethical behaviour. Monitoring can occur through internal accounting controls, regulator surveillance, legal liability, or financial product regulation. The other lever for mitigation is affecting the intrinsic value agents place on being ethical, e.g. instilling a duty of care, or affecting the culture of banking. The path to a better financial system will be built by retuning the mix of external and internal controls on financial agent behaviour. This is a mix that will not, in our opinion, rely heavily on incentive contracting.

References

Clementi, G. L. and Hopenhayn, H. A. (2006). 'A Theory of Financing Constraints and Firm Dynamics', *The Quarterly Journal of Economics*, 121(1): 229–65.

Foster, D. P. and Young, H. P. (2010). 'Gaming Performance Fees by Portfolio Managers', *The Quarterly Journal of Economics*, 125(4): 1435–58.

Foster, D. P. and Young, H. P. (2012). 'A Strategy-Proof Test of Portfolio Returns', *Quantitative Finance*, 12: 671–93.

Grossman, S. J. and Hart, O. D. (1983). 'An Analysis of the Principal-Agent Problem', *Econometrica*, 51(1): 7–45

Harrison, G. W. and Rutström, E. E. (2008). 'Risk Aversion in the Laboratory', in M. Isaac and D. Norton (eds), *Research in Experimental Economics*. Bingley, UK: Emerald Group Publishing, 41–196.

Hart, O. and Moore, J. (1990). 'Property Rights and the Nature of the Firm', *Journal of Political Economy*, 98(6): 1119–58.

Hölmstrom, B. (1979). 'Moral Hazard and Observability', *The Bell Journal of Economics*, 10(1): 74–91.

Jensen, M. C. and Meckling, W. H. (1976). 'Theory of the Firm: Managerial Behavior, Agency Costs and Ownership Structure', *Journal of Financial Economics*, 3(4): 305–60.

Noe, T. H. (2009). 'Tunnel-Proofing the Executive Suite: Transparency, Temptation, and the Design of Executive Compensation', *Review of Financial Studies*, 22(12): 4849–80.

Taleb, N. (2005). *The Black Swan: Why Don't We Learn That We Don't Learn?* New York: Random House.

4

A Short History of Crisis and Reform

Richard Davies

4.1 Introduction and Summary

Crisis and reform go hand in hand in banking. This chapter reviews five crashes, arguing that to understand modern financial systems we need to understand the fragilities that caused each crisis. Those crashes led to new rules, regulations, and institutions. In each case the reform process took just a few years. The impact of the reforms—intended and accidental—is felt today, centuries later.

The episodes covered include a familiar collapse, the period 1929–33, and four that are less well known: the crises of 1792, 1825, 1857, and 1907. In each of the five cases, the financial system in Britain or America was put in jeopardy or failed. The crises, and the reforms that followed, provide a number of lessons for today.

- **The search for yield.** Each crisis involves what Walter Bagehot called 'blind capital' and modern regulators call a 'search for yield' (Bagehot 1915). It involves the systematic underestimation of risk by *all* financial market actors including banks, investors, the public, and regulators. The search for yield explains the aggressive investments in Colombian debt in 1825, and in American railroads in 1857; it also explains the attractiveness of the flawed trust companies in 1907, and the run-up to the 1929 crash. It played a huge role in the crisis that started in 2007.

- **Creeping safety nets.** There is a tendency to increase the scale of the implicit state safety net that underpins finance after a crisis. This happened in 1792 with Alexander Hamilton's bailouts, and with the establishment of deposit insurance in 1934. The urge to support banks and depositors is understandable, especially when the payments system is put at risk. But it also changes incentives. Before American banks could lean on the Federal Reserve, they were likely to bail one another out. Before deposit insurance existed, banks chose to hold much higher capital levels because their depositors demanded that they do so.

- **Distorted incentives.** Cycles of crisis and reform have gradually driven a wedge between the economic interests of banks' managers and their owners and creditors. Before 1825, banks in England and Wales were owner-managed, so that if a bank failure wiped out depositors, it wiped out owners too. Various reforms have weakened these links, limiting the downside risk that bank managers face. Loosening the economic link between the stability of a bank and the returns its managers can expect changes the environment in which non-economic incentives like duties and social norms operate. This makes the push for regulation much harder.

- **Unintended consequences of regulation.** The crises of 1825 in England and Wales and of 1929–33 in America left regulators dissatisfied with atomistic and undiversified banking systems, and led to laws that promoted consolidation and merger. These new laws were strongly criticized at the time. The emergence of systemic institutions is, in part, a result of previous regulatory decisions. It shows the importance of a careful assessment of the consequences of new regulations.

4.2 1792—Wall Street's First Crisis

Systemic banking crises tend to have early warnings: market tremors that precede the seismic shifts that are on the way. The early warning for Wall Street's first crash was a mini boom which turned to bust in the summer of 1791. The bubble was in 'scripts', a type of option that gave the right to buy a share the Bank of the United States (BUS), the country's first central bank, due to be set up that December. The idea was that investors would pay $25 per script, and then, after further payments of $375, they would receive a full BUS share. If the investor decided not to invest in the BUS, the script could be sold to another investor. This was seen as a great opportunity: script prices shot up, rising by 100% in July and by a massive 950% (to $264) by 11 August 1791 (Sylla 2007).

But the run-up of prices was too rapid. Investors realized there was a bubble and prices began to fall sharply. This started to pull down the price of America's sovereign debt, which had only begun to trade in October 1790 but had already become an international asset, held by foreign banks. In response, the regulators in charge of a pool of emergency cash met on 15

August. They were concerned about the losses in value of the US debt and so between August and September 1791 they bought debt in New York and Philadelphia, its main markets. This propped up prices and helped prevent a market crash. But this was just a warm-up.

The prices of debt securities rose strongly in early 1792. Many accounts pinned the blame for the boom and the bust that followed on market manipulation (Davis 1917a). But more recent empirical studies put it down to excessive credit (Cowen, Sylla, and Wright 2006). The BUS opened in Philadelphia, then the American capital, in December 1791. The bank was by far the largest financial institution in the country: the total assets of all the other banks (there were five at the time) were around $3 million. And it didn't act with caution: within just one month its balance sheet had grown by $2.7 million through new loans. This was a massive credit boom.

The loose lending meant that the BUS had created $2.2 million of notes and deposits between December 1791 and January 1792. But these deposits—the BUS's liabilities—could be exchanged for hard cash. This is exactly what happened, and depositors began to claim their reserves as specie which fell rapidly.

The BUS and other banks had provided too much credit and created too much money. They were rapidly running out of reserves. The BUS had to lean on a private bank, the Bank of New York, for reserves (Wettereau 1937). It became clear that banks needed to reduce their lending. But this 'deleveraging' is dangerous: if done too fast it can lead to a depressing spiral. Alexander Hamilton, the Secretary of the Treasury, realised this, and wrote to all banks asking them to cut their lending in a gradual fashion. The banks ignored him, and cut credit sharply. BUS lending fell by 25% from the end of January to the start of March. This contraction caused a sharp drop in financial market prices.

Fortunately, Hamilton was a keen student of financial history (Chernow 2004). He had studied both the South Sea Bubble in England and the Mississippi Bubble in France, and knew that failure to act would weaken the American financial system, potentially for decades (Sylla 2007). Hamilton had also run a bank, founding the Bank of New York in 1784. In March 1792 he stepped in to manage the crisis. His crisis management had a number of prongs (Sylla et al. 2009):

- **Banks to continue lending.** Hamilton directed America's five banks to lend to merchants who owed money to the Treasury. He encouraged the use of deposit transfers, rather than hard cash (specie) in transactions. Customs collectors were reassured that BUS notes would be treated equally with specie. The BUS was told to issue notes which could be used in transactions as a way to stem the outflow of specie, which was draining its reserves.

- **Sovereign debt strong, and seen to be strong.** Hamilton ordered open market operations in which the emergency cash pool used in 1791 once again made purchases of government debt. He also took steps to signal the strength of the government finances. America had just borrowed £1.2 million in Amsterdam at just 4% interest. This lower interest rate signalled the strength of the fiscal position. Hamilton made sure that newspapers covered this.

- **Bagehot's rules.** Hamilton ordered a policy, most famously promoted by Walter Bagehot, in which the BUS would lend to commercial banks, against good collateral but at a penalty rate. The danger was that the banks would sell their holdings of US Government securities to meet their needs for reserves. Instead, Hamilton set up a plan whereby the banks, dealers, and merchants could use government securities as collateral. The loans would be made at 7% rather than the usual 6%.

By using multiple tools Hamilton prevented the crisis from spreading (Sylla 2008). His response worked: the panic of 1792 had ended by mid April. Confidence in the banks quickly returned and the impact on the US real economy was relatively mild (Davis 2004).

4.2.1 Reforms

One of the problems during the panic had been the informal system of share trading. It had not been clear, during the panic, who owed what to whom. In modern terms, the trading had been 'over the counter' rather than cleared centrally by an exchange. In response, in May 1792, a group of traders met on Wall Street. Many of them had taken part in the cooperative market operations earlier in the year. In the same spirit, they agreed upon the 'Buttonwood Agreement', the origin of the New York Stock Exchange (Sylla 2007).

The traders' attempt at a private-sector 'reform' showed that when incentives are aligned, members of the financial system will come together to create new institutions that support financial stability. The crash of 1792 also shows that this is not always the case though. In particular, despite Hamilton's urging that banks should not deleverage too fast, they all chose to cut lending quickly, failing to consider the impact that bank-wide deleveraging would have. This was an example of an externality, which should be corrected by regulators.

Hamilton's actions saved the banks. Indeed, the number of banks in America grew strongly, with no bank failure until 1809 (Cowen, Sylla, and Wright 2006). But the crisis also showed that when financial system volatility meant the sustainability of the Federal debt programme was put in doubt, the government would be likely to step in. It was an early demonstration of the existence of a state safety net in finance.

4.3 1825—Britain's Latin American Mania

In 1821 there were around 800 separate country banks in England and Wales. Of these, 552 held licences to issue banknotes (Clapham 1945). The fragmented system meant local service: Yorkshire had fifty-six issuing banks, Devon thirty-four, and Kent thirty-one (Pressnell 1956). The banks were small, issuing around £8,000 of notes on average per year. Ownership was concentrated—banks were limited to a maximum of six partners.

The small country banks were unstable. Even in the benign macroeconomic conditions in the decade preceding 1825, 2% failed each year. Nor were they the most skilled bankers, many seen as 'no more than jumped-up shopkeepers, with no knowledge whatever of banking principles' (King 1936). But the small size meant that while a bank's failure would bankrupt its six owners, it did not put the economy at any risk.

Scottish banking was organised on a completely different model. Scotland had around thirty banks, fewer than Yorkshire, but they were much bigger. The newly established National Bank of Scotland had 1,238 partners and was able to open thirteen branches in its first year (RBS 2012). The Scottish model was for large banks with many partners and many branches. Some in England, including the Prime Minister, Lord Liverpool, already favoured this model (Clapham 1945). Proposals to set up joint stock banks had been published (Joplin 1822).

The early 1820s was a period of solid growth and low inflation. Industrial output grew strongly between 1821 and 1825. Interest rates were low and getting lower, as the government borrowed more and more cheaply (Homer and Sylla 1991). Britain's debt securities (consols) had a consistently lower yield than those issued by the other leading economies (Neal 1992). And in 1822, £150 million of 5% consols were converted to 4%, and in 1824, £70 million of 4% were converted to 3.5%.

In these conditions of strong growth and low interest rates, a search for yield started in around 1822. Lending boomed. Some of the loans were pretty dubious. Spain had lost control of most of its empire, and the new states created from former Spanish colonies needed finance. London investors made loans to Brazil, Colombia, Mexico, and Guatemala. Taken at face value they were attractive. Mexican 6% bonds sold at the same price as the 3% British consol. The expected return abroad was double that offered at home. Over £18 million in loans were made to 'enterprises in South America which absorbed the hard-won savings of humble families, by thousands and tens of thousands, were nearly all chimerical, and some of them were grotesque in their absurdity' (Broderick and Fotheringham 1906).

Indirect exposures to Latin America also developed. Easy credit allowed lots of new companies to spring up in England and Wales. Many of these intended to pursue South American mining opportunities. Others were based on international trade. There were around 625 new companies in 1824 and 1825, with a capitalisation of £372 million (Neal 1998). This meant that investors and banks could be doubly exposed to developments in the New World: directly through the Latin American bonds and indirectly through loans to the new mining companies. The share prices of five leading mining companies rose by between 300% and 4,000% in just a month in December 1824.

But investors were taking little account of risk. They had limited information on their investments, and the detail that was available to them often came from journalists who had been paid to promote the new investments (Dawson 1990). Many investors expected the British Government, which had supported Latin American independence, to provide financial support to the new governments (Flandreau and Flores 2007). Investors were not distinguishing between the safe British consol and risky Latin America, and there was too little differentiation between the yields for each new country. It took a couple of years for investors to realise that successful fiscal states (Argentina, Brazil) had a capacity to collect taxes that others lacked (Mexico and Columbia).

Britain was then hit by its first emerging market debt crisis. The initial shock was political. In 1823 a previous monarch (Ferdinand) was reinstalled in Spain, and refused to recognise outstanding (Cortes) debt. The expectation of Spanish default hit frothy markets. Prices fell and yields spiked. While the boring British 3% bonds continued to pay interest, the majority of the more exciting South American bonds did not pay past 1826 or 1827.

As with the 2007 subprime crisis, the trigger was a relatively small fraction of the overall financial system. The scale of the foreign exposures (£43 million) and the total paid in capital for the new domestic firms (£49 million) was less than an eighth of the stock of £820 million government debt (Neal 1998). But stress moved though the banking system. The banks turned to the Bank of England, which began to lend for longer maturities and against a wider set of collateral. It also provided as much cash to the public as was possible.

But by December 1825 Lombard Street was full of people trying to withdraw cash from banks. A highly interconnected London bank, Sir Peter Pole & Co., was saved by the Bank of England (Clapham 1945). Despite these emergency steps, things got much worse. Six London banks suspended payments, forcing country banks to do the same, and a run on the country banks started (Neal 1998). In 1825 and 1826 the failure rate rose to 10% per year.

The financial crisis started to impact British business, and the Bank of England started a kind of 'credit-easing' policy, by lending directly to companies. Despite this there was a jump in the number of bankruptcies. It was another example of state support, but was worth it: virtually all of these funds were repaid by 1828 (Clapham 1945).

4.3.1 Lessons and Reforms

The crisis was, at the time, 'the most overwhelming revulsion in commerce that had ever happened' (Evans 1859). England had been thought of as 'within twenty-four hours of barter' (King 1936). The policy response flowed naturally from the interpretation of the crisis. There were two problems. First, irresponsible note issue by the country banks was blamed for fuelling the speculative boom. Second, England's banks had proved structurally inferior to those in Scotland which had been relatively stable in the face of this crisis (Kindleberger 1978).

The legislation that followed 'affected the whole landscape of banking and currency' (Clapham 1945). Three changes were important. First, banknote issuance was regulated. Legislation (the Notes Act), which limited the issue of notes by banks other than the Bank of England, became law in March 1926. This prohibited the issue of small notes by country banks. The legal restriction was reinforced by the Bank of England refusing to do business with any joint stock banks that issued notes (Neal 1998).

Second, the Bank of England gave up its monopoly as the sole joint stock bank in England. It retained a monopoly within a sixty-five-mile radius of London, but outside this banks would be permitted to form larger (more than six) partnerships. This would allow them to raise more capital. The new banking act was passed on 26 May 1826.

Third, the Bank of England moved quickly to establish branches. By the end of July, agents had been appointed for Gloucester, Manchester, and Swansea. The Bank took its cues from the Bank of Ireland, Bank of Scotland, and the Second Bank of the United States. The local branches did not compete directly with local banks for every type of business, focusing instead on discounting commercial bills that were short term and high quality. This changed the British payments system, meaning traders in one town could receive payment in another (King 1936).

The policy response was highly controversial. The note issue by country banks had been strong, but had only replaced the notes that had been withdrawn during the period 1818–22 (Presnell 1956). Looking back at the crisis *The Economist* was highly critical, pointing to the generalised search for yield rather than the role of pound notes, or the lack of joint stock banks (*The Economist* 1857). Others pinned the blame on private credit creation and a search for yield (Evans 1859).

Nor had the regulators done as well as they could have. The Bank of England's Court minutes suggest that the Bank's response had been 'much too little, much too late' (Neal 1998). The lending of £400,000 to Pole, Thornton & Co. had been done in secret, to prevent other banks from making claims. This was a mistake. Alexander Hamilton's experience suggested that communication of support is important. Perhaps the Bank should have shouted about its support for Pole (Neal 1998). As it was, the run on Pole continued until it failed. The failure became public knowledge, causing more demands from banks. The policy of secrecy did not work.

The events of 1825 and the regulatory response transformed British banking. The new joint stock banks developed slowly at first, with just four, in Huddersfield, Bradford, Lancaster, and Norwich, opening in 1827. But in 1829 a Somerset bank gave a glimpse of the future: its owner set up a new joint stock bank, absorbing five others in which he was a partner. A single, large bank replaced five smaller ones. Local banks became branches. This process was repeated, leading to an expansion of banking and a contraction of banks. Nineteenth-century economists said that 'changes in the banking structure... were responsible for every major influence upon market evolution in the succeeding twenty years' (King 1936). It would become perhaps the most important single trend in the evolution of British banking for the next 180 years (Davies et al. 2010).

4.4 1857—The First Global Financial Crisis

The early 1850s were a period of strong British growth. Exports were doing particularly well. But in 1857 the UK was hit by 'the most severe crisis that England, or any other nation, has ever encountered' (Evans 1859). Others lamented that 'we now unfortunately find ourselves ... in the midst of a crisis more severe and more extensive than any which has preceded it' (*The Economist* 1857). By the end of 1857 the shipyards and cotton factories were idling or on half-time, and the iron exports of South Wales were depressed. Britain had seen slumps before; the remarkable thing about this one was that its origins started 4,000 miles away, in the American Midwest.

In 1856 around a quarter of British exports went to America. Many British assets were there too. Britain held £80 million in American assets, comprised of stocks, bonds, and the credit that British firms extended to their American trading partners. And, in spite of a relatively high Bank Rate in the 1950s, trade bills—lending to companies for export and import of goods—expanded greatly (Hughes 1956).

The system of banking in Britain had changed since 1825. Joint stock banking had expanded, so that banks were fewer and larger. Indeed, there had been a 'monstrous development of the banking system as an instrument for the distribution of capital' (Evans 1859). The deposits of the London joint stock banks alone had risen from £8.9 million in 1847 to £43 million in 1857.

And a new player—the discount house—had become particularly important. Discount houses evolved from bill brokers, a kind of money-market intermediary that would find appropriate borrowers (bills) for investors. They developed into dealers who 'discounted on their own accord' (i.e. took risk on their own balance sheet) by lending to firms that needed cash to tide them over between the purchase of inputs and making of sales. Their liabilities included money 'at call' i.e. deposits that could be withdrawn at any time. While they had a different name, economically speaking, they were banks.

By the 1850s the discount houses had become a popular place for banks to place their excess funds. Banks needed to provide their own depositors with a decent rate of return, often the Bank Rate less one percentage point. So the minimum the discount houses could pay the banks was this rate. But the Bank of England was also an active lender, so the highest rate that the discount houses could charge borrowers was the Bank Rate. This squeeze gave the discount houses a cushion of just a tiny space of just one percentage point in which to compete.

This led to 'insane competition' and aggressive lending behaviour (King 1936). The discount houses needed to funnel banks' funds into investments as rapidly as they could. They actively sought out loan possibilities, lending to mine owners and manufacturers. Some of their agents 'scoured the countryside soliciting bills of exchange'. They also needed to minimise costs. Cash reserves—an asset which makes the balance sheet stronger, but pays no interest—represented money that could be lent out. So the discount houses operated with 'virtually no cash reserve' (Hughes 1960). The discount house, a financial innovation, was also a new source of weakness.

The new opportunity that excited lenders most was American railroads. By 1857 tracks joined Baltimore to Ohio and Chicago. More lines were being laid further west. In America, new banks were being set up to lend directly to railroads, many with dubious capitalisation (Gibbons 1858). American railroad bonds and stocks had started to appear on the London and Amsterdam stock exchanges in the 1840s. They were very popular: the total investment over the period 1852–7 made by foreign investors may have been as large as the total trade in goods with the United States. As *The Economist* reported in December 1857:

> A word of warning. It is estimated on good data, that the amount of railway bonds, and of bonds of other public speculative works in the United States, a great number of which, according to an American authority, are next to worthless, but have been placed in Europe, principally in England and Germany, at their full nominal value, during the last five years…exceeds *one hundred million dollars*. (Emphasis in the original)

The crisis started in mid 1857, with the failure of an insurance company, Ohio Life (Calomiris and Schweikart 1991). Its problems were due to a firm-specific fraud but its collapse 'struck on the public mind like a cannon shot'. In autumn, there was a banking collapse in America. The speed and number of failures is striking. In the last five working days of September, 150 banks located in East Coast states (Pennsylvania, Maryland, Virginia, and Rhode Island) refused to pay depositors (Evans 1859). In October another 1,415 refused payment. Overall, the number of commercial failures in America and in Canada was 5,123; the aggregate liabilities of the failed firms was $292 million. It happened at a time when steam navigation and telegraph communication were starting to connect stock markets (Sylla, Wilson, and Wright 2006). The news was quickly transmitted to Britain.

English merchants who were exposed to America began to fail in October 1857. This included several Glasgow firms involved in exports to America who owed money to the Western Bank of Scotland. On 7 November an American bank that had branches in Liverpool, Glasgow, New York, and New Orleans failed. This, in turn, brought down the Western Bank of Scotland and its ninety-eight branches, £1.5 million of capital, and £5 million of deposits. The situation in Glasgow created the 'wildest panic' and troops were needed on the streets (King 1936).

In general, the crisis in Britain was not one of retail bank runs as it had been in America. Rather, the banks caused a wholesale market run on the discount houses (Hughes 1960). Their balance-sheet fragility quickly became clear. One firm had just £10,000 of capital supporting a balance sheet of £900,000. The discount houses asked the Bank of England for help. In November 1857, two of the largest four discount houses failed. The largest discount house, Overend & Gurney, had close links to the Borough Bank of Liverpool and was in difficulty too (Hughes 1960). Overend & Gurney asked the Bank of England for unlimited discount. Between 10 and 12 November 1857 it received a total of £1.8 million from the Bank.

In 1825, non-financial firms were starting to be hit. Overall, 135 firms, with a total capital of £42 million, failed in last quarter of 1857 (King 1936). It caused a 'grave dislocation in every branch of commerce'. Again they applied for assistance from the central bank. In response, the Bank of England extended its discount policy to provide cash directly to firms. Advances to banks and discount houses continued but it was direct lending to companies that made up the majority of Bank of England emergency lending during the crisis.

4.4.1 Lessons and Response

The response to 1857 explicitly recognised that regulatory safety nets tend to distort behaviour. The discount houses had expected Bank of England support in the face of any difficulty. This resulted in moral hazard: in the expectation of state support they acted in a riskier way than the discount houses would have otherwise. They operated with little capital and low reserves, so that when the shock from America hit Britain, their illiquidity quickly turned into bankruptcy.

In response, the Bank of England changed its lending policies. Discount houses would no longer be able to borrow whenever they wanted, but would have to apply for funds on a quarterly basis. The idea was that this would force them to self-insure, keeping their own cash reserves, rather than relying on the Bank as implicit insurance. As the Bank's Court resolved:

> The habitual advances by Discount or Loan to Bill Brokers, Discount Companies and Money Dealers *being calculated to lead them to rely on the assistance of the Bank of England for their security in time of pressure*; Advances . . . shall be confined to Loans made at the period of the Quarterly advances, or to Loans made under special and urgent circumstances . . . . (Bank of England 1858, emphasis added)

Again, the regulation was controversial (King 1936). First, the Bank of England was 'obsessed' by the way discount houses relied on it, and the data it used was inaccurate. Second, the Bank rushed to reform: it did not wait for the verdict of a 1958 Committee or for the conclusion of the Governor's evidence to that Committee before setting up its new lending rules. *The Economist* thought the policy unprincipled—targeted at a specific type of financial intermediary, rather than looking at an institution's management and balance sheet on a case-by-case basis (*The Economist* 1858). And *Banker's Magazine* thought that the policy lacked credibility: would the Bank really allow a discount house to fail?

In 1866 this question was answered. The Bank of England allowed Overend & Gurney to fail rather than bailing it out. Following this there was an extended period of financial stability in Britain. Some have attributed this to a period in which moral hazard was absent from the banking system. Others think that British banks were too fearful and too cautious.

4.5 1907—The End of National Banking and the Birth of the Federal Reserve

In the early 1900s America had a fragmented system with over 22,000 banks, of which there were three main types. National banks, established by a Federal Act and under federal control, specialised in current accounts, and had to keep a reserve-to-deposit ratio of between 15% and 25%. They were the largest, with assets of $1.8 billion, which had grown 97% in ten years. State banks were under looser control than national banks. They had no legal reserve requirements and so held very low reserves (around 4–5%). They also had a large proportion of total deposits in the form of time deposits which meant they were less susceptible to runs.

A third type of financial firm was important in the 1907 crisis. Loan and trust companies were the financial innovation of the period. As with London's discount houses in the 1850s, they were banks in everything but name. They accepted deposits; they engaged in maturity transformation—loans had a longer maturity than deposits—and they held only a fraction of deposits as reserves. But, unlike banks, trust companies were lightly regulated, and allowed to hold shares in other companies as assets (Sprague 1908). Their higher returning assets meant they could pay higher interest rates on deposits. Trust companies therefore gathered deposits rapidly, growing by 244% in the ten years to 1907. They became comparable in size to national banks, with assets of $1.4 billion.

America had no central bank in 1907. This meant that private banks, through their lending decisions, directly controlled the money stock. The demand for money was highly seasonal, with a spike in demand each autumn when cash was needed to fund crop harvesting and moving, and to pay labourers' wages. Since supply was not as flexible as demand, there were often tight monetary conditions in the autumn.

The supply of broad money ballooned relative to currency. In 1879, banks held $1 in currency for every $2 in deposits. By 1907, the $1 in currency was magnified to $6 in deposits by the banking system. It all meant that by early 1907, financial America was 'riding for a fall' with 'Wall Street financiers, high and low... hypnotized by the long period of easy money, rising prices, quickly made fortunes, and successful promotions' (Moody 1919). Market murmurs in March and in July revolved around the concern that real factors—the demand for steel and railroad earnings—began to look weaker.

In October 1907, a failed attempt at market manipulation lit a spark. Two bankers—Charles Morse and Augustus Heinze—had built a large position in the shares of the United Copper Company (Tallman and Moen 1990). But the value of the firm had been falling as copper prices dropped. So Morse and Heinze began to buy more stock to prop up its value. Finally, they tried to corner the market and put in place a financial trick known as a 'bear squeeze'; this involved buying up huge quantities of stock to leave any short sellers of the stock needing to buy it back at any price. The plan, which failed, required them to borrow heavily from the complex network of banks which they had links to.

One of the banks that Heinze ran, Mercantile National, came under close scrutiny. A run started on it and two others. Fortunately, the bank was a member of a consortium—The New York Clearing House (NYCH)—that provided group insurance. Member banks would pay in to the clearing house, in return for support in times of need (Tallman and Moen 2012). As a member,

Mercantile received support. But this exposed other NYCH members to risk, so the help came with conditions: the NYCH required that Heinze and all the bank's directors, including Morse, resign. This action revealed the complex web of banking relationships. They led, via various other banks, to the Knickerbocker Trust Company.

Trust companies had been 'fancied by those who wanted to get rich quickly' (Clapham 1944). They were not members of the Clearing House and so could not rely on support from other financial institutions when faced with unusually large withdrawals. The Knickerbocker was the third largest trust and used the National Bank of Commerce, the second largest member of the Clearing House, as its bank. This meant that firms that held cheques written by Knickerbocker customers, who had purchased goods, could cash them at the National Bank. This would put the National Bank at risk, and on Monday 21st it announced that it would no longer clear for Knickerbocker.

There was no deposit insurance in 1907, and before Knickerbocker opened the next morning there were fifty depositors queuing outside (Silber 2007). The trust's management announced to the crowd that there was plenty of cash. This did not dissuade the crowd, and the trust paid out £8 million in two hours before suspending payment.

Contagion spread. That afternoon, money market rates spiked, reaching 70% (compared to an average of around 5%). Then, the next day, there was a run on the Trust Company of America, the second largest, with 1,200 depositors queuing that day (Silber 2007). This trust lost $14.5 million, or 25% of total deposits, in just two days. Some depositors had moved funds out of Knickerbocker, and into Trust of America, only to withdraw them once again. They began to hoard currency at home.

In the absence of a central bank, rescue attempts came from the banks themselves, led by J.P. Morgan (Bruner and Carr 2007). On 24 October 1907, depositors were running on the trust companies, and the stock market was in freefall. One cause was the very high prices of 'call money'—the short-loans traders would take to invest in stocks. This completely dried up, with only a few loans being made, and at a punishing 125% interest rate. In response, J.P. Morgan put together a pool of bankers that loaned $25 million to investors at a more reasonable 10%.

Despite the bankers' attempts, a period of 'currency famine' began. Businesses that previously accepted personal cheques began to demand hard cash. Banks in Brooklyn and Harlem suspended payments completely, and by the end of the week all the banks in New York City had imposed an upper limit ($50 or $100) on how much money depositors could withdraw. Between 31 October and the end of the year there was a currency premium, which reached 4% in November. It meant that in order to get $100 of cash from a broker, a customer would have to write a cheque for £104. In this period, 'currency was king' (Silber 2007).

In response, the NYCH declared that banks would no longer have to settle their accounts with one another in cash. Instead, Clearing House loan certificates could be used. These certificates were issued to all member banks that had posted collateral. The idea was to increase the available money supply for depositors, by ensuring that banks used these certificates, rather than cash, in their dealings with one another. The IOUs were acceptable because they were all members of the Clearing House.

But the hoarding continued. Country banks that normally relied on the New York banks to settle their accounts with other banks started to demand their deposits back. In the last ten weeks of 1907, $124 million was shipped to country banks, compared to a pre-crisis average of $1.6 million. Rentals of safe deposit boxes tripled. The users included businessmen withdrawing huge amounts to be used to pay wages. Nevada, Oregon, and California had to declare bank holidays to prevent further outflow (Friedman and Schwartz 1963).

All this meant that the payment system was impaired, the ultimate concern for financial stability. The Comptroller of the Currency, William Ridgley, expressed how financial woes hurt real economic activity.

> The greatest hardship to business generally has been the derangement of the machinery for making collections and remittances. As can be readily seen, this has interfered with every kind and class of business and led to a curtailment of business operations of every kind. Factories have suspended, workmen have been thrown out of employment, orders have been cancelled, [and] the moving of crops has been greatly retarded.

The speed with which real economic activity was hit was striking: 'It took hardly twenty-four hours from the disturbance...in New York for the difficulties to become national...the whole country's welfare is pretty much bound together in a financial way' (Vanderlip 1908).

4.5.1 Lessons and Response

The crisis of 1907 again shows that, in the absence of a central bank, leadership can come from the banking sector itself. The private-sector rescues included the actions of J.P. Morgan to support money markets that underpinned the stock exchange. It also included a system of joint insurance (the NYCH) that could issue emergency interbank money when needed. When private-sector interests are aligned with the needs of the overall economy (i.e. when both wish to avert a systemic crisis), public-sector support is not always needed.

But following the panic there was agreement that better currency control was needed. During the crisis the money supply had fallen by 10%, despite a 10% *increase* in the supply of currency, due to the hoarding by depositors (Friedman and Schwartz 1963). One step was the introduction of so-called 'emergency currency', which could be released to boost currency circulation when a crisis hit. It was used in 1914, when more than $200 million of Aldrich-Vreeland notes were issued, boosting the currency by 25% and preventing a collapse that year (Silber 2007).

But the lasting impact was the central control of the currency by a central bank. The emergency currency legislation included a clause establishing the National Monetary Commission, which sat for four years, issuing thirty reports between 1909 and 1912. It led to the creation of a new form of cash—Federal Reserve money—that would have a much more flexible supply. It replaced the existing currency (gold, silver dollars, greenback, and bank notes) of previous monetary regimes. And it set up the Federal Reserve System as the institution to control the new flexible-supply money. The crisis of 1907 gave America its central bank.

4.6 The Great Contraction, 1929–33

The events of 1929–33 are unique in banking history. America was hit by a stock market crash in 1929, followed by repeated waves of banking collapse between 1930 and 1933. Despite important international spillovers, America bore by far the most pain. At the end of the crisis it had lost a quarter of its real GDP and prices were a quarter lower. Bank failures meant that the money supply dropped by a third as well (Crafts and Fearon 2010). By contrast, in Britain, real GDP fell by 5% and there were no bank failures.

Once again, the run-up to the crisis was a golden period. Industrial production boomed: Ford was making Model T cars at a rate of 9,000 a day by 1925 (Brinkley 2003). Spending on building new homes ran close to $5 billion in 1926 (Crafts and Fearon 2010). With the car and construction boom came strong wage growth and rising consumption. Mild slowdowns in May 1923 and October 1926 both lasted a little over a year and did nothing to dent the overall expansion of 1921–9. And the newly set-up Federal Reserve appeared to be in control of inflation. In fact, prices were slightly lower in 1929 than in 1927, despite the latter year being the top of the economic cycle (Friedman and Schwartz 1963).

On the face of it, America's banks looked relatively sound. In 1929, total assets were around $62 billion, of which around 15% were cash assets, 60% loans, and 20% investments. The American investment securities they held seemed safe too: 80% were bonds, with around half of these being government bonds. The banks had allowed their capital buffers to drop, but this was justified by mergers that had diversified balance sheets (Saunders and Wilson 1999).

But the stock market was looking frothy. The share of firms operating exciting new technologies, including radios, aluminium, aeroplanes, and cars, were popular. Shares in General Motors were very heavily traded (Bordo and James 2010). Few of these firms paid dividends, so the investments were made in anticipation of future gains, rather than a track record of profits and payouts. Banks' foreign lending declined in quality (Friedman and Schwartz 1963); and they raised the cost of loans to brokers, suggesting concern about the state of the market. Premia on investment funds also looked high: another signal of optimism that was unjustified by the underlying results (Rappoport and White 1993). Looking back, this was a clear example of a search for yield.

But while stocks looked hot, business conditions were not booming, and prices continued to fall. The central bank faced a puzzle: should it tighten its policy, to halt the run-up of the stock market, or loosen its policy to maintain the expansion of business? This raised concern in the Federal Reserve System, where arguments about how to deal with this bifurcation of markets 'paralysed monetary policy'. Some economists wanted to refuse to lend central bank money to banks that were making large loans for investment in securities, but this policy was not followed. In 1928, the Federal Reserve began to tighten monetary policy, raising the discount rate from 3.5% to 5%. These rates were punishing for those firms in need of credit. But they failed to dampen the booming markets, in part because corporations that had excess cash started to lend to brokers, fuelling the speculation. In the end, the Federal Reserve's policy was 'not restrictive enough to halt the bull market yet too restrictive to foster vigorous business expansion (Friedman and Schwartz 1963).

Then the economy started to decline, partly due to tight monetary policy. The cycle peaked in August 1929, with production falling very sharply—at an annualised rate of 20%—in the next two months. A series of weak results from major firms started to concern investors. The real economic decline set for 1929 looked likely to be sizeable. But the banking collapse that followed made it far worse.

Things started to really worsen with the crash of October 1929 (Galbraith 1961). As prices started to fall, investors tried to dump stock. In September, for example, the average daily trading was 4 million shares, but on 29 October over 16 million shares were traded. From peak to trough the Dow Jones index lost close to 50% of its value, cutting chunks out of share owners' wealth. But despite its huge scale, and the fact that it deepened economic weaknesses America already faced, many economists argue the Great Crash plays too great a role in historical accounts of the Depression. It was the subsequent collapse of banks (and of the money supply) that would make things really bad.

A banking panic started in agricultural areas in the autumn of 1930, with over 500 bank failures in November and December. This included the largest bank failure in American history, when the Bank of the United States failed despite Federal Reserve efforts to save it. Public confidence in both banks and the authorities fell, and bank customers began to drain the banking system of deposits and hoard currency. Not long after the first banking panic, a second wave of failures appeared, starting in 1931. Again, bank customers withdrew deposits. Between February and September 1931, commercial bank deposits fell by close to 10%.

The failures started to subside in 1932. This was, in part, due to a Federal Reserve bond buying campaign. The policy, similar to quantitative easing, injected extra reserves into the system. The money stock decline slowed and there were some signs of a revival (Burns and Mitchell 1946).

But it was a short pause, because the banking system was now badly weakened. The banks' capital position had been hit hard. Actual capital was known to be lower than published capital because banks were valuing assets at the prices they had paid rather than depressed market values. And bank runs had become self-fulfilling. Once a deposit run started, the only way customers' demand for cash could be met was through quick sales of assets (Temin 1976). These emergency 'fire' sales lowered asset values: government bonds were down 10% and high-grade firms' bonds were down 20% in 1932 for this reason. These lower values depressed the value of banks' assets and eroded capital further, and made the bank's eventual failure inevitable. In response, a new institution—the Reconstruction Finance Corporation (RFC)—was set up in 1932 as an additional lender to banks in trouble.

But a fresh banking panic started in 1933. It was deeper and more widespread than those that went before it: others had been regional in nature, while this was national (Wicker 1966). It was exacerbated by the publication of a list of banks that had received bailout loans from the RFC. As bank runs engulfed the American states, they began to enforce bank holidays. During these breaks local banks were banned from paying funds to depositors. Nevada was first up, declaring a holiday in October 1832, then followed by Iowa, Louisiana, and Michigan in January and February 1933.

The fresh hunt for currency hit the New York City banks hard. These banks had huge interbank exposures, and during February 1933 inland banks drew $760 million from them. The conversion of deposits into currency meant the money stock fell by 12% in two months at the start of the year, an annualised rate of around 75%. The New York banks went to the Federal Reserve, which turned out to be a 'weak reed for a nation to lean on' because it was close to its own lending limits; the central bank's branches did not open on 4 March

1933. America's central bank had suspended payments, doing exactly what it had been set up to prevent.

The nationwide bank holiday lasted a week and until 15 March in some places. It wiped out a swathe of banks: over 2,000 banks that had existed before the emergency holiday never opened again. In total, around 9,000 banks failed during the four years from 1930 to 1933. The failures drastically cut the money supply, tightening monetary conditions, and exacerbating the decline of the real economy and markets. In the four years following the great crash, the decline in the total value of NYSE listed shares was around $15.5 billion. The bank failures resulted in a direct loss of wealth for banks' investors and depositors. Total losses due to bank failures were around $2.5 billion with more than half of this falling on bank depositors, i.e. holders of a supposedly safe asset.

4.6.1 Response and Lessons

The immediate task was to stabilise the banking system. A network of unlicensed lenders was either shut down, or forced to reopen with a licence and submit to regulations. Fresh equity was injected into the system with the RFC putting in $1 billion, or one-third of the nation's existing bank capital. Over 6,000 banks, half of those remaining, were given publicly supplied capital.

After a brief skirmish between Senators Glass and Steagall in 1932, the Banking Act of 1933 was passed. Arguably the most important change was the introduction of deposit insurance, which became active on 1 January 1934. The Federal Deposit Insurance Corporation (FDIC) would insure the customer deposits held by banks. The FDIC protected up to $2,500 per depositor (this rose to $10,000 by 1950) and charged banks a premium based on the amount of deposits insured. This had two effects. First, in the event of a bank failure, it reduced depositors' losses, protecting wealth and preventing drops in the money stock or consumption. Second, it meant bank runs were no longer self-fulfilling, thereby lowering the probability of the bad outcome—a bank failure—that it insured against.

The banking rules were tightened up too. In particular, the investment banking arms of commercial banks were barred from the system, and commercial banks were banned from acting as the agents of non-banks investing in the stock market. In parallel, the Federal Reserve Board was given powers to regulate banks that were granting credit to customers for stock market investment. These rules reflected the view that part of the weakness of the banking system lay in the late 1920s boom. The message was clear: the uses of credit are not all the same, and banks supported by the Federal Reserve System were not to funnel cash to those involved in speculation or trading in securities, property, or commodities.

The policy actions during and after the crash depression have been heavily criticised (Bordo and James 2010). In the run-up to the crisis, the Fed was trying to control consumer prices as well as market activity (real estate and equities) with just one interest rate. Then, when the crisis hit, it missed opportunities to aggressively loosen policy at moments when the economy looked strong (particularly in early 1931). It had not, critics say, taken account of the fact that deflation made the real value of debt and real interest rates more punitive (Crafts and Fearon 2010). And the very existence of the Federal Reserve may have prevented the kind of corrective action that the banks themselves would have imposed in its absence. Large banks would have simply suspended payments as they did in 1907 (Friedman and Schwartz 1963). The presence of the Fed meant they had access to discounting, or an 'escape mechanism'.

The longer-term reforms—especially the FDIC—have come under fire too. Banks, which previously advertised the strength of their capital positions, began to advertise that they were FDIC-insured. The safety net that had made deposits safer had also reduced depositors' incentive to check up on their bank. With the state safety net in place, banks' capital ratios declined over the next eighty years, reaching ratios far below those seen before the FDIC, another state safety net, was created (*The Economist* 2012).

References

Bagehot, W. (1915). *The Works and Life of Walter Bagehot*, vol. 2, ed. Mrs Russell Barrington. London: Longmans, Green, & Co.

Bank of England (1958). 'Minutes of the Court of Directors', 11 March.

Bordo, M. and James, H. (2010). *The Great Depression and the Great Recession: What Have We Learnt?* Mimeo.

Brinkley, D. (2003). *Wheels for the World: Henry Ford, his Company, and a Century of Progress, 1903–2003*. London: Penguin.

Broderick, G. C. and Fotheringham, J. K. (1906). *The History of England, 1801–1837* (The Political History of England, vol. XI). London: Longmans, Green & Co. Paperback edition: Charleston: Bibliobazaar, 2010.

Bruner, R. F. and Carr, S. D. (2007). *The Panic of 1907: Lessons Learned from the Market's Perfect Storm*. New Jersey: Wiley.

Burns, A. F. and Mitchell, W. C. (1946). *Measuring Business Cycles*. Cambridge, MA: National Bureau of Economic Research.

Calomiris, C. W. and Schweikart, L. (1991). 'The Panic of 1857: Origins, Transmission, and Containment', *The Journal of Economic History*, 51(4): 807–34.

Chernow, R. (2004). *Alexander Hamilton*. London: Penguin.

Clapham, J. H. (1945). *The Bank of England, A History, Volume II (1797–1914)*. Cambridge: Cambridge University Press.

Cole, A. H. (1927). 'Cyclical and Sectional Variations in the Sale of Public Lands, 1816–60', *The Review of Economics and Statistics*, 9: 41–53.

Cowen, D. J., Sylla, R., and Wright, R. E. (2006). 'The U.S. Panic of 1792: Financial Crisis Management and the Lender of Last Resort,' mimeo (July).

Crafts, N. and Fearon, P. (2010). 'Lessons from the 1930s' Great Depression', CAGE Online Working Paper Series, 23.

Davis, J. H. (2004). 'An Annual Index of U.S. Industrial Production, 1790–1915', *The Quarterly Journal of Economics*, 119(4): 1177–1215.

Davis, J. S. (1917a). *Essays in the Earlier History of American Corporations*. Boston: Harvard University Press.

Davis, J. S. (1917b). 'William Duer, Entrepreneur, 1747–1799', in J. S. Davis, *Essays in the Earlier History of American Corporations*. Cambridge, MA: Harvard University Press.

Davies, R., Richardson, P., Katinaite, V., and Manning, M. J. (2010). 'Evolution of the UK Banking System', *Bank of England Quarterly Bulletin*, Q4, 13 December, 321–32.

Dawson, F. G. (1990). *The First Latin American Debt Crisis: The City of London and the 1822–25 Loan Bubble*. Princeton: Princeton University Press.

The Economist (1857). 'The American President on the American Crisis', December 26, no. 748.

The Economist (2012). 'Strength in Numbers', 10 November.

Evans, D. M. (1859). *The History of the Commercial Crisis, 1857–1858 and the Stock Exchange Panic of 1859*. London: Groombridge.

Flandreau, M., and Flores, J. H. (2007). 'Bonds and Brands: Intermediaries and Reputation in Sovereign Debt Markets 1820–1830', *Journal of Economic History*, 69: 3646–84.

Friedman, M. and Schwartz, A. (1963). *A Monetary History of the United States, 1867–1960*. Princeton: Princeton University Press.

Galbraith, J. K. (1961). *The Great Crash 1929*. Harmondsworth: Pelican.

Gibbons, J. S. (1858). *The Bank of New York, the Dealers, the Clearing House, and the Panic of 1857*. New York: D. Appleton and Co.

Homer, S. and Sylla, R. (1991). *A History of Interest Rates*. New York: Wiley.

Hughes, R. T. (1956). 'The Commercial Crisis of 1857', *Oxford Economic Papers*, 8(2) (June): 194–222.

Joplin, T. (1822). 'An Essay on the General Principles and Present Practice of Banking in Scotland and England'. London: Printed for Messrs. Baldwin, Cradock, & Joy, Paternoster Row, and J. Ridgway, Piccadilly.

Kindleberger, C. P. (1978). *Manias, Panics and Crashes: A History of Financial Crises*. New York: Basic Books.

King, W. T. C. (1936). *History of the London Discount Market*. New York: George Routledge & Sons.

Moody, J. (1919). *The Masters of Capital: A Chronicle of Wall Street*. New Haven: Yale University Press.

Neal, L. (1992). 'The Disintegration and Re-integration of International Capital Markets in the 19th Century', *Business and Economic History*, 21: 84–96.

Neal, L. (1998). 'The Financial Crisis of 1825 and the Restructuring of the British Financial System', Federal Reserve Bank of St Louis, May.

Pressnell, L. S. (1956). *Country Banking in the Industrial Revolution.* Oxford: Clarendon Press.

Rappoport, P. and White, E. (1991). 'Was There a Bubble in the 1929 Stock Market?', Rutgers University.

RBS (2012). 'National Bank of Scotland', *RBS Historical Archive.*

Saunders, A. and Wilson, B. (1999). 'The Impact of Consolidation and Safety-Net Support on Canadian, US and UK Banks: 1893–1992', *Journal of Banking and Finance*, 23: 537–71.

Silber, W. L. (2007). *When Washington Shut Down Wall Street: The Great Financial Crisis of 1914 and the Origins of America's Monetary Supremacy.* Princeton: Princeton University Press.

Sprague, O. M. W. (1908). 'The American Crisis of 1907', *The Economic Journal*, 18: 353–72.

Sylla, R. (2007). 'Alexander Hamilton: Central Banker and Financial Crisis Manager', *Financial History*, 87 (Winter): 20–5.

Sylla, R., Wilson, J. W., and Wright, R. E. (1997). 'America's First Securities Markets, 1790–1830: Emergence, Development and Integration', paper presented at the Cliometrics Conference.

Sylla, R., Wilson, J. W., and Wright, R. E. (2006). 'Integration of Trans-Atlantic Capital Markets, 1790–1845', *Review of Finance*, 10 (4): 613–44.

Sylla, R., Wright, R. E., and Cowen, D. J. (2009). 'Alexander Hamilton: Central Banker', *Business History Review*, 83: 61–86.

Tallman, E. W. and Moen, J. R. (1990). 'Lessons from the Panic of 1907', *Federal Reserve Bank of Atlanta Economic Review*, 75 (May/June): 1–13.

Tallman, E. W. and Moen, J. R. (2012). 'Liquidity Creation without a Central Bank: Clearing House Loan Certificates in the Banking Panic of 1907', *Journal of Financial Stability*, 8: 277–91.

Temin, P. (1976). *Did Monetary Forces Cause the Great Depression?* New York: W. W. Norton.

Vanderlip, F. (1908). 'The Panic as a World Phenomenon', *The Annals of the American Academic of Political and Social Science*, 31: 2–7.

Wettereau, J. O. (1937). 'New Light on the First Bank of the United States', *Pennsylvania Magazine of History and Biography*, 61(3): 263–85.

Wicker, E. R. (1966). *Federal Reserve Monetary Policy, 1917–1933.* New York: Random House.

5

Failures of Regulation and Governance

Sue Jaffer, Susana Knaudt, and Nicholas Morris

The regulatory and governance arrangements which guide the activities of the UK financial services industry today have evolved in response to changing political and ideological forces. The immediate post-war regulatory system assumed the trustworthiness of participants, and encouraged this through a 'club-like' approach, whereby peer group pressure encouraged other-regarding behaviour. Governance arrangements at that time were simpler, because there were only limited degrees of separation between investors and borrowers, and firms were more specialised. Managers were often also owners, so that principal-agent problems were less severe than they have become today.

As discussed in Chapter 2, globalisation, changes to industry structure, and remuneration arrangements eroded the trustworthiness of participants. At the same time the systems which exerted peer-group pressure were dismantled and the self-regulatory regime was replaced by administrative control. However, an unintended consequence of this administrative control was the encouragement of selfish behaviour, which became widespread. Belief in efficient markets meant that trustworthiness was not seen as important, and strong trust was replaced by weak trust. Moreover, this belief in efficient markets led to the UK's 'light-handed' regulation which became a model for international regimes, with disastrous consequences.

In what follows, we explore the various failings of both the governance arrangements and the regulatory system which allowed and, in many cases, contributed to the decline in trustworthiness of the industry.

5.1 The Evolution of the Regulatory System

At the end of the Second World War, overdraft was the only instrument of lending. Deposit-taking and lending institutions could only operate as 'recognised' banks, with recognition granted either by the Bank of England (the Bank) or by the market, with ongoing supervision (Bank of England 1974). The Bank had moral authority in the City. This was facilitated through its role as the gateway to government business, which made up a substantial part of the City's revenue at the time. The leaders of the major financial services firms were conservative and risk-averse, receptive to the guidance provided by a respected Bank of England. As discussed in Chapter 2, trust and trustworthiness were key elements of the system.

However, the Bank's authority was weakened by the introduction of Department of Trade licensing of unregulated and often foreign-owned entities (moneylenders and 'fringe banks') in 1966. Quantitative controls were also removed in 1971, leaving the clearing banks able to compete for business which had previously been the preserve of secondary banks and finance houses. Internationalisation and the growth of global wholesale money markets (over which the Bank had less control) further weakened the status of the Bank.

The fringe banking crisis of the mid 1970s led the Bank to widen its supervisory powers to cover all the larger non-bank deposit-taking institutions. Data-reporting requirements for banks were increased, and within the Bank a new Banking Supervision Division was established. The Banking Act 1979 set up the first UK deposit protection scheme, financed by contributions from the banks and licensed institutions. The introduction of formal controls replaced previous reliance on the trustworthiness of market participants. In addition, the introduction of deposit insurance reduced the need for depositors to seek trustworthy institutions.

Following the election of the Thatcher Government in 1979, a series of enquiries led to further political pressure for change, with an underlying philosophy of reliance on competitive markets and administrative control. In 1980, a committee led by the former Prime Minister, Harold Wilson, argued for the establishment of a single regulatory body. This was followed in 1981 by the Gower Committee, which recommended a comprehensive regulatory regime for the securities and investment industry, aimed primarily at improving retail investor protection. A new Securities and Investment Board (SIB) was created by the Financial Services Act 1986. Self-regulatory bodies (SROs), the Personal Investment Authority (PIA), the Investment Management Regulatory Organisation (IMRO), and the Securities and Futures Authority (SFA) were also established.

Deregulation of London's financial markets, including abolition of fixed commission charges, the removal of the division between stockbrokers and stock-jobbers on the London Stock Exchange, and the change from open outcry to electronic-screen-based trading, took place on 27 October 1986. The mood of the time was to create 'a far more determined and professional approach to regulation', recognising that 'The City can no longer be run as a "club"' (Kynaston 2002). Although the SROs, overseen by the SIB, were presented as a mechanism for improved self-regulation of the industry, the new system introduced a multiplicity of different bodies, multiple levels of administration and greater complexity, and assumed only limited trustworthiness on the part of market participants.

Four key events worsened the situation further. The collapse of Johnson Matthey Bankers (JMB) in 1984 raised questions about the Bank's competence as supervisor, damaging relations between the Bank and the Treasury. On 5 July 1991, Bank of Credit and Commerce International (BCCI) had its operations forcibly shut down in five countries by coordinated international action. Also, in late 1991, Robert Maxwell's death led to the uncovering of around £400 million which had been removed from pension funds in order to support other companies, notably the Daily Mirror. The near-collapse of Barings Bank in 1995 led to further criticism of external auditors, supervisors, and regulators.

The various enquiries into JMB, BCCI, Maxwell, and Barings criticised the Bank's supervisory activities, and undermined its position as a regulator both with the government and in the City (Hadjiemmanuil 1996). The weak regulatory record of the Bank and a desire by the incoming Labour Government to be seen to be tough on the City brought the end of 'cosy' self-regulation. As a consequence, the Bank of England Act 1998 transferred responsibility for the supervision of deposit-taking institutions, including setting capital adequacy requirements, from the Bank to the Financial Services Authority (FSA). The Financial Services and Markets Act 2000 (FSMA) disbanded the SROs and also transferred their responsibilities to the FSA along with responsibilities for the prevention of market abuse. The Financial Services Compensation Scheme (FSCS) was set up covering both securities and banking. An ombudsman was established to respond to complaints.

The new regulatory system had, at its core, a tripartite system involving the FSA, the Bank, and the Treasury.[1] Responsibility for the supervision of deposit-taking institutions now rested with the FSA, including the process of deciding capital adequacy requirements for banking and investment

---

[1] As specified in the Memorandum of Understanding (MoU) between the Bank and the FSA, published in October 1997. This memorandum also set out the ground rules for coordination between the Bank, the FSA, and the Treasury in the event of a financial crisis.

businesses. The Bank retained responsibility for stability of the financial system as a whole, while the Treasury was responsible for the institutional structure and legislation, and in principle had a monitoring role over both the Bank and the FSA. However, in practice both the Bank and the Treasury left the majority of regulatory matters to the FSA, and coordination between the three authorities was difficult and sporadic (Davies 2010).[2] FSMA reflected the expectation of the various stakeholders that the FSA's regulation would continue to be 'light-handed' and not interfere unduly in the development of the UK's financial services industry.

As a result, sector-specific SROs, with clear rule books able to give practical guidance, were replaced by a large bureaucracy that did not give specific advice or guidance. In due course, fourteen volumes of complex rules appeared. Smaller city firms now had to deal with a 'help desk' and larger firms saw a constantly changing roster of supervisory staff. At the same time the EU released a flood of directives covering capital adequacy and conduct of business, all of which had to be negotiated and subsequently incorporated into UK rules.

Pressure to simplify the now complex system opened the door for industry lobbying to reduce regulatory oversight. Representation from the industry following the Sandler Review (Sandler 2002) encouraged the FSA to move further towards a light-touch regulatory regime in order to improve innovation and the UK's competitive position (Whittaker 2004). As part of this light touch approach, the FSA emphasised the importance and durability of 'principles-based' regulation and defined eleven 'principles for business'.

Perceptions that the UK ran a successful regulatory system had significant international implications. The European Commission also recommended and implemented 'light-handed' regulation. In 2005, the vast majority of Initial Public Offerings took place in London rather than in New York. Hank Paulson, then the US Treasury Secretary, suggested that the US move towards a more flexible UK-style approach. Canada also began a process of moving towards UK-style principles-based regulation.

Concerns about international flows of credit, and the potential for a regulatory 'race to the bottom', led to the negotiation and agreement of the Basel Accords. A Standing Committee of bank supervisors was set up under the Bank for International Settlements (BIS), and produced the Basel I Accord, issued in 1988, which set a minimum capital requirement (White 1996). The negotiation of Basel II was precipitated by banking industry lobbying, which

---

[2] In fact, the Tripartite Committee, which included Gordon Brown as Chancellor of the Exchequer, did not meet once at the level of the principals between 1997 and 2003. See 'Three people in the marriage', Chapter 18 of Davies (2010).

focused on how banks that used 'sophisticated risk models' should be able to reflect this sophistication in lower levels of prudential capital.

Basel II had limited impact on the financial crisis. In the first instance, the crisis was about liquidity rather than capital. Basel II's impact on capital requirements was modest (and normally reduced them) and its implementation was incomplete by the time of the crisis. Indeed Basel II had not been formally adopted in the United States by the time of the GFC. The history of the crisis and the impact of regulation was more about the 'elephants in the room'. These were those issues which either through feeble conceptual understanding, unwillingness to grasp nettles, or through industry pressure were simply never addressed by the regulators. For example, no regime regulating the liquidity mismatches of banks or branches of banks was even attempted until after the GFC, and no regime limiting levels of leverage existed at the time of the GFC. Lehman was leveraged some sixty times at the time of its failure (so that less than a 2% move in its asset value was all that was required to wipe out its capital). Yet its capital levels were in compliance to the end and subject to intense regulatory scrutiny. Lending activities, including mortgages, remained largely unregulated. Excessive interest rates and charges were openly tolerated and there was no requirement to disclose how interest was calculated.

5.2 The Decline of Trust and Trustworthiness

Up to the 1960s, regulation of the banking industry was orchestrated by the Bank of England in a largely informal manner. Regulation relied on trust, in that supervision operated through the relationships between key Bank of England personnel and senior industry figures. The Bank expected the banking community to take collective responsibility to avert any bank failure, with only limited funding contribution from the Bank (Capie 2010). In its 1974 memorandum, the Bank noted that: 'The sanction available to us, so strong that it is virtually unused, has been to let it be known that we were dissatisfied with the way a bank was being run' (Bank of England 1974).

Overall, the system assumed the trustworthiness of participants. It was also characterised by the type of 'intelligent accountability' discussed by O'Neill in Chapter 8. Financial executives were required to account for their actions and the performance of the industry. The formation of the SROs was intended to build upon the existing trust-based approach by introducing bodies which were trusted within the industry. The White Paper that followed Gower's report argued for a continued reliance on strong trust:

self-regulation has a continuing and crucial contribution to make. It means commitment by practitioners to the maintenance of high standards as a matter of integrity and principle, not because they are imposed from outside. (UK Government 1985)

In practice, the SROs instead implemented a detailed administrative system, the dangers of which were highlighted by numerous commentators. The *Financial Times* commented 'for even the most sympathetic and conformist investment firm, this SIB rule book will give a chilling impression of the sheer bureaucratic cost of the new regulatory regime', while Michael Prest, writing in *The Times*, observed 'The SIB rules are comprehensive and we are promised many more; and they are rules, not mere guidelines....By constructing the elaborate apparatus of SROs, the Government has skilfully disguised the true extent of the central direction. Orwell would have understood.' Andreas Whittam-Smith[3] remarked that 'the only means of securing compliance with the new rules may be by creating a great bureaucratic system of form-filling and inspection worthy of the old Austro-Hungarian Empire'.

FSMA, however, envisaged only a limited continuing role for self-regulation (FSA 1999b). The FSA thus implemented regimes for authorised persons who were subject to codes of conduct. Only the exchanges, the professional bodies, and the Society of Lloyds retained any self-regulatory role, but even these were subject to FSA direction. The original system of 'flexible and responsive' regulation based on relationships of trust and moral suasion, coordinated by the Bank and involving a large degree of self-regulation, had been replaced by a system with a single agency responsible for most aspects of regulation.

From its inception, the FSA's regulatory and supervisory philosophy was grounded on a strong belief in self-correcting markets which did not require strong trust or assume the trustworthiness of participants. As a result of the long period of stability (the Great Moderation), the Efficient Markets Hypothesis (EMH) became deeply embedded in regulatory philosophy, to the extent that it became essentially impervious to challenge. When raising concerns about EMH and its implications, Rajan (2010) found:

I exaggerate only a little bit when I say I felt like an early Christian who had wandered into a convention of half-starved lions.... the critics seemed to be ignoring what was going on before their eyes.

---

[3] Founder and first editor of *The Independent* newspaper. Quoted in Kynaston (2002: 682).

The benefits of increased financial intensity and financial innovation were not doubted, and securitisation was seen as delivering increased diversification of risk and more liquid markets. High profits and high bonuses were assumed to be justified by the market (Woolley 2010).

Thus the FSA believed that 'primary responsibility for managing risks lay with the senior management and boards of the individual firms' and that 'customer protection is best ensured not by product regulation or direct intervention in markets, but by ensuring that wholesale markets are as unfettered and transparent as possible, and that the way in which firms conduct business (e.g. the definition and execution of sales processes) is appropriate'.

By 2005, the merits of principles-based, 'light-handed' regulation were well established in the UK. The Treasury 'Hampton Review' praised FSA as 'an example of a consolidated regulator with an impressive risk-based approach'. By 2007, the political environment was unfavourable to any measures which tightened financial conditions. The prevailing view was that 'the best guarantee of financial stability was that market participants had the interests of their investors and shareholders at heart, and those interests were far more powerful than any regulatory intervention' (Davies 2010). As the GFC was to demonstrate, the misconception that markets govern themselves is greatest at the top of the cycle, where the danger is at its maximum. Similarly, faith in regulation is greatest at the bottom of the market, when it is needed least (Rajan 2010).

Regulation by the FSA focused on review of internal risk management systems, rather than on assessment of the underlying risks. Financial penalties for breaches of regulatory standards were fairly light during the period and more sophisticated activities, such as short selling and spinning, were regarded as supporting efficient markets. Suggestions to increase regulatory oversight were not pursued once adverse comment was received from the industry, and the FSA responded to industry pressure to further reduce restrictions.

At the heart of the FSA approach was an attempt to encourage and monitor adherence to a set of ethical principles. Yet there were repeated examples of breaches of the FSA's principles, extensive and unresolved conflicts of interest leading to the abuse of customers; extraction of rents through overpriced products and underpriced tail risks; deliberate mis-selling and the provision of misleading information; grossly and repeatedly inadequate risk management systems and risk models. Hector Sants, then CEO of the FSA, famously stated: 'a principles-based approach does not work with people who have no principles' (Sants 2009).

At the same time, monitoring degenerated into an administrative 'tick box' approach. Supervision was no longer based on personal relationships, given the dramatic expansion in the scale and globalisation of the industry, and the accountability of executives was no longer intelligent in O'Neill's terms (see Chapter 8 in this book).

While regulatory efforts focused on the technical aspects of the delivery of products and service to clients by financial institutions, governance was perceived by authorities to be an area where self-regulation seemed to be adequate. In reality, the colossal failings of Lehman, AIG, Northern Rock and others clearly unearthed serious leadership failings and, more importantly, a disconnect between management and the board, which gave bank executives free rein in their appetite for excessive risk taking.

5.3 Governance Arrangements

5.3.1 Failures of Governance

The failure of bank governance was an important contributory factor to the GFC, with the role, function, and effectiveness of the boardroom being inadequate on many levels. The OECD (2004) defines four key aspects of corporate governance. First, governance specifies the distribution of rights and responsibilities between different players involved in the firm, such as the board of directors, executives, and shareholders, establishing rules and procedures for decision making. Second, it is the set of relations between management, the board of directors, shareholders, and other stakeholders. Third, it is the structure through which a company sets its strategy and objectives. Fourth, it is the system of incentives offered to the board of directors and management in order to pursue these objectives in the interest of shareholders and society.

In Britain prior to the GFC, corporate governance architecture followed the recommendations of the Cadbury Committee (1992). The Cadbury recommendations defined the responsibilities of the board, proposed the separation of Chair and CEO roles, and formed part of a largely self-regulatory environment. As we discuss further below, there was almost universal belief in efficient markets, with a concomitant desire to minimise the burden of regulation on a seemingly competitive financial sector. At the same time, however, there were strong incentives for banks to shift towards high-risk high-leverage strategies. High leverage delivered high returns to shareholders, and high remuneration to executives, and in turn created incentives for them to create risk as it was creditors who bore any downside risk. Development of derivatives and structured investment vehicles ballooned and boards rode the wave apparently oblivious of the dangers to come. The government's implicit guarantee further encouraged firms to engage in excessively risky behaviour.

The size and complexity of banks made them difficult to manage and regulate. Boards, managers, auditors, and supervisory authorities seem to have had limited information as to the true state of the financial condition of each firm. This was compounded by complex and internationally diverse accounting practices, which enabled multinational banks to transfer losses to subsidiaries and/or to keep them off their balance sheet. Ard and Berg (2010) point out that the 'central irony of the governance failures that became apparent in the crisis is that many took place in some of the most sophisticated banks operating in some of the most developed governance environments in the world, such as the United States and the United Kingdom'.

Ard and Berg identify five broad areas of corporate governance failure preceding the GFC: risk governance; remuneration and alignment of incentive structures; board independence, qualifications, and composition; disclosure and transparency; and shareholder engagement.

- *Risk governance*: Weak and inexpert boards had limited risk awareness, while management did not adequately consider the risks involved or make the boards aware of them. The risk management functions did not have enough authority, stature,[4] and/or independence.[5] Board structures, such as risk committees, were not able to challenge management.

- *Remuneration and alignment of incentive structures*: Compensation schemes encouraged excessive risk taking and executives pursued short-term gains at the expense of the firm's long-term stability and value.

- *Board independence, qualifications and composition*: Boards suffered from erosion in independence and objective oversight, while management became more powerful[6] with some banks having 'imperial CEOs' who performed dual roles of CEO and Chairman. Deferential boards with few executives and low technical expertise were no match for

---

[4] See the case of Paul Moore, sacked in 2004 from being HBOS's head of group regulatory risk for highlighting the bank's risky lending strategies and the failure of KPMG, the bank's auditors, to report on it. <http://www.bbc.co.uk/blogs/thereporters/robertpeston/2009/02/why_crosby_resigned.html>, accessed 3 March 2014.

[5] Parliamentary Commission on Banking Standards *'An Accident Waiting to Happen': The Failure of HBOS*, April 2013 states: 'The risk function in HBOS was a cardinal area of weakness in the bank. The status of the Group risk functions was low relative to the operating divisions. Successive Group Risk Directors were fatally weakened in carrying out their duties by their lack of expertise and experience in carrying out a risk function, by the fact that the centre of gravity lay with the divisions themselves rather than the group risk function, and by the knowledge that their hopes for career progression lay elsewhere in the bank.'

[6] See the case of J.P. Morgan's CEO and Chairman Jamie Dimon which caused controversy in his dual role at one of the largest global investment banks: <http://www.ft.com/cms/s/0/51ce0cb2-c21b-11e2-ab66-00144feab7de.html#axzz2WEHc7j4S>, accessed 3 March 2014.

management. Becht et al. (2012) note that government rescues have masked the extent of bank problems and make specific governance failure difficult to ascertain.

- *Disclosure and transparency*: Weaknesses and inconsistent accounting standards enabled multinational banks to arbitrage regulations to fit their strategies and practices and made the disclosure of risks insufficient.
- *Shareholder engagement*: In the UK, parliamentary evidence showed that there was an absence of formal shareholder engagement and dissent (Becht et al. 2012), which left banks free to pursue self-serving goals.

As discussed in Chapter 2, the failures observed by Ard and Berg can be explained at least in part by the counterproductive nature of governance arrangements, in which the interests of management and shareholders were not properly aligned. Authors such as Mayer (2013) and Stout (2012) further argue that the primacy given to shareholders is also mistaken and damaging, and has led to a situation where shareholders can abuse the commitment of other stakeholders (such as creditors and employees) to the corporation. Management is unable to balance the interests of stakeholders, because of the threat posed by hostile takeovers, and key decisions are decided by short-term shareholders at the expense of those concerned about longer-term performance. Stout has likened the implication for shareholders and other stakeholders to 'fishing with dynamite'—the catch goes up in the short term, but in the longer term you run out of fish.

5.3.2 Policy Response and Future Prospects

Following the GFC, governments in western economies engaged in a wide-ranging review of governance in financial institutions, with authorities in the US and Europe requiring banks to change fundamentally the way they conducted their affairs. Implementation of the resulting policy changes is still in progress. In the UK, the Walker Report (2009) investigated the role, limitations, and failures of bank boards, and set out a series of recommendations to establish new ethical standards in for bank behaviour. It called for active, accountable, and hands-on boards, able to question and assess management's risk objectives and results. It also demanded a more intrusive regulatory and supervisory role for the government in the risk governance of banks. The Review's key recommendations were to enhance remuneration controls, improve risk management, and recognise the need for non-executive directors to be better prepared for their role and better supported while in post.

Ferreira et al. (2011), however, note that regulatory initiatives so far have been based on circumstantial evidence as there is not enough knowledge about the characteristics of boards of banks and their relation to firm and country characteristics. The authors find that prior to the GFC there was emphasis on board independence rather than board competence, and that the former was not enough to prevent failure in the US, UK, and Ireland.

The Treasury Committee's Report on the Royal Bank of Scotland (RBS) highlighted the limitations of the Financial Services Authority's ability to objectively assess the failures both of RBS executives and the board of directors. It also identified governance issues in the supervisory authority itself (House of Commons Treasury Committee 2012). In response, the Parliamentary Commission on Banking Standards (2013) addressed the individual responsibilities of senior management and the board of directors. The report's recommendations aimed to make executives and board members personally accountable for decisions, paving the way for criminal proceedings in cases of failure and neglect. The report recommended reducing incentives for risky and abusive behaviour by increasing equity requirements and reforming remuneration arrangements to tie more closely to the long-term interests of the bank. The report's recommendations also included the creation of a 'Senior Persons Regime', incentives for better behaviour, enforcement powers against individuals, and reforming governance to reinforce individual responsibility.

Re-establishing trust in banks will depend critically on solid and accountable governance. Improving personal incentives and giving effect to personal accountability are key requirements. Once the recommendations of the Parliamentary Commission are implemented, this will mark a step forward in the removal of the incentives and culture that have worked actively against trustworthiness. By ascribing personal responsibility to banks' registered senior persons, with possible criminal consequences in case of failure, and reforming remuneration, the incentives for reckless behaviour would be mitigated. As we discuss in Chapter 16, this is an essential step but is unlikely to be sufficient. Few of the governance proposals will engender improvements in strong trustworthiness, since they do not provide for the introduction of other-regarding motivations. Rather they are focused largely on removing countervailing incentives and/or providing incentives for executives to avoid punishment (which at best gives rise to a weak form of trustworthiness).

Allen et al. (2006) view good governance practices as an 'essential form of self-regulation', and they argue that the alignment of bank decision-makers with the public good can ameliorate the difficulties of central bank oversight, especially in the case of multi-jurisdictional entities. Writing before the GFC they saw the need for regulatory intrusion in banks' boards in order to protect the country's financial infrastructure. To achieve this, the authors favoured the appointment of an external stakeholder representing the public interest on the board of financial institutions. Such appointments would work directly towards improving strong trustworthiness, by increasing the focus on other-regarding motivations.

This recommendation echoes an earlier recommendation made by Stone (1975) for the appointment of public-interest directors. It is consistent with Mayer's recommendation for 'Trust Firms', whereby the board of directors is complemented by a board of trustees which is responsible for setting firm values and ensuring that these are delivered. There is also some similarity with the suggestion made by Awry and Kershaw in Chapter 13 of having a board-level ethics committee, which sets standards and provides a channel of accountability. These options are discussed further in Chapter 16, as examples of mechanisms that might be used to improve strong trustworthiness in the financial sector.

5.4 The Failures of Regulation

Why did external regulation fail to rise to the challenges? How was it that a regulatory system long based on securing the integrity and probity of its constituents failed to elicit trustworthy behaviour?

In some cases, the problem was in essence an error of omission: the regulatory authorities had not focused on the implications of asset price bubbles and patterns of risk taking for the system as whole. Nor had they identified the extent of the implicit subsidies building up as financial institutions became too big and too interconnected to be allowed to fail. The view that markets worked also led regulators to believe that competition was sufficient to protect customers from poor quality and/or excessively expensive products.

In other cases, the problems that arose were intrinsic to the regulatory process, although (as discussed in Chapter 2) they were worsened by changes to industry structure and incentives. Regulation inevitably suffers from incentives to arbitrage formal rules, and such problems are worsened by the presence of regulatory borders.

Moreover some of the problems were created or seriously exacerbated by regulation itself. Misplaced faith in the EMH, and in the risk models developed in response, allowed systemic pressure to go unchecked. Regulation not only failed to secure genuine accountability—in some cases it contributed towards the abrogation of responsibility by important players, or served to distract management attention from the key issues. Similarly, not only did regulation fail to secure the information required by customers to allow the placing of warranted trust, but the emphasis on disclosure created a proliferation of data ill-suited to the needs for users (Kay 2012). We address these failings below.

5.4.1 Macro-prudential Failures

A widely acknowledged failure of regulation was that the tripartite system was 'confused and fragmented', and macro-prudential oversight slipped through the cracks (Conservatives 2009). None of the regulatory authorities were focused on the systemic risks building up within the financial system. The FSA and the Basel Accords were intended to bring risk management up to best practice, yet failed to have sufficient impact. No one was focused on the system as a whole. In particular, no one was focused on the implications of the explosion in securitised credit for asset prices and systemic stability. While it was recognised that equity ownership was a necessary loss absorber, in retrospect the capital requirements imposed by Basel II were woefully inadequate. Prudent levels of capital to address black swans and fat tails were out of reach of the majority of banks and also completely out of step with the returns achieved in many forms of banking activities. More capital is not necessarily the magic bullet.

This lack of attention is partly explained by the widespread faith in efficient markets and the perceived political importance of financial services to the strength of the economy that existed at the time. But in fact information about performance is imperfectly known and speculative, creating the scope for asset price bubbles and busts. Cognitive biases exist so that players are not always rational, and there is the potential for misalignment of incentives given the number of intermediaries in the investment chain (Kay 2012).

5.4.2 Moral Hazard, 'Too Big to Fail' (TBTF), and Externalities

Arrangements for lender of last resort and deposit insurance were introduced to prevent liquidity problems turning into insolvency. It has long been recognised that deposit insurance creates moral hazard, because depositors no longer have to monitor the behaviour of the banks in which they are depositing money. In turn, the banks had a restraint removed from their risk taking (Ngo 2007). However, the moral hazard created by deposit insurance was reinforced by the sheer scale of risk taking and by the TBTF phenomenon.

As discussed in Chapter 2, the extent of leverage, the merger of deposit-taking activities with high-risk trading activities, excessive risk taking, and the interconnectedness of bank lending increased the risk of systemic collapse considerably. Once enough risk was taken, governments became unable to stand by and let the wider public suffer the externalities that would result from banking collapses (Rajan 2010). Market discipline was reduced, and further risk taking was encouraged. The advent of universal banking spread the moral hazard problem much wider, with taxpayer guarantees being extended to the risk-taking activities of investment banks.

It is not necessarily true that firms thought they would be bailed out if trading conditions deteriorated. Rather, they were *'rationally careless'* about the pricing of risk and hence the market ceased to work (Wolf 2011). The moral hazard problem also extended to creditors. Creditors had been bailed out consistently in past crises, lessening their incentive to monitor and price the risks being taken. Haldane (2011) describes this as a 'time inconsistency' problem. The authorities know that making the creditors bear losses may make things worse in a time of crisis. However, if the creditors realise that their contracts will not be enforced in the event of failure, the debt market also fails to provide any market discipline.

Now that the bailouts have been done, the moral hazard is increased, unless it is possible to break expectations that they will be repeated. The government has become the implicit and unpaid insurer of the TBTF banks, providing a massive subsidy to those banks, and too big to fail is now explicit (Kay 2010). Savers, investors, and the economy at large are forced to endure artificially depressed returns while bank balance sheets are rebuilt. Indeed, the consolidation of banks that was brokered by governments following the GFC has exacerbated the TBTF problem. Moreover, there is concern that the current reform measures are unlikely to be sufficient to stop a repeat of the cycle and prevent economic collapse in future (Boone and Johnson 2010).

There was also little appreciation of the potential size of the external costs that would be imposed in the event of banking failure, and the size of the consequential implicit liabilities accruing to governments and taxpayers. These external costs included the subsidies paid by taxpayers to TBTF institutions as well as the consequences of the recession which followed the GFC, which impacted on production, employment, and wealth.

It is worth noting that the problem of external costs is a recent phenomenon. Originally, banking institutions were incorporated with unlimited liability. Owners could be bankrupted, and hence exerted strong pressure for a conservative approach to risk taking. Likewise, depositors used to be at risk of losing their funds given the absence of any deposit insurance. Both encouraged reliance on trust mechanisms. As a consequence, there was no call upon public funds to bail out failing banking institutions. Even up to and including the JMB failure in 1984 the consequences of bank failure were contained. Prior to this, the Bank coordinated rescue attempts which were largely funded by the banking sector. With the JMB failure, however, the American banks refused to participate, and the English clearing banks agreed to contribute only that one last time (Goodhart 2004).

5.4.3 Regulatory Arbitrage

Regulatory rules are always susceptible to arbitrage, and this was true of the Basel capital requirements. The Basel Accords required a minimum of total capital equal to 8% of banks' assets, weighted to reflect relative riskiness. However, the risk weights adopted were arbitrary. Capital regulation encouraged the use of off-balance-sheet vehicles, as well as restricting some relatively safe kinds of lending while encouraging an oversupply of other more risky lending—such as securitised subprime lending in the US. Basel II relied on credit ratings provided by credit-rating agencies (CRAs), which also turned out to be flawed.

The extent of regulatory arbitrage is indicated by the fact that the risk-weighted value of assets fell over a prolonged period—right up until the crisis hit (Independent Commission on Banking 2011). Trading book capital requirements (measured by value-at-risk—vaR) reflected the fact that assets could be sold off rapidly (FSA 2009b). They did not address what happened if a market simply froze. Moreover, the VaR measures generated pro-cyclical behaviour (in combination with mark-to-market accounting) and failed to capture low-probability, high-impact tail events (Goodhart 2008).

However, the problem was not only that the rules proved inadequate in constraining behaviour. They also relieved finance executives from taking responsibility for managing their capital levels. For example, Northern Rock borrowed heavily in wholesale markets between 2004 and 2007 to fund its queue of mortgages pending securitisation through its ironically named off-shore funding conduit 'Granite'. As the demand for mortgage-backed securities declined in 2007, it became unable to repay its existing borrowings, eventually holding 75% of assets in the form of mortgages. The fact that it would be compliant with Basel II was the reason Northern Rock gave for its now infamous decision to increase dividends shortly before its collapse. Thus, compliance with a (flawed) international regulatory system blinded management, and the FSA, to the perils they faced.

Commentators such as Noel Whiteside (2010) have concluded that the evolution of detailed regulatory rules in response to market pressures is ineffective. Regulatory staff are at a disadvantage in terms of technical competence and the quality of information they have available, and supervision is subject to both regulatory creep and regulatory capture. The resulting administrative complexities 'destroy the very market signals that were the supposed advantage of new systems' (Whiteside 2010). For these and other reasons, Kay (2010) argues that regulation needs to work with incentives and not against them. Moreover, when regulatory mistakes are made, there is a risk that all regulated firms are together coordinated into making the same mistake (Rajan 2010).

5.4.4 Regulatory Borders

To date, regulation has also failed to deal effectively with borders, both national and between the regulated and unregulated financial sectors. Regulation across national borders is needed to prevent regulatory standards from falling to the lowest common denominator:

> National policies such as strict business regulations lower profits by raising the costs of production. Firms will therefore engage in regulatory arbitrage, moving to countries with lax standards. Fearing a loss of their tax base, nation-states have little choice but to lower their regulatory standards to entice foreign investment and avoid capital flight. The end result is a world where regulatory standards are at the lowest common denominator. (Drezner 2002)

Indeed, in the light of recent scandals involving Libor (Barclays and others), money laundering (HSBC), and inadequate compliance processes (J.P. Morgan) the need for effective global oversight is even more pressing.

However, despite this imperative the principle of a single market in banking services presents major problems for implementation. The Turner Review identified that:

> The crisis has shown this philosophy to be inadequate and unsustainable for the future...These current arrangements, combining branch passporting rights, home country supervision, and purely national deposit insurance, are not a sound basis for the future regulation and supervision of European cross-border retail banks. (FSA 2009b)

The key issue is that while banking institutions may be global in coverage, it is the role of national governments to provide fiscal support in the event of a crisis. Bankruptcy laws are national in nature, which has major implications for creditors. No one knows how the loss burden from the failure of an international cross-border financial institution would be handled (Goodhart 2008). The failure of (inadequately supervised) international groups has destroyed local subsidiaries which may be crucial to the local economy. Overcomplex systems and products may be beyond the limited resources of local agencies to understand. Interdependency can cause liquidity problems in markets far removed from the cause, and global communications can enable vast quantities of money to be moved between jurisdictions in seconds.

The problem of regulatory arbitrage applies equally to the border between banking and its shadow sector. Goodhart (2010) has described the process as follows:

> In particular, if regulation is effective, ... the returns achievable within the regulated sector are likely to fall relative to those available on substitutes outside. There will be a switch of business from the regulated to the non-regulated sector. In order to protect their own businesses, those in the regulated sector will seek to

open up connected operations in the non-regulated sector, in order to catch the better opportunities there.

As Wolf (2011) states, 'There is little point in making banks safer if the financial system as a whole becomes less safe.'

5.4.5 Quality of Information

Consistent with the belief in efficient markets, the regulatory approach relied heavily on disclosure. However, many of the possible sources of information available to investors failed to support their placing of trust. In particular, there is widespread agreement that information about asset securitisation and derivatives was insufficient for investors to assess value and risk (Barth 2010). Thus, during hearings on the Goldman Sachs Abacus case, the SEC said:

> In the private market we believe that, in many cases, investors did not have the information necessary to understand and properly analyse structured products, such as CDOs, that were sold in transactions in reliance on exemptions from registration. (O'Brien 2012a)

Indeed the Kay Review argued that regulatory assumptions (focused on how greater disclosure of information can solve the problem of information asymmetry) have been damaging, swamping users with information that is not useful and increasing the amount and volume of 'noise' generated in the financial system (Kay 2012). This has served to worsen the cognitive biases that are part of the real problem (such as excessive optimism, anchoring, and loss aversion).

The performance of various agents whose role is to provide independent information has also been criticised. Financial audits are intended to provide reasonable assurance that the financial statements give a true and fair view in accordance with financial reporting requirements. The criticisms of auditors that followed the GFC included that the audit process missed early warning signs of developing problems. Audits were conducted in an overly mechanistic way, with insufficient professional judgement. Auditors also acquiesced in banks' inclusion of assets at inflated values and accepted the use of derivatives to inflate profits by hiding losses and risks (Sikka 2009).

In addition, auditors failed to challenge non-disclosure of off-balance-sheet liabilities and raise more questions about the risk of default. For example, the court-appointed examiner into the Lehman bankruptcy noted that the auditors Ernst and Young 'failed to question and challenge improper or inadequate disclosures in the firm's reports and accounts', and 'Ernst and Young took no steps to challenge the non-disclosure by Lehman of its use of $50 billion of temporary off-balance-sheet transactions' (Davies 2010).

At the root of these problems was the fact that auditors suffered from a lack of independence, facing strong incentives to temper critical opinions of accounts if there was a risk that non-audit work might be jeopardised (House of Commons Treasury Committee 2009). This is now being addressed in the UK through new legislative requirements for the separation of audit and consulting services. However, there remains a lack of transparency in financial reports, which tend to contain a mass of detail but no easily understood 'story' as to gains, losses, and future risks.

5.4.6 The Role of the Credit-Rating Agencies (CRAs)

The CRAs also played an important role in the regulation and risk management of the financial services industry. Credit ratings are intended to reduce information asymmetries and to assist in management and investment decisions. However the World Bank noted:

> In the United States and Europe faulty credit ratings and flawed rating processes are widely perceived as being among the key contributors to the global financial crisis. (Katz, Salinas, and Stephanou 2009)

A key failure of the CRAs in the run-up to the GFC concerned conflicts of interest related to securitisation. CRAs often earned consultancy fees advising on how to structure an issue in order to achieve a predetermined rating. Further, as Willem Buiter has noted, CRAs 'got into a line of business that they did not understand. They were reasonable at rating sovereign risk and large corporates but not at rating complex structures, but they did it anyway' (Davies 2010). As the GFC unfolded, the ratings agencies suddenly downgraded some assets which they had previously rated AAA to 'junk' status, which fund managers were then forced to sell, exacerbating the collapse. In response, the Bank of England has signalled a move away from reliance on ratings, and industry experts have also begun to call for the ratings agencies to be used less.

Securitisation also had the undesirable effect of reducing the information value contained within market prices. Since the originator of the securities was no longer liable for losses, securitisation reduced the incentive for good underwriting, while at the same time making any form of independent analysis by the purchaser impossible. The complexity involved in tranching also made the assessment of creditworthiness much harder. The spreads on credit default swaps were assumed to provide useful information on creditworthiness, which further discouraged credit analysis, but actually provided no useful warning of the impending collapse (Turner 2012).

5.4.7 Compliance and Enforcement

A further issue which has contributed to a loss of trust in the financial services industry is the failure of compliance and enforcement regimes to secure much more than strict technical compliance. O'Brien argues that one of the central problems is a cultural terms of reference that has allowed 'technical compliance with legal obligation but derogation from the underpinning spirit' (O'Brien 2011).

Much of what went on prior to the GFC was legal, but allowed actions that have been called 'deceptive and immoral'. Despite the fact that firms such as Goldman Sachs and Citigroup sold unsuitable products and did immense harm to their customers, enforcement action through the courts has until recently failed. In the US, the Department of Justice recently decided that there was no case against Goldman Sachs. The SEC has dropped a further case against Goldman Sachs, and in Australia, action by ASIC against Citigroup failed. In all of these cases the courts held that fiduciary duties could be contracted around, in that sophisticated investors had contracted out of the protections afforded by legislation. However, as described by O'Brien in Chapter 10, the Australian Federal Court has recently found that Lehman Brothers Australia did engage in deceptive and misleading conduct, rejecting the privileging of *caveat emptor* over fiduciary duties towards the local councils (for whom Lehman provided asset management advice).

In the UK, the FSA concluded that there was no reasonable prospect of bringing a successful enforcement action against RBS executives. The FSA found errors of judgement and execution on the part of the board and management, but such errors were not regarded as sanctionable. Either the processes and controls which governed how the decisions were made would need to be proven deficient, or their judgements shown to be outside the bounds of reasonableness bearing in mind the information available at the time (FSA 2011b). In the absence of any codes or standards against which to judge their performance (in particular in regard to due diligence on the ABN AMRO merger), legal action was felt to have little chance of success.

Recent evidence of wrongdoing has further damaged trust in the industry. The collusion implicit in the LIBOR rate rigging and other scandals are said to indicate a collapse of integrity, providing evidence of the failure of internal systems as well as external supervision and enforcement (O'Brien 2012b). Compliance and enforcement mechanisms failed to restrain unethical conduct, and there remains concern that bankers regard fines simply as a cost of doing business rather than representing a punishment which is deserved.

5.4.8 Product Regulation

In the past, the FSA has been reluctant to regulate financial products, either retail or wholesale, for fear that regulation would stifle innovation (FSA 2009b). There was also concern that product intervention could lead to less choice for customers and increase uncertainty for the industry (HM Treasury 2011). Instead, reliance was placed on conduct of business rules coupled with confidence that customers would choose products which serve their needs and that firms would not create excessively risky products.

However, this approach has failed at both the wholesale and retail levels. The GFC was in large part generated by ill-conceived products designed for sophisticated investors which, in effect, detached pricing from true risk. At the retail level, the last two decades in the UK have seen various 'waves of major customer detriment' leading to enormous compensation payments— around £3bn for mortgage endowments, £11.8bn for pension mis-selling and £195m for split capital investment trusts (Turner 2010a). In response, regulators are now taking a more intrusive role to protect consumers from products deemed detrimental to their interests. The FSA and the Financial Conduct Authority (FCA) now plan to be involved with the industry at all stages of the product cycle (FSA 2011a).

Since then, the FCA has announced that its product regulation role will focus on the pricing of products so that they reflect consumer value, enhancing disclosure to limit information asymmetries and on product governance. Notably, the bulk of regulatory initiatives are geared toward retail consumer protection, with only limited initiatives addressing wholesale conduct.

The most notable wholesale regulatory initiative has been changes to over-the-counter (OTC) derivatives, which played a key role in the GFC. This market, as described by Lawton (2012), had grown 'rapidly without appropriate regulatory scrutiny, posing problems of inadequate risk management and lack of transparency'. In 2009, the G20 countries agreed to implement four changes to this market (FSA and HM Treasury 2009), whereby standardised OTC derivative contracts would be traded on exchanges or electronic trading platforms, and controls and reporting requirements would be strengthened. These changes are being implemented in the European Union, Basel, and through the European Market Infrastructure Regulation (EMIR).

UK financial regulators have yet to determine the extent of intervention in the product design phase, both in the retail and wholesale markets. While the emphasis has been on consumer protection, the GFC was in part created by derivative products that were traded by non-retail participants. These products have been equated to gambling because of their futures-based characteristics. Posner and Weyl (2011) argue that 'financial products are socially beneficial when they help people insure risks but when these same products are used for gambling they can instead become socially detrimental' and that therefore they should be subject to the same scrutiny that the FDA applies to the approval of drugs prior to sale to the public. However, determining whether potential new products are beneficial to customers is not an easy task. Others propose that a drive towards the simplification of financial products should be pursued instead (Carlin and Davies 2012).

Posner and Weil also suggest that regulators ought to 'deter financial gambling because it is welfare-reducing and contributes to systemic risk'. In order to do so, however, the regulator has to accurately pronounce judgement as to whether a product fits certain criteria for approval. This implies that in order to do so, regulators must have the technological capacity to ascertain the potential riskiness of the product both to the customer and to the system throughout the life cycle. It also means that, were an approved product to fail, the regulators could find themselves partly liable for faulty design. Moreover, pre-launch regulator involvement could also have the unintended consequence of creating moral hazard by removing incentives to the firm to manage the product through its cycle. Pre-approved products could potentially be seen as 'certified' and therefore of guaranteed quality. For these reasons the FCA has stated that it will not be involved in product approval, or in prescribing returns for financial products, but rather that it will supervise adequate product governance.

However, the difficulty of striking the right balance between consumer protection and encouraging innovation remains. Experience suggests that regulators lack the resources to be effective on their own, and that understanding the dynamics of the industry and embedding effective compliance mechanisms are difficult in the absence of trust (O'Brien 2010).

5.4.9 Rent Extraction

One role of regulation is to limit the advantages that can be obtained by market players through market power or asymmetric information. Different societies use different methods of making the legal and regulatory system effective against rent-seeking abuses by firms and individuals. As discussed in Chapter 16, self-regulatory arrangements and professional standards have been made to work in other industries.

However, the modern financial sector is unusual in the dominance it exerts over national economies, in the size of the rents that are available through unprincipled behaviour, and in the complexity of its products and industrial structure. Today, the health of the financial services sector is crucial to most nations, and governments have assumed huge liabilities in order to support failed financial firms. Politicians are attracted by promises of growth and high returns, and are often blind to the downside or longer-term consequences of inappropriate incentives for excessive risk taking.

There is particular concern over the role of increased complexity, in terms of both the cross-border structure of the industry and of the products that it sells. The ability of those in positions of authority—which may be politicians, regulators, the courts or corporate boards—to implement and enforce appropriate controls and suitable disclosure is weakened, sometimes substantially, by the lack of understanding of products, processes, and industry structures. Greater complexity tilts the negotiation in favour of rent-seekers. In extremis, if the rent-seekers are permitted to design the system to maximise complexity then their ability to extract rents will be largely unconstrained. The international nature of both staff and management also dilutes any sense of social compact.

5.5 Regulation and Trustworthiness

Prior to the GFC, there was a widespread consensus that financial markets were efficient: that the markets were self-correcting, that market participants were rational, and that government intervention was largely unnecessary. In this world, the finance sector was seen to provide an efficient pass-through of intermediation costs, and high salaries and profits were justified by the benefits of financial innovation. The long period of stability, the 'Great Moderation', supported this consensus and provided legitimacy to the 'light touch' regulatory approach adopted by the FSA.

This was also a world in which trustworthiness was not regarded as important. Efficient markets worked on the basis of self-interest and delivered good outcomes. Regulation focused on the prevention of market failures and the improvement of market processes—for example, through requirements for disclosure.

Following the crisis there is evidence that far from being controlled by self-correcting markets, the risks were misunderstood and mispriced. Instead of contributing to stability and growth, financial innovation was mostly used as a method of extracting rents. And there are concerns that there still are systemic pressures pushing the industry towards excessive levels of risk.

However, repeated crises indicate that there are deep-seated problems in regulating financial systems. Politicians naturally favour looser regulation as they are concerned about growth. The financial sector has very substantial resources available to lobby against regulatory restrictions.

> When regulation is tight, banks naturally spend much money and time lobbying against it. The banks have the money, they have the best lawyers, and they have the funds to finance the political system. (Boone and Johnson 2010)

Moreover, it is the countries with the largest financial sectors, such as the UK, that find it most difficult to fight the pressures (Kay 2010).

Considerable effort is being made to address the identified regulatory failures:

- Explicit responsibility for macro-prudential regulation is being given to the Financial Policy Committee in the UK, with consideration being given to regulatory tools which are able to act in a counter-cyclical manner.
- Methods to reduce the future probability and cost of externalities from financial failure are being sought through a raft of proposals, ranging from increased capital requirements, convertible debt, and methods to reduce the extent of moral hazard such as the retail ring fence, the Volcker rule, and living wills. These include proposals to make the decision-maker personally liable for the safety of the bank balance sheet, using a variety of remuneration hold-back and claw-back provisions.
- Proposals to improve accountability through automatic sanctions against directors of failed banks in the form of bans from future positions of responsibility in financial services, possible criminal charges for recklessness, and the Senior Persons and Licensing regimes recommended by the Parliamentary Commission on Banking Standards.
- Continued efforts are being made to improve the international dimension of financial regulation, through revised Basel Accords. Efforts to apply regulation more consistently across the shadow banking system are also under consideration.
- More intrusive regulation intended to protect consumers from products deemed detrimental to their interests. Thus, the Financial Conduct Authority (FCA) plans to be involved with the industry at all stages of the product cycle in order to ensure early identification of the sources and nature of risks to customers, to use intensive supervision to mitigate any risks, improve redress to customers, and where necessary change incentives in the markets.

The successful introduction of such reforms is essential. However, many of the limitations of regulation identified above remain inevitable without improvements to the trustworthiness of the individuals and institutions within the financial industry:

- Regulatory arbitraging and lobbying based on the threat of cross-border movements of banking services will continue to weaken the effectiveness of regulation.
- Complexity and information asymmetries are unavoidable, perennially placing regulators behind the game and customers at continued risk of abuse.

- Regulation undermines the other-regarding motivations which are needed to underpin trustworthiness, encouraging weak rather than strong trustworthiness. Actions are regarded as acceptable provided they are legal, and the probability of being caught becomes a driver of decision taking rather than concern for the obligations owed.

These limitations lay behind the failure of both principles-based regulation and rules-based regulation, and the danger is that they will continue to do so. Kay talks about the importance of regulation working in concert with incentives and the market, rather than trying vainly to counter them—'it is much easier to channel a flow of water into appropriate downhill channels than to push it uphill' (Kay 2010). However, Noe and Young (Chapter 3 in this book) make it clear that incentives cannot work.

The story told in the remainder of this book concerns the need for trustworthiness: both its importance and how to enhance it within financial services, for example:

- How to ensure that institutions operate for the benefit of their customers rather than at their expense.

- How to define the obligations in a way that enable the benefits of financial intermediation to be enjoyed, while ensuring that financial agents do not abuse the trust that is intrinsic in their function.

- How to ensure that the information available to regulators, and users of financial services, is sufficient to enable intelligent judgements to be made on where to award trust, and to ensure that trust where given is warranted.

Resolution of these issues would support the regulatory reforms aimed at improving financial stability, by tempering some of the pressures for excessive risk taking. They would also ensure that the financial industry could be trusted to deliver financial intermediation services that can be relied upon by customers.

References

Allen, H., Christodoulou, G., and Millard, S. (2006). *Financial Infrastructure and Corporate Governance*, Bank of England Working Paper No. 316, Bank of England.

Ard, A. and Berg, A. (2010). 'Bank Governance: Lessons from the Financial Crisis', *The World Bank: Financial and Private Sector Development Vice Presidency*, Note 13.

Bank of England (1974). 'The Supervision of Banks', internal memorandum.

Barth, M. (2010). 'How Did Financial Reporting Contribute to the Financial Crisis?', *European Accounting Review*, 19(3): 399–423.

Becht, M., Bolton, P., and Röel, A. (2012). 'Why Bank Governance is Different', *Oxford Review of Economic Policy*, 27(3): 437–63.

Boone, P. and Johnson, S. (2010). 'Will the Politics of Global Moral Hazard Sink Us Again?', in *The Future of Finance: The LSE Report*. London: London School of Economics and Political Science, 247–88.

Capie, F. (2010). *History of the Bank of England 1950s to 1979*. New York: Cambridge University Press.

Carlin, B. I. and Davies, S. W. (2012). 'Political Influence and the Regulation of Financial Products', mimeograph, <https://wpweb2.tepper.cmu.edu/wfa/wfasecure/upload/2012_PA_631384_602900_688351.pdf>, accessed 25 February 2012.

The Committee on the Financial Aspects of Corporate Governance (The Cadbury Committee) (1992). *Report of the Committee on the Financial Aspects of Corporate Governance*. London: Gee—A division of Professional Publishing Ltd.

Conservatives (2009). 'From Crisis to Confidence: Plan for Sound Banking', Policy White Paper, <http://www.conservatives.com/News/News_stories/2009/07/~/media/Files/Downloadable%20Files/PlanforSoundBanking.ashx>, accessed on 2 December 2012.

Davies, H. (2010). *The Financial Crisis: Who Is to Blame*. Cambridge and Malden, MA: Polity Press.

Drezner, D. W. (2002). 'Who Rules? The Regulation of Globalization', University of Chicago, <http://danieldrezner.com/research/whorules.pdf>, accessed 5 September 2013.

Ferreira, D., Kirchmaier, T., and Metzger, D. (2011). 'Boards of Banks', ECGI Finance Working Paper, <http://www.lse.ac.uk/fmg/workingPapers/discussionPapers/DP664_2010_BoardsofBanks.pdf>, accessed 4 September 2013.

Financial Conduct Authority (FCA) (2011). *Approach to Regulation*.

FSA (1999). *Consultation Paper 2: Practitioner Involvement and the Treasury Progress Report on FSMB*.

FSA (2009a). *Mortgage Market Review DP09/3*.

FSA (2009b). *The Turner Review: A Regulatory Response to the Global Financial Crisis*.

FSA (2011a). *Discussion Paper DP11/1*.

FSA (2011b). *The Failure of the Royal Bank of Scotland: Financial Services Authority Board Report*.

FSA and HM Treasury (2009). *Reforming OTC Derivative Markets: A UK Perspective*.

Goodhart, C. (2004). 'The Bank of England 1970–2000', in R. Michie and P. Williamson (eds), *The British Government and the City of London in the Twentieth Century*. Cambridge: Cambridge University Press, 340–72.

Goodhart, C. (2008). 'Regulatory Response to the Financial Crisis', CESifo Working Paper No. 2257.

Goodhart, C. (2010). 'How Should We Regulate the Financial Sector?', in *The Future of Finance: The LSE Report*. London: London School of Economics and Political Science, 165–86.

Hadjiemmanuil, C. (1996). *Banking Regulations and the Bank of England*. London: LLP.

Haldane, A. G. (2010). 'Fair Value in Foul Weather', mimeograph, Bank of England.

Haldane, A. G. (2011). 'Control Rights (and Wrongs)', Wincott Annual Memorial Lecture, 24 October 2011.

HM Treasury (2011). *A New Approach to Financial Regulation: Building a Stronger System*. London: HM Stationery Office.

House of Commons Treasury Committee (2009). *Banking Crisis: Reforming Corporate Governance and Pay in the City*. London: HM Stationery Office.

House of Commons Treasury Committee (2012). *The FSA's Report into the Failure of RBS*. London: HM Stationery Office.

Independent Commission on Banking. (2011). *Independent Commission on Banking: Interim Report: Consultation on Reform Options*.

Independent Commission on Banking (2012). *Independent Commission on Banking: Final Report: Recommendations*.

Katz, J., Salinas, E., and Stephanou, C. (2009). 'Credit Rating Agencies', *World Bank: Crisis Response Note 8, Public Policy Journal* [online journal], <http://rru.worldbank.org/PublicPolicyJournal>, accessed 5 December 2012.

Kay, J. A. (2010). 'Should We Have Narrow Banking?', in *The Future of Finance: The LSE Report*. London: London School of Economics and Political Science, 217–34.

Kay, J. A. (2012). *The Kay Review of UK Equity Markets And Long-Term Decision Making: Final Report, BIS*, <www.bis.gov.uk/kayreview>, accessed 30 July 2012.

Kynaston, D. (2002). *The City of London, Volume IV: A Club No More 1945–2000*. London: Pimlico.

Lawton, D. (2012). *Markets*. London: IDX International Derivatives Expo.

Mayer, C. (2013). *Firm Commitment*. Oxford: Oxford University Press.

Ngo, P. (2007). 'International Prudential Regulation, Regulatory Risk and the Cost of Bank Capital', *International Journal of Banking and Finance*, 5(1): 27–58.

O'Brien, J. (2010). 'The Future of Financial Regulation: Enhancing Integrity through Design', *Sydney Law Review*, 32: 63–85.

O'Brien, J. (2011). 'The Price of Sophistication: Wholesale Investor Protection in the Aftermath of the Global Financial Crisis', mimeograph.

O'Brien, J. (2012a). 'The Façade of Enforcement: Goldman Sachs, Negotiated Prosecution, and the Politics of Blame', in S. Will, S. Handelman, and C. Brotherton (eds), *How They Got Away with It: White Collar Criminals and the Financial Meltdown*. New York: Columbia University Press, 178–203.

O'Brien, J. (2012b). 'Banking Scandals: Where the Buck Stops: Updated 27 July 2012', *Financial Review* [online newspaper], <http://www.afr.com/p/lifestyle/review/enforcement_facade_P9ktF6hpSWWgRZ4vmx7UtJ>, accessed 27 August 2012.

Organisation for Economic Cooperation and Development (2004). *OECD Principles of Corporate Governance*. Paris: OECD Publications.

O'Neill, O. (2005). 'Accountability, Trust and Professionalism', in N. Ray (ed.), *Architecture and its Ethical Dilemmas*. London: Taylor and Francis, 77–88.

Parliamentary Commission on Banking Standards (PCBS) (2013). *Changing Banking for Good: First Report of Session 2013–14*. London: HM Stationery Office.

Posner, E. A. and Weyl, E. G. (2011). 'An FDA for Financial Innovation: Applying the Insurable Interest Doctrine to 21st Century Financial Markets', *Northwestern University Law Review*, 107(3): 1307–57.

Rajan, R. G. (2010). *Fault Lines*. Princeton and Oxford: Princeton University Press.

Sandler, R. (2002). *Medium and Long-Term Retail Savings in the UK: A Review*. London: HM Treasury.

Sants, H. (2009). 'Delivering Intensive Supervision and Credible Deterrence', speech delivered at the Reuters Newsmaker Event, London, 12 March.

Sikka, P. (2009). 'Financial Crisis and the Silence of the Auditors', *Accounting, Organisations and Society*, 34(6–7): 868–73.

Stone, C. (1975). *Where the Law Ends: The Social Control of Corporate Behavior*. New York: Harper and Row.

Stout, L. (2012). *The Shareholder Value Myth*. San Fransisco: Berrett-Koehler Publishers.

Turner, A. (2010a). 'Protecting Customers and Winning Trust', speech given at the British Bankers' Association Conference, 13 July.

Turner, A. (2010b). 'What Do Banks Do? Why Do Credit Booms and Busts Occur and What Can Public Policy Do About It?', in *The Future of Finance: The LSE Report*. London: London School of Economics and Political Science, 5–86.

Turner, A. (2012). 'Securitisation, Shadow Banking and the Value of Financial Innovation', The Rostov Lecture on International Affairs, School of Advanced International Studies (SAIS), John Hopkins University.

UK Government (1985). 'Financial Services in the United Kingdom: A New Framework for Investor Protection', Cmd. No. 9432.

Walker, D. (2009). *A Review of Corporate Governance in UK Banks and Other Financial Industry Entities: Final Recommendations*. London: HM Treasury.

White, W. R. (1996). 'International Agreements in the Area of Banking and Finance', Bank for International Settlements Working Paper 38.

Whiteside, N. (2010). 'Creating Public Value: The Theory of the Convention', in J. Benington and M. H. Moore (eds), *Public Value Theory and Practice*. London: Palgrave Macmillan, 74–85.

Whittaker, D. (2004). 'Sandler Review: Revelation or Revolution?', speech at the Institute and Faculty of Actuaries, Younger Members Convention, 29 November.

Wolf, M. (2011). 'Comment on Andrew G. Haldane, "Control Rights (and Wrongs)"', Wincott Annual Memorial Lecture, 24 October.

Woolley, P. (2010). 'Why Are Financial Markets So Inefficient and Exploitative—and a Suggested Remedy', in *The Future of Finance: The LSE Report*. London: London School of Economics and Political Science, 121–44.

Part II
Trustworthiness, Motivations, and Accountability

6

Trustworthiness and Motivations

Natalie Gold

6.1 Introduction: The Principle of Self-Regard

In 1836, John Stewart Mill wrote of political economy, as it was then called, that it presupposes 'an arbitrary definition of man, as a being who inevitably does that by which he may obtain the greatest amount of necessaries, conveniences, and luxuries, with the smallest quantity of labour and physical self-denial with which they can be obtained' (Mill 1836: V.46). Despite the rise of behavioural economics, this is still the standard picture. As a widely used graduate textbook in microeconomic theory states: 'A defining feature of microeconomic theory is that it aims to model economic activity as an interaction of individual economic agents pursuing their private interests' (Mas-Colell, Whinston, and Green 1995). Standard models assume not only that people are *self-interested*, in the sense of being concerned with their own well-being—they are also assumed to be *selfish*, in the sense of *only* being concerned with their own well-being, and even *self-regarding*, in that their well-being merely concerns themselves and does not reference any other agent—a kind of solipsism or 'unsympathetic isolation'.[1] Hence I will call this assumption about motivation the *principle of self-regard*.[2] It is often traced back to Adam Smith's *Wealth of Nations*, where he famously wrote, 'It is not from the benevolence of the butcher, the brewer, or the baker that we expect our dinner, but from their regard to their own interest. We address ourselves,

---

[1] The term 'unsympathetc isolation' is due to Edgeworth (1881: 12).
[2] This definition of self-regard follows from Mill's definition of self-regarding conduct in *On Liberty* (I.9), as that which 'merely concerns oneself'. Mill's concern was with actions, and whether they would have any harmful effect on others, but his adjective could just as well be applied to people's interests.

not to their humanity, but to their self-love, and never talk to them of our own necessities, but of their advantages' (Smith 1776: ch. 2).

The principle of self-regard became increasingly important in the late nineteenth century, with the work of economists such as Alfred Marshall and Francis Edgeworth, whose analyses emphasised the way in which the interaction of individual agents causes economic outcomes. They pioneered a mathematical model of behaviour in which individuals maximise utility and firms maximise profits, subject to constraints on their budgets and resources. This is the core of neoclassical economics, which is in the current mainstream of the subject.[3] In terms of the underlying mathematics, 'utility' is an empty placeholder which includes anything that might make an agent choose one option over another. In other words, the theory of behaviour that the model represents is one where individuals pursue their interests, where 'interests' can be understood in the loosest possible sense of the term, as anything that a person would like to achieve.[4] However, in practice, the content of 'utility' needs to be specified if models are to have any predictive or descriptive power—which is equivalent to delimiting a person's interests. When interpreting and applying economic models, utility is usually taken to be a function of the agent's own consumption of goods and services, and agents to be self-regarding. Agents are, as Edgeworth put it, in a state of 'unsympathetic isolation' (Edgeworth 1881: 12).

The principle of self-regard was not supposed to be taken as a theory of human nature. Although it is often attributed to Adam Smith, he most certainly did not endorse it. Despite the above, often quoted, passage from the *Wealth of Nations*, Smith opened his earlier *Theory of Moral Sentiments* with a contradictory empirical claim, 'Howsoever man may be supposed, there are evidently some principles in his nature, which interest him in the fortune

---

[3] Specifically, it is the mainstream way of modelling individuals and firms. But not all mainstream economics papers model individuals or firms.

[4] The 'utility' terminology can cause confusion because of its etymology. It was introduced into economics alongside formal methods, in the so-called 'marginalist revolution', which showed how prices depend on the value of the last (or marginal) unit consumed or produced. In the influential work of William Jevons, marginalism was associated with a theory of value that was based on Bethamite utilitarianism and the idea that there is a monistic and measurable pleasure–pain index: hence 'marginal utility' (Jevons 1871). However, as Bentham's theory fell out of favour, economists also distanced themselves from it, culminating in the 'ordinal revolution' of the 1930s, when economists rejected the idea that there was a cardinal scale of utility. Utility functions were still used but they only represented an ordinal valuation, i.e. consumers were assumed to be able to rank commodity bundles but not to be able to quantify these judgements. The fact that these ordinal preferences could be represented with a mathematical function meant that, in the formalism of the model, consumers are represented as 'maximising utility'. However, despite the continued use of the word 'utility', economics had been decoupled from utilitarianism: the primitive concept was that of a preference ranking, and no assumptions were made about what considerations underpinned the ranking. To maximise utility is just to choose the most preferred consumption bundle from those available.

of others, and render their happiness necessary to him, though he derives nothing from it except the pleasure of seeing it' (Smith 1759). For Smith, humans are fundamentally social beings and have other-regarding motivations. Furthermore, *The Wealth of Nations* builds on the discussion that was in *The Theory of Moral Sentiments*, where it is made clear that self-interest is set within the wider context of social obligations and that it is associated with the classical virtue of prudence, not the vice of greed (Smith 2013). It has become commonplace to take passages from *The Wealth of Nations* out of context and to forget that Smith's writings pre-date the neoclassical idea of individuals as utility maximisers.

Even the fathers of neoclassical economics merely took the principle of self-regard to be a good approximation of motivation in certain domains. Mill acknowledged that conduct could depend on 'the feelings called forth in a human being by other individual human or intelligent beings, as such; namely, the *affections*, the *conscience*, or feeling of duty, and the love of *approbation*' (Mill 1836: V.34, italics in the original). However, he considered these motivations to be the subject matter of philosophy. Edgeworth thought that people care about the welfare of others, even indicating how concern for others could be incorporated into his mathematical framework, but he believed that the principle of self-regard was a reasonable assumption in both war and trade (Collard 2001).

The original neoclassical economists were also reticent about the domain of economic theory. Early formulations of the theory required cardinal measurement of utility and it was more plausible that people could make the required numerical comparisons if they only had to compare material satisfactions. However, once the original cardinal foundations (and the association with utilitarianism) were rejected in favour of the modern ordinal ones, which only require a ranking of outcomes, that paved the way for the utility-maximising model to become an all-encompassing theory of human behaviour (Lewin 1996; Mandler 2001). But, if the ordinal framework is augmented with the principle of self-regard, then the expansion of the economic approach looks more dubious.

In the policy domain, the popularity of the principle of self-regard may owe something to Smith's idea that a person who intends only his own gain is led by an 'invisible hand' to pursue the good of society, 'more effectually than when he really intends to promote it' (Smith 1776: ch. 2). Not only has the principle of self-regard seemed like a reasonable assumption but, if people would act according to it, then it would promote good outcomes. However, the principle of self-regard narrows the range of tools that are available for policymakers. A consequence of using Mills' 'arbitrary definition' is that interventions are limited to financial incentive schemes, or regulations that are enforced by the threat of fines or prison. One argument of this chapter is that excessive focus on the principle of self-regard obscures other—potentially very effective—policy interventions.

Even within the domain of political economy, both Marshall and Mill explicitly recognised that the principle of self-regard was a simplification. Marshall thought that the focus on self-regard was justified because 'the steadiest motive to ordinary business work is the desire for the pay which is the material reward of work' (Marshall 1890: Book 1, ch. 2, V1). However, he immediately followed this with the statement that, 'Everyone who is worth anything carries his higher nature with him into business.' Similarly, Mill conceded that the principle of self-regard was a simplification, 'treating the main and acknowledged end [of behaviour] as if it were the sole end' (Mill 1934: V.38). This led Mill to conclude that the resulting 'approximation' of behaviour might need to be corrected to take account of other impulses (Mill 1934: V.34). To the extent that we are influenced by other motives, models based on the principle of self-regard will fail to explain or predict events, and policies based on the principle of self-regard will not have the desired effects.

In this chapter, I will argue that we need to move beyond self-regard when we formulate regulations for finance. Self-regard is not a good assumption and behaviour that is based on it will not produce good outcomes. That is because the principle of self-regard precludes an important sort of trust and trustworthiness, which is based on non-self-regarding motivations, and which we rely on in finance. This implies that, when formulating policy, we should consider how to design institutions and regulations so that they induce the relevant non-self-regarding motivations, and that we should design financial institutions so that they attract employees who are more likely to have those motivations.

6.2 Beyond Self-Regard: A Richer Account of Motivations

In economics, it is standard to assume that an agent is only motivated by her own material rewards and punishments, and to investigate the optimal way to structure incentives given these self-regarding motivations. There are two cross-cutting objections to this: that people are not only motivated by *their own rewards*, and that people are not only motivated by their *material rewards*. My focus is on the first of these objections, but before I explore some of the ways in which people may be non-self-regarding, it is worth explaining how the two objections relate to each other.

When a person acts in order to get an 'apparent reward' (or avoid a punishment), psychologists say that she has an *extrinsic motivation* (Deci 1975). This is in contrast to *intrinsic motivation*, which does not involve apparent external rewards. Examples of intrinsic motivation include completing a task because it is fun or because one is obliged, as opposed to doing a task because one will be paid or punished depending on completion. We might think of extrinsically motivated behaviour as that which aims to get an external reward, supplied by some other agent.

The distinction between intrinsic and extrinsic motivations divides up behaviour differently from that between self-regarding and non-self-regarding behaviour. For instance, Marshall acknowledged that, in the economic domain, as well as being motivated by the desire for pay some people are motivated by a desire for approbation or by the pleasure of doing skilful work (Marshall 1890). The pleasure of doing skilful work is clearly an intrinsic motivation, but it is also a self-regarding one. The desire for approbation is arguably an extrinsic motivation, but it is certainly other-regarding, as it challenges the assumption of unsympathetic isolation.

My concern is with the self-regard of neoclassical agents: their goals never depend on other people, and their behaviour is always about the achievement of those goals, never about how they act in the pursuit. Hence neoclassical economics neglects some of the goals that we pursue which, whilst selfish, essentially depend on other people. It also entirely disregards two important classes of motivation, pro-social and procedural, where the goals pursued are not the narrow (selfish) self-interest of the agent.[5]

6.2.1 Pro-Social Motivations

People are not only concerned with *their own* outcomes. They may be concerned with the outcomes of others. (In the economic model: agents' utility may be a function of others' outcomes as well as their own.) The desire to improve the outcome of others is a *pro-social* motivation; its opposite, which is rarely studied, could be considered an *antisocial* motivation, the desire to diminish the outcomes of others.[6] These are types of other-regarding motivations.

Pro-social motivation covers a variety of ways in which we may be concerned about the outcomes of others. The one that has attracted most attention from researchers is *altruism*, the concern for the outcomes of another or others (e.g. Collard 1978; Fehr and Fischbacher 2003). Another pro-social motivation that is increasingly attracting attention is the concern for the

---

[5] Note that my concern is with proximate goals. People may get a 'warm glow' from non-self-regarding behaviours, so that pursuing such goals is still, in a sense, self-interested or welfare-enhancing. I do not have a stake in the debate about whether such self-interest is always the ultimate goal of action. For more on that debate, especially arguments and evidence that helping behaviours are not always the result of an ultimately self-interested motivation, see Sober and Wilson (1998), Batson and Shaw (1991), and Batson (2011).

[6] For some exceptions, see Zizzo and Oswald (2001) and Abbink and Sadrieh (2009).

outcome of one's group (e.g. Bacharach 2006; Sugden 1993). This differs from altruism because it stems from a common category membership and is a concern for the collective outcome of 'our' or 'my' group, whereas altruism is the interpersonal promotion of 'your' or 'their' welfare (Brewer and Gardner 1996). The outcome of the group need not necessarily reduce to the outcomes of the individual members, nor must improvements in the group outcome reflect improvements in the outcomes of individual members, although we might think that it is likely to do so, or that it will do so in a well-functioning group (Gold 2012). Experimental manipulations that increase group identity lead to more pro-social behaviour (e.g. Brewer and Kramer 1986). It is difficult to disentangle whether this is caused by concern for the outcome of the group or by altruism because, particularly in small groups, increasing group identity may also increase interpersonal altruism between members of the group. However, it is important to distinguish the two concerns conceptually because they may lead to different outcomes (Bacharach 1999; Gold and Sugden 2007).

6.2.2 Procedure-Regarding Motivations

People are not only concerned with their own *outcomes*. The aims of human behaviour are not always focused on end states. For example, people may want to behave fairly, to behave morally, to follow norms, or to abide by standards (e.g. professionalism, doing a good job according to standards in one's field). They are not so much interested in the outcome per se as in the way in which it is achieved or the principle on which they act. These motivations are procedure-regarding.

It may be possible to interpret some cases of procedure-regard as the achievement of outcomes or end states (for instance, we might think of fairness as being about achieving equal outcomes, or morality—on consequentialist views—as being about implementing the best outcomes), or to fit them into a modelling framework of means–end reasoning.[7] However, even if that is possible, it will get the order of explanation wrong. Sometimes people desire to follow a procedure, often a normative rule, for its own sake, not as a means to an end; the ensuing outcome is secondary to the choice of procedure.

6.2.3 Selfish Yet Other-Regarding Motivations

Even allowing that agents are completely selfish and concerned with their own outcomes, these outcomes may reference other people. For instance,

---

[7] For the possibilities and limits of this modelling approach, see, e.g., Broome (1992) and Brown (2011).

agents may care about being esteemed by others, and pursuit of esteem may motivate their behaviour (Brennan and Pettit 2004; Offer 1997 and Chapter 7 in this book). Here we have a sense in which agents may be other-regarding despite being completely selfish: they are concerned with the opinions of others.

We can use esteem and regard to incentivise behaviour; they increase our repertoire of extrinsic rewards. Even if undertaken for purely selfish reasons, the pursuit of esteem and regard may indirectly lead people to care about the outcomes of others—because how others perceive your intentions and your contributions to their outcomes will affect the attitudes they hold towards you.[8] In George Eliot's *Mill on the Floss* (Book 1, ch. 6), Tom and Maggie Tulliver split a jam puff. Tom does his best to divide it equally but fails, and Maggie urges Tom to take the best bit. However, Eliot remarks 'I fear she cared less that Tom should enjoy the utmost possible amount of puff, than that he should be pleased with her for giving him the best bit', establishing that Maggie is not an unselfish character, despite her other-regarding behaviour.

We are not purely self-regarding creatures. As well as copious experimental evidence, we know this from introspection and by observing everyday life. Furthermore, as I will go on to argue, non-self-regarding motivations are essential to a proper understanding of trustworthy behaviour.

6.3 Trust, Trustworthiness, and Motivations

Trusting is a risky business. A truster makes herself vulnerable to her trustee, exposing herself to the risk that her trust will not be fulfilled. We can think of trust as a three-place relation: A trusts B to X. A is the truster, B the trustee, and X is an undertaking with an outcome that A cares about. A person (or institution) who fulfils the trust that is placed in them is trustworthy.

In economics, this minimal definition is taken as sufficient: trust and trustworthiness are defined as behaviours (see, e.g., Fehr 2009) and the neoclassical way of studying trust is to ask to how trustworthy behaviour can be sustained, based on self-regarding motivations. According to this approach, trustworthiness can be ensured by threatening punishments and offering rewards, structuring the trustee's incentives so that it is in her self-regarding interest to be trustworthy. One type of reward is the expected benefit from future encounters, so if the truster and the trustee have a continuing relationship, then there is an incentive for a self-regarding agent to be trustworthy (Hardin 1996, 2004).

---

[8] See Rabin (1993) for a classic economic model that includes intentions, and Falk, Fehr, and Fischbacher (2008) for recent evidence that intentions matter.

However, the idea that trustworthiness is based on self-regard is empirically and theoretically inadequate. Empirically, there is plenty of evidence that people behave in a trustworthy manner, even when that leaves them worse off. (See the discussion of the 'trust game' below.) Theoretically, most philosophers reject the neoclassical analysis of trust. Philosophical analyses also use the behavioural definition of trust but they take it as a starting point: a necessary condition that must be further augmented because, as it stands, the neoclassical analysis conflates trustworthiness with reliability.

The concern to distinguish trustworthiness from reliability stems partly from the fact that, unlike reliability, trustworthiness is often considered to be a moral virtue. Reliability is a property that may be possessed by mechanical objects. For example, we may rely on our alarm clock to wake us up in the morning, but we do not trust it. However, reliability is not just a property of mechanical objects—it can also apply to human agents performing intentional actions. For instance, the philosopher Kant was in the habit of taking a walk at 3.30 pm every day, and he was so punctual that his neighbours could set their clocks by him. Imagine a neighbour who used Kant's walk to time the school run, almost as though he were an alarm clock. She would have been relying on him in order that her children would not be left waiting by the school gates, but it would be wrong to say that she trusted him. Furthermore, if Kant had been late for his walk, causing her to be late for the children, then he would not have been culpable. But someone who breaches a trust is prima facie culpable. This difference between reliability and trustworthiness is reflected in the moral psychology of trust. When someone we trust lets us down, we feel betrayed; but disappointment is the appropriate attitude to being let down by someone or something we rely on. There is a normative element to trust, which is not present in reliance.

It is tempting—but wrong—to conclude from the above examples that the difference between trustworthiness and reliability relates to 'intending to X'. After all, a car does not intend to start and, although Kant did something intentionally, what he intended was to 'take a walk at 3.30 pm' and not 'ensure that his neighbour be on time for the school run'. The neighbour is simply relying on Kant's predictable punctuality, in much the same way that she would depend on a predictable alarm clock. So it seems that 'intending to X' is necessary for trustworthiness. However, in most of the philosophical literature it is not sufficient that the trustee intends to X, she must also do X for the right sort of reason.

There is widespread agreement amongst philosophers that behaviour that is motivated by the pursuit of rewards or the avoidance of punishment is reliable rather than trustworthy. As Annette Baier puts it, 'We may rely on our fellows' fear of the newly appointed security guards in shops to deter them from injecting poison into the food on the shelves, *once we have ceased to trust them'* (Baier 1986: 234, my italics). This stipulation relates to issues of moral psychology and culpability. If we use an incentive system to motivate someone and it fails to work, then the fault lies with our design of the system and we should feel disappointed, not betrayed. Hence the general agreement that trustworthy behaviour must be sufficiently 'internally driven' (Holton 1994: 66).

Philosophers disagree about what the intrinsic motivation involved in trustworthiness must be. A popular account is given by Annette Baier (1986), who argues that trustworthy behaviour is motivated by 'good will', a motivation to take care of something the trustee cares about. Baier identifies trustworthy behaviour as driven by a concern for the truster's outcomes, i.e. it is a type of pro-social behaviour. Karen Jones (1996) argues that goodwill is not enough and that, in addition (in order to exclude cases where someone is reliably benevolent), the trustworthy person must be directly and favourably moved by the fact that someone is counting on her.

In contrast, a compelling recent account of trust, due to Katharine Hawley (2012), locates the difference between trust and reliance in terms of 'commitments'.[9] According to Hawley, trusting someone is a matter of relying on them to meet their commitments, and trustworthiness is a matter of adjusting one's behaviour to one's commitments. Hence the virtue involved in trustworthiness is that of living up to one's commitments. It is obvious that we can acquire commitments through explicit promises and contracts, but commitments may also arise without an explicit agreement—for example, through accepting a role or via social conventions. Hawley says that to ascribe trustworthiness in some specific instance, it is enough for the trustee to behave in accordance with her commitment. She need not be motivated by the commitment. However, when we talk of the virtue of trustworthiness, we indicate a general trustworthiness, someone who will fulfil whatever commitments they have. So we might expect that 'a generally trustworthy person will often meet her commitments simply because they are her commitments' (Hawley 2012: 16). We can classify this as a procedure-regarding motivation, for fulfilling commitments.

Unlike the self-regarding account of trust used in economics, most philosophers favour an account that involves non-self-regarding motivations.

---

[9] Note that this is a different usage from the one that is most commonly used in economics. In philosophy, 'commitment' is a normative term and, for Hawley, it is supposed to connote something similar to an obligation (although commitments and obligations are different and she argues that it is commitment, and not obligation, that is important for trustworthiness). This normative usage differs from the use of 'commitment' which is often found in economics, whereby 'commitment' is a descriptive term connoting a form of binding, in contrast to 'discretion' or 'flexibility'. It also differs from the well-known use of the word by Amartya Sen (1977), where 'commitment' is an attitude that transcends self-interest and may result in a choice that does not maximise the agent's welfare.

However, there is disagreement about how best to formulate a motivational account of trustworthiness—whether it involves a species of pro-social motivation or whether the motivation is ultimately procedure-regarding. As a philosophical theory, I favour the procedural account. But much of what I will go on to argue is compatible with either account because the fiduciary duties that exist in finance involve the commitment to promote the client's interests. What the goodwill and the commitment accounts have in common is that trustworthy (as opposed to reliable) behaviour stems from non-self-regarding and non-selfish motivations.

6.4 Strong Trust

The behavioural definition of trustworthiness used in economics will label some actions as 'trustworthy' that an account of trustworthiness that also stipulates motivations would label 'reliable'. Rather than get into a disciplinary dispute about terminology, we can grant a behavioural use of the word trust (and trustworthiness) but distinguish between 'strong trust' and 'weak trust' (and strong and weak trustworthiness), where *strong trustworthiness* must include a non-self-regarding motivation on the part of the trustee, but *weak trustworthiness* can be the result of any motivation. Hence, weak trust will include cases that some philosophers would claim are only instances of reliance and are not 'really' trust.

Even my definition of strong trust will fail to satisfy most philosophers because it incorporates all non-self-regarding motivations (including selfish but other-regarding motives, such as the pursuit of esteem). I do not need to be invested in the dispute about which non-self-regarding motivation is the 'correct' one because I am concerned with the psychology of trustworthy behaviour and the motivations that are its wellspring, not the sources of its normativity. So, for instance, the fact that people have a 'sense of moral duty' is relevant, but whether people really have such duties or whether their moral psychology reliably tracks them are of no import to my argument. My argument for using strong trust is consequentialist, that it gets good results. I am sure that sometimes we have a moral duty to be trustworthy. But the foundation of morality is a thorny issue; philosophers don't even agree about why trustworthiness is a virtue. So it is a good thing that we can construct an argument for strong trust in finance without straying into the terrain of moral duties.

We need strong trust. It is more efficient than weak, and we rely on it in most everyday transactions. It has a priority over weak trust, as I will explain below. I will also argue that, in at least some financial transactions, strong trust is important because weak trust may not be a possibility.

6.4.1 The Existence of Strong Trustworthiness

We can be sure that strong trustworthiness exists: experimental economics gives us the evidence. The 'trust game' has two players, a 'sender' and a 'receiver'. The sender is endowed with $10. She may choose to transfer some or all of it to the receiver. Any money that is transferred is multiplied up by the experimenter. Then the receiver gets to choose whether to send any of that money back. By sending money, the sender opens up the possibility of mutual gain because the experimenter increases the pot of money. But, by sending, she also exposes herself to risk because there is no guarantee that the receiver will send any of that money back. If the sender sends money and her trust is not fulfilled, then she is worse off than if she had sent nothing.

If both agents in a trust game are rational and self-regarding, then the receiver will never transfer any money back, the sender can predict that there would be no back-transfer if she sent money, and hence she sends none. The sender correctly anticipates that any trust would be breached, so she never places any trust.

However, people trust and are trustworthy. In the original trust experiment conducted by Berg, Dickhaut and McCabe (1995), virtually all senders sent at least some money, the average amount sent was over $5, and roughly one-third of the receivers reciprocated by sending back more than was originally sent. The game was only played once, so there was no tangible benefit of sending back money. Therefore those who reciprocated were strongly trustworthy. This is even more noteworthy because the experiment was 'double blind', i.e. participants were anonymous to the experimenters as well as to each other.

6.4.2 The Efficiency of Strong Trust

Strong trust is both more demanding than weak trust and more stable: it is robust to a wider range of counterfactual situations. Trustworthy behaviour that is only compelled by a desire to avoid punishment will no longer be trustworthy in the absence of that punishment. Robustness is an important property. For example, imagine two parties trying to broker an agreement for mutual benefit. If they can only rely on each other's weak trustworthiness, then they need to construct a contract containing clauses to cover every possible eventuality. If they are motivated by strong trust, then an incomplete contract may suffice. Since most contracts are by necessity incomplete, in the absence of strong trust contractors would often have to fall back on costly legal processes. It is clear from this that where strong trust is available, it is more efficient than weak.

6.4.3 The Priority of Strong Trust

Strong trust is ubiquitous. It is involved in virtually all market transactions. When we hand over our money to the butcher, the brewer, or the baker, we expect that they will hand over the goods in exchange. According to the principle of self-regard, this behaviour must be motivated by reputation—if it is known that a tradesman does not hand over the goods then people will not trade with him in the future—or by the threat of recourse to legal action. But this is not what really motivates people to complete transactions. When we hand over our money to the butcher, the brewer, or the baker, we trust that they will hand over the goods in exchange, and that is based on the expectation of strong trustworthiness.

In case you are in doubt about this, consider another example—that of taking a taxi. Payments for services always have an element of asymmetry, with the payment point being either before or after the service (and the situation where payment is split between these two points in time is relatively rare). The party who performs their part of the bargain first must trust the other party to complete. When hailing a cab on the street, it is normal to pay for the ride after being dropped off at one's destination and it is unlikely that the rider will ever be picked up by the same taxi driver again, or could be identified and excluded by the community of taxi drivers. But it is extremely rare for the rider to run off at the end without paying.[10] I have never even considered doing that; nor, I suspect, have most people.

This brings us to the relation between trust and laws, and the priority of strong trust. When we receive goods and services, a legal framework for enforcement of payment does exist and, *in extremis*, we could have recourse to the law. But the neoclassical idea that we need the law in order to trust (in a weak sense) gets things the wrong way round. Effective laws codify behavioural standards that (most) people are already motivated to live up to and, when there is widespread disagreement with the standard, then the law is not enforced—think of laws against cannabis, homosexual intercourse, and tax evasion in some Mediterranean countries. A consequence of this is that legal changes alone, without corresponding changes in social norms, have limited efficacy as a mechanism for behaviour change, as has been found by those who seek to eradicate female genital cutting (Mackie ms). Only when the majority of people are already prepared to comply with the law can the authorities enforce it on a minority of deviants. In other words, it is only

---

[10] One might argue that, across the whole population, it is better if riders pay as otherwise no one would become a taxi driver. But it would still be in any individual rider's financial interests not to pay: we have an n-person prisoner's dilemma, and a purely self-regarding person would never pay for taxi rides.

because the majority of people are trustworthy in a strong sense that the law can be used to ensure that everybody is trustworthy in the weak sense.

6.5 Strong Trust in Finance

Strong trust is a feature of all transactions, but it is particularly important in finance. Financial products are often very complicated, there is a whole chain of transactions between the initial seller and the end user, and the end user typically is not in a good position to assess the product. There is *asymmetric information*, where the seller knows important facts about the product that are unknown to the buyer. Asymmetric information is not unique to finance, and it has been much studied by economists. The standard example of asymmetric information is the *market for lemons*, a model of the used-car market (Akerlof 1970). The amount that a buyer is willing to pay depends on the quality of the car she is being offered, but she does not know whether the car is good quality or whether it is a 'lemon'. If she buys a car then she bears a risk of overpayment—which may mean she does not buy. In the used-car market, it is possible to overcome asymmetries of information without trust. Sellers can ameliorate the risk (and get what their car is worth) by offering devices such as warranties. Even with asymmetric information, *caveat emptor* or 'buyer beware' is the norm. But the situation in finance is not a simple market for lemons. We can identify at least two differences.

The first difference relates to the types of product that are for sale. In the market for lemons there are high-quality cars and low-quality lemons; the low-quality lemons are still cars that someone would want to buy, at the right price, and the risk is that of overpaying. But there is a third type of car, which does not enter the marketplace. We can distinguish a lemon from a death trap, a car that has a potentially fatal fault, which is known to the seller. Death traps are not a feature of the used-car market; they go on the scrap market instead. But in the run-up to the crash, the financial equivalent of death traps were sold, products that were not fit for purpose—for example, vehicles for retirement savings that were expected to be completely wiped out in thirteen years (as discussed by Peyton Young in this volume).

The market for lemons is a simplified depiction of the used-car market, and neither the model nor the market itself is characterised by the existence of death traps. This may be partly due to the long arm of the law, the existence of warranties, and the fact that (in the UK) buyers are savvy enough to insist on seeing a recent MOT certificate. But, importantly, most people would agree that it is simply wrong to sell a car that is a death trap to an unknowing or unwitting buyer. It would not even cross their minds to try to sell their death trap as a working car. We can trust people not to sell cars that are death traps, in the strong as well as the weak sense. But, before the financial crisis, some bankers knowingly sold the financial equivalent of death traps. There was not even the basic level of trust that is assumed in the market for lemons model.

A second difference between finance and the market for lemons is the modes of product assessment that are available. The market for lemons is really a story about matching products to buyers, ensuring that buyers have enough information to make a relatively precise valuation of the product. A warranty is a signal of a high-quality product, which is worth paying more money for. But warranties do not exist in finance. There are no guarantees; products come with a health warning stating that they can go down as well as up. Potential buyers need reliable information about risk and returns in order to purchase appropriate products.

An alternative device for getting product information is third-party assessment. This sometimes operates in the used-car market. When people buy and sell cars through personal ads there is unlikely to be a warranty, nor are most buyers competent to assess a car themselves. They may engage the services of a mechanic, a third party with the expertise to assess the car. In the 'assessor model' the burden of trustworthiness is shifted to the assessor and the relationship between buyer and seller is governed by *caveat emptor*. Another example of this model is the housing market. A potential buyer pays third parties, in the UK a surveyor and a solicitor, to get all the relevant information. Estate agents, who represent the seller, are generally considered untrustworthy.

We can distinguish assessment from advice. Mechanics and surveyors give information about quality, possibly including a valuation, but they don't generally give advice about whether the car or house will meet the buyer's needs, and whether or not to purchase it. In contrast, we sometimes expect not only information but also advice. In medicine, patients rely on the advice of doctors to make an informed choice between treatments. Sometimes, the doctor makes the choice for the patient—for instance, choosing which of a number of possible drugs to prescribe. In the legal profession, we may expect our lawyer both to represent us and to advise us on the best course of action. The relationship between advisor and advisee involves strong trust. An advisor is supposed to take the advisee's interests into account, providing advice about how best to further them. Professions that operate on the advisor model often have a professional ethic, an idea of the standards of good service and a commitment to uphold those standards.

However, advice and assessment are not completely distinct. Assessors do not necessarily advise, but advisors must to be able to make an assessment in order to give good advice.

The existence of competent third-party assessors allows the relationship between buyer and seller to remain *caveat emptor*. But third-party assessment failed in the run-up to the financial crisis. External ratings agencies completely underestimated the risk of some products. There are a variety of reasons for this failure, but it seems that at least some financial products are not amenable to third-party assessment. They are so complicated that only those who construct them (or not even those who construct them!) are in a position to know all their implications.

The situation in finance may involve 'asymmetric expertise'. The market for lemons model concentrates on asymmetric information, knowing 'that' a product is a lemon. In order to know that a product is a lemon (if there is no way of signalling it) we require the existence of an expert, who knows 'how' to assess the product.[11] If a product is so complicated that only the seller is in a position to provide a reliable assessment, then there is an asymmetry of expertise between the seller and everyone else, an asymmetry of knowing 'how' to make an assessment. On that case, only the seller is in a position to know relevant information about the product, so we need sellers to be trustworthy providers of information. (This may involve not just giving truthful information, but also revealing all relevant information to a buyer who does not know what information she should ask for.)

Finance is not simply a market for lemons. In the run-up to the crisis some people in the sector lacked even the basic level of trustworthiness assumed by the lemons model; and yet strong trust is particularly important in finance because there may be asymmetric expertise as well as asymmetric information. Of course, one response to these problems is simply to regulate financial products—to ban death traps and to prevent products from becoming too complicated for third-party assessment—in order to ensure that sellers are weakly trustworthy. However, regulation is only a partial solution. Regulations can be gamed and, whilst we can easily agree that some products are not fit for purpose, such as the savings vehicles discussed above, it will not always be so easy to distinguish what counts as a financial death trap as opposed to simply a very risky product that some informed consumer might buy; or to decide whether to allow the sale of a product that most people consider an unacceptable risk, even though the odd risk-seeker might choose to invest. Too much emphasis on regulation obscures a second way we can prevent untrustworthy behaviour, namely to increase strong trustworthiness.

---

[11] For more on the relation between knowing that and knowing how, see Stanley (2011).

6.6 Preventing Untrustworthy Behaviour

In order to design effective policies to prevent untrustworthy behaviour, we need to understand the causes of that behaviour.[12] The most salient cause of untrustworthy behaviour is the deliberate breaching of trust, where someone who knows that a trust has been placed in her purposefully breaches that trust for her own private gain. But that is not the only or maybe even the most prevalent cause of breaches of trust. We cannot always assume that everyone—the truster, the trustee, and any theorist or third-party observer to the transaction—frames the situation the same way. If we recognise the role of 'framing' in decision making, then we can identify a second cause of breach of trust: when the truster and trustee frame the situation differently.

In our everyday lives, we negotiate many different relationships—our roles may include family member, friend, neighbour, worker, employer, client, consumer etc.—which are governed by different norms. These most obviously include norms of conduct, or behavioural norms, but there may also be norms about what emotions or motivations are appropriate, even if emotions and motivations are not something that we can always control. For instance, in market exchanges the range of motivations is not much restricted and there is licensed self-regard; at home the balance is tilted much more towards other-regarding-ness; and at work we may be committed to a professional ethic. It may be possible to abide by the behavioural norm without the expected motivation and emotion, but the lack of appropriate motivation and emotion is often seen as problematic (imagine parents who do not love their children, or doctors who are not motivated by the well-being of their patients, even if they perform all the behaviours that we expect from people occupying those roles).

A prerequisite for deciding to abide by the norms of a particular relationship is seeing that they apply. Hence the considerations that motivate a person depend on the relationship that she takes herself to be in, how she 'frames' her situation, and hence the norms that govern her interactions. A person can fail to be trustworthy because she does not frame an interaction as one that requires strong trust, even though she would have been motivated to be trustworthy had she framed it differently. This contrasts with the

---

[12] What we should do to encourage trustworthy behaviour also depends on the motivation that underpins strongly trustworthy behaviour. For example, imagine a charity wanting to increase donations. If potential donors are motivated by esteem then the charity should offer to acknowledge the donations publicly; if donors are motivated by sympathy then the charity should make salient the plight of those who will be helped by the donation; and if donors are motivated by commitment then the charity should remind potential donors of the relevant normative imperative. But we can still come to some general conclusions and recommendations, even in the absence of a complete and accurate picture of what motivates human behaviour.

paradigm of untrustworthy behaviour, which involves the recognition that a trust has been placed followed by a deliberate breach of that trust. As applied to finance, imagine a transaction where the buyer of a product believes the buyer–seller relationship operates on an advisor model, so she expects strong trustworthiness on the part of the seller. Contrast the situation where the seller knows how the buyer frames the transaction and sells her an unsuitable product anyway, in order to make a profit from a client, with the situation where the seller believes that the pair are merely buyer and seller, in a *caveat emptor* relationship, so it is the buyer's job to get her own assessment of the product.

It does not matter to the neoclassical agent how anyone frames a transaction because the principle of self-regard dictates that agents will always pursue their private advantage. However, most people are not 'knaves', to use Hume's term for people who are only ever motivated by their private interests (Hume 1741). Nowadays, psychologists use 'psychopath' as a label for people who lack empathy and conscience, and measure these tendencies on a 'psychopathy scale' (Hare and Vertommen 2003; Levenson, Kiehl, and Fitzpatrick 1995). The idea is that psychopathy is a personality trait, which people may have to varying degrees, and 'psychopaths' are people with pathologically high levels of the trait.[13] Only 1% of the population are psychopaths. The vast majority of people are capable of non-self-regarding motivations.

Non-psychopaths are *trust-responsive*, tending to fulfil trust when they believe that it has been placed in them (Bacharach, Guerra, and Zizzo 2007). The trust game probably underestimates people's capacity for trustworthiness because the laboratory is an artificial situation with no cues from real life and what constitutes appropriate behaviour is ambiguous. Researchers phrase their instructions in 'neutral' terms and normatively laden labels are avoided. For example, subjects are referred to as 'actors' or 'participants', not 'trusters' and 'trustees'; the actions are called 'transferring money' rather than 'placing and fulfilling trust'. The typical subject is a student who has agreed to participate at least partly in order to make money. (In fact, in the trust game, CEOs are more trustworthy than students; Fehr and List 2004.) The action of sending money is open to multiple interpretations: it could be seen as placing a trust, but it could also be seen as a gamble undertaken in the hope of making more money. Even if it is seen as placing a trust, the receiver may think that the interaction is not properly framed as a trust situation, that placing

---

[13] Scored according to the Hare Psychopathy Checklist–Revised (PCL–R), a psychopath is some-one who scores more than 30 out of a possible 40. The mean score in the general population is 2–4 out of 40, with more than half the population scoring zero or one and females scoring lower than males (Neumann and Hare 2008). Note that the PCL–R is not a psychiatric diagnosis—although we might expect that people who have high levels of psychopathy will also be diagnosed with 'antisocial personality disorder'.

trust is not appropriate in the laboratory, and therefore not be motivated to respond in a trustworthy manner. These tendencies can be exacerbated by *motivated construal*, when an ambiguous situation is interpreted in a way that is consonant with a person's interests, without the person necessarily even being conscious of this.[14] The more ambiguous and atypical a situation is, the more we can expect there to be motivated construal.

The trustworthiness of non-psychopaths can be enhanced by making it clear that the situation is one of strong trust, and furthermore, that it is one where strong trust and trustworthiness are appropriate. However, there is a small percentage of psychopaths, who always act according to the principle of self-regard and who would deliberately breach trust whenever it was to their advantage. These people will only ever be weakly trustworthy. Material incentives are needed to ensure their trustworthiness. As we might expect, psychopaths are over-represented in the prison population, a widely quoted estimate is 15–25% (Hare 1996).[15]

Unfortunately, whilst psychopaths may need sanctions to elicit weakly trustworthy behaviour, sanctions can have a negative effect on strong trustworthiness. There is an inherent tension between strong trust and material incentives: if trusters use incentives then they are not placing strong trust. Imagine someone taking the role of truster in a trust game who says, 'I trust you to return money and I will sanction you if you don't.' The sentence makes sense if we parse it as 'I (weakly) trust you to return money because I will sanction you if you don't.' But it is strange to say 'I (strongly) trust you to return money and I will sanction you if you don't', because if the person really (strongly) trusted the trustee, then she wouldn't need to threaten sanctions. The sanction is a signal that the relationship is not governed by strong trust. Sanctions substitute for strong trust.

Evidence from laboratory experiments on trust confirms this: using the threat of punishment in order to enforce high returns in the trust game backfires (Fehr and Rockenbach 2003; Fehr and List 2004). In a version of the trust game where trusters stated their desired back-transfer and were allowed to impose a fine if they received less than the desired amount, imposing a fine led to *less* money being sent back. (Note that the proceeds from the fines did not go to the truster, so there was no financial benefit to imposing fines

---

[14] An infamous example is found in Hastorf and Cantril (1954), where fans of opposing teams in a dirty game each saw the other side as being the perpetrators of most fouls.

[15] Hare's (1996) estimate is based on his experience of testing the US prison population. Obviously the figure depends on factors such as the rate of incarceration and how prisoners are split between gaols and mental institutions, but studies on other prison populations agree that the rate of psychopathy in prison is higher than in the general population, finding proportions of 3%–49% (Sullivan and Kosson 2006). The mean score amongst US prisoners is 22–4 (Hare 1996), which is also substantially higher than the mean score of 2–4 in the general population (Neumann and Hare 2008).

other than any effect on the amount of money sent back.) The threat of sanctions also led to less money being returned when the sanctions were imposed by the experimenter, without the knowledge of the trusters (Houser, Xiao, McCabe, and Smith 2008) This finding is consistent with a large literature which demonstrates that monetary rewards and punishments sometimes backfire—for instance, payments reduce work effort and the offer of monetary compensation reduces willingness to do civic duty—known as the 'motivation crowding effect' (Frey and Jegen 2001).[16]

In contrast, those subjects who forewent the punishment option in favour of strong trust found that their trust was rewarded (Fehr and Rockenbach 2003; Fehr and List 2004). In the trust game with the punishment option, if the fine was not imposed then the trustees sent more money back and trusters were better off—both compared to when the fine was imposed *and* compared to the version where there was no possibility of a fine. Not imposing a threat of punishment when one is on offer is a signal that the relationship involves strong trust.

However, the majority of subjects threatened sanctions, even though the threats decreased their expected earnings (Fehr and List 2004). This may be related to an overly pessimistic view of other people's motivations: people believe that others are more motivated by extrinsic incentives than they are themselves (Heath 1999). In fact, the overwhelming majority of people have motivational structures that include both self-regarding and non-self-regarding elements, and most people have a large capacity for non-self-regarding behaviour. Whether or not they behave in a non-self-regarding and hence strongly trustworthy manner depends the institutional structures and the types of relationships they perceive they are in.

When designing institutions, there is a tension between the need to threaten sanctions, in order to keep psychopaths in line, and the need to reinforce the perception of non-psychopaths that strong trust is appropriate. To some extent, the conflict in approaches is unavoidable. But it is not as bad as it looks, or as it is sometimes made out to be.

The tension between strong trust and the need for sanctions occurs when there is a mixture of psychopaths and non-psychopaths. But the composition of organisations is not fixed. We can increase strong trust in organisations by making them a less attractive place for psychopathic types. It is an open question whether there are more psychopaths in finance than in other sectors. Psychopathy is more prevalent amongst business leaders than in the population as a whole, with the proportion of psychopaths rising to 4% (Babiak and Hare 2009; Babiak, Neumann, and Hare 2010; Board and Fritzon 2005).

---

[16] For more on the role of prices in shaping frames and the connection of this to the motivation crowding effect, see Gold (ms).

However, to my knowledge there is no study comparing business leaders to leaders in other fields and it seems likely that psychopaths, being ruthless and manipulative, will be over-represented in leadership positions in any field. But it is also plausible that professions offering high financial rewards are particularly attractive to psychopaths, since they do not get satisfaction from non-self-regarding aspects of a job. In general, we can affect the type of people that we attract into roles by varying the currency in which rewards are offered (Brennan and Hamlin 2000). This is something to bear in mind when considering executive compensation, and other types of compensation that society can bestow such as honours and esteem.

Even within a sector that is composed of a cross-section of society, including some psychopaths, the tension between strong trust and sanctions is less than it seems from the experiments cited above. The literature on the counterproductive effect of sanctions focuses on financial penalties, abstracting from the social or moral sanctions which are often attached to punishment. For instance, in experimental trust games with sanctions, there is no mention of fines or any normative language, only 'conditional pay-off cuts' (e.g. Houser, Xiao, McCabe, and Smith 2008). A pay-off cut could be seen as a price, not as a punishment. Even fines operate in an ambiguous space between price and punishment. I certainly know people who regard risking a parking ticket as taking a gamble and the possibility of a fine as the price of parking. In a well-known experiment, fining parents who were late picking up their children up from nursery led to an increase in lateness; the parents treated the fine as a price that was worth paying (Gneezy and Rustichini 2000). The idea that a punishment is a price is embodied in the economic analysis of crime. In those models, when a fine is threatened the cost of the prohibited activity is the amount a violator can expect to pay (the level of fine weighted by probability of getting caught), and agents treat this cost like the price of engaging in the activity. The natural extension of this approach, as noted by the economist Tyler Cowan (2013)—possibly tongue in cheek—would be to charge VAT on fines, as a consumption tax on the fined activity.

If agents are completely self-regarding, then thinking about sanctions in wholly material terms makes sense. But non-self-regarding agents will also be sensitive to social sanctions, like opprobrium or disapproval, and the moral sanctions of their own conscience. These social and moral aspects of sanctioning can be hugely important. Since punishment is usually accompanied by opprobrium and guilt, studying financial sanctions in isolation is distorting. In the absence of accompanying social sanctions, it may be natural to interpret financial sanctions as a price rather than a punishment, and prices elicit different behaviour to punishments. The law threatens punishment for murder and theft, but people do not usually argue that these laws increase the incidence of crime. In these cases it is clear that the behaviours are wrong, that there is a social consensus that they are inappropriate, and that the material sanctions are targeted at a small minority of deviants. Material punishments do not necessarily have counterproductive effects if they are embedded in a clear social and moral framework. If we have that framework then, in the same way that some have advocated using different types of rewards to motivate different types of people (e.g. Brennan and Hamlin 2000), we can use different types of sanctions to motivate different types of people.

Of course, the reaction to the financial crisis has included moral opprobrium—from the general public. But general opprobrium alone may not be sufficient. People may have a generic dislike of criticism and censure but, in order to strongly motivate, opprobrium needs to come from those whose opinion they care about. The same point can be made about the motivating power of esteem: a complete theory will specify whose esteem is being pursued. Often the people whose approbation is sought are not members of society in general, but of a smaller group of people who are close to or connected with the agent. For instance, in the professional domain, people may seek approbation from others within their organisation or employment sector. These are also the people who set the norms of conduct within the workplace. So social sanctions that would effectively prevent untrustworthy behaviour in finance need to be imposed from within the sector, and strongly trustworthy behaviour needs to be supported by the culture of organisations.

These two approaches—changing the composition of organisations and changing their culture—are complementary. The entry and exit of those who are motivated by more than self-regard can be self-reinforcing (Bruni and Smerilli 2009). To the extent that the people at the top of an organisation are particularly influential in setting the tone, their behaviour and the sort of behaviour that they endorse can be disproportionately important. It is alleged that some leaders of financial institutions either deliberately breached the trust of their clients or tacitly endorsed the untrustworthy behaviour of those further down the organisation. It seems that some business leaders do need to be motivated by sanctions. However, even amongst business leaders, the vast majority of people have a capacity for empathy and conscience. We shouldn't expect that they are all looking to take advantage of trusters. Regulation change is part of the response to the financial crisis, but culture change is also a useful part of the policy toolbox.

6.7 Conclusion

When Mill introduced the 'arbitrary definition' that was to become the neoclassical economic agent, his idea was that the principle of self-regard was an approximation, which 'is then to be corrected by making proper allowance for the effects of any impulses of a different description, which can be shown to interfere with the result in any particular case' (Mill 1836). The principle of self-regard abstracts away from the non-self-regarding motivations that result in strong trustworthiness. Strong trust is ubiquitous, efficient, and has a priority over weak trust. If we want to encourage trustworthy behaviour in finance, then we should not discount non-self-regarding motivations, and we should design policies and institutions that encourage strong trustworthiness.

References

Abbink, K. and Sadrieh, A. (2009). 'The Pleasure of Being Nasty', *Economics Letters*, 105(3): 306–8.

Akerlof, G. A. (1970). 'The Market for "Lemons": Quality Uncertainty and the Market Mechanism', *The Quarterly Journal of Economics*, 84(3): 488–500.

Babiak, P. and Hare, R. D. (2009). *Snakes in Suits: When Psychopaths Go to Work*. New York: HarperCollins.

Babiak, P., Neumann, C. S., and Hare, R. D. (2010). 'Corporate Psychopathy: Talking the Walk', *Behavioral Sciences & the Law*, 28(2): 174–193.

Bacharach, M. (1999). 'Interactive Team Reasoning: A Contribution to the Theory of Cooperation', *Research in Economics*, 53: 117–47.

Bacharach, M. (2006). *Beyond Individual Choice: Teams and Frames in Game Theory*, ed. N. Gold and R. Sugden. Princeton: Princeton University Press.

Bacharach, M., Guerra, G., and Zizzo, D. J. (2007). 'The Self-Fulfilling Property of Trust: An Experimental Study', *Theory and Decision*, 63(4): 349–88.

Baier, A. (1986). 'Trust and Antitrust', *Ethics*, 96(2): 231–60.

Batson, C. D. (2011). Altruism in Humans. Oxford: Oxford University Press.

Batson, C. D. and Shaw, L. L. (1991). 'Evidence for Altruism: Toward a Pluralism of Prosocial Motives', *Psychological Inquiry*, 2(2): 107–22.

Berg, J., Dickhaut, J., and McCabe, K. (1995). 'Trust, Reciprocity, and Social History', *Games and Economic Behavior*, 10(1): 122–42.

Board, B. J. and Fritzon, K. (2005). 'Disordered Personalities at Work', *Psychology, Crime & Law*, 11(1): 17–32.

Brennan, G. and Hamlin, A. (2000). Democratic Devices and Desires. Cambridge: Cambridge University Press.

Brennan, G. and Pettit, P. (2004). *The Economy of Esteem: An Essay on Civil and Political Society*. Oxford: Oxford University Press.

Brewer, M. B. and Gardner, W. L. (1996). 'Who Is This "We"? Levels of Collective Identity and Self-Representations', *Journal of Personality and Social Psychology*, 71: 83–93.

Brewer, M. B. and Kramer, R. M. (1986). 'Choice Behavior in Social Dilemmas: Effects of Social Identity, Group Size, and Decision Framing', *Journal of Personality and Social Psychology*, 50(3): 543.

Broome, J. (1992). 'Deontology and Economics', *Economics and Philosophy*, 8(2): 269–82.

Brown, C. (2011). 'Consequentialize This', *Ethics*, 121(4): 749–71.

Bruni, L. and Smerilli, A. (2009). 'The Value of Vocation: The Crucial Role of Intrinsically Motivated People in Values-Based Organizations', *Review of Social Economy*, 67(3): 271–88.

Collard, D. A. (1978). *Altruism and Economy: A Study in Non-Selfish Economics*. Oxford: Martin Robertson.

Collard, D. A. (2001). 'Edgeworth's Propositions on Altruism', *Economic Journal*, 85(338): 355–60.

Cowan, T. (2013). 'How You Know that Singaporeans Are Really Serious About Microeconomics', <http://marginalrevolution.com/marginalrevolution/2013/08/how-you-know-that-singaporeans-are-really-serious-about-microeconomics.html>, accessed 19 August 2013.

Deci, E. (1975). *Intrinsic Motivation*. New York: Plenum Press.

Edgeworth, F. Y. (1881). *Mathematical Psychics: An Essay on the Application of Mathematics to the Moral Sciences*. London: Kegan Paul.

Falk, A., Fehr, E., and Fischbacher, U. (2008). 'Testing Theories of Fairness—Intentions Matter', *Games and Economic Behavior*, 62(1): 287–303.

Fehr, E. (2009). 'On the Economics and Biology of Trust', *Journal of the European Economic Association*, 7(2–3): 235–66.

Fehr, E. and Fischbacher, U. (2003). 'The Nature of Human Altruism', *Nature*, 425(6960): 785–91.

Fehr, E. and List, J. A. (2004). 'The Hidden Costs and Returns of Incentives—Trust and Trustworthiness Among CEOs', *Journal of the European Economic Association*, 2(5): 743–71.

Fehr, E. and Rockenbach, B. (2003). 'Detrimental Effects of Sanctions on Human Altruism', *Nature*, 422(6928): 137–40.

Frey, B. S. and Jegen, R. (2001). 'Motivation Crowding Theory', *Journal of Economic Surveys*, 15(5): 589–611.

Gneezy, U. and Rustichini, A. (2000). 'A Fine Is a Price', *Journal of Legal Studies*, 29: 1–17.

Gold, N. (2012). 'Team Reasoning and Cooperation', in S. Okasha and K. Binmore (eds), *Evolution and Rationality: Decisions, Cooperation and Strategic Behaviour*. Cambridge: Cambridge University Press, 185–212.

Gold, N. (ms). 'Shared Valuations and the Market', unpublished paper.

Gold, N. and Sugden, R. (2007). 'Theories of Team Agency', in F. Peter and S. Schmidt (eds), *Rationality and Commitment*. Oxford: Oxford University Press, 280–312.

Hardin, R. (1996). 'Trustworthiness', *Ethics*, 107(1): 26–42.

Hardin, R. (2004). *Trust and Trustworthiness*, vol. 4. New York: Russell Sage Foundation.

Hare, R. D. (1996). 'Psychopathy: A Clinical Construct Whose Time Has Come', *Criminal Justice and Behavior*, 23(1): 25–54.

Hare, R. D. and Vertommen, H. (2003). *The Hare Psychopathy Checklist–Revised*. Toronto: Multi-Health Systems.

Hastorf, A. H. and Cantril, H. (1954). 'They Saw a Game: A Case Study', *The Journal of Abnormal and Social Psychology*, 49(1): 129.

Hawley, K. (2012). 'Trust, Distrust and Commitment', *Noûs*, 48(1): 1–20.

Heath, C. (1999). 'On the Social Psychology of Agency Relationships: Lay Theories of Motivation Overemphasize Extrinsic Incentives', *Organizational Behavior and Human Decision Processes*, 78(1): 25–62.

Holton, R. (1994). 'Deciding to Trust, Coming to Believe', *Australasian Journal of Philosophy*, 72(1), 63–76.

Houser, D., Xiao, E., McCabe, K., and Smith, V. (2008). 'When Punishment Fails: Research on Sanctions, Intentions and Non-Cooperation', *Games and Economic Behavior*, 62(2): 509–32.

Hume, D. (1741). 'Of the Independency of Parliament', in *Essays Moral, Political, and Literary*, <http://www.gutenberg.org/files/36120/36120-h/36120-h.htm>, accessed 19 August 2013.

Jevons, W. S. (1871). *The Theory of Political Economy*. New York: D. Appleton, reprint 1880, <http://www.gutenberg.org/ebooks/33219>, accessed 19 August 2013.

Jones, K. (1996). 'Trust as an Affective Attitude', *Ethics*, 107(1), 4–25.

Levenson, M. R., Kiehl, K. A., and Fitzpatrick, C. M. (1995). 'Assessing Psychopathic Attributes in a Noninstitutionalized Population', *Journal of Personality and Social Psychology*, 68(1): 151.

Lewin, S. B. (1996). 'Economics and Psychology: Lessons for Our Own Day from the Early Twentieth Century', *Journal of Economic Literature*, 34(3): 1293–1323.

Mackie, G. (ms). 'Effective Rule of Law Requires Construction of a Social Norm of Legal Obedience', unpublished paper.

Mandler, M. (2001). 'A Difficult Choice in Preference Theory: Rationality Implies Completeness or Transitivity But Not Both', in E. Millgram (ed.), *Varieties of Practical Reasoning*. Cambridge, MA: MIT Press, 373–402.

Marshall, A. (1890). *Principles of Economic Thought*. Reprint at Rod Hay's Archive for the History of Economic Thought, McMaster University, Canada, <http://socserv2.socsci.mcmaster.ca/~econ/ugcm/3ll3/index.html>, accessed 19 August 2013.

Mas-Colell, A., Whinston, M. D., and Green, J. R. (1995). *Microeconomic Theory*, vol. 1. New York: Oxford University Press.

Mill, J. S. (1836). 'On the Definition of Political Economy; and on the Method of Investigation Proper to It', *London and Westminster Review*, 26 (October): 1–29. Reprinted in *Essays on Some Unsettled Questions of Political Economy*. London: J. W. Parker, 1844, <http://www.gutenberg.org/ebooks/12004>, accessed 19 August 2013.

Mill, J. S. (1859). *On Liberty*, reprinted as Harvard Classics, vol. 25. New York: P. F. Collier, 1909, <http://ebooks.adelaide.edu.au/m/mill/john_stuart/m645o/>, accessed 19 August 2013.

Neumann, C. S. and Hare, R. D. (2008). 'Psychopathic Traits in a Large Community Sample: Links to Violence, Alcohol Use, and Intelligence', *Journal of Consulting and Clinical Psychology*, 76(5): 893.

Offer, A. (1997). 'Between the Gift and the Market: The Economy of Regard', *The Economic History Review*, 50(3): 450–76.

Rabin, M. (1993). 'Incorporating Fairness into Game Theory and Economics', *The American Economic Review*, 83(5): 1281–1302.

Sen, A. K. (1977). 'Rational Fools: A Critique of the Behavioral Foundations of Economic Theory', *Philosophy & Public Affairs*, 6(4): 317–44.

Smith, A. (1759). *The Theory of Moral Sentiments*. London: A. Millar and Edinburgh: J. Bell. Reprinted at Metalibri, 2005, <http://metalibri.wikidot.com/title:theory-of-moral-sentiments:smith-a>, accessed 19 August 2013.

Smith, A. (1776). *An Inquiry into the Nature and Causes of the Wealth of Nations*. London: W. Strahan and T. Cadell, <http://www.gutenberg.org/ebooks/3300>, accessed 19 August 2013.

Smith, V. (2013). 'Adam Smith: From Propriety and Sentiments to Property and Wealth', *Forum for Social Economics*, 42(4): 283–97.

Sober, E. and Wilson, D. S. (1998). *Unto Others: The Evolution and Psychology of Unselfish Behavior*. Cambridge, MA: Harvard University Press.

Stanley, J. (2011). *Know How*. Oxford: Oxford University Press.

Sullivan, E. A. and Kosson, D. S. (2006). 'Ethnic and Cultural Variations in Psychopathy', in C. J. Patrick (ed.), *Handbook of Psychopathy*. New York: Guilford Press, 437–58.

Sugden, R. (1993). 'Thinking as a Team: Toward an Explanation of Nonselfish Behavior', *Social Philosophy and Policy*, 10: 69–89.

Zizzo, D. J. and Oswald, A. J. (2001). 'Are People Willing to Pay to Reduce Others' Incomes?', *Annales d'Economie et de Statistique*, 63–4: 39–65.

7

Regard for Others

Avner Offer *

> It is the great precept of nature to love ourselves only as we love our neigh-
> bour, or what comes to the same thing, as our neighbour is capable of
> loving us.
>
> Adam Smith, *The Theory of Moral Sentiments* (6th edn. 1790, I. i. 5. 5)

Since the 1980s, public policy in English-speaking countries has been
guided by two doctrines. The first is selfishness (or more grandly, 'rational
choice'), namely that people are motivated primarily by self-regarding interests which they pursue in market exchange. The second is that the primacy
of self-regard is good. Adam Smith's 'invisible hand' ensures that market
exchange is socially efficient. Wherever possible, therefore, production,
distribution, and exchange should be transacted in markets, and should
respond to prices. I call these doctrines 'market liberalism'. There is, however,
a long-standing question as to whether Adam Smith's notion of the invisible hand can be reconciled with his ethical motive of 'sympathy' in the *The
Theory of Moral Sentiments* (Montes 2003). I argue here that what matters in

* First published in 2012 (with slight differences) as 'Self-Interest, Sympathy and the Invisible
Hand: From Adam Smith to Market Liberalism', *Economic Thought*, 2(1): 1–14.

Smith's conception of sympathy is not our sympathy *for* others. Rather, it is approbation, the sympathy of others *for ourselves*. This reading reconciles selfishness and sympathy and is altogether more credible. It also has a bearing on the efficiency attributes and on the ethical authority of current norms of self-interest and market freedom.

Despite their venerable lineage and normative centrality, we do not know whether the doctrines of self-interest and market efficiency are true. Their core premises are insecure. It has never been proven that unfettered markets are always more efficient than other arrangements; it is not even easy to define what such efficiency would consist of. And self-interest is either an a priori axiom, or a psychological speculation. In reality, personal choices are not always intended to maximise economic advantage. Financial motivations are often crowded out by intrinsic ones, such as obligation, compassion, and public spirit. As for aggregate efficiency, those who buy and sell for their own advantage have no incentive to seek it, and it has never been proven that efficiency just happens by itself.

The doctrines of selfishness and of market efficiency are sometimes presented as hard-nosed conceptions of immutable reality. It is supposedly not the business of economists to make moral judgements. Implicitly, however, and often openly as well, these doctrines also imply ethical claims: self-regard and market pay-offs are presented not only as true, not only as efficient, but also as just and proper. Milton Friedman wrote, 'The ethical principle that would directly justify the distribution of income in a free market society is, "To each according to what he and the instruments he owns produces"' (Friedman 1962: 161–2). An alternative view is that both types of claims, from reality and from justice, are asserted because they are self-serving. Indeed that is what we should expect if we truly believed them. This critical view is also developed here.

Since selfishness and the invisible hand remain unvalidated, they provide a bad model of reality. Like other bad models, and because they are bad models, in a normative role they can serve to justify harm. How these doctrines inflict harm is described in Chapter 15, and an alternative normative model is set out below, which is the one that really comes out of Adam Smith. Economics today has arrived at what appears to be a blind alley: the doctrines of efficient markets and the policy norms they endorsed have failed repeatedly and badly. They are not sufficient to explain the success of capitalism and its variants, and they do not account for its failures.

I dwell on Smith here at some length, because his authority is claimed by market liberals as providing support for their doctrines, and also because his real doctrine is different, more attractive ethically, and more compelling empirically. In his view, the drive for personal advantage is tempered by the quest for approbation. Individual well-being arises from social acceptance.

In contrast, according to Smith, market exchange is efficient only when it is impersonal and truly competitive. In reality, and even in modern societies, such competitive and impersonal settings are not the rule. Whenever there is personal interaction (as in a good deal of economic and social exchange), mutual obligation enters the calculus of advantage.

I

Every economic exchange creates a transient condition of dependence. Much of the time, this makes no difference: buyers and sellers have ways to police each other. Conventions, law, morality, and regulation keep defectors in check. But when knowledge and bargaining power are unequal, opportunities for duplicity and defection can open up. The doctrine of self-interest provides an adequate motive. Another justification for defection is that self-interest promotes collective welfare. As Bernard de Mandeville put it in 1714, 'Private Vices, [are] Publick Benefits'. 'The worst of all the multitude', he wrote, 'did something for the common good' (Mandeville 1714: 9, l.17).

The two interlocking doctrines of self-interest and market efficiency carry through to the present day. But they remain unvalidated. The primacy of self-interest is only a speculation. The invisible hand remains an article of faith. As norms for conduct, these two doctrines are asymmetric in time. Self-interest is a licence for defection now. In contrast, the 'Publick Benefits' promised are delayed and uncertain.

The concept of an 'invisible hand' is identified with Adam Smith. The two most famous passages in *The Wealth of Nations* align it with the interests of the businessman who

> ...intends only his own gain, and he is in this, as in many other cases, led by an invisible hand to promote an end which was no part of his intention. Nor is it always the worse for the society that it was no part of it. By pursuing his own interest he frequently promotes that of the society more effectually than when he really intends to promote it. (Smith 1776 [1976]: IV.ii, 456)

Note that Smith's criterion is not the benefits for the individual, but for society. The other famous passage says:

> It is not from the benevolence of the butcher, the brewer, or the baker, that we expect our dinner, but from their regard to their own interest. We address ourselves, not to their humanity but to their self-love, and never talk to them of our own but of their advantages. (Smith 1776 [1976]: I.ii, 27)

These lines can be taken as a warrant for self-seeking. In the spirit of Mandeville, do your worst; it is only for the best.

But Smith held Mandeville in contempt. Mandeville, he wrote disapprov-
ingly in his first book, *The Theory of Moral Sentiments*, 'seems to take away
altogether the distinction between vice and virtue, and of which the tendency is, upon that account, wholly pernicious... All public spirit, therefore,
all preference of public to private interest, is, according to him, a mere cheat
and imposition upon mankind' (Smith 1759 [1976]: VII.ii.4.6, 308).

Smith's first chapter, 'Of Sympathy', opens resonantly: 'How selfish soever
man may be supposed, there are evidently some principles in his nature,
which interest him in the fortune of others' (Smith 1759 [1976]: I.i.1, 9). In
this passage, 'sympathy' is independent of and as real as selfishness. These
generous words impart a benign aura to the book. But the claim is a little
puzzling. Howsoever admirable such impulses of innate sympathy might be,
they are not entirely credible as a prime motivator.

The primacy of sympathy is more believable, however, if what really matters
is not our sympathy *for others*, but the sympathy of others *for ourselves*: 'nothing pleases us more than to observe in other men a fellow-feeling with all the
emotions of our own breast' (Smith 1759 [1976], I.i.2.1, 13). Note that 'nothing pleases us more'. The motivational primacy of other people's sympathy
is meant here literally. Likewise, in the passage below, it is described as the
prime mover of economic activity:

> What are the advantages which we propose by that great purpose of human life
> which we call bettering our condition? To be observed, to be attended to, to be
> taken notice of with sympathy, complacency, and approbation, *are all* the advan-
> tages which we can propose to derive from it. It is the vanity, not the ease, or the
> pleasure, which interests us. (Smith 1759 [1976], I.iii.2.1, 50; italics added)

As a motive that is equally compelling as self-interest, the approbation of
others is more credible than benign altruism. But in order to give satisfaction,
the approbation of others has to be genuine. Unmerited approbation is not
worth having (Smith 1759 [1976]: 115). So the approbation of others needs to
be authenticated. And that is why Smith opens his argument by asserting the
existence of unilateral sympathy. To make it clear, approbation is not an alternative to sympathy, it is animated by sympathy. To make the model work,
for the sympathy of others to be credible to us, we need to believe that they
have a capacity for unilateral sympathy. And for this capacity to be credible
in others, we need to observe it in ourselves. Our capacity to sympathise *with*
others has to be assumed in order to make the sympathy *of* others credible to
us. This need for approbation is wired in: 'Nature, when she formed man for
society, endowed him with an original desire to please and an original aversion to offend his brethren... She rendered their approbation most flattering
and most agreeable to him for its own sake; and the disapprobation most
mortifying and most offensive' (Smith 1759 [1976]: III.ii.6, 116).

How to authenticate the approval of other people? We do not have access to their minds. But we can see into our own. Smith uses the device of 'the impartial spectator'. Approbation needs to be deserved (in an echo of the Golden Rule, 'As every man doth, so shall it be done to him' (Smith 1759 [1976]: II.ii.1.10, 82). In order to take satisfaction in praise, one needs to have earned it. Individuals know whether they are praiseworthy better than an external observer. They should wish for no more praise than a well-informed and fair-minded stranger might be willing to accord: 'We endeavour to examine our own conduct as we imagine any other fair and impartial spectator would examine it...We suppose ourselves the spectators of our own behaviour, and endeavour to imagine what effect it would, in this light, produce upon us' (Smith 1759 [1976]: III.1.2, 110; III.1.5, 112). The agent views his own conduct as other people might see it, and cannot, in fairness, claim any special consideration, unless it was truly deserved. This point of view, of the 'impartial spectator', is internalised, so that the sense of desert no longer depends on the presence or absence of actual praise (Smith 1759 [1976]: III.1.5, 115). For this model to work, Smith needs to assume that the individual not only has a natural desire for praise, but also an innate desire to *be* virtuous: 'Nature has endowed him not only with the desire of being approved of, but with the desire of *being* what ought to be approved of' (Smith 1759 [1976]: III.2.7,117). But that may be a step too far: is this really credible? Even Smith admits that the capacity for sympathy is not restricted to the virtuous and the humane (Smith 1759 [1976]: I.i.1.1,9).

A similar concept to Smithian approbation is provided in my own account of 'the economy of regard' (Offer 1997). In economics it is assumed that individuals form their preferences independently of each other. In contrast, the concept of 'regard' implies that they form their preferences in response to each other. The ultimate benefit is self-worth. As Smith argued, self-worth requires the validation of others. The term 'regard' has two meanings: The first is 'to be noticed'. The second is 'to be valued'. Validation needs to be independent and impartial. Instead of relying on self-validation by the 'impartial spectator', in my model it is achieved by evaluating the signal of approbation. A good signal, in theory, is one that is difficult to make and difficult to fake. Hence, the recipient should be in a position to evaluate it (Camerer 1988). Approbation is communicated as a signal from the counterparty, by means of a 'gift' (the term is applied to any voluntary transfer). The glow of acknowledgement in the cycle of reciprocal exchange is the authentication device.

Regard takes many forms: attention, acceptance, respect, reputation, status, power, intimacy, love, friendship, kinship, and sociability. Withholding signifies indifference and rejection. To convey authentic regard, a genuine signal requires discrimination and effort. But it does not require virtue. Regard can motivate anyone, villains as well as the virtuous, and is sustained so long as it is reciprocated. The reciprocal motive of regard is less demanding, and more realistic, than assuming, as Smith needs to do, that people are imbued with 'the real love of virtue, and the real abhorrence of vice' (Smith 1759 [1976]: III.2.7, 117). But Smith was right to perceive that some level of shared virtue helps to motivate the cycle of reciprocity. If social norms are benign, then a good deal of cooperation, pro-social behaviour, and reciprocity can be motivated by the quest for approbation alone.

For Smith, ethical obligation does not mean self-denial: it is grounded in the pursuit of personal benefit, in 'reflected self-interest' (Montes 2003: 74). The value of benevolence is not diminished even if it is motivated partly or wholly by self-love (Smith 1759 [1976]: VII.ii.3.16, 304). Ethical norms have consequently evolved as part of human nature. This is also consistent with recent experimental findings, which have a shown that the commitment to fairness is widespread, but falls short of being universal (Camerer and Fehr 2004). For Smith, extending sympathy is guaranteed to pay off:

> No benevolent man ever lost altogether the fruits of his benevolence. If he does not always gather them from the persons from whom he ought to have gathered them, he seldom fails to gather them, and with a tenfold increase, from other people. Kindness is the parent of kindness; and if to be beloved by our bretheren be the great object of our ambition, the surest way of obtaining it is, by our conduct to show that we really love them. (Smith 1759 [1976]: VI.ii.1.19, 225)

In other words, the best way to obtain the regard of other people is to provide them with our own.

The 'invisible hand' is invoked only once in *The Wealth of Nations*. Its effectiveness is understated: it is merely 'not always the worse for society'; and it does not *necessarily* promote the interests of society, it only does so 'frequently'. The miraculous powers it has subsequently acquired may not have been intended by its author (Grampp 2000; Rothschild 2001: ch. 5; Samuels, Johnson, and Perry 2011). In contrast, the 'impartial spectator' (the internalised norm of propriety), is invoked sixty-six times in Smith's first book, *The Theory of Moral Sentiments*, and its authority, the authority of conscience, is taken as binding. It was also Smith's final word: a revised sixth edition was published just before his death.

The contradiction is real. How to square the doctrines of laissez-faire and 'natural liberty' with those of moral obligation that seem to coexist in Smith, and even more so, how to square the difference between Smith and Mandeville? My response is that much of the time there is no contradiction. The invisible hand applies where markets are impersonal and competitive, and where they trade in uniform commodities. In contrast, the impartial spectator's ethical norms apply whenever exchange is mediated by personal relations. Approbation may be valued highly, but impersonal markets cannot supply it (Offer 1997: 454–67).[1]

This is demonstrated in Smith's chapter, 'Digression concerning the Corn Trade and Corn Laws', in *The Wealth of Nations* (Smith 1776 [1976], IV.v.a–b, 524). In the British *ancien regime*, the grain trade was regulated by means of maximum prices and restrictions on export and hoarding. Their purpose was to prevent extreme price rises in times of shortage. E. P. Thompson regarded these arrangements as a reciprocal 'moral economy', in which the poor provided deference, and the rich guaranteed subsistence (Thompson 1971). Smith argued that these regulations were misguided, and that a free market was more likely than any regulator to ensure subsistence, except in the most extreme circumstances. Grain production and trade, the largest industry in the country, was too extensive for any monopolist to capture. Merchants who raised prices above the competitive level would be undercut by the others.

The popular belief that merchants hoarded grain deliberately in times of dearth gave rise to food riots; the fear of riot deterred respectable traders and the business therefore attracted 'an inferior set of dealers... together with a number of wretched hucksters' (Smith 1776 [1976], IV.5.b.8, 528). The accusation of impropriety became self-fulfilling. The implication is that in impersonal, competitive markets, virtue does not matter; it makes no difference that the grain trade middlemen are short on virtue. The impersonal discipline of competitive markets made them serve the public good. This chapter demonstrates how the invisible hand can operate when markets are impersonal.

II

The advocates of market liberalism naturally concurred in this analysis. The Mont Pelerin Society is an influential and well-funded global society of academics, businessmen, and their acolytes, all of them hostile to the welfare state, which has assembled annually since 1947 (Hartwell 1995; Walpen 2004; Mirowski and Plehwe 2009). In 1976, it went to Scotland to commemorate the bicentenary of *The Wealth of Nations*. In one of the papers presented, the Chicago economist Ronald Coase explained:

> For that extensive division of labour required to maintain a civilised standard of living, we need to have the co-operation of great multitudes, scattered all over the world. There is no way in which this cooperation could be secured through the exercise of benevolence. Benevolence, or love, may be the dominant, or, at any

[1] Nieli (1986) applies the impartial spectator in the case of personal intimacy, the invisible hand for impersonal relations. Viner (1972: 80–2) has an analogous concept of 'social distance'. Both cited in Montes (2003).

rate, an important, factor within the family or in our relations with colleagues and friends, but as Adam Smith indicates, it operates weakly or not at all when we deal with strangers... The great advantage of the market is that it is able to use the strength of self-interest to offset the weakness and partiality of benevolence. (Coase 1976: fol. 13)

Milton Friedman also differentiated between the intimate sphere, where obligation was appropriate, and the impersonal one, where it was impractical. On the moral level, Smith regarded sympathy as a human characteristic, but one that was itself rare and required to be economised. He would have argued that the invisible hand was far more effective than the visible hand of government in mobilising not only material resources for immediate self-seeking ends but also sympathy for unselfish charitable ends (Friedman 1976: fol. 9).

Friedman's assertion that love is scarce may have come from an essay by Robertson, 'What do Economists Economize On?' (Robertson 1956) (they economised on love). But Smith himself never regarded sympathy as being scarce. He considered it to be innate and universal.

Like Friedman, Coase also twisted the existence of benevolence into an argument against collective provision:

> ...this should not lead us to ignore the part which benevolence and moral sentiments do play in making possible a market system. Consider, for example, the care and training of the young, largely carried out within the family and sustained by parental devotion. If love were absent and the task of training the young was therefore placed on other institutions, run presumably by people following their own self-interest, it seems likely that this task, on which the successful working of human societies depends, would be worse performed. (Coase 1976: fol. 13)

So much for education and schools. In this market-liberal argument, everything hangs on the relative scale of impersonal markets, which are supposedly much larger than the aggregate scale of those forms of exchange that involve personal interaction.

Chicago economists assume that impersonal markets predominate. This is also suggested by the common usage which implies that we live in competitive market societies. But a good deal of commercial activity is anything but competitive. And incentives of interpersonal regard continue to pervade large sectors. They dominate production and exchange within the household (including the creation and raising of children), and those segments of production which depend on personal interaction: health, education, personal care, small teams, relational salesmanship, family farming, the military, the professions, and hierarchical bureaucracies of various kinds. The boundaries of self-regard, pseudo-regard, and authentic regard shift in response to technological conditions, modes of production, cultural norms, and personal

preferences. Overall, taking the imputed money value of household production (including childcare), not-for-profit activity, and public and collective
goods, less than half of the imputed money value of final output is allocated
through markets.[2]

In advanced societies, people have deliberately avoided impersonal markets for most of their satisfactions. Even within markets, a good deal of
exchange involves interpersonal interaction, e.g. in marketing, hospitality,
and personal services. The share of services has come to dominate output
in western developed societies, and services typically require interpersonal
interactions and trust. Teachers, doctors, lawyers, waiters, hairdressers, sales-
people, and financial managers too, all owe the client a duty of care. Hence,
both Mandeville and Smith can be right at the same time, in different sectors
and activities. The challenge for policy is not to get the invisible hand to
displace the impartial spectator, or vice versa, but to identify the appropriate
sphere and scope for each. As the relative share of commodity production
declines in advanced societies the impartial spectator's duty of care only gains
in importance.

III

In view of the enduring influence of the invisible hand doctrine, and of
Smith's authority, one might assume that it is founded on compelling analysis. Most of his argument, as in the Corn Trade chapter, is descriptive: Smith's
'System of Natural Liberty' is appropriate to competitive markets, which can
discipline market traders. Analytically, however, invisible hand statements
take the form of causal propositions: action A leads to result B—they imply
a mechanism at work. But Smith did not try to show *how* it worked, except,
as above, by anecdote, example, or assertion. The invisible hand itself is
alchemy—a felicitous phrase but without any transcendental clockwork to
support it.

And so it has remained. The invisible hand is at the heart of economics,
and provides a social justification for the primacy of self-regard. But it is no
more than an article of faith. Taken as a formal theorem, for almost two
centuries nobody was able to prove it. In the 1950s, the 'Two Theorems of
Welfare Economics' were proven mathematically by Arrow and Debreu.
These theorems were proclaimed as the final demonstration of the invisible hand theorem (Arrow and Hahn 1971: 5). They show that every general
equilibrium is associated with a state of Pareto efficiency (in which no one

---

[2] Roughly quantified in Offer (1997).

can be made better off without someone else being made worse off). This notion of efficiency has generally been adopted as the touchstone of economic performance. Like other economic terms which diverge from their ordinary meanings, Pareto efficiency is quite different from the lay concept of efficiency, which is defined by the relation between input and output. The Two Theorems, the purported proof of the invisible hand postulate, are not in fact such a great advance: the proof is clever and difficult, but it only obtains if (at the time of exchange) there are markets open for all goods and prices until the end of time. Such conditions are not easy to satisfy. Furthermore, the criterion of Pareto efficiency is not particularly attractive (Bromley 1990). The point of departure is a demonstration by Edgeworth that for two persons trading with each other there is a deal that maximises their joint pay-off (in fact, the deal has such a single solution only under restrictive assumptions, and is otherwise indeterminate) (Mirowski 1994: 24–9). Likewise, in the two theorems of welfare economics, there is a general equilibrium (of all simultaneous trades in the economy) that maximises collective pay-offs for every set of initial endowments. When the butcher and the baker are trading bread and meat in order to make their sandwiches, the joint maximum is easy to measure. But what units can be used to measure *everybody's* satisfaction or utility? How can we compare even the value of a single dollar, for the rich and for the poor? If it is 'willingness to pay', that surely depends on 'ability to pay'—that is to say, on initial endowments and their ownership. The rich can always outbid the poor. And why should the property rights of the rich be taken as prior? As Bentham pointed out, property is created by society and depends on it (Bentham 1838: 307, 309). If one person has everything and everybody else has nothing, then welfare will be raised by redistributing from one to all, even at the expense of pre-existing claims.

The Pareto criterion of so-called efficiency endorses existing property rights and the status quo, and does not take into account what other distributions might be more equitable or could provide more welfare overall. Indeed, no objective criterion for maximising welfare overall is provided. Every person is the sole judge of their own welfare. Every person has a veto and can cry a halt. The criterion is undemocratic. It is equivalent in this respect to the principle of unanimity demanded by Public Choice advocates such as James Buchanan. And like Public Choice doctrine, its main effect is to provide legitimacy and protection for the existing distribution of property, however acquired and however unequal.

But the prerequisites even for this underwhelming notion of efficiency are non-existent. Kenneth Arrow (himself one of the two authors of the welfare theorems) has written that 'a complete general equilibrium system, as in Debreu (1959), requires markets for all contingencies in all future periods'. Another High Theorist (and Arrow's co-author), Frank Hahn, wrote that 'the complete market hypothesis is completely falsified' (Arrow and Hahn 1971: 72; Hahn 1984: 121). John Williamson, the senior IMF economist who coined the term 'Washington Consensus', has written:

> One does not have to be some sort of market fundamentalist who believes that less government is better government and that externalities can safely be disregarded in order to recognize the benefits of using market forces to coordinate activity and motivate effort. This is a proposition that is such a basic part of economic thinking *that it is actually rather difficult to think of a work that conclusively establishes its truth*. But there are a variety of indirect confirmations. (Williamson 2008: 26; italics added)

This is just it. Theorists agree that general equilibrium cannot be made to work (Ackerman and Nadal 2004). A set of analytical results (Sonneneschein–Debreu–Mantel) from the 1970s showed that individual preferences could not be aggregated reliably into a unique and stable general equilibrium (Kirman 1992; Rizvi 2006). That markets are the best systems of delivery is not a universal truth, and depends on local circumstances. And perfection cannot be achieved incrementally. It is all or nothing. Short of the invisible hand there is only the 'Second-Best' (Lipsey and Lancaseter 1956). Even in theory, the economy does not improve incrementally as railways (for example) are privatised.

In classical economics from Adam Smith to John Stuart Mill, the object of policy was not the interests of disparate individuals, but the welfare of society. Smith insisted on the primacy of the common good over self-interest,

> The wise and virtuous man is at all times willing that his own private interest should be sacrificed to the public interest of his own particular order or society. He is at all times willing, too, that the interests of this order or society should be sacrificed to the greater interest of the state sovereignty, in which it is only a subordinate part. (Smith 1759 [1976]: VI.ii.3.3, 235)

Note the role for virtue and wisdom: man is not the slave of desire. He is capable of self-command, and of acknowledging a greater good beyond himself. This is also consistent with nineteenth-century utilitarianism, an other-directed ethical doctrine endorsed by most English Victorian economists, whose precept was 'The Greatest Good of the Greatest Number.' Like Smith and Hume, Bentham, Mill, Jevons, Sidgwick, Marshall, Edgeworth, and Pigou also held a view not unlike the Stoic doctrine that, in the words of Smith, 'We should view ourselves, not in the light in which our own selfish passions are to place us, but in the light in which any other citizen of the world would view us' (Smith 1759 [1976]: III.3.11, 140–1).

In contrast, more recent economics makes a virtue of self-regard: it prides itself on being counter-intuitive. Concern for others is soft-minded 'cheap talk'. It may be an ethical injunction, but that is only a 'value'. Those who want to understand the world are told to separate 'ought' from 'is'. Modern social science prides itself on 'value freedom' (Bromley 1990: 89–91). Scientists describe things as they are, not as they ought to be. But the tough-minded economist with no time for ethics is also making an ethical stand. The Pareto-efficiency criterion has nothing to say about prior distribution, which it takes as given. It is silent about equity. That is an ethical position, which relies on the counter-intuitive assumption that well-being is entirely subjective and cannot be compared from one person to another. For Lionel Robbins, an influential exponent of neoclassical doctrine in the 1930s, 'me-first' was founded on the 'Indisputable Facts of Experience' (Sugden 2009). Following on Robbins, in standard microeconomic theory, e.g. in the theory of household consumption, 'me-first' is simply taken as a premise which needs no justification.

But the facts of experience are no such thing. Others have different intuitions (Sugden 2009). As an empirical postulate, self-interest is tautological: any choice observed can be attributed to self-interest. If, however, it means that everyone is always maximising a material or financial or market advantage, then it is manifestly untrue. The psychological model of unbounded self-regard is not credible. Friendship, love, loyalty, charity, patriotism, civility, solidarity, integrity, and impartiality (which are ubiquitous and compelling) depend on the premise of unbounded self-regard being wrong. The family, religion, the workplace, the judiciary, the state, the nation, and military service—some of the most powerful and enduring institutions assume that people will not always put themselves first. And values are not inscrutably subjective. The focal points of market prices and their elasticities indicate a broad social consensus on what is valuable. Market-liberals themselves have realised that for microeconomics to have any predictive power, it is necessary to assume that preferences are 'assumed not to change substantially over time, not to be very different between wealthy and poor persons, or even between persons in different societies and cultures' (Becker 1976: 5). They have extended this into macroeconomics with the device of 'representative agent', i.e. a model of the economy as a whole in which multitudes of people are assumed to act as one. And in advocating business-friendly deregulation, market liberals are happy to use cost–benefit analyses based on 'willingness to pay', and have no problem aggregating dollars which have very different subjective values to different people.

IV

The self-regarding actor reappeared in a particularly de-socialised guise in the 1940s. He featured in early game theory and in the Savage axioms of rationality, laid down in the 1950s. Duncan Black defined the self-seeking rational voter, and laid the foundation for Anthony Downs's *Economic Theory of Democracy* in the 1950s. In the 1960s, Mancur Olson argued the futility of collective action. By the 1970s, methodological individualism and rational choice had become the standard assumptions in economics and political science. These doctrines are so pervasive now that it is easy to overlook how radical they were initially. This 'selfish turn' may neutrally be described as sociopathic, i.e. inimical to social cooperation. In social science discourse, the criterion of common good was simply set aside. Rational choice theory does not even need to be blessed by the invisible hand (Elster 2001). The 'hand' is bolted on as an afterthought.

There is a puzzle as to why, from the 1950s onwards, such an extreme form of self-regard should have beguiled academics in economics, political science, and philosophy, as being so manifestly self-evident. In evolutionary biology as well, the tide flowed from group to individual selection. Even John Rawls's *Theory of Justice*, the dominant work in moral and political philosophy, took individual self-interest, 'behind the veil of ignorance', as its point of departure. It is not generally known that Rawls was briefly a member of the Mont Pelerin Society. Rawls was put forward for membership by Milton Friedman in 1968, and withdrew from the Society three years later, before the publication of the *Theory* in 1971.[3] In keeping with the Society's orientation, Rawls privileges 'freedom' as the highest good. Many other philosophers and political scientists have followed his lead. But other social sciences, notably sociology, anthropology, and psychology, maintained a sceptical distance, and earned the disdain of 'tough-minded' rational choice colleagues.

Maybe this posture of 'toughness' is a clue. Decisiveness can be attractive, and it is only a short step to extol the rough virtues of manliness. In American culture in particular, 'toughness' is held out as a virtue. A robust Social Darwinism coexisted in nineteenth-century America with an intense religiosity—indeed the two were regarded as being complementary. Success was Godly, failure deserved (Hofstadter 1955).[4] The British gentlemanly ideal was the opposite: self-control rather than self-assertion, 'gentility' rather than hardness (Girouard 1981; Mason 1982).

Toughness is worthy of admiration when it signifies the ability to *endure* pain. But in the social and political rhetoric since the 1970s, toughness has mutated into a willingness to *inflict* pain: the rhetoric is 'hard choices' (hard

---

[3] Mont Pelerin Society, Proposals for Membership, September 1968, Mont Pelerin Society Papers 44/1, Hoover Institution Archives; Mont Pelerin Society, 'List of Members' [1970], Friedman Papers 87/5, Hoover Institution Archives; Mont Pelerin Society, list of lapsed members, 1972, Friedman Papers 87/2.

[4] See especially chapter 3 on William Graham Sumner.

for me to hurt you), 'cruel to be kind', or more directly 'if it ain't hurting, it ain't working'. When combined with a license for self-seeking, such 'toughness' might well inspire wariness rather than admiration.

The ideal of 'freedom' is associated with toughness, to the extent that it means a 'rugged' independence, 'standing on one's own feet'. Freedom has an exalted lineage in the historical struggle against religious oppression and in resistance to external and domestic tyranny. The historical quest for freedom is replete with martyrdom. In the European tradition of Rousseau and Kant, 'freedom' is also about the scope for moral or personal autonomy. In the Anglo-Saxon tradition, however, it stands primarily for the security of property rights, although both other meanings are implied as well (MacPherson 1962; MacGilvray 2011). In the American and British traditions, 'freedom' was compatible with the ownership of slaves: indeed, it dignified the ownership of slaves (Brown 2010a, 2010b). Chicago economist Robert Fogel won the Nobel Prize in part for a book that argued that slavery was 'efficient' (Fogel and Engerman 1974). No Pareto efficiency veto for the slaves; no more than for the subjects of the Pinochet dictatorship, lauded for its market liberalism and advised by Milton Friedman and James Buchanan. For market liberals, freedom does not extend to speech: both the Mont Pelerin Society and the Chicago Department of Economics, the sectarian incubators of market liberal thought, have restricted access to those with like-minded opinions and have not gone out of their way to debate with their critics. Protection of property is commonly conflated with individual autonomy and discretion, although possession of property and freedom for some, as Bentham once recognised, limits the freedom of others. In the market discourse of the twentieth century, 'freedom' has become just another term for self-interest, ubiquitous on right-wing mastheads. As in the case of 'toughness', personal virtue has transformed into social license: freedom from tyranny has mutated into freedom from obligation. In its more extreme form, as among the followers of Ayn Rand, it is a kind of juvenile revulsion from parental tutelage—indeed, 'paternalism' is one of the freedom advocates' greatest evils.

For all its rhetoric of freedom, neoclassical economics, at both micro and macro level, is not comfortable with actual choice. In microeconomic consumer theory, the agent has a set of innate preferences. He or she is presented by reality with a complete set of opportunities, prices, and their probabilities. Given their immutable preferences and the information they have, consumers can only make one choice, the one that maximises their preferences. They have no more discretion than a piece of clockwork. This rigid determinism leaves no room for ethical choice, and justifies any outcome as being inevitable. Likewise, at the macro level, policymaking is delegated to so-called 'independent' central banks with a rigid and narrow mandate, to achieve a given rate of inflation. Even that discretion is a concession designed to hold down the unruly pressure of wage demands. When it comes to asset prices, no intervention is warranted at all. In other words: one rule for labour, another for capital.

In reality, choice is never so easy. In contrast with the premises of deterministic economic modelling, a good deal of the future is unknowable, and time-inconsistent discounting means that choice is often genuinely intractable, with no optimising algorithm available (Offer 2006: ch. 3). In the face of such imponderables, choices still have to be made (Bhide 2010). This indeterminacy opens up room for genuine discretion, including an ethical choice, for 'doing the right thing'. In the absence of clockwork procedures, people fall back on established commitment devices, which allow them to place a larger conception of welfare beyond what might seem to be their own immediate interests. These commitment devices are established social conventions and strategies which often embody ethical norms, and which make it possible to overcome myopic preferences. Examples of this at a personal level are marriage, education, insurance, prudence, and patriotism; at the social level, constitutions, law, religion, money, calendars and clocks, government, and taxes. Before the relativism of Robbins and his amoral successors, the utilitarian doctrines of Victorian economists were also commitment devices of this kind.

Many of these commitment devices can be thought of as 'ethical capital'. They form a reliable inventory of expectations about how people are likely to act. They underpin trust and facilitate exchange. They economise on monitoring and enforcement. Ethical capital takes us back to Adam Smith, the impartial spectator, and the assumption of innate virtue.

Seen this way, the 'selfish turn' of the 1960s and 1970, the rise and acceptance of rational choice doctrines, constituted a wholesale destruction of ethical capital, an episode of normative demolition that still continues. 'Freedom' has a transcendental appeal in American culture and politics. But for a self-regarding rational individualist, it comes down to calculation: how much self-seeking is it useful to allow, if the same license is available to others. The choice depends on socio-economic standing: freedom from obligation is more valuable to the rich and powerful than to others, because there is more for them to lose.

References

Ackerman, F. and Nadal, A. (eds) (2004). *The Flawed Foundations of General Equilibrium: Critical Essays on Economic Theory*. London and New York: Routledge.

Arrow, K. J. (1987). 'Economic Theory and the Hypothesis of Rationality', in J. Eatwell, M. Milgate, and P. Newman (eds), *The New Palgrave Dictionary of Economics*. London: MacMillan, 70–4.

Arrow, K. J. and Hahn, F. (1971). *General Competitive Analysis*. Amsterdam and Oxford: North-Holland.

Becker, G. S. (1976). *The Economic Approach to Human Behavior.* Chicago: University of Chicago Press.

Bentham, J. (1838). 'Principles of the Civic Code', in J. Bowring (ed.), *The Works of Jeremy Bentham*, vol. 1. Edinburgh: William Tait.

Bhide, A. (2010). *A Call for Judgment: Sensible Finance for a Dynamic Economy.* Oxford: Oxford University Press.

Bromley, D. W. (1990). 'The Ideology of Efficiency: Searching for a Theory of Policy Analysis', *Journal of Environmental Economics and Management*, 19(1): 86–107.

Brown, M. (2010a). 'Adam Smith's View of Slaves as Property', *Real-World Economics Review*, 54: 124–5.

Brown, M. (2010b). 'Free Enterprise and Economics of Slavery', *Real-World Economics Review*, 52: 28–39.

Camerer, C. (1988). 'Gifts as Economic Signals and Social Symbols', *American Journal of Sociology*, 94: S180–S214.

Camerer, C. and Fehr, E. (2004). 'Measuring Social Norms and Preferences Using Experimental Games: A Guide for Social Scientists', in J. Henrich, R. Boyd, S. Bowles, C. Camerer, E. Fehr, and H. Gintis (eds), *Foundations of Human Sociality: Economic Experiments and Ethnographic Evidence from Fifteen Small Scale Societies.* New York: Oxford University Press, 55–95.

Coase, R. (1976). 'Adam Smith's View of Man', in the Hayek Papers, 163/4. Hoover Institution: Stanford University.

Debreu, G. (1959). *Theory of Value; an Axiomatic Analysis of Economic Equilibrium.* New York: Wiley.

Elster, J. (2001). 'The Nature and Scope of Rational Choice Explanation', in M. Martin and L. C. McIntyre (eds), *Readings in the Philosophy of Social Science.* Cambridge, MA: MIT Press, 311–22.

Fogel, R. W. and Engerman, S. L. (1974). *Time on the Cross: The Economics of American Negro Slavery.* London: Wildwood House.

Friedman, M. (1931–91). Milton Friedman Papers. Hoover Institution Archives, Stanford University.

Friedman, M. (1976). 'Adam Smith's Relevance for 1976', in the Hayek Papers 163/3. Hoover Institution: Stanford University.

Friedman, M. and Friedman, R. D. (1962). *Capitalism and Freedom.* Chicago: University of Chicago Press.

Girouard, M. (1981). *The Return to Camelot: Chivalry and the English Gentleman.* New Haven: Yale University Press.

Grampp, W. D. (2000). 'What Did Smith Mean by the Invisible Hand?', *Journal of Political Economy*, 108(3): 441–65.

Hahn, F. (1984). 'Reflections on the Invisible Hand', in F. Hahn, *Equilbrium and Macroeconomics.* Oxford: Blackwell, 111–32.

Hartwell, R. M. (1995). *A History of the Mont Pelerin Society.* Indianapolis: Liberty Fund.

Heller, J. (1962). *Catch 22.* London: Jonathan Cape.

Hofstadter, R. (1955). *Social Darwinism in American Thought.* Boston: Beacon Press.

Kirman, A. P. (1992). 'Whom or What Does the Representative Individual Represent?', *Journal of Economic Perspectives*, 6(2): 117–36.

Lipsey, R. G. and Lancaster, K. (1956). 'The General Theory of Second Best', *Review of Economic Studies*, 24: 11–32.

MacGilvray, E. (2011). *The Invention of Market Freedom*. New York: Cambridge University Press.

Macpherson, C. B. (1962). *The Political Theory of Possessive Individualism: Hobbes to Locke*. Oxford: Clarendon Press.

Mandeville, B. (1714 [1988]). *The Fable of the Bees, or, Private Vices, Publick Benefits*. Indianapolis: Liberty Classics.

Mason, P. (1982). *The English Gentleman: The Rise and Fall of an Ideal*. London: André Deutsch.

Mirowski, P. (1994). 'Introduction', in P. Mirowski (ed.), *Edgeworth on Chance, Economic Hazard, and Statistics*. Lanham, MD: Rowman & Littlefield.

Mirowski, P. and Plehwe, D. (2009). *The Road from Mont Pelerin: The Making of the Neoliberal Thought Collective*. Cambridge, MA: Harvard University Press.

Mont Pelerin Society. Papers. Hoover Institution Archives, Stanford University.

Montes, L. (2003). 'Das Adam Smith Problem: Its Origins, the Stages of the Current Debate, and One Implication for Our Understanding of Sympathy', *Journal of the History of Economic Thought*, 25(1): 63–90.

Nieli, R. (1986). 'Spheres of Intimacy and the Adam Smith Problem', *Journal of the History of Ideas*, 47(4): 611–24.

Offer, A. (1997). 'Between the Gift and the Market: The Economy of Regard', *Economic History Review*, 50(3): 450–76.

Offer, A. (2006). *The Challenge of Affluence: Self-Control and Well-Being in the United States and Britain Since 1950*. Oxford: Oxford University Press.

Offer, A. (2012). 'A Warrant for Pain: Caveat Emptor vs. the Duty of Care in American Medicine, c. 1970–2010', *Real-World Economics Review*, 61: 85–99.

Rizvi, S. A. T. (2006). 'The Sonnenschein–Mantel–Debreu Results after Thirty Years', *History of Political Economy: Agreement on Demand: Consumer Theory in the Twentieth Century*, 38 (annual supplement): 228–45.

Robbins, L. R. (1932). *An Essay on the Nature and Significance of Economic Science*. London: Macmillan.

Robertson, D. H. (1956). 'What Do Economists Economize On?', in D. H. Robertson, *Economic Commentaries*. London: Staples Press, 147–54.

Rothschild, E. (2001). *Economic Sentiments: Adam Smith, Condorcet and the Enlightenment*. Cambridge, MA: Harvard University Press.

Samuels, W. J., Johnson, M. F., and Perry, W. H. (2011). *Erasing the Invisible Hand: Essays on an Elusive and Misused Concept in Economics*. Cambridge and New York: Cambridge University Press.

Smith, A. (1759 [1976]). *The Theory of Moral Sentiments*, 6th edition. Oxford: Clarendon Press.

Smith, A. (1776 [1976]). *An Inquiry into the Nature and Causes of the Wealth of Nations*. Oxford: Clarendon Press.

Sugden, R. (2009). 'Can Economics Be Founded on "Indisputable Facts of Experience"? Lionel Robbins and the Pioneers of Neoclassical Economics', *Economica*, 76(304): 857–72.

Thompson, E. P. (1971). 'The Moral Economy of the English Crowd in the Eighteenth Century', *Past and Present*, 50: 76–136.

Viner, J. (1972). *The Role of Providence in the Social Order: An Essay in Intellectual History*. Philadelphia: American Philosophical Society.

Walpen, B. (2004). *Die Offenen Feinde und ihre Gesellschaft: Eine hegemonietheoretische Studie zur Mont Pelerin Society*. Hamburg: VSA-Verlag.

Williamson, J. (2008). 'A Short History of the Washington Consensus', in N. Serra and J. Stiglitz (eds), *The Washington Consensus Reconsidered: Towards a New Global Governance*. Oxford: Oxford University Press, 14–30.

8

Trust, Trustworthiness, and Accountability*

Onora O'Neill

8.1 Trust or Accountability?

Discussions of compliance and non-compliance, and of sanctions and penalties, have always formed part of discussions of justice and of the philosophy of law. Yet there is all too little philosophical discussion of profound changes in the ways in which compliance with required standards is institutionalised that have been introduced in the last thirty years. In particular, there is too little discussion by political philosophers of several important aspects of the shift from cultural and social approaches to compliance to widespread reliance on formalised structures of accountability and corresponding duties of accountability.

In many public-sector and professional contexts this transition has supposedly introduced forms of accountability that were more often found in commercial than in professional and public life. Traditional approaches to compliance in the professions and in the public services relied heavily on cultures of trust, backed by considerable reliance on prescribed process and selective and sparing use of sanctions. Contemporary approaches both in professional life and in public services, in financial services and more broadly in corporate life, often use more elaborate, formalised structures of accountability, typically backed by an array of financial and other non-criminal sanctions, and sometimes by a wider use of criminal sanctions. These innovations are often seen as a reasoned response to cultural changes that have

* An early version of this paper appeared as 'Gerechtigkeit, Vertrauen und Zurechenbarkeit', in O. Neumaier, C. Sedmak, M. Zichy, and O. Verlag (eds), *Gerechtigkeit: Auf der Suche nach einem Gleichgewicht*. Frankfurt: Ontos, 33–55.

culminated in a 'crisis of trust' in developed societies. Many who comment on this crisis claim that trust is obsolete: we have eroded the social capital that traditional societies had accumulated, so now have to do without it. In complex and sophisticated societies, trust can no longer provide the cohesion and compliance that it provided in traditional societies. So a substitute for trust is needed, and that substitute requires more formal accountability for performance.

Those who hold such views typically see trust as a matter of attitude and affect.[1] On such views, the paradigm of trust is an infant's blind trust in its mother, and relations of trust have their proper place in one-to-one, face-to-face relationships, pre-eminently in relations of mutual goodwill. Beyond such intimate or personal relationships, trust is seen as risky, and those who trust are often depicted as immature or deferential, and as risking disappointment, if not betrayal (Holton 1994; O'Neill 2002a,b; Jones 2012).

It is rather obvious why this conception of trust looks questionable in complex institutional settings, where relationships are usually neither face-to-face nor one-to-one, and where affect and attitude are not prime considerations. If we were wedded to this conception of trust, it would be foolish to seek an end to the supposed 'crisis of trust'. For that crisis would be a proper reaction to a (supposedly recent) realisation that many relationships offer no basis, or no longer offer a basis, for this conception of trust. If we conceive of trust simply as a matter of (blind) acceptance or deference, and similar attitudes, we can reasonably conclude that trust should play little part in the public life of a mature democracy, or in its institutional and professional life, or anywhere else where relationships are not or no longer personal. Attitudes of trust should be replaced by a stance of *caveat emptor*: the proper model of accountability should be closer to that taken to prevail in commercial life.

As I see it, this conclusion is purchased at the price of accepting and promoting a specific, contentious, and fundamentally unintelligent conception of trust, whose obsolescence is then taken as reason to look for a *replacement* or *successor* to relations of trust. Setting up a straw person for (pointless) destruction is a poor substitute for engaging with the topic in a fuller and more intelligent way. A better account of trust that sees it as an intelligent response to evidence of trustworthiness is needed not only in public and professional, but in financial and more broadly in commercial life.

---

[1] Much discussion of the 'crisis of trust' is advanced by sociologists, journalists, and pollsters, but some philosophical approaches also see it as a matter of attitude. See Baier (1996) and Jones (1996) for accounts of trust as an attitude.

8.2 Managerial Accountability as Successor to Trust

Those who are keen to do without trust typically argue that it should be replaced with accountability. Unfortunately many of them then adopt an unintelligent conception of accountability. They identify accountability with a specific, managerial conception of accountability that centres on establishing systems for *controlling* performance by *setting targets* for individuals and institutions, *measuring* success (or lack of success) in meeting targets, *publicising* that success or failure, and then *sanctioning* failure and *rewarding* success.

The phrase *managerial accountability* can be read in two ways. On one view the thought behind it is only that those who manage must be held to account—as, for example, the managers of a company may be accountable to the board, and ultimately to shareholders, or those who manage a school may be accountable to governors and parents. On this *broad* reading there is much to be said for managerial accountability, and very little to be said against it.

However, many advocates of managerial accountability interpret it more narrowly. They demand not only that those who manage be held to account, but specifically that they be held to account *by managerial methods*: managers should be managed. In the United Kingdom, for example, government has sought to hold those who manage in the public sector to account by applying managerial methods. These have typically included setting targets, measuring performance against these targets, and sanctioning defective performance, for example, by adjusting funding or imposing extra controls.

The real significance of this approach can be obscured. It may seem that all that is at stake is *accountability for managers*—and who would disagree with that? —and that the adjective has, as it were, slipped sideways. But this is not what is meant. Contrast the case with the grammatical slide of the adjective in the common phrase 'disabled toilets'. When you read that phrase you do not (unless chronically pessimistic) assume that the toilets are disabled. You assume that they are *for the disabled*. And when you read the phrase 'managerial accountability' you may think that it means *accountability for managers*. But it doesn't. It actually means accountability organised on managerial lines, or at least on what are taken to be managerial lines.

So the reasonable claim that managers should be held to account is commonly replaced by the much more specific (and questionable) claim that managers (and through them others) should be held to account by managerial methods—or in short by further management. All too palpable evidence for this way of looking at matters can be found in the adoption of managerial vocabulary in public life. It is now used by government, by the opposition, and by the media, who all speak unembarassedly of government not as governing or holding public bodies to account, or as regulating, but as managing: government is to 'deliver' services, 'meet targets'—and to be lambasted for failing to do so. The accusations of overcentralisation and of 'control freakery' now often levied against government are a corollary of assuming that 'delivering' outcomes and services is the proper task of govern-ment, and that the proper or preferable conception of public accountability is managerial in this narrow sense.

The arguments for embracing this specific conception of the way in which managers should be held to account are astonishingly sparse. Contrary to common assumptions, there is no ready analogy with ways in which manag-ers are held to account in the commercial world, where they are ultimately held to account by processes of corporate governance that are *not* managerial in structure (Garratt 1996). Nor is an extension of managerial accountability to ever more senior managers of managers of managers...at all plausible as a way of improving performance. Yet this system has been borrowed from the private sector, and now takes the form of zealous hyper-regulation not only of the public service but of professional life. This has become a matter for complaint not only within the public sector and the professions, but in parts of the private sector that find themselves hoist by their own petard, as regulators adopt quasi-managerial approaches to their task. The United Kingdom provides a shining example of an approach to improving account-ability that has had some unhappy consequences—although changes were often imposed with the best of intentions.[2]

Proponents of managerial accountability—in the narrow, presently fash-ionable sense of the term—think that it has a number of merits. Supposedly it is readily integrated with managerial processes, cheap, objective, fair, easy to publicise and dovetailing well with 'transparency' or 'openness'. These sup-posed merits, however, add up to less than one might hope.

But it is at least true that managerial accountability integrates well with managerial process: it is, after all, simply an extension of managerial process. It is a specific form of vertical, up–down accountability, differing from some others in its reliance on target setting. It envisages that managers will set *targets* (from *above*) for individuals and institutions (working *below* them), and that their performance will then be *measured* against those targets and *sanctioned* if inadequate. In short, it is basically a continuation of manage-ment. Managerial accountability is not the only form of vertical accountabil-ity. Bureaucratic accountability is also vertical but focuses on adherence to

---

[2] And this despite the efforts of the 'Better Regulation Taskforce' and its successors which aim to ensure that regulatory regimes meet the so-called five principles of good regulation, which they identify as *Proportionality, Accountability, Consistency, Transparency, Targeting*. Despite their efforts, a huge quantity of complex and often ill-drafted legislation and regulation that does not meet these standards is churned out each year. Details of the activities of the Better Regulation Executive may be found at <https://www.gov.uk/government/policy-teams/better-regulation-executive>.

prescribed procedures; military accountability is also vertical but focuses on execution of commanded action.

A central difficulty with taking managerial accountability as the general form of accountability is that, unlike (for example) manufacturing processes, many professional and institutional activities lack obvious or easily measurable outcomes or targets. So the targets *actually* set are often *proxies* for the real objectives, chosen less for their merits than because they are nicely measurable. Supposedly, proxy measurements provide *performance indicators* that can be used where there is no easily measured target. Much can go wrong here.

Proxy indicators that are chosen because they are easy to measure may not be accurate proxies for what really matters. Yet, simplistic and misleading proxies are often chosen. We know, for example, that school quality is not adequately measured by pupils' exam scores. We know that measuring waiting times for non-urgent surgery is not a good measure of hospital performance. We know that institutions can choose and publicise indicators of achievement that flatter the needs of the moment or provide good publicity. Sometimes performance will be represented—or misrepresented—as outstanding because it has grown, or because its rate of growth has grown, or because 'customers' in a carefully selected time period, or of a carefully chosen type, are more numerous: in a complex field careful selection of indicators can suggest that there are many winners.

In saying this I do not suggest that performance indicators always mislead. For example, the use of upper-arm circumference as a proxy measure of malnutrition in children is quick, cheap and reasonably accurate; and it is hard to manipulate without blatant dishonesty. It uses a genuine unit of measurement—centimetres—to provide a reliable proxy for a quite different variable. In other cases, proxy indicators are not even robustly numerical (e.g. 'customer' satisfaction scores!), or are poorly related to the variables of real interest, so are poor indicators.

Even when performance indicators are reasonably closely connected to the real targets, and do not use bogus units of measurement, they create problems. Even well-chosen performance indicators can create perverse incentives. If exam marks are taken as an indicator of school achievement, this will have unintended and ultimately perverse effects. Pupils will be guided into the areas where high marks are easier to get; exam performance will be stressed at the expense of other educational objectives; schools will find ways to 'game' the system.

Given that performance indicators have these well-known problems, why are they so prized? Several advantages are often mentioned. First, performance indicators *seemingly* substitute (cheap and objective) inexpert for (expensive and possibly subjective) expert judgement: quality of performance is measured objectively in simple ways, and recorded merely by ticking boxes or recording scores. Quality control then seemingly becomes both cheap and objective. Second, the very simplicity of scores on performance indicators makes them easily aggregable into rankings and league tables that are useful for forms of *transparency* and *openness* that can supposedly be used to secure accountability to wider publics and to demonstrate the fairness of resource allocation and other decisions.

Yet the very demand for easy 'measurement' and simple record keeping may undermine objectivity. Recording performance by requiring ticks or numbers in boxes may turn out to be neither cheap, nor objective, nor transparent. A car is well serviced only when the mechanic does an expert job, whether or not he ticks all the boxes. The tick in the box may be objective enough: but what counts is whether it accurately represents an expert underlying performance. Management by performance indicators, and checking success by ticking boxes to represent scores on these indicators, makes expertise redundant, but may not secure objectivity. The price can be high.

Nor is management by performance indicators cheap. If expert performance is not eliminable, it will be an *additional* cost to monitor performance by scores on proxy indicators that are remote from the real tasks to be judged. Where tick box recording is introduced into systems of accountability, other more intelligent ways of securing good performance and holding people to account either have to be maintained in the background—or dispensed with. Unsurprisingly, the *added* value of managerial accountability can be less than its advocates hope.[3]

Finally, even if (for some perverse reason) we persist with this fundamentally unintelligent approach to accountability, there is no reason to assume that it can replace trust. On the contrary, if not ultimately based on relations of trust, managerial accountability will spiral into an infinite regress of deferred accountability. Unless *at some point* trust is placed in some claims or some persons, institutions, or processes, there will be *no* reason to place it in any procedures for securing accountability, however Byzantine.

This suggests that it might be worth looking for more intelligent forms of accountability. For example, depending on context, it might be appropriate to hold managers accountable by relying variously on democratic or corporate forms of governance, or on legal, financial, or professional forms of accountability. We may not need to invent the wheel. We do need to get beyond discussions that take narrow and ultimately *stupid* views both of accountability and of trust. What could change if we took a different view of each? What would serious approaches to *intelligent trust* and *intelligent accountability* require?

---

[3] This is hardly a new point. Michael Power (1997, 2009) has repeatedly shown the real cost of ill-designed systems of accountability across to some twenty years.

8.3 Placing Trust Intelligently: Claims and Commitments

An intelligent conception of trust would, I think, start with the thought that *except in rare and atypical cases* (the infantile case) both placing and refusing trust is a matter of *judging* either *truth claims* or *commitments to action (promises)*. Trust in others' truth claims is *well placed* if their words are, or turn out to be, true of the world. Trust in others' commitments is well placed if they duly act to shape the world, making some part of it true to their word and specifically to their commitments. Regardless of the direction of fit, trust is badly placed where words and the way things turn out do not fit. It is well placed when conferred *on trustworthy truth claims* and *trustworthy action*; ill placed when conferred on *untrustworthy truth claims* and *untrustworthy action*.

Trust is rarely a matter of mere responsiveness to others: it is rarely blind. An infant's trust in her mother is not an illuminating paradigm of trust: it would be more accurate to see it as a paradigm of powerlessness and dependence. By contrast, a decision to trust a neighbour or colleague to post a letter or to deposit money in a bank account may be well- or ill-judged, just as a refusal to place trust in the amazing financial proposals that arrive in electronic form from various exotic places may be well- or ill-judged. In placing and refusing trust, agents act on the basis of evidence: attitudes and affect may (or may not) follow on decisions to place or refuse trust, but are not the basis for doing so. I may trust my neighbour to post a letter although I am not particularly intimate with or fond of her, and I may refuse to trust others of whom I am genuinely fond, but whom I know to be forgetful, to do so.

There need be nothing peculiar about placing trust in the claims and commitments of institutions or officials or complex processes, when there is appropriate evidence of their trustworthiness in the relevant matters. Equally, there need be nothing absurd in refusing to trust the claims and commitments of others with whom we are close and of whom we are fond: the parents of drug addicts and the friends of spongers have excellent reasons for withholding trust in certain respects, despite their affection, and despite protestations of reform. Well-placed trust requires discrimination: it is directed selectively at specific claims and specific undertakings. Although we often speak loosely of trusting a person, we typically place trust in somebody for some but not for other truth claims, for some but not for other sorts of undertakings to act. Our aim is to align trust with others' trustworthiness.

Placing and refusing trust, whether in others' truth claims or in their commitments, requires judgement of available evidence, including judgement of their speech acts, their track record, and their likely willingness to live up to their word. But it does not need complete evidence, let alone proof.

On the contrary, where I have complete evidence or proof, trust becomes redundant: I do not need to trust that I am now writing, or that I have hands, or that two plus two is equal to four. Trust is also redundant where I have effective guarantees or control of outcomes: I do not need to trust others to act where I control their action. Small wonder that tight managerial accountability is thought of as superseding trust, since it destroys its very context!

Since trust *must* run ahead of proof or control, it is always *possible* to place it badly. Unavoidably trust carries risk. So controlling the level of risk by placing it intelligently matters. A lot of different things can go wrong. My judgement may be poor. I may place my trust in the claims of lifestyle gurus or the predictions of market analysts; I may place it in the commitments of con artists, or pyramid selling schemes, such as the one devised by the aptly named Mr Madoff who made off with others' money on such a grand scale. Even if my judgement is not poor, I may still get matters wrong because the available evidence for truth claims is poor, or the commitments that I had good reason to think trustworthy turn out to be deceptive.

Misplaced trust may reflect either lack of information, or one's own incompetence in judging information to hand, or others' insincere and deliberate fabrication of misleading evidence, including false testimony and false promises. We are, I think, likely to be most upset where we place trust badly as a result of others' deliberate fabrication or false testimony, or their false promises or insincere commitments. These are the cases where we think that we were duped and deceived, where we feel betrayed and that our trust was abused. (Yet, might it not also be reasonable to feel dismay if one's own incompetence leads one to place trust badly? Do we perhaps not mind this so much in the fond, if false, assumption that *at least in matters of judgement* we have as much or more competence as the next person? (Hobbes 1651 [1991]: I, 13, para. 2))

Does the fact that we have to place trust without guarantees suggest that it is always a mistake to trust? Could we perhaps lower risks by refusing to trust what others say or the commitments they make? Such caution might reduce the risk of being let down or disappointed. We can be more or less prudent in placing and refusing trust. But, as I have argued, we cannot do without trust. What we can do is to look for some reasonable evidence in placing trust in others' claims and commitments. We need evidence that their claims are likely to fit the world, or that they are likely to fit the world to their commitments. In short, we judge trustworthiness in order to place trust intelligently. The basic reason why managerial forms of accountability are misdirected is that they often make it *harder* to judge whether claims or commitments are trustworthy, so do not support but undermine the intelligent placing and refusal of trust.

8.4 An Intelligent Approach to Accountability

More intelligent systems for securing accountability could support rather than supersede the placing and refusal of trust. Intelligent structures of accountability should provide good—or at least *moderately* good!—evidence whether it is likely that others will fit their words to the world or the world to their commitments. An intelligent approach to accountability should support the intelligent placing—and refusal—of trust. It should focus on judging others' *trustworthiness* in the relevant matters.

Accountability forms part, but never the most fundamental part, of a set of interlinked normative ideas. As I see matters, the most fundamental normative idea is that of a *requirement*, or more accurately of *required action*. Required action may be of many sorts: we commonly distinguish, for example, between legal, institutional, instrumental, customary, and ethical requirements, and this list is not exhaustive. However, for the limited analytic purposes that I have in mind here, I shall not say much about the differences between distinct types of required action, or about the contexts that they presuppose, or about the arguments which might support specific requirements. The common and in my view most fundamental feature of requirements is that they can only be specified by describing the *type(s) of action* required, hence propositionally.[4]

From the point of view of an agent of whom certain types of action are required, requirements constitute *obligations* or *duties*. In some (but not all) cases, others may be entitled to the performance of required action. From the point of view of those on the receiving end, the required action appears as an *entitlement* or *right* in the latter sort of case. We can think of those who have obligations or duties as *obligation bearers* and of those who have rights or entitlements as *right holders*. Again, I shall not spend time distinguishing obligations and rights of various types, but note that obligations and rights are specified by using act descriptions—that is, propositionally.

Obligations and rights are asymmetric: a requirement to act may or may not be matched by a right to claim, but a right to claim is underspecified if not matched by a requirement to act. The thought that obligations need not have counterpart rights has been a commonplace of most writing on ethics and politics through the centuries, although often obscured in recent rights-centred writing, which commonly neglects all but claimable obligations (this is not to say that contemporary rights-centred literature is clear about the allocation of obligations: alas, the reverse is commonly true).

---

[4] Can there also be accountability for non-required action, such as conformity to good practice? Or is what is described merely as 'good practice' in fact required, or required absent special justification? Matters are often left obscure on this crucial set of issues.

Rights and claimable obligations—including the obligations of justice—form the figure and ground of a single normative pattern. Since 'imperfect' obligations lack counterpart rights and cannot be claimed, accountability for their discharge is not easily formalised.[5]

Conceptions of accountability form a third but distinct extension of *some* normative structures, and in particular of *some* claimable obligations (such as the obligations of justice). An agent is accountable (often we might say *answerable*) for performance or non-performance of some primary obligation when he or she (often overseen or assisted by others) has a further obligation to render an account of (non-)performance of the primary obligation to some other agent or institution, who holds an obligation to hold the agent to account for that (non-)performance. An agent or institution to whom or to which an account is owed may in turn be accountable to some further agent or institution for discharging their obligations to hold to account.

Clearly accountability too is fundamentally propositional: it is a matter of *rendering* and *receiving accounts* of what has been done, and of *holding to account* where there are discrepancies between the account rendered and the obligations that were to be discharged. Accountability, as its etymology suggests, rests on giving *an account* of performance to the person or institution charged with judging the fit (or lack of fit) between that performance and the relevant obligations, and with taking action on that basis. Accountability is propositional, anchored in providing accounts of what has been done (or not done), in receiving and judging those accounts, and in holding individuals and institutions to account for their performance.

Accountability for (non-)performance of some obligation may or may not be to right holders. For example, a person may promise a friend to deal with a problem, whereby the friend acquires a right to have her deal with the problem, and the agent will be accountable to that friend for so doing—or for failing to do so. On the other hand, within a legal order those who violate others' rights will be accountable to the courts, rather than to those whom they wrong. Absent a legal order, wrongdoers might be accountable either to those whom they wrong, or to their friends and relations, who might have a right (even a duty!) to hold to account by taking revenge.

In setting out these points I have avoided the word *responsibility*, because it is commonly used as a synonym **both** for *primary obligations or duties*, **and** for *second-order obligations to account for performance of primary obligations*. For example, we may say that parents are *responsible for* their children's safety, meaning that they have a duty to make sure that their children are safe; but we may say that employees are *responsible to* their employers, meaning that

---

[5] Imperfect obligations are important, but do not fall within the sphere of justice. Often they are construed as virtues. See Schneewind (1990) and O'Neill (1996).

they are accountable to their employers for discharging their primary obligations. Could the difference between first-order obligations and second-order obligations to render account and hold to account be captured by equating the former with *responsibility for* (some action) and the latter with *responsibility to* (some agent or institution) for some action? Unfortunately there are contexts, especially where the noun forms (*responsibility, responsibilities*) are used, where this way of drawing the distinction can become ambiguous. So I avoid the terms *responsible* and *responsibility*.

The important thought is simply that if duties and rights are specified propositionally, then accountability for their performance must build on those specifications. Accountability is unintelligent if it is undertaken in ways that suppress or omit an intelligible account of what ought to be done. Managerial accountability, with its focus on proxy indicators of performance, is an unintelligent form of accountability because it does exactly this. The points set out in this section are listed more formally in the Appendix to this chapter.

8.5 The Opacity of Transparency

An intelligent approach to accountability sheds some light on further difficulties with managerial conceptions of accountability. Managerial conceptions of accountability, and the quasi-numerical types of information which they deploy, are supposedly useful for accountability to wider, non-expert audiences. The information given by scores on performance indicators is simple, so can be aggregated and disclosed to those audiences. This disclosure achieves *transparency* or *openness*. It supposedly allows wider publics to tell whether performance has been adequate or inadequate, even whether process has been fair or unfair.

For example, performance indicators provide information of a (supposedly) objective and simple numerical type, which can be ranked in *league tables*. This makes it possible to rank the (relative) performance of institutions (schools, hospitals, universities) or of professionals (lecturers, surgeons, teachers). League tables can be published and publicised. Since anybody can read a ranking, this allows wider publics to tell who is performing well and who badly. League tables supposedly provide accountability to the public at large.

In my view this sort of transparency is *not always a necessary and never a sufficient basis for accountability to wider publics*. Consider first why transparency is not necessary. Transparency cannot be a necessary element of accountability because it sometimes damages accountability. Such damage occurs whenever transparency creates a layer of perverse incentives. Where transparency creates selective incentives to concentrate on some rather than other matters it may distort what is done. Where it requires institutions to publish some rather than other sorts of material (sometimes including working papers and internal memoranda) candid discussion within institutions may be damaged. Time and energy will be diverted to defensive activity. Position papers may minimise or omit serious discussion of options that might get a bad press, depress share prices, or provide information that helps competitors. Minutes may be drafted to support public relations rather than to provide accurate working records. Even more damagingly, demands for ubiquitous transparency create incentives to do more outside meetings, whether in private conversations, as chairman's action, or in unminuted telephone calls. Misplaced transparency requirements can damage good work on policy, sound management, institutional integrity, and even democratic process.

Transparency is also not sufficient for accountability to wider publics. Merely 'making information available' will not achieve adequate standards of communication. Communication that works for some audiences may not work for others. The advocates of transparency are often wildly over-optimistic in thinking that mere requirements for public, commercial, or other institutions to disclose more and more information to more and more 'stakeholders' will make their work more and more transparent to those audiences.

On the contrary, since transparency is *only* a matter of making material available, of disclosure, it does not mandate and often does not achieve good communication with specific audiences. Shovelling facts and figures onto websites is not usually a good way of communicating, except with fellow professionals who have the time and expertise to sift and use what is disclosed. Transparency may be a boon for related or rival institutions, for NGOs, and for others with professional capacity who specialise in criticising others' performance. It is less useful for wider publics. Less expert audiences may be unable to find the relevant information, to see the wood for the trees, to assess what they understand, and to see what is missing or to judge how the parts fit together. They are unlikely to have the time to take an active and constructive part in any debate. Unlike carrier pigeons, information does not automatically seek out relevant audiences.

In the end, one of the main limitations of the transparency culture—and, more generally, of the managerial accountability culture to which it is so closely linked—is that it takes a trivialising view of communication. Good communication has to take account of the *specific capacities and concerns of actual audiences*. This is necessary to achieve *intelligibility to* and *assessability by* the relevant audiences, and so an adequate basis for placing or refusing trust. Transparency is only a matter of distributing information, and not of communicating with specific audiences.

The illusory quest for objective and quantitative methods of measuring all performance and for total transparency provides no more than spurious

precision and an illusion of accountability. It can obscure significant obligations, and risks undermining the work of those who seek to honour their
obligations. More intelligent forms of accountability would begin from an
account of the action that is required of specific obligation bearers. They
would aim to reach an informed judgement of the adequacy of performance
in particular cases, and to provide evidence of trustworthiness or untrustworthiness. They would seek and communicate intelligible evidence of performance, so enabling the intelligent placing and refusal of trust. This is hardly
revolutionary, and I finish by setting out some standards for intelligent
approaches to accountability.

8.6 Informed, Independent, and Intelligible

Intelligent accountability, I suggest, is a matter of holding agents to account
for meeting their primary obligations, and this invariably needs judgement.
Those who hold to account must discharge second-order obligations to judge
others' performance of their primary obligations. They must judge others'
performance competently and fairly. To do this they must be both informed
about the performance required and independent of those of whom it is
required. If they are also to secure accountability to wider audiences, they
must also communicate their judgements intelligibly to those audiences. The
benchmarks for intelligent accountability are *informed* and *independent* judgement of performance, complemented by *intelligible* communication of those
judgements. Each of these standards is worth considering in more detail.

(a) **Informed Judgement.** *Intelligent accountability* begins with an informed
judgement of what ought to be done, what was actually done, and
whether it meets basic obligations. Neither rendering an account nor
holding to account is possible without an informed grasp of the obligations for which agents are to be held to account, which can be compared to the actual performance achieved. Those who hold to account
have to grasp both *what* ought to have been done and *what* was actually
done. Expert judgement of action against intelligible standards cannot
be replaced by superficial scores on performance indicators, let alone
ticks in boxes.

(b) **Independent Judgement**. By itself, informed judgement is not enough
for intelligent accountability. Accountability will also fail if those who
judge are not adequately independent. They must not be in the pockets
of those whose performance they judge; they must not judge unfairly;
they must not be corrupt. There is an old saying that those who know
cannot judge fairly, while those who can judge fairly know too little to

provide an informed judgement. This is no doubt an exaggeration, but the tension between informed and independent judgement is real. Do experts inevitably have (too many) interests in common with those whose performance they are asked to judge? Must we always fear that they will judge unfairly, that they will favour some and discriminate against others? Can expert judgement match the open and simple information that performance indicators ostensibly offer? These concerns form the core of the complaint that used to often be made of public-sector institutions, experts, and professions—that they suffer from *producer capture*, whereby hospitals are run for the convenience of doctors, schools for the convenience of teachers, universities for the convenience of academics, courts for the convenience of lawyers, and so on. As I see it, the dangers of corruption, producer capture, and professional cosiness are real, but it is absurd to try to remedy them by dispensing with informed judgement of performance. To do so would be like disbanding the police because police corruption occurs, or prohibiting manufacturing because defective products are sometimes made and sold. The proper remedy for corruption, producer capture, and professional cosiness is to institute and maintain robust ways of securing judgement of performance that is both informed and independent. There are ways of requiring inspectors, examiners, auditors, and other experts to whom account must be rendered, and who are charged with holding to account, to be and to demonstrate that they are independent of those whom they judge. Inspectors, examiners, and auditors must not be colleagues of, paid for, or dependent on those whom they inspect. They must declare relevant interests and stand down where there is a conflict of interest. They must have powers to initiate the removal from office of those who do not meet adequate standards. This is the appropriate approach for efforts to raise standards of accountability, in finance as elsewhere.

(c) **Intelligible Communication.** Those who hold to account are themselves accountable to further individuals and institutions, and often to the wider public. To discharge these obligations, they need to provide intelligible accounts of the achievements and failings of those whose performance they have judged. They must communicate intelligibly to relevant audiences, thereby enabling those with less expertise, less proximity, or less time, to judge the performance of those who are held to account. Communication needs to be both intelligible to and assessable by relevant audiences, so has to differ for different audiences: a corollary of the fact that communication requires more than mere transparency.

8.7 Institutions, Professions, and Professionalism

In recent years, some professions and institutions that used to carry many obligations of accountability have been widely criticised for failing to discharge these obligations. A standard remedy has been to replace professional with managerial accountability. As we have seen, this remedy has had heavy costs. Those who devised and imposed it may not have made the wrong diagnosis, but they have prescribed a debilitating remedy.

The supposed 'crisis of trust', for which the widespread introduction of managerial accountability proved an inadequate remedy, was driven in some part by the difficulties professions and professionals faced in maintaining and discharging their obligations in changing institutional landscapes. Personal bonds and professional structures were weakened, and professions and professional bodies sometimes indeed failed to exercise independent judgement. These more traditional forms of accountability were then supposedly remedied by superimposing new forms of managerial accountability. Even where these failures were exceptional they were often assumed to be widespread. Professional leaders were deprived of many of the methods by which they had previously been able to keep professional performance up to the mark. Senior professionals were kept so busy by new managerial demands that they had less time—and dramatically less authority—for introducing younger colleagues to the demands of professional life, let alone disciplining them. Some aspects of professionalism atrophied. Yet seen with partial hindsight—for all of this is still going on around us still—the introduction of managerial accountability often proved partly self-defeating.

As the remedy has failed, it may be time for a new prescription. A strength of well-structured professions and professional bodies is that they can provide cultural support for meeting obligations that managerial forms of accountability do not provide. Much professional work is pretty unglamorous; some is poorly rewarded (although the converse has been the problem in financial services). There are always temptations to cut corners, to hurry procedures, to do a less good job than is needed, and to cover up for friends and colleagues. If a revival of serious professionalism is to provide a part of the remedy for the evident problems of relying on unintelligent forms of accountability, this will not be because it magically secures professional integrity, let alone because it comes with pretty professional codes. Genuine professional integrity grows out of tough institutional structures. It requires rigorous institutional and financial separation, robust systems for dealing with conflicts of interest, serious remedies for failure, and serious support for professional cultures. If professionalism in financial services is to be renewed it will need all of these structures.

Structures of accountability that secure adequate independence for professional judgement will only be robust enough if they provide strong reasons for those who are to hold others to account to meet their obligations. Managerial forms of accountability backed by detailed financial incentives and criminal sanctions have sometimes proved to be burdensome and an unreliable way of securing trustworthy performance. In the long run and in the small hours of the morning, the realities of earning professional respect, or losing professional respect, of being respected or shamed, ultimately expelled and ostracised, can have greater weight. Unintelligent forms of accountability damage the ways in which this sort of respect is gained—and lost. They demoralise professionals—and damage the very professional performance which those who impose managerial forms of accountability probably covet and imagine they are supporting. The realisation that some professional cultures were failing in some ways was not a sufficient reason for dismantling those cultures. It was a good reason for reforming and strengthening both professions and professional bodies, and for aligning the interests of professionals with those of the publics whom they are meant to serve. Parallel changes could matter hugely for financial services.

These demands have implications not only for professionals, but for professional bodies. Professionals risk losing independence and integrity if their professional bodies see their obligations only as a matter of providing for professional defence for those who fail or fall short. Serious professional bodies take responsibility for professional standards and performance, not only at the point of entry, but beyond. They take both professional training and continuing professional development seriously. They establish ways of resolving complaints that are actually and demonstrably independent—for example, by including powerful 'lay' members in their processes for resolving complaints. None of this is rocket science: but it does require some rigour about identifying and declaring interests and conflicts of interests, and about ensuring that complaints bodies are demonstrably independent and effective. The point is well illustrated by considering requirements for auditors to be independent of the institutions they audit—and the dire consequences of permitting commercial relationships that incentivise giving a soft 'audit' rather than a genuinely 'true and fair view' (cf. the Enron scandal and other notorious cases).

If we persist in using unintelligent forms of accountability, the public—who are not unintelligent—will judge, with some accuracy, that they cannot place or withhold trust intelligently. They will find that they cannot distinguish trustworthy from untrustworthy institutions and individuals. In these circumstances, the very basis for placing and withholding trust intelligently will be continually eroded. It will not be surprising if a 'crisis of trust', in which credulity and cynicism are weirdly mixed, persists. Yet a serious effort to reinvigorate intelligent forms of accountability, including robust forms of professional accountability, might help re-establish a basis for placing and withholding of trust intelligently, not only in the professions and in public service, but in financial services and even in industry. If this could be achieved we might find better ways of securing certain obligations without imposing self-defeating or ineffective controls or proliferating legal sanctions.

Appendix: The Formal Structure of Accountability

These distinctions can, I think, usefully be set out a little more formally as follows:
1. The most elementary feature of any normative claim is that some type of action, A, is required, which we may render:
   A ought to be done.
2. However, normativity is vestigial unless there are agents—individuals or institutions—who ought to do what ought to be done. Requirements must be held by obligation bearers, which we may render:
   A ought to be done by X.
3. Where those obligations are claimable, i.e. owed to some right holder, Y (again either an individual or an institution), this may be rendered:
   A ought to be done by X, and Y has a right to A being done by X.
4. Where obligation bearers are accountable for their performance of *primary* obligations to do A, this accountability is a further *second-order* obligation that refers to the *primary* obligation:
   A ought to be done by X, Y has a right to A being done by X, and X is accountable to Z for doing A.
4* As a special case of 4. We may note that sometimes obligation bearers are accountable to right holders for their performance, in which case:
   A ought to be done by X, Y has a right to A being done by X, and X is accountable to Y for doing A.
5. Putting these together, where obligation bearers have *second-order* obligations to account for their performance to others, those others have corresponding obligations to hold them to account, so:
   A ought to be done by X, Y has a right to A being done by X, X is accountable to Z for doing A, and Z ought to hold X to account for doing A.
6. More systematically, and in simplified form, since there are *many* required act types, *many* obligation holders, *many* right holders, and *many* agents and institutions to whom obligation bearers are accountable, a system of accountability has the formal structure:
   $A_1 \ldots A_n$ ought to be done by the Xs; the Ys have rights to $A_{1 \ldots} A_n$ being done by the Xs; the Xs are accountable to the Zs for doing $A_1 \ldots A_n$; and the Zs ought to hold the Xs to account for doing $A_{1 \ldots} A_n$.

Obligations and rights cannot be specified without intelligible descriptions of required act types and ways of identifying the relevant obligation bearers and right holders. First-order obligations for action of certain types and second-order obligations to render and hold to account for performance of first-order obligations both build on and require intelligible act descriptions.

References

Baier, A. (1996). 'Trust and Anti-Trust', *Ethics*, 96: 231–60, 235.

Garratt, B. (1996). *The Fish Rots from the Head: The Crisis in our Boardrooms.* London: Profile Books.

Hobbes, T. (1651 [1991]). *Leviathan*, ed. Richard Tuck. Cambridge: Cambridge University Press.

Holton, R. (1994). 'Deciding to Trust, Coming to Believe', *Australasian Journal of Philosophy*, 72: 63–76.

Jones, K. (1996). 'Trust as an Affective Attitude', *Ethics*, 107: 4–25.

Jones, K. (2012). 'Trustworthiness', *Ethics*, 123: 61–85.

O'Neill, O. (1996). *Towards Justice and Virtue*. Cambridge: Cambridge University Press.

O'Neill, O. (2002a). *Autonomy and Trust in Bioethics*. Cambridge: Cambridge University Press.

O'Neill, O. (2002b). *A Question of Trust*. Cambridge: Cambridge University Press.

Power, M. (1997). *The Audit Society: Rituals of Verification*. Oxford: Oxford University Press.

Power, M. (2009). 'The Audit Explosion', *DEMOS* [online commentary], <http://www.demos.co.uk/files/theauditexplosion.pdf>, accessed 4 March 2014.

Schneewind, J. B. (1990). 'The Misfortunes of Virtue', *Ethics*, 101: 42–63.

Part III

Problems with the Legal and Regulatory System

9

Financial Crisis and the Decline of Fiduciary Law

*Joshua Getzler**

9.1 Newt Gingrich's Theory of Fiduciary Duty

Fiduciary law demands that managers of the affairs of others should avoid conflicts of duty or interest that might distract them from pursuing their beneficiaries' best interests. This ideal—that powerful managers should offer disinterested fiduciary service to those who depend on them—is still evoked on occasion in our political and business culture, even if the notion of what fiduciary duties demand of us can be a little hazy. For example, in the 2012 presidential primaries Mr Newt Gingrich, a notable conservative figure in American politics, assailed Mr Mitt Romney for his profit taking as a partner at the private equity firm Bain Capital, focusing on one case where some $180 million in value was stripped out from a company that was then put into administration:

> [T]o what extent did they [i.e. Bain] have some obligation to the workers? Remember, these were a lot of people who made that $180 million, it wasn't just six rich guys at the top, and yet somehow they walked off from their fiduciary obligation to the people who had made the money for them. (Gingrich, interview with Rush Limbaugh on *Fox News*, 10 January 2012)

* My initial ideas for this chapter were presented in late 2010 to the Supreme Court of Western Australia and the Western Australian Bar Association, and I thank my Perth colleagues and particularly Matthew Howard and Christopher Zelestis for stimulating debate. For further fruitful discussion I thank John Armour, James Edelman, James Goudkamp, Avner Offer, Lionel Smith, Nicholas Morris, David Vines, and the members of the Oxford Duty of Care in Finance Study Group.

Gingrich's theory of fiduciary obligation was intended more as political rhetoric than precise legal analysis; but he was justified in claiming that something had gone astray in the way that managerial and financial executives viewed their role in the modern economy, and that weakened fiduciary standards might have some bearing on the problem.

We will start our analysis by looking at how misaligned incentives contributed to the crisis in the financial economy, and then turn to the possible solutions afforded by fiduciary law. The argument is then offered that we need to repair fiduciary law before we can use it to repair the financial system.

9.2 What Went Wrong?

From the late 1970s the profit-taking financial sector in the western economies, notably in Britain and the United States, took over the stewardship and management of a greatly increased share of society's capital. The financiers benefited from a new politics wedded to free market ideologies, coinciding with new information technologies that facilitated trade in assets and their financial derivatives on a hitherto unimagined scale and at warp speeds. In these conditions finance was able to penetrate and extract value from the housing and welfare systems of the west as well as the privatised industries and service sectors that had once resided within the public or non-profit sectors. The financiers profited mightily from that vast entrustment of assets, and they increased their fees still further through multiple leveraging and rapid turnover of investments, presented as a highly skilled quantification of risk engineered by the best and brightest (Noe and Young 2012). To invent a phrase, the financiers engaged in 'immaturity transformation' of capital: they used wealth entrusted to them for long-term security and steady growth in order to make high profits at high risks through rapidly turning trades. Those risks were hidden by a complex web of insurance transactions that generated further arrangement fees and manufactured fresh classes of asset that could be marketed in turn; but these mechanisms for the reassignment and recalibration of risk could not survive a systemic downturn. Even if the financial intermediaries appreciated the nature of the risks they were creating, they had little incentive to do otherwise, for the risk of capital loss fell on the entrusting parties rather than the fee-taking managers. This misalignment of incentives and interests was the devil in the system that led to its downfall.

The scale of 'financialisation' of the economy driven by this multiplication of asset trading was truly vast; in the United Kingdom it can be measured by the statistic that the share of Gross Domestic Product accorded to finance went from 5.2% in 2000 to 10.1% by the time of the crash (Crowley and Choudhury 2012, citing figures from the Office of National Statistics).

In the United States financialisation began perhaps two decades earlier, eventually topping 8.4% of Gross Domestic Product at the height of the recent bubble. Barring the period of speculation that ended in 1929, the share of finance in the American economy from 1900 to 1980 moved from 2% to 4% (Greenwood and Scharfststein 2013).

When the great bubble burst in 2007–8 following a downturn in the US housing market, swathes of entrusted capital invested in the new and rickety financial assets were destroyed, and the guardians of the financial system groped for tools to contain the crisis. In September 2008 the US Government's attempt to apply market discipline to the overleveraged financial sector through denial of support to Lehman detonated a crisis of debt contagion, necessitating massive state capital support of failing investment houses and insurers. The crisis in Britain was every bit as severe, with the state having to take into public ownership some of the largest banks in the world, nationalising enormous losses but clawing back very little of the profits extracted in the fat years. The state rescue of finance may have been necessary in the crisis, but the terms of the rescue could be condemned as inequitable and unsustainable; this debate continues as the government tries to find a way to return the banks to the private sector.

For all the recklessness and incompetence now exposed, very few of the financiers responsible for this crash have suffered legal censure for the destruction they helped to cause. This contrasts with the spate of litigations and prosecutions that followed ruptures in the corporate sector the decade before, with the failures of Enron, WorldCom, Global Crossing, Adelphia, and other new technology conglomerates in 2001–2. The difference in legal response calls for explanation. In the wake of the 2008 crisis the financiers claimed that the investment risks that now seemed obvious with hindsight were rational enough at the time of investment even if they had turned out badly; that measured by the standard practices of the market there was little actionable fraud or negligence in the preceding years of exuberance; and that generally all participants in the financial sector, including investors and regulators, had consented to the fatal complexities and interdependencies of modern financial engineering. As Bob Diamond, the head of Barclays, put it four years after the crash, with invincible charm: 'There was a period for remorse of banks but I think this period is over... The question for us is how do we put some of the blame game behind us' (Werdigier 2011). With help from the taxpayer to rebuild the shattered financial system[1] and support from central banks to keep

---

[1] It is fair to note that of all the large banks, Barclays did not immediately take UK Government support to maintain its liquidity in 2008. But its appearance of independence was conjured: instead of accepting home government support it entered into a concealed deal with Qatar to secure the necessary capital injection, a deal now being investigated as a major act of fraud (Robinson 2013).

open the taps of credit, the financiers advocated a return to business as usual. Perhaps the scale of the disaster was so great that legal sanctioning of any particular participant individuals seemed otiose. It was common enough for the top executives of the failed investment houses to claim that they had not fully understood what was happening around them; responsibility seemed diffused through the entire financial system. Prosecutors seemed happy to accept promises from finance houses to improve internal management and do better next time, and chary of launching investigations of frauds that were difficult to prove, and that often exposed concomitant failures of government oversight (Rakoff 2014).

Occasionally the complacency, greed, and recklessness of the top financiers did lead to disciplinary action. One notorious case in 2010 involved the investment bank Goldman Sachs. Goldman in 2007 had arranged the Paulson CDO subprime trade, a deal executed on the brink of the US housing market collapse. The deal enriched Goldman and its client Paulson at the direct expense of other Goldman clients who were counterparties to the CDO trade; the sting was that Goldman executives had privately predicted this course of events, designing the CDO product with Paulson in order to bilk the Goldman clients on the other side of the deal. At the US Senate hearing into Goldman's conduct in the Paulson trade, the following exchange occurred with the head of the bank, Mr Lloyd Blankfein:

> 'Why would the clients believe in Goldman Sachs?' the senator asks.
> Mr. Blankfein meanders in his answer. He says he wishes he were better at explaining the situation, the idea that his firm has many different roles.
> 'There are parts of the business where you are a money manager where you owe a duty to the client, and there are parts of the business where you are a principal' he says. (*The New York Times*, 27 April 2010)

The Goldman executives at those hearings could not bring themselves to acknowledge that they had any duty to act in clients' best interests and avoid conflicts of duty or interest. They could not conceive (not even Harvard-law-educated Mr Blankfein) that there was a problem in having the bank invest in the same trades as its clients, or trade against its clients, or as the evidence revealed, help one client sell to another client and simultaneously join the seller in speculative trading against that buying client, in return for handsome remunerations from both sides. After all, this multiple and conflicted trading is precisely what an investment bank does; it has 'skin in the game', and by participating in the broadest spectrum of commercial activity through syndicates and proprietary trading it generates the information, expertise, and capital that makes it useful to clients, despite the dangers of dealing with such a conflicted and rapacious type of business partner.

Broad-spectrum investment banking, in short, has no room for fiduciary duties. It is a business model *founded* on conflicts of duty and interest—but the conflicts are seen as controlled and beneficial ('managed conflict' in the jargon)—until they go badly wrong. In 2010, under pressure from the public and politicians over the Paulson trade and other major profiteering before and after the crisis, Goldman eventually conceded 'mistakes' of non-disclosure and paid a settlement including hefty fines of over half a billion US dollars (US Securities and Exchange Commission 2010). The capital markets were simply relieved that Goldman had not been de-licensed or its executives jailed, and the share value of the bank went up by a sum considerably more than the fine exacted. Other banks had to sacrifice greater amounts of their profits in fines; at the end of 2013 J.P. Morgan topped the bill, paying some $20 billion to the regulators (Hussain 2013). By some estimates bank expenditure on legal defences actually exceeded the fines and compensation paid (Harress 2013).

Back in the United Kingdom, the exposure of the rigging of the London Interbank Offered Rate in 2012 provided a jolting reminder of how badly the London banks had behaved in the years before the crash—and indeed afterwards as they continued to extract value from the weakened economy through access to state subsidies. But the financial sector went into further decline as the financial crisis of 2008 segued into the sovereign debt crisis late in 2009, depressing the already weakened economy of the UK as well as the Eurozone. The scale of financial activity and employment in the western centres shrank rapidly, especially in the highly internationalised City of London. Many of the financial titans—including Bob Diamond himself—were finally pushed out of their leadership roles as embarrassing emblems of all that had gone wrong.

9.3 Can Fiduciary Law Help?

Today, years on after the crisis, and with only a partial and fragile recovery in train, the legal and regulatory cultures that permitted the skewed incentives and poor accountability of the financiers are largely unchanged. Finance and banking remain deeply troubled, with profits in decline, public subsidy and risk underwriting still at high levels, and rewards to individual financiers still shockingly inflated. As a call to action, the 2008 crisis has gone to waste, with the political classes continuing to dither over even the mildest reforms of the financial sector (Mirowski 2013; Vickers 2013). The pity of it is that effective re-regulation of the financial sector is not all that difficult to conceive and execute, using existing tools of the law. We do not have to start from scratch, imposing fresh and untried rules and regulations on a recalcitrant and powerful financial class; we only have to remember and grasp what is already to hand. The law has for centuries applied fiduciary duties to those entrusted with the affairs and assets of others, and the jurisprudence is well-elaborated and effective. Fiduciary law aligns the incentives of fiduciaries and beneficiaries by a strategy of negation. Its first instinct is not to give the fiduciary agent rewards in parallel with the beneficiaries, but rather to guide the fiduciary away from self-reward and conflicts of duty and interest entirely so that a due positive performance can be rendered. Rewards to the fiduciary must be openly agreed, and any self-interested or conflicted conduct must be duly authorised and win fully informed consent from all affected parties (Getzler 2006b). A restoration of these classical fiduciary duties would go some way to preventing the kinds of agent irresponsibility that fuelled the financial crisis. But first we need to know more about how fiduciary duties work.

The law of fiduciaries is based on the simple moral and practical insight that strong powers must be allied to strong duties. We will often need to appoint someone to manage activities on our behalf. The manager may be selected because his probity, skills, and abilities allow him to deal with the affairs or assets of the beneficiary far better than the beneficiary could have done unaided. A manager of another person's affairs and assets can often do best when armed with a strong set of powers to act on his beneficiary's behalf. For example, a fiduciary with custody of investment assets must hold the assets securely, convey them to the right persons at the right times, and invest them in order to harbour and increase their value. These tasks are best performed where the fiduciary has extensive control powers to defend assets and independent discretion and authority to act swiftly and decisively in reaction to real-world events, without having to run back to the beneficiary for instructions at every moment. Indeed the beneficiary may not understand what is at stake in complex decisions, or be too partial to make intelligent decisions, and so must trust the fiduciary to decide on his behalf in his best interests. Fiduciary law counterbalances the very strong managerial powers with a very strong set of counterbalancing duties, requiring that the manager serve the beneficiary with unswerving loyalty and due competence. This means that decisions are to be insulated from all extraneous reasons of self-interest or the interests of third parties; and that decisions should be taken with due care and with all relevant information being applied to the decision-making process. Fiduciary duties tend to be applied where there are steep information asymmetries in favour of the manager, and inhibitions on the beneficiary's ability to monitor the discretionary power of that manager. Not every relationship involving trust, reliance, and asymmetries of skill and information requires fiduciary protections. I do not regard my car mechanic as a fiduciary even though the mechanic's decisions involve skills I lack and that I rely upon for my safety. But I can monitor and verify my mechanic's work by taking the car to the garage down the road for a second check; and moreover contractual warranties guaranteeing defined results can be incorporated into the dealing. In the heartland of fiduciary responsibilities—such as financial management—the tenor of the relationship is very different to the case of the car repairer down the street. Key information about the conduct of the managerial relationship will be generated by the manager himself, and it is difficult for the beneficiary to monitor this bottled-up information and verify the performance, which in any case will involve high levels of judgement that cannot easily be measured against objective outside standards (Frankel 2010).

The solution fiduciary law offers to resolve the twinned problems of monitoring the fiduciary and constraining the fiduciary's judgement is the requirement of *accountability*. Accountability in law has two aspects. First, it means being required to tell the story of how one discharged one's managerial trust—to *give* an account, whether to the beneficiary, or to some third party who is appointed to hear the story, an auditor. Second, accountability means ensuring that the results of one's stewardship match what one ought to have done—to *render* an account. The fiduciary remedy of account directs the fiduciary to carry out or perfect the performance he ought to have rendered; it defends a performance interest, to use the language of legal analysis (Getzler 2011).

The distinctive nature of fiduciary duties and remedies derives ultimately from this equitable concept of accountability, of having to explain one's use of power or management of a fund, to show a due balance, and to purify or perfect one's performance. So if assets under fiduciary management go missing due to fraud or incompetence or have fallen into the wrong pocket, the fiduciary has to pay into the beneficiary's account to bring it to the level it ought to have been. If unauthorised transactions have been made in breach of fiduciary duty, for example involving unauthorised profit taking by the fiduciary, then any profits from the transaction have to be paid in, and any losses ensuing from the illegal conduct have to be compensated; moreover the beneficiary can also demand rescission or cancellation of the offensive dealing. The fiduciary remedies are therefore quite different to the norms of tort law (compensate for harm you have caused) or contract law (carry out your promises or else pay for any loss caused by a performance shortfall). For these common-law obligations the gist of the action is *compensation* for damage or harm to interests, not *accountability* or due performance. Thus a fiduciary can be forced to surrender personal gains, or to rescind inconsistent contracts or conveyances, when there is no loss whatsoever and no breach of any promise or harm to any vested interest. What is being sought from the fiduciary is a decent process of decision making rather than a defined or prescribed result. We tolerate a poor end result where a financier has shown care, skill, and loyalty in serving us, yet events turn out badly; but we do not tolerate a bad process involving conflicts of duty and interest, even where there is no unavoidable harm inflicted and even where the illegal profits taken may not have been available to the beneficiary. This process-oriented accountability helps explain why fiduciary law is not obviously reducible to contract, which typically sets out the bargained exchange of services and performances as a set of verifiable terms. The uncertainty and lack of verifiability of fiduciary performances defeat such attempts at specific or complete contracting. Moreover contract law has no reporting mechanism in the sense of a duty of disclosure; and only very nascent good-faith controls on the tenor of performances.

Fiduciary law thus has enormous power and potential as a body of rules shaping the incentives of managers and creating norms of disinterested service. The challenge is to understand why the classical fiduciary duties were not applied to finance over the past thirty years, and that makes for some interesting contemporary legal history.

9.4 How Was Fiduciary Law Diminished?

Since the mid 1980s, there has been a steep reduction in the incidence and intensity of fiduciary duties, a movement occurring across the common-law world but especially notable in American and English law. Part of the story involves plain and simple rent-seeking by the financial community, which successfully agitated to cut back fiduciary constraints through a programme of lobbying and litigation. A powerful example of how the ground rules might be changed by industry pressure was afforded by the American Uniform Prudent Investor Act of 1992, permitting uninhibited investment of fiduciary funds in any class of financial asset. This statutory reform, trumpeted as one of the great achievements of the application of economic reasoning to the law, in turn influenced the English Trustee Act of 2000, a major raft of legislation that was passed with active encouragement and input from the City of London. The result of these particular legislative changes was that institutional funds could now be moved without special licence into any sort of market trade, and were no longer directed toward the historic categories of safe and balanced long-term investments, typically gilts, stable listed companies, and land securities on wide margins of safety. Under the new legislation open-ended standards of 'prudence' or 'reasonableness', defined in terms of objective market rationality, were to do the necessary work of preserving value and avoiding undue risk (Langbein 1996; Getzler 2009).

Another part of the story involved a shift in the intellectual commitments of the legal caste, which came to see classical fiduciary law as an archaic hangover. In America the new disposition was driven by economic ideology, namely the belief that unconstrained financial markets would be guided by rational self-interest and informational efficiencies to reach optimal results without the heavy guiding hand of prescriptive legal rules. The law was there to assist actors in making and enforcing their own bargains, not to make the bargains for them. This was the central claim of the influential Chicago economist Ronald H. Coase (1960), and his reasoning came to be applied not only to the law of investment management (Posner and Langbein 1976) but to fiduciaries generally (Easterbrook and Fischel 1993). Lawyers came to accept that actors in supposedly rational and transparent markets could dispense with many of the standard legal obligations in partnership, agency, corporate, or other fiduciary relations, and contract to formulate the governance rules that best suited their self-perceived business interests. In a separate stream of economic theory it came to be appreciated that fiduciary agents armed with power to govern the affairs of others could not easily be monitored and controlled since they possessed most of the information and power within the relationship. Clients, such as investors, were highly dependent on their agents' probity and skill but had few means to monitor agent conduct. The solution was to push even further down the contractarian road and recommend incentive contracts that would optimally reward agents if they maximised benefits for their principals (Jensen and Meckling 1976; Langbein 2005; Sitkoff 2004, 2011). So awareness of the principal-agent problem involved not an embrace of traditional fiduciary discipline but rather its total rejection in favour of the profit motive.

Outside America, common lawyers did not think about fiduciary law in overtly economistic terms. But contract law, with its voluntarism, appeal to party autonomy, and formal properties of doctrinal clarity, exerted a great intellectual appeal, and lawyers began using contract principles to nibble at the foundations of classical fiduciary law until eventually the edifice collapsed. The seeds of this movement were sown by the distinguished Australian jurist Paul D. Finn, who having rejected the notion of intrinsically fiduciary statuses or relationships in his acclaimed doctrinal study of 1977, went on to argue that fiduciary duties were imposed simply when it was legitimate for transacting parties to expect such duties (Finn 1977, 1989). There was no essential fiduciary core or stereotypical fiduciary relationship (cf. Hayton 1996). This opened the door to a view of fiduciary duties not as a bundled set of rigid principles, imposed by law upon certain close voluntary relationships as mandatory conditions essential to the health of those relationships, but rather as a set of presumptive undertakings based on the will and expectations of the parties (Edelman 2010).

The idea that fiduciary duties should resemble voluntarily assumed con-tractual relations and be completely malleable at the will of the parties was finally grounded in the common law in a case from 1984. In *Hospital Products Ltd v United States Surgical Corporation*, Mason J, later to become Chief Justice of Australia, gave a minority judgement holding that fiduciary duties involv-ing profit disgorgement could be ordered against a corrupt distributor of med-ical equipment who had gone into secret competition with his supplier. The core of his judgement was this:

> That contractual and fiduciary relationships may co-exist between the same par-ties has never been doubted. Indeed, the existence of a basic contractual relation-ship has in many situations provided a foundation for the erection of a fiduciary relationship. In these situations it is the contractual foundation which is all important because it is the contract that regulates the basic rights and liabilities of the parties. The fiduciary relationship, if it is to exist at all, must accommodate itself to the terms of the contract so that it is consistent with, and conforms to, them. ((1984) 156 CLR 41, 97)

Here we have one of the most influential passages in the entire canon of modern fiduciary law, all the more remarkable since Mason J was writing in dissent. The passage was picked up by English, Australian, and other common-law courts to form the basis for a new view that parties could readily contract out of any or all of the fiduciary responsibilities, either by excluding fiduciary duty completely, or diminishing the scope or subject matter to which the duties applied, or by reducing the intensity or standard of demand imposed by the duty. There was a certain irony in this development, for Justice Mason's aim in his *Hospital Products* judgement was to inject some level of fiduciary obligation and remedy into normal contract law, in order to make the corrupt distributor segregate and surrender profits made through breach of contrac-tual obligation. Instead the traffic went the other way; contract powers were to be allowed to squeeze out fiduciary duties even in the heartland of close managerial relationships. The law was now taken to permit financial manag-ers to engage in conflicts of interest including direct profit taking alongside or even in competition with clients (the result Mason J had argued *against*). The law could now allow conflicts of duty involving service to multiple and sometimes rivalrous beneficiaries, reversing over two centuries of case law condemning double employments. And in most jurisdictions the law per-mitted fiduciaries to use widely drafted exclusion clauses taking away any actionable duty to take care in their provision of financial services.[2] Perhaps

---

[2] Trustee Act 2000 (England and Wales), Sch. 1 s. 7, allowing the objective standard of care set out in s. 1 to be excluded by agreement, ratifying the controversial decision in *Armitage v Nurse* [1998] Ch. 241, [1997] EWCA Civ 1279. In 2003 the Law Commission of England and Wales proposed restricting the ability of trustees to exempt themselves from duties of care, but their pro-posals were heavily criticised by City lobbies, and instead in 2006 a voluntary code was proposed,

the most adventurous change was to hold that business context or custom could of itself remove fiduciary duties from any relationships contracted in that business context. This reversed the rule requiring informed, conscious, and independent consent to the exclusion of fiduciary duties. Examples of this shrinking of the scope of fiduciary duties included where one contracted with an agent already serving multiple clients, or obviously trading on his own account into the same market as the beneficiary; fiduciary duties in such circumstances could not be expected in the first place (Getzler 2006a, 2007).

The courts not only eviscerated the content of fiduciary obligations by applying contract rules to normal fiduciary relations; they also undermined the potency of the special fiduciary remedies, again imitating the rules of contract. Three distinct procedural rules were at stake: the strict fiduciary causal rules applying full solidary liability for any effective breach, without apportioning blame amongst multiple wrongdoers; the evidential presumptions that favoured beneficiaries over fiduciaries whenever there was any possibility of wrongdoing or exploitation; and the strong remedies of equitable account, encompassing aggressive profit stripping, rescission to undo illicit transactions, and compensation to restore the status quo ante. Historically each of these remedies had been used to repress breach by upholding the due performance of fiduciary relationships, rather than permitting efficient breach and derogation of duty followed by *ex post* compensation for harm done. Each of these distinctive fiduciary procedures was read down in a series of difficult and controversial cases. Now, instead of forcing the fiduciary miscreant to render a due performance via the traditional equitable remedies, it became possible for the fiduciary to make an 'efficient breach' of his or her obligations with an eye to profit, hoping that the forensic penalty would be offset by the rewards flowing from the wrongdoing (Getzler 2005).

After the contractarian revolution a certain amount of fiduciary rhetoric continued to be broadcast by the judges as if to reassure that legally supported levels of trust would still be enforced, but the content of the duties as actually applied was all too often weakened. In the English Court of Appeal case of *Bristol Building Society v Mothew* [1998] Ch 1, Millett LJ pursued exactly such a rhetoric, affirming the high loyalty and service required of the fiduciary agent, whilst in effect partitioning and downgrading those duties to hold that if a fiduciary avoided overt conflict of interest or duty, there was no further applicable fiduciary duty to take care or promote the best interests of a beneficiary (in that particular case, a client who lost capital through mortgage fraud that the fiduciary agent negligently failed to detect was denied compensation;

suggesting disclosure of the contents of such exemptions at the time of entrustment, but with no restrictions as to the content of the exemptions. Scottish law bans exemptions of the trustee duty of care outright.

recovery would have been possible had the breach been regarded as an abuse of the fiduciary duties). *Mothew's case* was immediately acclaimed as a revelatory clarification of the law, even though it strained against venerable authorities of the nineteenth and earlier twentieth centuries (Birks 2000; Conaglen 2010; Edelman 2012). Some saw *Mothew* as virtually eliminating fiduciary loyalty as any type of positive duty at all; the loyalty prescriptions only existed in order to help agents carry out their positive duties of agency, contract or property management without undue distraction; they were 'parasitic' or merely adjunct duties (Birks 2000; Conaglen 2010; cf. Getzler 2002), and the law should put no bar on parties excluding any or all of those adjunct duties if they did not wish to assume them.

Since 2008 the adherence of the courts to the new paradigm of attenuated fiduciary law has hardly been shaken by the revelations of financiers' abuse of their powers over clients; only recently have there been signs of a tightening up with some decisions holding financial advisers and intermediaries to account in the lower and intermediate courts.[3] But in the highest courts the main contractarian direction of the law has not been reversed, and the mild tightening of legal regulation could easily be undone in a number of pending appeals.

All of this suggests that fiduciary law itself must be repaired before it can properly carry out its role in regulating financial entrustment and management. For that to occur, the courts and legislators must have a clearer vision of what a healthy fiduciary law would look like. Advocating a return to classical fiduciary principles must therefore be justified.

9.5 The Goals of Fiduciary Accountability and the Proper Role of Consent

Law at its best can set behavioural standards that are internalised as norms which can guide group and individual behaviour effectively *without* monitoring, litigation, and enforcement. Fiduciary law with its vocabulary of service and loyalty is particularly well-placed to perform this hortatory, norm-promoting function. Classical fiduciary law, simply put, holds that there is a gamut of risky, exploitative, and disloyal behaviour that an entrusted person with power over others should not and cannot engage in. Fiduciary law aims to *disable* those in positions of control from abusing or exceeding

---

[3] *Rossetti Marketing Ltd v Diamond Sofa Company Ltd* [2013] 1 Bus LR 543, [2012] EWCA Civ 1021; *In Re El Paso Corporation Shareholder Litigation*, Civil Action No. 6949-CS, Ch Ct of Delaware (dec'd 29 Feb 2012, Chancellor Strine); *Wingecarribee Shire Council v Lehman Brothers Australia Ltd (In Liq)* [2012] FCA 1028; *Bathurst Regional Council v Local Government Financial Services Pty Ltd (No 5)* [2012] FCA 1200.

their power by a twin strategy: first, by denying fiduciaries all gain from their misconduct, and second, by requiring them to undo wrongful actions and restore their beneficiaries to the position they would have been in had proper performance been rendered. By treating the fiduciary *as if* he were honest, fiduciary law helps to *make* him honest (Getzler 2011; Holton 2011).

This strategy of seeking counterfactual, legally enforced trust as a workable surrogate for true, extra-legal trust is perhaps the distinctive quality of classical fiduciary law, and marks that body of law off from the more familiar regimes of contract, tort, crime, and regulatory law. One implication of this counterfactual form of trust is that fiduciary law properly eschews punishment as a remedial strategy. It seeks to guide parties to right conduct, not impose sanctions for wrongdoing. We do not punish those whom we hope to trust.[4] Again, this classical insight has been lost in the recent cases.

Finally, fiduciary law is also distinct from other legal categories in that classically it demands a well-informed subjective consent to any departures from its characteristic duties. There is a kind of double entrenchment at work: a fiduciary owes a beneficiary disinterested and loyal service; any attempt to depart from that standard in a presumptive fiduciary relationship must apply the same protections, so that the beneficiary is advised in negotiating any variation of duties according to the same standards of disinterestedness and loyalty. The demanding requirement of informed consent lies behind the evidential presumption that any profit made in a fiduciary office is likely to be made at the expense of due performance of the obligation, unless it has been fully understood and permitted by the beneficiary *ex ante*. Where the demands of fully informed consent are not met, all profits must be handed over or held on trust for the beneficiary if they have the slightest connection to the office of the fiduciary (Bryan 2012; Nolan 2012). Recent case law that moves the test of consent to an objective contractual basis is therefore a heresy that is inimical to fiduciary principle.

Economic reasoning can be invoked to justify this stringent vision of fiduciary law, alongside the classical legal language. The suite of demanding fiduciary duties can be described as a 'penalty default rule'. This denotes a rule set at an equilibrium that perhaps the majority of market actors would not have chosen in free and well-informed bargaining with infinite resources to discover and express their preferences, because the pre-packaged duties are set—on purpose—either too high or too low. The penalty of sticking to the default rule therefore encourages release of information and revealing of preferences by

---

[4] In the context of an egregious breach of a fiduciary duty where penal damages were sought on top of simple profit disgorgement, Heydon JA denied the penal remedy, stating that in the context of upholding fiduciary obligations '[e]quity does not bear the same relationship to the instinct for revenge as the institution of marriage does the sexual appetite': *Harris v Digital Pulse Pty Ltd* (2003) 56 NSWLR 298, [2003] NSWCA 10 at [470].

self-aware and rational actors who will renegotiate terms and tailor the level of protection to their special needs (Ayres and Gertner 1989). In fiduciary law the default rule sets a very high, perhaps too high protection against conflict of interests and duties; the parties are free to adapt these rules where this brings countervailing advantages. The law can then leave in place a highly protective default position for less sophisticated actors who cannot easily bargain or do not know which equilibrium to bargain for (Whincop 1997; Conaglen 2010: 219–21). Moral hazard and temptation to abuse fiduciary power to redraw relationships in favour of the fiduciary is reduced when the law applies stringent disclosure rules to ensure that any departures from the default rule are well understood and consent is well informed. The costs of forcing many or most parties to bargain around the overstringent fiduciary default position are therefore justified because the pay-off to individuals and society of honest and faithful service is very high. The fiduciary disclosure and consent rules ensure that the balance of risk and protection is set to the level the parties actually accept with full information and eyes wide open; where such well-informed and independent consent cannot be given, the default position should be very demanding of the fiduciary. There may be a good case for setting efficient rather than penalty default rules in normal contracting, where the majority of parties do not win much value from having to release information and dicker over the precise setting of contractual standards. Objective consent there suffices to shift the goalposts (Posner 2006). But in fiduciary relationships, it makes sense to require the parties in the first instance to bond to give up self-interest and divided loyalties as a condition of service.

9.6 Afterword

Is there a case against a revival of classical fiduciary principles? Would the techniques of counterfactual trust enforcement and setting of penalty default rules impose an inordinate burden? It is often argued that many actors in the world of financial management and intermediation might be driven from business if the rigorous requirements of classical fiduciary duties were built back into our law. The arguments presented here suggest that such actors had no worthwhile business to do within finance in the first place.

References

Ayres, I. and Gertner, R. (1989). 'Filling Gaps in Incomplete Contracts: An Economic Theory of Default Rules', *Yale Law Journal*, 99: 87–130.

Birks, P. (2000). 'The Content of Fiduciary Obligation', *Israel Law Review*, 34: 3–38.

Bryan, M. (2012). *Boardman v Phipps (1967)*, in C. Mitchell and P. Mitchell (eds), *Landmark Cases in Equity*. Oxford: Hart Publishing, 581–610.

Coase, R. H. (1960). 'The Problem of Social Cost', *Journal of Law and Economics*, 3: 1–44.

Conaglen, M. (2010). *Fiduciary Loyalty: Protecting the Due Performance of Non-Fiduciary Duties*. Oxford: Hart Publishing.

Crowley, K. and Choudhury, A. (2012). 'London Shrinks Faster Than Any Financial Center as Banks Come Under Attack', *Bloomberg News*, 17 January.

Easterbrook, F. H. and Fischel, D. R. (1993). 'Contract and Fiduciary Duty', *Journal of Law and Economics*, 36: 425–46.

Edelman, J. J. (2010). 'When Do Fiduciary Duties Arise?', *Law Quarterly Review*, 126: 302–27.

Edelman, J. J. (2012). *Nocton v Lord Ashburton (1914)*, in C. Mitchell and P. Mitchell (eds), *Landmark Cases in Equity*. Oxford: Hart Publishing, 473–98.

Finn, P. D. (1977). *Fiduciary Obligations*. Sydney: Law Book Co.

Finn, P. D. (1989). 'The Fiduciary Principle', in T. G. Youdan (ed.), *Equity, Fiduciaries and Trusts*. Toronto: Carswell, 1–56.

Frankel, T. (2010). *Fiduciary Law*. New York: Oxford University Press.

Getzler, J. (2002). 'Duty of Care', in P. Birks and A. Pretto (eds), *Breach of Trust*. Oxford: Hart Publishing, 41–74.

Getzler, J. (2005). 'Am I My Beneficiary's Keeper? Fusion and Loss-Based Fiduciary Remedies', in S. Degeling and J. Edelman (eds), *Equity in Commercial Law*. Sydney: Thomson/LBC, 239–77.

Getzler, J. (2006a). 'Inconsistent Fiduciary Duties and Implied Consent', *Law Quarterly Review*, 122: 1–8.

Getzler, J. (2006b). 'Rumford Market and the Genesis of Fiduciary Obligations', in A. Burrows and A. Rodger (eds), *Mapping the Law: Essays in Honour of Peter Birks*. Oxford: Oxford University Press, 577–98.

Getzler, J. (2007). 'ASIC v Citigroup: Bankers' Conflict of Interest and the Contractual Exclusion of Fiduciary Duties', *Journal of Equity*, 2: 62–70.

Getzler, J. (2009). 'Fiduciary Investment in the Shadow of Financial Crisis: Was Lord Eldon Right?', *Journal of Equity*, 3: 219–50.

Getzler, J. (2011). '"As If": Accountability and Counterfactual Trust', *Boston University Law Review*, 91: 931–48.

Greenwood, R. and Scharfststein, D. (2013). 'The Growth of Finance', *Journal of Economic Perspectives*, 27(2): 3–28.

Harress, C. (2013). 'Banks Have Been Fined Nearly $3 Billion by the SEC and Have Spent $66 Billion on Litigation, but One Major Bank Hasn't Paid a Dime and Expects to Pay $0 in Litigation this Year', *International Business Times*, 29 August, <http://www.ibtimes.com/banks-have-been-fined-nearly-3-billion-sec-have-s pent-66-billion-litigation-one-major-bank-hasnt>, accessed 1 April 2014.

Hayton, D. (1996). 'The Irreducible Core Content of Trusteeship', in A. J. Oakley (ed.), *Trends in Contemporary Trust Law*. Oxford: Oxford University Press, 47–62.

Holton, R. (2011). 'Fiduciary Relations and the Nature of Trust', *Boston University Law Review*, 91: 991–4.

Hussain, S. (2013). 'JP Morgan in Record $13bn Settlement with US Authorities', *BBC News*, 20 November, <http://www.bbc.com/news/business-25009683>, accessed 1 April 2014.

Jensen, M. C. and Meckling, W. H. (1976). 'Theory of the Firm: Managerial Behavior, Agency Costs and Ownership Structure', *Journal of Financial Economics*, 3(4): 305–60.

Langbein, J. H. (1996). 'The Uniform Prudent Investor Act and the Future of Trust Investing', *Iowa Law Review*, 81: 641–69.

Langbein, J. H. (2005). 'Questioning the Trust Law Duty of Loyalty: Sole Interest or Best Interest?', *Yale Law Journal*, 114: 929–90.

Langbein, J. H. and Posner, R. A. (1976). 'Market Funds and Trust-Investment Law', *American Bar Foundation Research Journal*, 1: 1–34.

Mirowski, P. (2013). *Never Let a Serious Crisis Go to Waste: How Neoliberalism Survived the Financial Meltdown*. London: Verso.

Nolan, R. (2012). '*Regal (Hastings) Ltd v Gulliver (1942)*', in C. Mitchell and P. Mitchell (eds), *Landmark Cases in Equity*. Oxford: Hart Publishing, 499–528.

Posner, E. A. (2006). 'There Are No Penalty Default Rules in Contract Law', *Florida State University Law Review*, 33: 563–88.

Rakoff, J. S. (2014). 'The Financial Crisis: Why Have No High-Level Executives Been Prosecuted?', *New York Review of Books*, 61(1), 9 January.

Robinson, M. (2013). 'Barclays Under Investigation Over Claims It Lent Qatar £6bn to Buy Its Own Shares and Avoid a Government Bailout at Height of 2008 Financial Crisis', *Daily Mail*, 1 February.

Sitkoff, R. H. (2004). 'An Agency Costs Theory of Trust Law', *Cornell Law Review*, 89: 621–84.

Sitkoff, R. H. (2011). 'The Economic Structure of Fiduciary Law', *Boston University Law Review*, 91: 1039–49.

US Securities and Exchange Commission (July 2010). 'Goldman Sachs to Pay Record $550 Million to Settle SEC Charges Related to Subprime Mortgage CDO', <http://www.sec.gov/news/press/2010/2010-123.htm>, accessed 12 October 2012.

Vickers, J. (2013). 'Where Are We on Banking Reform?', *The Anglo-German Annual Lecture*, Berlin, 27 June.

Werdigier, J. (2011). 'It's Time to Stop Criticizing Bankers, Barclays Chief Says', *The New York Times*, 11 January.

Whincop, M. J. (1997). 'Of Fault and Default: Contractarianism as a Theory of Anglo-Australian Corporate Law', *Melbourne University Law Review*, 21: 187–236.

Young, H. P. and Noe, T. (2012). 'The Limits to Compensation in the Financial Sector', *Oxford Economics Discussion Paper*, 635 (December): 1–14.

10

Professional Obligation, Ethical Awareness, and Capital Market Regulation

*Justin O'Brien**

10.1 The Nature of Professional Obligation

At the heart of the disclosure paradigm governing market conduct regulation is a compromise that differentiates between classes of investors. The regulatory architecture presupposes that markets cannot function in a sustainable manner unless two core conditions are met. First, participants must act with integrity. Second, there is adequate disclosure to facilitate informed decision making. What constitutes effective disclosure and whether certain core obligations transcend investor classification remain, however, exceptionally contested. All too often, disclosure is reduced to technical considerations. This emasculated approach ignores the fact that disclosure was initially conceived as a means to an end rather than an end in itself. The paradigm was explicitly built on an ethical and normative foundation (e.g. Landis 1938). Reclaiming this lost heritage is essential if we are to ensure that within capital markets professional obligation meshes with rather than erodes societal welfare. When it comes to policing financial markets, consumer protection mandates have traditionally focused on retail markets. This is legitimated on the basis that these participants lack sufficient knowledge or experience to decide what information they need. Conversely, financially sophisticated participants in wholesale markets have been expected to attend to their own informational needs. The objective of regulating wholesale markets has, therefore, been

* I acknowledge the support of the Australian Research Council for the award of a Future Fellowship, which facilitated research visits to the United Kingdom and the United States. In addition I wish to thank the staff at the Harvard Law School Special Collection Unit for their unstinting support in tracking down the lost papers of James M. Landis.

primarily limited to ensuring that market infrastructure is sound and that markets are free from abuses. This approach is no longer sustainable in legal or policy terms.

In a remarkable ruling handed down in 2012, the Australian Federal Court, for example, found no legal basis for bifurcating between sophisticated or professional investors and retail clients (*Wingecarribee Shire Council v Lehman Brothers Australia*). Such an approach, it maintained, facilitated misleading and deceptive conduct. It brought the market into disrepute. The significance of the case lies in the fact that it was the first time globally that the differentiation between investor classes was subject to judicial determination. All prior cases had been settled without any admission of liability. Likewise, in the policy realm, there can be little doubting the significance of the final report issued by the Parliamentary Commission on Banking Standards (2013) in the United Kingdom. The Commission explored forensically how the interplay between corporate, regulatory, and political culture led inexorably to the Global Financial Crisis (GFC). In so doing, it has torn asunder prior rationales for and limitations to external intervention. It advocates a fundamental reframing of regulatory purpose. It does so on the basis of profound scepticism of protestations from the finance industry that it has learnt the lessons of the past. The Commission is equally suspicious of the stated commitment by the sector to the development of higher professional standards. While noting the critical importance of culture, the Commission rightfully recognises that effective reform and oversight cannot be outsourced from core regulatory authorities. The Commission argues that adequate accountability structures must be put in place to guard against any further deterioration of public confidence because of either a lack of political will or regulatory capacity. The approach is designed to break the desultory cycle that often accompanies financial crises. Unfortunately the formal government response, released in July 2013, has ignored many of the enhanced accountability mechanisms proposed, privileging instead the introduction of a new criminal charge of reckless conduct (Treasury 2013), which in practice is going to face enormous barriers to effective usage. In part this can be explained by the desultory cycle of regulatory politics within the financial sector. Extended regulatory reach in the aftermath of crisis, often underpinned by legislative change, leads inexorably to accusations of overreach (see O'Brien 2003, 2007, 2009). The GFC is no different. Indeed, the only remarkable thing was the speed of the pendulum shift until the revelation of further misconduct temporarily shifted the balance of material and ideational power within core regulatory regimes (Hood, Rothstein, and Baldwin 2001).

This chapter explores these competing dynamics and the impact on regulatory engagement, design, and strategies. This evaluation takes place in the context of a broader investigation into the roles played by the professions as actors in the framing and implementation of regulatory rules, a heretofore under-researched dimension to the crisis. Why, for example, were the professions so close to the executive suites unwilling or incapable of exercising scepticism, the hallmark of expertise? This is an existential question for both the established professions and those who would like to see the establishment of a professional standards board for banking, an idea canvassed but discounted (with cause) by the Parliamentary Commission on Banking Standards. The chapter, therefore, assesses a critical question. What is the nature of professional obligation in the context of capital market regulation? Particular reference is made to the legal and audit communities, both of which play pivotal, though contested 'gatekeeper' roles in upholding market integrity.

The chapter is structured as follows. First, the approach by the banking industry to the reform agenda is outlined. It is argued that such was the power of the lobby that without the subsequent revelation of huge derivative trading losses, the manipulation of key financial benchmarks, and the breaching of trading embargos, it had the capacity to limit meaningful change. These revelations, which post-date the GFC itself and have changed, temporarily, the nature of political discourse, are then explored in an evaluation that links contemporary concern to the initial framing of debates of market conduct regulation. In the third section, the policy and regulatory implications of judicial rejection in Australia of a reliance on differentiating between investor classes as a defence are evaluated, as well as the efficacy of regulatory strategies designed to improve audit quality. This provides an evidential foundation to assess the extent to which codes of conduct can lead to an improvement in integrity, the long-stated goal of market conduct regulators—a subject addressed in the fourth section. Tracing the contours of the political debates from the inception of the Securities and Exchange Commission in 1934 to the submissions to the Banking Standards Commission in 2012 and 2013 reveals a core conceptual flaw in the disclosure paradigm. It has not and cannot work without commitment by industry to facilitate and work with regulatory purpose. This commitment was not there in 1933–4 and it remains absent. The chapter concludes that unless duties and obligations are given as much attention as rights, commitments to uphold market integrity will remain hollow, making it likely that we will lurch once again into crisis.

10.2 Regulatory Pendulums and the Dynamics of Design

By 2011 bankers on both sides of the Atlantic had maintained that the time for apologies was over. The then Chief Executive of Barclays used a public lecture to warn 'it sounds controversial to suggest banks must take risk, in the wake of a near collapse of the financial system, but banks serve little economic or social purpose unless they do so' (Diamond 2011). In New York, his counterpart at J.P. Morgan Chase, Jamie Dimon, complained bitterly that plans to restrict proprietary trading were being championed by those who did not understand capital markets (*Fox News* 2012). Within months the reputations of both executives and their respective institutions were to go into free fall.

Radical departures from internal procedures at J.P. Morgan's London-based Chief Investment Office severely compromised Dimon's assertion that the bank could and did control risk. Initially dismissed by the bank as a 'tempest in a teacup', a subsequent Congressional investigation found that 'inadequate derivative valuation practices enabled traders to hide substantial losses for months at a time; lax hedging practices obscured whether derivatives were being used to offset risk or take risk; risk limit breaches were routinely disregarded; risk evaluation models were manipulated to downplay risk; inadequate regulatory oversight was too easily dodged or stonewalled; and derivative trading and financial results were misrepresented to investors, regulators, policymakers, and the taxpaying public who, when banks lose big, may be required to finance multi-billion-dollar bailouts' (Permanent Sub-Committee on Investigations 2013: 1). Dimon has, to date, survived the controversy. Bob Diamond was not so fortunate. Following the revelation of systematic attempts to manipulate the London Interbank Offered Rate (Libor), for which Barclays negotiated a settlement in July 2012 without admitting liability, Diamond was forced to resign. He was seen as primarily responsible for driving a culture within Barclays that privileged the transactional over the relational. His definition of culture in the BBC lecture as being 'how people behave when no-one is watching' (Diamond 2011) was treated with derision in scathing reports issued by the Treasury Select Committee (2012) and the Parliamentary Commission on Banking Standards (2013).

The manner in which the banking industry conceives of culture, however, remains exceptionally vague and self-interested. This calls into question whether self-referential reports on improving practice are in themselves sufficient to rebuild trust. In May 2013, for example, the major New York investment bank Goldman Sachs published the results of its *Business Standards Committee Impact Report*. Goldman Sachs' intention was to present to the markets a reframed conception of business ethics and accountability. The gravity of the task was indicated by the prodigious workload undertaken. Goldman Sachs (2013: 3) claimed that its report was the result of 'tens of thousands of hours of discussion, analysis, planning and execution, and importantly training and development, which alone totalled approximately 100,000 hours'. Drawing upon the bank's experience of the Global Financial Crisis (GFC), the report begins with a stated recalibration of the firm's strategy. It emphasises the need to put the interests of clients first. Two additional drivers are also referenced, namely 'reputational sensitivity and awareness and the individual and collective accountability of our people' (Goldman Sachs 2013: 3). Curiously, there is no mention of the fact that the stated commitment to reform derives from a settlement agreement with the Securities and Exchange Commission. The settlement dealt with allegations that the pre-existing standards and practices at the bank in relation to the design, marketing, and sale of complex financial products violated each of these noble objectives (see O'Brien 2013a). In August 2013 a former Goldman Sachs junior trader, Fabrice Tourre, was found guilty of violating securities law by failing to disclose to investors the identity of the counterparty in the notorious Abacus transaction. The transaction involved the construction of a basket of referent securities chosen in part by a hedge fund controlled by John Paulsen. It was not disclosed to investors that Paulsen's fund was betting that the investment would fail. One of the most remarkable aspects of the court proceedings, which this author attended, was the open characterisation by both prosecution and defence of the Collateralised Debt Obligation market as a speculative gamble devoid of real economic benefit.

Goldman Sachs was, of course, far from being the only offender. The GFC demonstrated in startling detail the externalities caused by emasculated conceptions of responsibility and accountability. Corporate executives and their professional advisors conspired to push through deals and strategies informed by legal technicalities and accounting conventions as well as market norms. These strategies led to suboptimal results for both the sustainability of specific corporate models and the professional standing of their advisors. Existing codes of conduct at corporate, industry, or professional level proved incapable of addressing hubris, myopia, and the decoupling of ethical considerations from core business. The failure to articulate and integrate purpose, values, and principles within a functioning ethical framework created or exacerbated socially harmful corporate cultures. These cultures elevated technical compliance over substance. Ethical obligation was stated but not delivered. Deterrence was defective and ineffective. There was little or no accountability. No credible mechanisms to identify institutional or systemic risk were put in place. The fact that the statute of limitations has run in most jurisdictions without the bringing of criminal charges for wilful blindness poses a series of fundamental and unresolved questions. Has the panoply of reform initiatives at national, regional, and global level addressed the core normative problem of systemic unethical conduct? Alternatively, have we privileged the politics of symbolism, creating the illusion of a robust architecture capable of withstanding a crisis of similar magnitude? It is in this context that the revitalised Goldman Sachs Business Standards initiative, linked directly to a strengthening of its code of conduct, is so interesting? The critical question, therefore, is whether the revised approach, which covers client relationships, conflicts of interest, structured products, transparency and disclosure, broader governance, and training and development, is a robust improvement or a cynical privileging of symbolism? On this front, the evidence is decidedly mixed.

In sharp contrast to earlier reliance on *caveat emptor*, the bank now claims that its suitability framework has been enhanced. This, it is claimed, will 'help us [i.e. Goldman Sachs] better assess whether our clients have the background, experience and capacity to understand the range of outcomes from transactions they execute with us, particularly those transactions that are strategic or complex'. Second, the firm has introduced what it claimed to be a 'systematic, integrated and comprehensive firm-wide framework for reputational risk monitoring and management'. Third, there is an explicit emphasis on culture. 'We know that while formal processes and rules are important, they cannot alone substitute for sound judgment and experience and an environment in which every person in the firm feels equally accountable for the firm's reputation', the report concludes. So far so good one might say. Reputation, however, is determined by risk. In this regard the report reads much more defensively.

The defensive tone rings—or should ring—alarm bells. It suggests the commitment to enhanced disclosure and transparency reflects only external imposition. Indeed, the report is explicit on this point. Goldman Sachs (2013: 7) notes that 'the uncertain impact of regulatory reform on both our clients and the firm currently is a consistent theme across our businesses'. Simultaneously it seeks refuge in a highly selective reading of its illustrious past. It notes that 'suitability will always be an important focus for us as will conflicts and business selection' (Goldman Sachs 2013: 7). The failure to provide effective mechanisms to deal with this fundamental problem within a functioning ethical framework, however, is what got Goldman Sachs into such trouble in the first place. Moreover, presenting enhanced levels of disclosure and transparency as voluntary initiatives when in fact they are mandated through legislative change and regulatory settlement negotiations is dissembling of the first order. It takes much away from the authenticity of the report. Paradoxically, the report itself goes on to spell out the forced nature of change. 'Our Investment Management Division has been concentrating on new regulations and requirements related to suitability, many of which impact a broader range of clients than in the past and call for enhancements to disclosure, documentation and controls' (Goldman Sachs 2013: 7). At the same time, Goldman Sachs (2013: 14) remains sanguine that 'professional investors generally have the background, experience and risk profile to make their own investment decisions'. As the Tourre civil proceedings made clear, however, this was manifestly not the case. It has, nonetheless, established vetting procedures related to the design and purpose of specific instruments offered by the firm. These are designed to ensure 'the instrument is appropriate for the markets and that the relevant risk factors associated with the instrument are adequately addressed and disclosed' (Goldman Sachs 2013: 15). The unmistakable message is that Goldman will design, market, and sell the product if it thinks it can get away with it, not on whether it is appropriate or socially useful. *Plus ça change, plus c'est la même chose*—the more things change, the more they stay the same.

This extended vignette tells us much about the corporate and regulatory response to the GFC. Six years on from August 2007 and the vaporisation of the securitisation market, regulatory authorities across the globe remain mired in crisis rather than engaged in strategic management. Within that time frame, we have moved progressively from a rubric of 'too big to fail' to a dawning recognition that systemically important financial firms are not only too big to manage, to regulate, but also to litigate effectively against and arguably now too complex to insure. At the same time, the global investigation into the manipulation of the London Interbank Offered Rate (Libor) suggests the problem is systemic. The Libor investigation, which remains at an early stage, has exposed corruption in the rate-setting process, as most recently noted by an umbrella grouping of financial regulators in the United States:

> Recent investigations uncovered *systematic false reporting and manipulations* of reference rate submissions dating back many years. This *misconduct* was designed to either increase the potential profit of the submitting firms or to convey a misleading picture of the relative health of the submitting banks. These actions were *pervasive, occurred in multiple bank locations around the world, involved senior bank officials at several banks, and affected multiple benchmark rates and currencies*, including LIBOR, EURIBOR, and the Tokyo Interbank Offered Rate (TIBOR). Each of the banks that faced charges engaged in a *multi-year pattern of misconduct that involved collusion* with other banks. These revelations have undermined the public's confidence in these benchmarks [emphasis added]. (Financial Stability Oversight Council 2013: 137)

Similarly, the Parliamentary Banking Standards Commission in the United Kingdom has expressed grave concern at the failure of restraining forces. It links 'prolonged and blatant misconduct' in the Libor and associated scandals to a 'dismal' and 'striking limitation on the sense of personal responsibility and accountability' (Parliamentary Banking Standards Commission 2013: 16). The paucity of institutional memory in leading banks and the fact that such manipulative activities continued even after bailouts have made business ethics appear as little more than an oxymoron. While unethical conduct was widespread, it is important to note that much that occurred in the GFC was deemed to be technically legal or compliant with accounting standards. With the partial exception of the Tourre case, enforcement has been lacking. Given that the statute of limitations has run in the United States, the reality is that no criminal or civil prosecutions will be staged to test this belief or bring those responsible to account (Rakoff 2013). No cases relating to the initial crisis have been mounted in the United Kingdom, a decision justified on the basis that there was no credible expectation of securing a guilty verdict (Financial Services Authority 2011). In Australia, however, one significant and revealing case has been litigated to a judicial determination. The case, *Wingecaribee v Lehman Brothers Australia*, and its implications are discussed in detail below. First, however, it is necessary to evaluate the extent to which continued public unease has contributed to an acute legitimacy crisis for both the capital markets and the disclosure paradigm itself.

10.3 Reclaiming Disclosure's Normative Underpinnings

Political intervention in financial regulation tends to be most effective when anchored to sources of legitimacy and authority. Notwithstanding the corrosive and deeply disturbing abuse scandals that have weakened, with cause, the standing of the Catholic Church, the reputation of Pope Francis remains untarnished. An advocate for the poor and the dispossessed, every step of his reign to date has been marked by the astute exercise of the power of symbolic voice. His intervention in the debate on the regulation of global finance is no different. Pope Francis (2013) warned that 'certain pathologies are increasing, with their psychological consequences; fear and desperation grip the hearts of many people, even in the so-called rich countries; the joy of life is diminishing; indecency and violence are on rise; poverty is becoming more and more evident'. In identifying as a causal mechanism 'our relationship with money, and our acceptance of its power over ourselves and society' the speech had clear echoes of Franklin Delano Roosevelt's inaugural presidential address in the midst of the Great Depression. Although separated by eighty years, the danger of the elevation of 'false idols' remains an exceptionally potent and eerily apposite message for the regulation of capital markets.

Roosevelt (1933) anchored the New Deal architecture that underpins the disclosure paradigm on the need to put 'an end to a conduct in banking and in business, which too often has given to a sacred trust the likeness of callous and selfish wrongdoing...Restoration calls, however, not for changes in ethics alone. This Nation asks for action, and action now'. Pope Francis (2013) elevated the pitch to a global level, noting that the 'worship of the golden calf of old (cf. *Exodus* 32:15–34) has found a new and heartless image in the cult of money and the dictatorship of an economy which is faceless and lacking any truly humane goal'. This privileging of monetary value over moral values did not happen by accident. It is the result of conscious ordering. For the pontiff this state of affairs has practical ideational roots. It derives from corruption, fiscal tax evasion, and 'ideologies which uphold the absolute autonomy of markets and financial speculation, and thus deny the right of control to States, which are themselves charged with providing for the common good. A new, invisible and at times virtual, tyranny is established, one which unilaterally and irremediably imposes its own laws and rules' (Francis 2013). Critically, these battles over mandates tend to be fought at the crucial implementation stage of regulation. This is largely but erroneously conducted on a technical basis. The complexities contribute to opacity rather than transparency and as a consequence a reduction in public confidence and trust. Nowhere is this more apparent than in the United States, a point made with great erudition by Paul Volcker, the legendary former chairman of the Federal Reserve. For Volcker (2013), the regulatory architecture in the United States is a 'recipe for indecision, neglect and stalemate, adding up to ineffectiveness. The time has come for change'. What is needed is a process of ethical and political renewal. Both Pope Francis and Paul Volcker identify fundamental flaws in conceiving of regulatory purpose, which must be addressed if confidence in capital market conduct is to be warranted. This necessitates conceptual as well as practical reform. As could be expected, Pope Francis (2013) stressed the normative dimension:

> There is a need for financial reform along ethical lines that would produce in its turn an economic reform to benefit everyone. This would nevertheless require a courageous change of attitude on the part of political leaders. I urge them to face this challenge with determination and farsightedness, taking account, naturally, of their particular situations. Money has to serve, not to rule...In this way, a new political and economic mindset would arise that would help to transform the absolute dichotomy between the economic and social spheres into a healthy symbiosis.

This is far from an exercise in handwringing. It is a deliberate and cautious attempt to change the narrative governing the purpose of regulation. Pope Francis is rescuing from history the claim that 'the principle of freedom to contract...is...merely the expression of an ingrained prejudice in favor of a definite kind of interference, namely such as would destroy non-contractual relations' (Polanyi 1944: 171). Change of this magnitude necessitates recognition by the financial services sector itself that the bifurcation between the economic and the political and social spheres has been disastrous to societal cohesion and, indeed, its own self-interest. Not for the first time, understanding what could be the future of financial regulation necessitates reclaiming and stating its rationale. This core fact informed the calculation of its initial framers. None speaks more directly to the problems facing the industry and society today than James M. Landis, its key architect. An inaugural member of the Securities and Exchange Commission who became its chairman in 1935, Landis was an outstanding practitioner and theoretician of regulatory design.

From the beginning Landis stressed purpose over regulatory form, cooperation over coercion. Critically, he saw the role of administrative agencies as not only policing but also guiding industry to understand, accept, and work cooperatively in providing socially beneficial outcomes. Within this framework, disclosure was designed to inform the investing public of actual practice, thereby incrementally changing the boundaries of what could be constituted as acceptable. Extending far beyond the narrow realm of banking and securities regulation, the New Deal was designed to recalibrate society itself through the guidance of neutral experts. Experience, experiment, and avowed faith in the rule of experts to solve the complexity of modern society underpinned a powerful interdisciplinary intellectual movement. It provided the opportunity to simultaneously translate theory into practice and generate theory from practice. It was to be in the financial sector, however, where the New Deal had the most pronounced influence. The result was a profound recalibration. Private interests were rendered subservient—if only temporarily—to societal obligation. Moreover, it was to be the progressive erosion of that compact, with the explicit support of political agency, which has, in large part, brought us to the current crisis. Seen in this context, the GFC is what happens when the needs and cultural framing of specific communities of practice gain ideational support for what purports to be communal virtues but more accurately reflects unsustainable (and ultimately failed) commercial virtues.

The cult of money has many acolytes. Credible reform necessitates that the ethos of responsibility percolates much deeper than bankers and their regulators. This is because many other actors are involved within the creation and legitimation of a given regulatory regime (Fligstein and Dauter 2007; Hood, Rothstein, and Baldwin 2001). Sustainable reform requires understanding and challenging the assumptions that delimit the range of options governing the world view of finance. We also need much more granular definitions of what constitutes integrity and the responsibilities and duties of the professions, as critical purveyors of advice to market participants. Through ideological privileging, neglect, or wilful blindness they failed to either identify or safeguard market integrity and societal welfare. In so doing they brought into doubt both the utility and legitimacy of their function. If capital markets are to restore the faded lustre of respectability, attention must focus on the moral principles of the professions. These are the 'gatekeepers' of market integrity (Coffee 2006; Loughrey 2011). They derive prestige and standing from identification with professional obligation. They appear, however, to have misunderstood its true meaning. The placing of legal permissibility over ethical judgement relied upon professional guidance from audit and legal communities. Such guidance was possible only because responsibility was conceived on a narrow technical rather than normative basis. It is this broader question of potential complicity that remains the least developed in the aftermath of the Global Financial Crisis. Before ascertaining how that process can be reversed, it is essential to evaluate how it occurred. It is in this context that evaluation of the Australian experience of the GFC and its aftermath is of particular relevance. Australia escaped the calamity of a major institutional collapse. Malpractice was, however, evident. Two case studies detailed below raise very real concerns about the manner in which the professions operated: (a) the marketing and sale of complex financial products; and (b) a gradual but pronounced deterioration in audit quality, which has resulted in the revocation of professional liability caps for the Institute of Chartered Accountants.

10.3.1 Complex Financial Products

'How was it that relatively unsophisticated Council officers came to invest many millions of ratepayers' funds in these specialised financial instruments? That is the fundamental question at the heart of these proceedings', reflected an Australian judge before pronouncing judgement in a case that has far-reaching implications for the regulation of financial services.[1] *Wingecarribee Shire Council v Lehman Brothers Australia* directly addresses a critical issue: what specific duty of care does a financial services provider owe to its clients and can these be voided by contractual terms or legislative exceptions? The Rares judgement provides the first definitive affirmative answer to the former and a negative to the latter. It holds that a critical bifurcation in the Australian financial services legislation between sophisticated or professional and unsophisticated investors cannot be used to evade responsibility of financial services providers to act in the best interest of clients. It finds that Grange Securities, a wholly owned subsidiary of Lehman Brothers Australia, breached its fiduciary duty in facilitating individual transactions for complex products to sophisticated clients without explaining the risks. Of potentially greater significance, in what is a robust indictment of financial engineering and the methods used by its leading practitioners, it holds that the placing of highly complex collateralised debt obligations in the investment portfolios of councils represented misleading and deceptive conduct.

The litigation's significance focuses on the interplay between three factors. First, the judgement revealed a serious and unresolved conflict over policy implementation of legislative intention in determining how complex securities instruments can and should be marketed. As will be explored more fully below, this has been only partially addressed by the Future of Financial Advice

---

[1] *Wingecarribee Shire Council v Lehman Brothers Australia (in liq)* [2012] FCA 1028, [14].

reform agenda, precisely because the Department of Treasury (2011) has not released the outcome of a consultation process on whether the bifurcation between sophisticated and retail investors should be repealed. Second, the litigation derives from rather than spawns a class action. The testing of obligation was left to commercial funders, listed on the Australian Stock Exchange for profit, rather than the regulator funded by the taxpayer to uphold the public interest. This is rendered even more surprising given that the entities represented in that action are themselves an arm of government. This opens the question of why the market conduct regulator, the Australian Securities and Investments Commission did not risk litigating a case that the judge himself found to be of acute public importance. In part the answer lies in a policy decision not to intervene when a class action has been initiated. Third, as Lehman Brothers Australia is in liquidation, it is unlikely to appeal. The legal advisors to the litigation funders, IMF, have already signalled intention to file suit against other solvent providers of complex financial products. The ruling is, therefore, likely to herald future litigation.

The United States investment bank Lehman Brothers had entered the Australian market through its acquisition of Grange Securities and Grange Asset Management in March 2007. In so doing, it took responsibility for the management of ongoing and prior relationships. These included the provision of transactional services and asset management for a number of local councils, each governed by a specific Individual Management Protocol (IMP). The Australian Federal Court found that 'the improvidence, and commercial naivety, of Grange's Council clients in entering into these transactions that were highly advantageous to Grange' (para. 266) could only have occurred because the financial services firm was dealing with individual officials variously described as 'financially quite unsophisticated and completely out of his depth' (para. 483), 'uninformed' (para. 491), and 'careless' (para. 462). Notwithstanding the carelessness, the Federal Court did not find grounds to reduce liability through contributory negligence. It did so because the Court held that the financial services firm had used a deliberate strategy to take advantage of its asymmetrical knowledge of product and regulatory complexity. That it could do so indicated a capacity to circumvent the legal rules and a failure of the audit process to ascertain the material risks of such a strategy for the financial services provider.

'The contrast between the actual, and patent, lack of financial acumen of the various Council officers at each of Swan, Parkes and Wingecarribee [the local councils representing the class action] and the intelligent, shrewd and financially astute persons at Grange was striking' (para 752). 'Generally, risk-averse people do not take bets with substantial assets held for public purposes', the judge concluded (para. 895). That they did so could be explained by the fact that they were victims of an elaborate deception. 'Grange financed itself when it required cash by borrowing from its Council clients at a rate of interest or on terms as to security that Grange was not likely to achieve in an informed, arm's length transaction with a commercial financier' (para. 264). The clients had no 'real appreciation of the true risks of SCDOs [Synthetic Collateralised Debt Obligations] or the financial wisdom of its [i.e. Grange's] recommendation' (para. 265). The judge is disarmingly forthright as to how and why this could happen:

> The nature and risks of a SCDO are concepts that are beyond the grasp of most people. Indeed, after the benefit of expert reports, concurrent expert evidence and the addresses of counsel, I am not sure that I understand fully how SCDOs work or their risks. Nonetheless, Grange portrayed itself as an expert in these investments. Most certainly, none of the seven Council officers who gave evidence had any expertise in these financial products. And, Grange knew and preyed on that lack of expertise and the trust the Councils placed in its expert advice. (para. 410)

The 445-page judgement highlights again and again how Grange actively circumvented the stated objection of its clients to investing in illiquid instruments through a combination of deception and obfuscation. This is made manifest in the evaluation of specific dealings with Wingecarribee Council, a rural shire in New South Wales. 'Grange tested the water' and when the official 'bit' he was 'reeled in' by 'words of comfort' (para. 662). According to the Court, the council believed that it 'had the best of both worlds: principal protection and increased interest. For Grange, this manner of allaying risk averse, financially unsophisticated council officers' fears of CDOs, was as easy as shooting fish in a barrel' (para. 662).

There can be no doubting the level of judicial disquiet at corporate interpretation of the bifurcation between sophisticated and unsophisticated investors 'given the subject matter involved, the prudent investment of public money' (para. 790). The severity of the misconduct and the robustness of the judgement calls into question the sufficiency of the options canvassed by the Australian Department of Treasury (2011: 8–10) on how complex financial products are systematically sold to mid-market participants (i.e. those that were deemed sophisticated or professional in legal terms but were, arguably, nothing of the sort).

The ability to contract out of investor protection mechanisms is central to the rationale behind the bifurcation between sophisticated (i.e. wholesale or professional) and unsophisticated (i.e. retail) investors. In many developed markets much greater disclosure is required when products or financial advice are offered to retail clients. Traditionally, the restraints on the retail side are designed to protect the naive and the unwary from unscrupulous action by those with asymmetrical advantage. Sophisticated or professional investors, by contrast, have traditionally been assumed to have the resources to make informed decisions. The Department of Treasury (2011) outlined four primary options: (a) retain and update the current system, including the introduction of extra requirements for specific complex financial products; (b) remove the distinction between wholesale and retail clients, making disclosure obligations consistent across the investment universe; (c) introduce a new sophisticated investor test based on the actual financial literacy of the specific investor; or (d) no nothing. The final option, despite having the advantage of compliance costs that are not increasing, is effectively ruled out. The review notes inaction does not 'address the problems with the current system...and would be inconsistent with what comparable jurisdictions are doing'.[2] The ruling in *Wingecarribee Shire Council v Lehman Brothers Australia* casts significant doubt on the sustainability of each of the others, with the exception of option (b). It is now incoherent from a legal and policy perspective to limit the demand for greater integrity to one component of the marketplace. Can we seriously suggest that *product A, when offered to customer B is ethical, unethical when offered to customer C, but that entity D, if offering both simultaneously, has a cohesive integrated operating framework and a warranted (as opposed to stated) reputation for integrity*? As with pregnancy, it is impossible to be semi-ethical.

Given the propensity for pension funds to include a proportion of alternative assets within their portfolios, it is essential that asset managers given authority to invest mandatory defined contributions understand the risks involved. This suggests that much greater emphasis needs to be placed on articulating and delineating more precisely where responsibility and accountability lies in financial product design. It is in this context that the lawyer, in particular, has the capacity to play an important role. If the lawyer's obligation is to the institution rather than the individual executive involved in the design and authorisation of a specific project, it is necessary to take into account the broader risk externalities and report, where necessary, those risks to the board of directors. As with the litany of scandals in the United States, no evidence was provided in the Lehman case in Australia that this was done. The financial regulator has signalled that this will not be tolerated: 'My position on this is clear—those selling complex products to unsuspecting investors need to wise up and do the right thing. They might get away with it for a while, but government and courts will inevitably rule in favour of investors' (Medcraft 2013). Removing the distinction and relying on disclosure alone is not, however, going to change practice—unless there is cultural change

---

[2] In this regard it is interesting to note the expansive definition of 'consumer' by the Director of Markets at the Financial Conduct Authority in the United Kingdom, which suggests past bifurcation has limited prior regulatory capacity to restrain activity that may contribute to an erosion of market integrity (Lawton 2013).

within the financial sector. Emasculated conceptions of responsibility have not, however, been solely the preserve of financial product designers and transactional lawyers. Similar lack of judgement has also informed the operation of the audit.

10.3.2 Deterioration in Audit Quality

On 4 December 2012 the Australian Securities and Investments Commission (2012a) released a review of audit performance that raised distinctly uncomfortable questions for the profession. The ASIC Chairman, Greg Medcraft, described as 'disappointing' the results, which showed an increase in failure to provide reasonable assurance that financial reports were not materially mis-stated from 14% to 18% over an eighteen-month period (Australian Securities and Investments Commission 2012b). This was mild compared to oral evidence presented the previous day at the Joint Parliamentary Committee investigating the governance and operation of ASIC. Then he was characteristically blunt: 'I consider what we are seeing now as [a] second strike for the audit sector and it is clearly one I think the profession should consider itself on notice: it needs to lift its game' (Medcraft 2012). While it is very much open to question whether the severity of the criticism was designed to offset broader criticism of the agency before parliament, there was no doubting its effectiveness in reframing the debate on the parameters of professional obligation within the audit community.

The ASIC review found three critical areas that highlighted dissonance between public expectations and actual practice: the sufficiency and appropriateness of the evidence on which judgement was exercised; the level, or more accurately the lack of, professional scepticism; and, concomitantly, the unwarranted reliance on the work of others, in particular in the compliance programmes of managed investment schemes. The evidence produced in the report is somewhat alarming. It is rendered more so because the deficiencies correspond to what the regulator sees as a global trend (ASIC 2012a: 5). For ASIC the importance of the evaluation lies not in whether the results were, in fact, misleading. The concern is more fundamental. Has the profession even the competence to gather the evidence on which to make a considered judgement? ASIC believes not. Crucially the lack of sufficient control was prevalent across the spectrum. Size of audit firm is not a precondition of quality (ASIC 2012a: 6).

The review process generated what ASIC (2012a: 9) termed 'a high level of concerns about the sufficiency and appropriateness of evidence obtained by auditors to support their conclusions on significant areas of the audit'. These included basic criteria such as external evaluation of impairment testing, fair value measurement, and assessment of the capacity of the audited entity to establish its viability as a going concern. Unquestioning use of data when deploying substantive analytical procedures, as well as the failure to ascertain directly from executives the material risk of fraud, compromised audit quality. The unquestioning use of data was most pronounced in the audit of financial institutions, arguably the most systemically important in a domestic, regional, and global context (ASIC 2012a: 11).

ASIC (2012a: 17) accepts that 'leaders remain committed to an appropriate "tone at the top" that emphasises the importance of audit independence'. However, it finds reliance on such pronouncements alone an implausible guarantee of probity. It is far from a ringing endorsement of expertise and judgement, the cornerstone of professional standing and legitimacy, that ASIC feels obliged to spell out what constitutes scepticism:

> Professional scepticism must be maintained and exercised throughout the planning and performance of an audit. Engagement partners and staff should have questioning minds, obtain a full understanding of all relevant facts, not be over-reliant on management's explanations and representations, and not just seek to obtain audit evidence that corroborates rather than challenges management's judgment. Partners and staff must have a sound knowledge of the accounting standards and framework to conduct an effective audit. When considering accounting treatments, partners and staff should consider the substance of arrangements, alternative views and the principles and intent of accounting standards in making their judgments. (ASIC 2012a: 21)

Not surprisingly, the content and tone of the report prompted an ongoing public relations battle, waged through the parliament and subsequently the media. The head of the CPA, Alex Malley, condemned what he termed a persistent 'propensity [on the part of ASIC] to make statements in a range of public forums that are sensationalised and driven by a media grab mentality rather than seeking constructive outcomes and working collaboratively with the profession' (Parliamentary Joint Committee 2013: 13). Rather than awaiting the outcome of the parliamentary inquiry, Malley (2013) then repeated his concerns to *The Australian*. If the approach was to influence the final findings of the Joint Committee, he was to be mistaken. In adjudicating on this debate, the Committee did little more than note but then disregard industry concern, largely and ironically enough, on the basis of scepticism. Critical in this regard is the overarching conclusion of the parliamentary investigation: 'The committee acknowledges the evidence provided by industry and professional bodies about what an audit actually encompasses, but it remains concerned about the gap that exists between what the public expects and what the public gets with regard to an audit' (Parliamentary Joint Committee 2013: 23). The Big Four auditing firms responded to the 'nudging' of ASIC by setting up action plans to improve the quality of auditing.

ASIC (2013) notes that the 'firms responded to encouragement from ASIC for the action plans to particularly focus on: the culture of the firm, including messages from firm leadership focusing on audit quality and consultation on complex audit issues' and that the plans should be regarded as 'living documents'. This action, however, was insufficient to prevent the auditing firms falling foul of another key Australian regulatory body, the Professional Standards Council (PSC).

The unexpected decision by the PSC to not approve a scheme capping the professional indemnity insurance put forward by the Institute of Chartered Accountants Australia (ICAA) reflects ongoing regulatory concern about audit quality and professional standards more generally within the audit and accounting profession. The decision is a major blow to the chartered accountants and, by extension, the other associations representing the profession. The PSC operates its licensing arrangement on a five-year basis, with the possibility of one-year extensions. Put simply, the framework governing the accountancy profession is now up for complete review. Second, that review is conducted by the PSC, which has the power not to recommend the renewal or approval of a scheme if it believes it deficient. The question for the PSC was whether the ICAA accounted for the deleterious decline in audit standards and quality identified by ASIC and endorsed by the Joint Parliamentary Committee. The PSC appears to have believed not. As of 30 June 2013 on a rolling basis the cap on professional liability will be revoked across all states and territories. With remarkable understatement the ICAA advised that 'members may wish to consider their risk profile in relation to the structure of their existing professional indemnity insurance levels'.

As the statutory authority responsible for encouraging regulated professional communities to improve standards, the PSC is well placed to evaluate how the conflict between commercial imperatives and the public interest is navigated. It is essential that those standards are effective if the efficacy of self-regulation or the meta-regulatory framework underpinning the PSC is to be demonstrated and legitimated. Failure to close the gap between perceived obligation and actual practice risks undermining the authority of the professional model itself. Armed with national and international evidence, perhaps this was a risk the PSC were not prepared to countenance. It was also a risk that animated the British Parliamentary Commission on Banking Standards' discussion on professional values but against which the British Government appears sanguine (Treasury 2013). Whether this represents caution or capture remains very much an open question. What is also clear, however, is that reliance on self-policing codes of conduct is both myopic and a dangerous rejection of evidence.

10.3.3 Codes of Conduct: Design, Efficacy, and Evaluation

Any successful proposal to extend responsibility and accountability to those involved in product design rather than clarifying the enabling conditions governing marketing and sale would constitute a major shift in the structure of the financial services industry. The integration of more interventionist normative objectives such as societal welfare with enabling ones may also significantly change the ethical boundaries of global finance. It is essential to move *efficiency* (i.e. lower transaction costs). Three additional distinct but overlapping normative dimensions must be applied. First, *permissibility* (i.e. whether a particular product can be sold and if so to whom and on what basis); second, *responsibility* (i.e. who carries the risk if the investment sours and on what terms); and third, *legitimacy* (i.e. does the product serve a legitimate purpose). As John Kay (2012: 9) has persuasively argued, sustainable reform must be predicated on capability to 'restore relationships of trust and confidence in the investment chain, underpinned by the application of fiduciary standards of care by all those who manage or advise on the investments of others'. The Kay formulation builds on an insight first advanced by the former managing director of the United Kingdom Financial Services Authority, Hector Sants (2009, 2010). Sants had famously complained that it was impossible for principles-based regulation to work when those charged with informal authority to maintain the integrity of the system had no principles. This was not simply a particularly memorable aside. It recognised the importance of what Oliver Williamson (2000: 597) has termed the 'non-calculative social contract'. In the aftermath of the GFC, public trust in technical expertise is understandably unforthcoming. What is, therefore, required for regulator and regulated alike is an articulation of a renewed 'non-calculative social contract' capable of embedding ethical restraint of the kind identified by the leading British philosopher Derek Parfit (2007: 25): 'an act is wrong just when such acts are disallowed by the principles that are optimific, uniquely universally willable, and not reasonably rejectable'. Paradoxically it is this very imperative that underpinned the initial (but lost) normative basis of the disclosure paradigm. As one of its key architects pointed out, eighty years ago the disclosure paradigm was:

> informed by a moral idea, a realisation that our ills have been due also to the weakening of our moral fibre, leading to easy temporising with traditional and tried standards of right and wrong. The only act that is founded upon a moral background, that has been passed in the past twenty years, is the Securities Act. The permeating character of such forces was slow to be comprehended, but with its discovery came a grim determination to restore to a numbed national conscience some semblance of sensitivity. It was of a spirit such as this that the Securities Act was born, free of vindictiveness that might easily have been attached to it,

reasonable in its demands and built upon tried experience in their formulation. It would be idle to pretend that it does not ask something of the security world, but it also promises much in return the opportunity of creating a true and honorable profession by the assumption and adequate discharge of public responsibilities. (Bane 1933)

What also becomes clear from a recently released archive of James M. Landis' personal papers at Harvard Law School is that across a whole swathe of industries, there was early recognition at the Federal Trade Commission (FTC), which initially had carriage of securities regulation, that far from weakening power, the early reliance of the Roosevelt Administration on the development of codes of conduct provided industry with an opportunity to retain it (see O'Brien 2013c). This history must be taken into consideration given the fact that the British Banking Association canvassed the idea of developing a code of conduct underpinned with statutory authority to the Parliamentary Banking Standards Commission as evidence of good faith. History tells us that self-policing and self-referential determination of obligation can be exceptionally problematic.

An example of how codes could militate *against* change comes from the Code of Fair Competition for Investment Bankers (1933). The code had ensured that power to determine the extent of compliance would remain with the banks themselves. It mandated that the management committee would contain twenty-one voting members: fifteen appointed by the President of the Investment Banking Association of America; six through a 'fair method to represent employers not members of the IBA; and a representative appointed without vote by the President of the United States of America'. Landis, by then heavily embroiled in disputes over the operation of the Securities Act, was horrified by the way in which industry was behaving. 'How truly despicable some of their tactics are. I really thought they were essentially decent though somewhat misguided people, but I have my doubts now', he wrote to Felix Frankfurter on 13 December 1933 (O'Brien 2013c). Those doubts were, in part, informed by unease about the willingness of industry to engage in meaningful partnership.

This unease was captured by an internal report prepared for Landis and the other members of the FTC on the workings of the National Recovery Administration (NRA), which was charged with oversight of the codes. Assigned the chief legal liaison to the NRA, Millard Hudson (1933a) was flabbergasted by what he termed the 'chaotic conditions' at the agency. 'There is hardly an important form of monopolistic practices which the Federal Trade Commission and the courts have endeavored to prevent in the past, that is not authorised and more or less explicitly provided for in these codes; not of course by individuals, but what is a great deal worse, by the cooperative activities of whole industries. It would be an exaggeration to say that any remonstrances against these things have resulted in any substantial improvement' (Hudson 1933a). Two weeks later, Hudson provided a more in-depth account of regulatory failure. 'The industries, having got the bit in their teeth, are running amok, and are bent upon destroying the good work accomplished by the Commission in the past and to prevent its doing any more in the future' (Hudson 1933b). Four principal reasons were attributed. First, no representative of the Commission had power to draw up and enforce a model code. Second, legal representatives were 'practically all young, inexperienced men, many of whom knew nothing whatever about the Commission's work. It was easy for the industries to put things over on them'. Third, 'having given the industries in the early codes practically everything they asked for, it was difficult to refuse those which came later. But the most alarming development is the unwillingness of the Administrator to set up any effective form of control over the administration of the codes. He is leaving it, by his own statement, as far as possible to the boards set up within the industries themselves. This means that matters in which they are interested will receive attention and probably little else will' (Hudson 1933b). Such an approach was diametrically opposed to the form and substance of Landis' regulatory design.

For Landis, 'the art of regulating an industry requires knowledge of the details of its operations [and the] ability to shift requirements as the condition of the industry may dictate' (Seligman 2002: 62). The power of the disclosure model, first set out in the Securities Act (1933) and reinforced by the Securities Exchange Act the following year, was the capacity to set, evolve, and frame broader discourse. The aim was not to mandate organisational change as some early commentators advocated (e.g. Douglas and Bates 1932). Instead, disclosure was presented as a necessary response to systemic failure and a manifestation of societal obligation. On his retirement from the SEC, Landis told *The New York Times* (1937), somewhat optimistically, that brokers 'are beginning to realize more clearly that their interest is tied up with the public interest. They are beginning more often to subordinate their own interest to the larger interest. People are beginning also to look upon the exchanges not so much as private institutions as public utilities'. The real tragedy here is not the misplaced optimism of Landis but the misplaced trust in financial services sector statements that, through their disclosures, they had recognised their obligations. The banking industry proved incapable of rising to the level of a profession. The result was a draining of legitimacy and authority. The exceptionally critical report by the Parliamentary Banking Standards Commission (2013) in the United Kingdom has laid bare the extent of that legitimacy crisis.

Throughout the report there is evidence of continued suspicion of both banks and their regulators. In a critical passage, the Commission warns against the myth that the problem in British banking is the result of individual failure or that banking has indeed learnt from its mistakes, thus requiring no further action. 'If the arguments for complacency and inaction are heeded now, when the crisis in banking standards has been laid bare, they are yet more certain to be heeded when memories have faded. If politicians allow the necessary reforms to fall at one of the first hurdles, then the next crisis in banking standards and culture may come sooner, and be more severe' (para. 273). The Commission is exceptionally cautious about the stated ambition of the banking industry to develop a professional standards body. While seeing potential value, it is exceptionally concerned that this too could become an exercise in regulatory gaming. 'There are also very substantial risks of duplication between the powers and role of a professional standards body and those of regulators as well as risk that the creation of such a body could become a focus of public policy, diverting attention from the changes that are urgently needed within the existing regulatory framework' (para. 598). It is a risk that the Commission is not prepared to countenance. 'On the basis of our assessment of the nature of the banking industry, we believe that the creation of an effective professional body is a long way off and may take at least a generation', it concludes (para. 601). The official response by the government is, however, much more accepting of the opportunity for responsibility to be transferred in due course (Treasury 2013: para 2.21). As with the rejection of the proposed appointment to the Financial Policy Committee of someone with historical knowledge of past crises and regulatory responses (Treasury 2013: para 5.32), it is a shortsighted response. The reform of British banking remains a work in progress, conducted within terms of reference that remain undisturbed by history or experience.

10.4 Conclusion

The enormity of the Global Financial Crisis has demonstrated just how misplaced confidence in market ordering was. As such, it represents a *fin de siècle* moment. The material and ideational certainties associated with the privileging of financial capitalism have evaporated. The *Wingecarribee Shire Council v Lehman Brothers Australia* decision highlights the suboptimal effect of a prior retreat to technicalities in dealing with substantive ethical considerations (i.e. the bifurcated protection offered to sophisticated or professional investors and their retail counterparts that remains embedded in the legislative framework). A point underscored by the successful civil proceedings taken against Fabrice Tourre, proceedings financed by Goldman Sachs notwithstanding the fact that it settled on similar charges. Moreover, as we have seen, structural problems in the audit process along with emasculated conceptions of responsibility to society have done much to weaken trust in the professions. In this context, the decision by the Professional Standards Commission in Australia to demand a higher standard of accountability from the audit community sends an unmistakable message that failure to act threatens not just the credibility of the professions but also the oversight mechanism itself.

As the Goldman Sachs Business Standards Committee Impact Report has revealed, the norms governing finance's conception of itself remain exceptionally powerful. To address them necessitates challenging the discourse that frame and legitimate its norms and its underpinning assumptions. In this context it is particularly striking that the Securities and Exchange Commission chose not to litigate its case against the bank to a judicially determined conclusion. The agency's timidity has been shown to be a costly mistake, a timidity that is also reflected across the Atlantic in the Parliamentary Commission on Banking Standards critique of regulatory capture. Sustainable reform necessitates fashioning a different narrative in an agonistic dialogue and partnership. As we have seen, a command and control approach to regulation without industry recognising and accepting its rationale and purpose has profound limitations. Rules are too easily transacted around. Likewise, reliance on principles without ongoing external validation and oversight is difficult to enforce. The policy question is how to render an alternative framework operational in a systematic, dynamic, and responsive way. To be successful, the alternative framework needs to balance specific economic efficiency (i.e. benefits to business) and professional rights to self-governance with explicit requirements that society should not be held responsible (or liable) for the failures of the former. At corporate, professional, and regulatory levels the framework needs to be mutually reinforcing. It needs to be capable of evaluating the calculative, social, and normative reasons for behaving in a more (or less) ethically responsible manner. It also requires reciprocal obligations from each institutional actor to maintain (and certainly not contribute through omission or commission to the erosion of) the integrity of the governance arrangements. These must articulate common understandings of what constitutes the core ethical problem. Moreover, it must generate a framework in which disputes over interpretation can and should be resolved in a manner that is proportionate, targeted, and ultimately conducive to the building of warranted trust in the operation of the financial sector. What is also apparent, however, is that those rules and procedures cannot be vouchsafed by allowing the communities of practice themselves to set what constitutes best practice and monitor effectiveness.

Tackling ethical deficiencies requires we pay much more attention to the moral dimension of market conduct, which I have argued is core rather than incidental to the disclosure paradigm. It is essential to once again stress the ethical component of corporate and professional obligation. In so doing we can rejuvenate the paradigm and provide a meaningful basis for trust. Without it we are destined to repeat past mistakes at precisely the point that society literally cannot afford to pay for them.

References

Australian Securities and Investments Commission (2012a). 'Audit Inspection Findings for 2011–2012', press release, Sydney, 4 December.

Australian Securities and Investments Commission (2012b). 'Audit Inspection Program Report for 2011–2012', Report 137, Sydney, December. <http://www.asic.gov.au/asic/pdflib.nsf/LookupByFileName/rep317-published-4-December-2012.pdf/$file/rep317-published-4-December-2012.pdf>, accessed 8 September 2013.

Australian Securities and Investments Commission (2013). 'ASIC Welcomes Audit Firm Plans to Improve Quality', press release, Sydney, 13 June.

Bane, B. (1933). 'The Securities Act of 1933', *The Certified Public Accountant*, 1: 587–92.

Coffee, J. (2006). *Gatekeepers: The Professions and Corporate Governance*. Oxford: Oxford University Press.

Department of Treasury (2011). *Wholesale and Retail Clients: The Future of Financial Advice*. Canberra: Commonwealth of Australia.

Diamond, B. (2011). 'The Radio 4 Today Business Lecture 2011', *BBC Radio 4*, 4 November, <http://news.bbc.co.uk/today/hi/today/newsid_9630000/9630673.stm>, accessed 30 March 2014.

Douglas, W. and Bates, G. (1932). 'The Federal Securities Act of 1933', *Yale Law Journal*, 43(2): 171–217.

Financial Services Authority (2011). *The Failure of the Royal Bank of Scotland*. London: Financial Services Authority.

Financial Stability Oversight Council (2013). *Annual Report*. Washington, DC: Department of Treasury.

Fligstein, N. and Dauter, L. (2007). 'The Sociology of Markets', *Annual Review of Sociology*, 33: 105–28.

Fox News (2012). 'Dimon on Price Wars, Volcker Rule, Stock Prices', 13 February, <http://video.foxbusiness.com/v/1450367194001/dimon-on-price-wars-volcker-rule-stock-prices/#sp=show-clips>, accessed 10 March 2014.

Goldman Sachs (May 2013). 'Business Standards Committee Impact Report'. New York: Goldman Sachs. <http://www.goldmansachs.com/a/pgs/bsc/files/GS-BSC-Impact-Report-May-2013.pdf>, accessed 8 September 2013.

Hood, C., Rothstein, H., and Baldwin, R. (2001). *The Government of Risk*. Oxford: Oxford University Press.

Hudson, M. (1933a). 'Memorandum for the Commission: Work at the NRA', 6 December, papers of J. M. Landis, Harvard Law School, Box 18-8.

Hudson, M. (1933b). 'Memorandum for the Federal Trade Commission', 22 December, papers of J. M. Landis, Harvard Law School, Box 18-8.

Institute of Chartered Accountants (2013). 'Proposed Professional Standards Scheme Summary Document', <http://www.psc.gov.au/agdbasev7wr/psc/documents/pdf/scheme_icaa_summary_2013.pdf>, accessed 8 September 2013.

Investment Banking Association of America (1933). 'Code of Fair Competition for Investment Bankers', papers of J. M. Landis, Harvard Law School, Box 18-8.

Kay, J. (2012). *The Kay Review of Equity Markets*. London: HM Government.

Lawton, D. (2013). 'Investor Relations in an Increasingly Regulated and International World', speech delivered at the Investors Relations Society Annual Conference, London, 18 June.

Loughrey, J. (2011). *Corporate Lawyers and Corporate Governance*. Cambridge: Cambridge University Press.

Landis, J. (1938). *The Administrative Process*. New Haven: Yale University Press.

Malley, A. (2013). 'Watchdog Out of Touch with Investors', *The Australian*, 17 April.

Medcraft, G. (2012). 'Oral Evidence to the Parliamentary Joint Committee on Corporations and Financial Services', Federal Parliament, Canberra, 3 December.

Medcraft, G. (2013). 'Opening Address', speech delivered at the ASIC Annual Forum, Sydney, 25 March.

New York Times (1937). 'Landis Retiring, Reviews SEC Acts', 10 September.

O'Brien, J. (2003). *Wall Street on Trial*. Chichester: John Wiley & Sons.

O'Brien, J. (2007). *Redesigning Financial Regulation: The Politics of Enforcement*. Chichester: John Wiley & Sons.

O'Brien, (2009). *Engineering a Financial Bloodbath*. London: Imperial College Press.

O'Brien, J. (2013a). 'The Façade of Enforcement: Goldman Sachs, Negotiated Prosecutions and the Politics of Blame', in S. Handelman, S. Will, and D. Brotherton (eds), *How They Got Away With It: White Collar Criminals and the Financial Meltdown*. New York: Columbia University Press, 178–204.

O'Brien, J. (2013b). 'Back to the Future: James M. Landis and the Rationale for Intervention in Capital Market Regulation', in J. O'Brien and G. Gilligan (eds), *Integrity, Risk and Accountability in Capital Markets: Regulating Culture*. Oxford: Hart Publishing, 41–62.

O'Brien, J. (2013c). 'Culture Wars: Rate Manipulation, Institutional Corruption and the Lost Normative Underpinnings of Market Conduct Regulation', *Seattle University Law Review*, forthcoming.

Parfit, D. (2007). *On What Matters*. Oxford: Oxford University Press.

Parliamentary Commission on Banking Standards (2013). *Changing Banking for Good*. London: HM Parliament.

Parliamentary Joint Committee on Corporations and Financial Services (2013). *Statutory Oversight of the Australian Securities and Investments Commission*. Canberra: Commonwealth of Australia.

Permanent Sub-Committee on Investigations (2013). *JPMorgan Chase Whale Trades: A Case History of Derivatives Risk and Abuses*. Washington, DC: United States Senate.

Polanyi, K. (1944). *The Great Transformation*. Boston: Beacon Press.

Pope Francis (2013). 'Address of Pope Francis to the New Non-Resident Ambassadors to the Holy See', speech delivered at Clementine Hall, The Vatican, Vatican City, 16 May.

Rakoff, J. (2013). 'Address on Judicial Activism and Regulatory Enforcement', speech delivered at Centre for Law, Markets and Regulation, UNSW Law, Sydney, 15 May.

Roosevelt, F. D. (1933). 'Inaugural Address', speech delivered at Capitol Hill, Washington, DC, 7 March.

Sants, H. (2009). 'Delivering Intensive Supervision and Credible Deterrence', speech delivered at the Reuters Newsmaker Event, London, 12 March.

Sants, H. (2010). 'Annual Lubbock Lecture in Management Studies', speech delivered at the Said Business School, 12 March.

Seligman, J. (2002). *The Transformation of Wall Street*. New York: Wolters Kluwer.

Treasury (2013). *The Government's Response to the Parliamentary Commission on Banking Standards*. Cm 8661. London: Stationary Office.

Treasury Select Committee (2012). *Fixing Libor: Some Preliminary Findings*. London: Stationary Office.

Volcker, P. (2013). 'Central Banking at a Crossroads', speech delivered at the Economic Club of New York, 29 May.

Williamson, O. (2000). 'The New Institutional Economics: Taking Stock, Looking Ahead', *Journal of Economic Literature*, 38: 595–613.

11

Systemic Harms and the Limits of Shareholder Value

*John Armour and Jeffrey N. Gordon**

11.1 Introduction

The generally accepted framework for analysing corporate law and governance implies that those running a corporation should seek to maximise the value of shareholders' claims, as measured by the stock price. We refer to this as the norm of 'shareholder value'. Its attraction is not hard to see. Under generally plausible assumptions, maximising the stock price has the very appealing consequence of also tending to enhance social welfare (Friedman 1970). As a result, the shareholder value norm has acquired an almost axiomatic status in discussions about corporate governance. For example, policy thinking about executive pay and the market for corporate control are largely premised on tying managerial welfare to the performance of the share price (Murphy 1999; Bebchuk and Fried 2004: 15–22). In keeping with this, early policy responses to the financial crisis assumed that problems arose because managers of financial firms were not sufficiently focused on shareholder value (e.g. Walker 2009: 82–7). In contrast, an emerging body of academic research suggests that the financial crisis gives us cause to reflect on whether these managers were *too* focused on the share prices of their firms (e.g. Beltratti and Stulz 2012; Erkens et al. 2012).

For share price maximisation to enhance social welfare, two key assumptions must be satisfied. The first is that the share price does in fact give the best

* We thank Dan Awrey, Rob Jackson, Reinier Kraakman, Terry Lyons, Alan Morrison, Arad Reisberg, Roberta Romano, and Nicolas Serrano-Verlarde for helpful comments and discussions in relation to this material, and Alex Imas for excellent research assistance. We are grateful for comments received following presentations of earlier versions of this work at Columbia, Frankfurt, and Oxford.

available estimate of the value of the shareholders' claims. To the extent that the stock market is not informationally efficient, it may be possible for managers to do a better job of maximising the value of the shareholders' residual claims by other means than maximising the stock price. The debate about this issue, which has been widely canvassed elsewhere (e.g. Stout 2012) does not form part of our critique.

The second assumption is that a range of mechanisms—contracts, liability rules, and regulation—act to ensure that any costs a firm's activities impose on other parties are internalised into that firm's profit function. If these do their job, there will not be significant externalities. We argue that the extent to which they fail to do so in relation to 'economic' or indirect harms has been underappreciated. The activities of certain sorts of firms—of which banks are a striking example—can cause economic losses to large numbers of parties through indirect and diffuse causal channels. This is outside the boundaries of what tort law, with its focus on direct physical harm to individual plaintiffs, is about. Turning to regulation, we observe that the shareholder value norm creates incentives for firms systematically to undermine the efficacy of regulatory internalisation mechanisms. The easiest way to maximise shareholder returns may simply be to exercise political influence to achieve a lower rate of regulatory 'tax'.

We propose an 'internal' or corporate governance solution to this problem; that is, one which affects directly the pay-offs of parties controlling the firm, as opposed to external measures designed to affect the firm's profit function. In particular, we make the case for liability rules for directors and officers of banks. Negligence liability, appropriately structured, is likely to make managers behave in a more risk-averse fashion. We argue that this is likely to be desirable in the context of firms capable of inflicting significant social losses.

The rest of this chapter is structured as follows. In section 11.2, we consider limitations in the ordinary mechanisms for control of externalities. In section 11.3, we turn to solutions, making the case for a duty of care in relation to the directors and officers of banks. Section 11.4 concludes. At the outset, we should emphasise that we are far more sure of the significance of the problem we document than we are of the efficacy of our proposed solutions, which we present primarily as a heuristic framework for debate.

11.2 Controlling Externalities

11.2.1 Externalities in the Banking Sector

Our motivation for writing this chapter lies in the recent financial crisis. Banks (and other similar financial institutions) carry on activities which have the potential to impose losses on other actors. These losses are 'systemic' in the sense that they adversely impact a wide cross-section of actors in the economic system; they are widely diffused, indirect, and very large.

The occasion for triggering such losses is bank distress. In the first instance, this is because of the possibility of contagion to other financial firms—that is, the failure of one triggers the failure of others. Many financial institutions are structurally fragile, because they rely on short-term financing to support long-term investments. For example, the basic business model of a commercial bank involves raising money from depositors and then lending it to businesses at a higher interest rate. This 'maturity transformation' means that there is a liquidity mismatch: depositors require liquidity, but the money is invested in illiquid loans (Turner 2009: 11–22). If too much liquidity is demanded by depositors, long-term assets must be liquidated in a way that is destructive of value. Of course, institutions actively manage this mismatch, but they remain vulnerable to events that trigger a sudden decline in the value of their liquid assets or a sudden increase in demand for liquidity (Freixas and Rochet 2008: 217–42).

Financial institutions are also typically highly interconnected, meaning that problems at one are transmitted to others. Most obviously, direct connections between balance sheets mean that the liabilities of one institution are assets of others that devalue if the first institution becomes financially distressed (Schwarcz 2008: 247). Contagion can also be driven by correlation in investment strategies. Fire-sale liquidation of securities by a distressed institution depresses market prices and consequently affects other institutions' balance sheets (Acharya 2009). Contagion can also occur across the liabilities side of firms' balance sheets, if short-term funders (such as depositors) infer from the failure of one financial institution that others are also likely to face difficulties (Chari and Jagannathan 1988; Gorton 1988).

Contagion to other financial institutions is particularly problematic because these firms are crucial to the functioning of the real economy. To see this, imagine an economy with just a single bank, through which all funding for business projects is channelled. If the bank suffers a shock that causes it to fail or simply reduces its liquidity, then borrowers' channel of access to credit will be impeded (Friedman and Schwartz 1971). Good business projects will go unfunded, or face premature liquidation before they have had the opportunity to generate worthwhile returns (Bernanke 1983). Banks also contribute to the payments system, the smooth operation of which is a public good for the economy at large (Independent Commission on Banking 2011).

The losses imposed by bank failure on the real economy are far larger than those suffered by bank shareholders. For example, the market capitalisation of Lehman Bros, Inc. peaked on 29 January 2007 at approximately $60 billion, and the high-water market capitalisation of the 'crisis banks', those who either failed or required special assistance in order to survive,[1] was approximately $1.2 trillion.[2] These numbers put an upper bound on the value of these firms' business activities from the perspective of their shareholders. Whilst these are large sums by any measure, the fallout from the crisis was much larger. Across the various stimulus programmes, the US suffered *net* fiscal outlays of 3.6% of GDP, or $5 trillion, in 2008 (Schildbach 2010). Moreover, despite these efforts, the US economy still contracted by 3.5% in the immediately following year 2009, down from a positive growth rate of 2.8% in 2007—a fall equivalent to approximately $9 trillion (IMF 2011: 2). By these estimates, the gross social loss approaches $14 trillion, and net of the shareholders' losses, were still nearly $13 trillion. These of course do not include costs incurred elsewhere around the world.

Why did the mechanisms ordinarily deployed to control externalities not restrict the pursuit of such strategies? We now consider each in turn.

11.2.2 Contractual Internalisation

Ronald Coase (1960) famously pointed out that in many cases, supposed 'externalities' can in fact be impounded into a firm's cashflows by contract. If the firm's activities impose costs on others, then those others have reason to seek to contract with the firm so as to give it an incentive to reduce those costs to the socially optimal level.

In the context of banks, bondholders and other creditors adjust the pricing of their loans according to the expected risk of the bank's default. This forces the bank to take into account the expected costs to creditors *ex ante*. For one class of creditor, namely depositors, this internalisation process does not operate smoothly. It is widely believed that retail depositors make systematic errors in the pricing of risk *ex ante*, leading them to 'underprice' the level of risk undertaken by a bank. As a consequence, the US like many other countries operates a system of deposit insurance, whereby individual depositors have their claims against banks insured by a regulatory agency—in the US, the Federal Deposit Insurance Corporation (FDIC). In the event of bank failure, the agency pays out to the depositors and is subrogated to the latter's claims against the bank. However, the 'premium' paid to the agency for insuring deposits often does not reflect the risk of a particular bank's default, likely

---

[1] The 'crisis banks' comprised Citigroup, AIG, Bank of America, Lehman Brothers, Bear Stearns, Merrill Lynch, Goldman Sachs, Morgan Stanley, Wachovia, and Washington Mutual: see Calomiris and Herring (2011).

[2] Stock market capitalisation data are derived from Wolfram Alpha, Yahoo! Finance, and author computations from firms' quarterly financial statements. This 'high-water' mark sums the highest market capitalisation reached by each of the crisis banks individually during the 2006–8 period. As these peaked at different points, this measure exceeds the highest aggregate capitalisation of the group and consequently tends to understate net social losses.

a result of the sort of limitations of regulatory intervention described in the preceding subsection. Thus neither retail depositors, nor the deposit insurers who fill their shoes, seem able effectively to contract with banks so that the latter internalise the costs their default would impose.

Incomplete pricing of risk by depositors or their insurers is a well-known problem. Clearly, it can give banks incentives to take on excessive levels of risk. However, it is only a small part of the larger picture. The costs of bank failure also fall upon parties who do not—and cannot—contract with the bank. Anyone who directly or indirectly relies on the payments system, or who might like in the future to obtain credit to fund investment or current consumption, will suffer a loss if the bank ceases to operate. The problem is not only the *quantity* of credit but also its *allocation*. Banks provide specialised services in assessing creditworthiness *ex ante* and in monitoring project performance *ex post*. Failure of a large bank disrupts these activities and leaves would-be borrowers without substitutes.

The desire to avoid such costs motivated governments to bail out banks in the US and Europe. In the winter of 2008–9, developed world governments made commitments to support the financial sector that peaked at 50% of GDP in the US, 70% in the UK, and averaged 40% across the EU (Bank of England 2009: 6; European Commission 2011: 2). Whilst the bailouts likely reduced the impact of bank distress on the world economy, they themselves create another well-known problem: creditor moral hazard. We have suggested that non-depositor creditors of banks are able to price in the expected costs to them of bank failure. However, the effect of bailouts is to provide *ex post* insurance to such creditors. Moreover, although creditors of large banks may be unable to foresee the particular forms of government support, they can safely predict its arrival. This reduces the borrowing costs that such banks would otherwise have to pay to engage in increased risk taking (Baker and McArthur 2009). It is by now a familiar argument that bank mergers were strongly motivated by the desire to attain 'too-big-to-fail' status to get the advantage of this funding discount (Brewer and Jagtiani 2013). Consequently, even those creditors who are in a position to cause banks to internalise part of the social costs of their risk taking will fail to do so (Stern and Feldman 2004: 23–8).

11.2.3 Tort Law

The greater the number of persons affected by the harmful activity in question, the more difficult it becomes for contracts to internalise the costs of bad outcomes. Under these circumstances, tort law is ordinarily supposed to play a role in internalising social costs by imposing liability on those whose activities have harmful externalities (Calabresi 1971).

However, tort law suffers from important limitations as a mechanism for internalising social costs. Most significantly, there is a general restriction on awarding damages for 'pure economic losses' (Bernstein 1998; Stapleton 2002). This rule, which might be more intuitively described as a restriction on liability for 'indirect' losses, imposes a bar on recovery for losses caused otherwise than as a direct result of physical damage caused to one's person or property.[3] To take the case of an oil spill: businesses whose property is physically contaminated are able to recover for business profits that are lost in direct consequence. For example, a beachfront hotel might find ingress of oil into its swimming pool, necessitating a period of closure to permit clean-up. The lost profits for this period of closure might be recoverable (to the extent they are foreseeable) as well as the direct costs of the clean-up. However, those whose property is not physically harmed are ordinarily unable to recover for lost profits. For example, a hotel operating several streets back from the beachfront, which experiences no direct contamination, nevertheless suffers a sharp fall in profits because holidaymakers avoid the area en masse having seen the oil spill on television.

Applied to the financial sector, the bar on recovery of economic loss rules out any possibility of tortious liability grounded on negligent risk management at financial firms leading to lost credit-contracting opportunities (or other losses associated with financial firm failure). There is no physical harm, only economic. Consequently, mandating higher levels of assets or unlimited shareholder liability would not force the internalisation of costs, as there would be no liability for these costs in any event. The lost contracting externalities are serious, but other remedial approaches must be pursued.

The leading rationalisation of the bar on recovery of pure economic losses is based on the extreme difficulty of calculating the net social losses of an indirect variety. To return to our previous example, the net social losses may be rather less than the extent to which the hotelier fails to earn profits otherwise expected. The hotelier might take action to mitigate his losses. Moreover, suppliers of substitute accommodation—say in another part of the country where the tourists go instead—might benefit from these circumstances. The complexity of the calculation exercise is viewed by some as justification enough for the exclusion of recovery for pure economic losses (Bishop 1982; Goldberg 1994: 14–27).

---

[3] *Cattle v Stockton Waterworks Co.* (1875) 10 QB 453, 457–8; *Robins Dry Dock & Repair Co. v Flint* 275 US 303 (1927); *Union Oil Co. v Oppen* 501 F 2d 558 (9th Cir. 1974); *Murphy v Brentwood District Council* [1991] 1 AC 398.

11.2.4 Regulation and Shareholder Value

A third well-known response to the problem of social costs, which owes its origins to the work of Arthur Pigou, posits that regulators should impose a penalty or 'tax' on an activity that generates negative externalities, such that the full social cost of its activities are imposed upon the firm (Pigou 1920: 168–71). The firm then has incentives either to reduce the level of the activity in question, or to take precautions against harm up to the extent to which they are socially cost-justified. Under such circumstances, the shareholder value norm operates virtuously. Because social costs have been factored into the firm's bottom line, then the share price will reflect residual returns *after* social costs are taken into account. Shareholder value maximisation therefore focuses managers' attention on ways of reducing the social cost of the activities in question.

More precisely, shareholder value maximisation focuses managers' attention on ways of reducing the *regulatory 'price'* the firm pays for its activities. One way of doing this is to innovate new ways of performing the activity in question that yield lower social costs. This will both reduce social costs and increase profits to shareholders, and so is clearly a desirable outcome. Innovation of this sort is commonly assumed by proponents of regulation to be one of the desirable side effects of the imposition of Pigouvian taxes. However, there is an alternative way in which shareholder value might be enhanced, which is not socially desirable.

The alternative is for the firm to exploit differences between textbook and real-world regulators, which generate what we term 'regulatory slack'. These differences comprise first the underspecification of regulatory terms, which can leave considerable space for firm-level discretionary action; second, the underenforcement of regulation because of the scarcity of regulatory resources; and third, information asymmetries between managers and regulators regarding the firm's conduct, which favour actors within the firm over the regulators. In other words, weaknesses in the implementation of real-world regulation leave gaps in the extent of the activities which are priced into the regulatory tax. A firm focused on minimising the regulatory price of its activities now has a choice: either to innovate new processes (as conventional theory implies) or to reorient its activities so that they fall more squarely within the gaps. Of course if arbitrage, rather than innovation, is pursued, then the social costs of the firm's activities will fail to be internalised.

Firms focused on minimising their regulatory costs can also seek to influence the production and enforcement of regulation so as to maximise the effective amount of slack. The constitutional framework partially determines the extent to which firms are able to exert influence of this sort—encompassing political donations, lobbying campaigns, sponsorship of directed research, revolving door employment opportunities for regulators, and aggressive legal challenges to regulatory decisions, to name but a few.

The firm's real choice when it comes to cost minimisation is therefore innovation versus influence. There are strong reasons for thinking influence is likely to dominate. If the firm invests in innovation, it will then be exposed to the risk of renegotiation or recalculation by the regulator, whereby an *ex post* increase in the level of regulatory tax will reduce the net returns to shareholders. If the firm cannot be certain *ex ante* that such renegotiation will not occur, then it will be hard to price the expected returns to investment in innovation. Investments in influencing the regulator will be much easier to price, however, because of the extent to which they are successful, they will give the firm certainty over the likely regulatory costs *ex post*. In other words, it is likely that a firm committed to minimising its regulatory costs will always want to pursue a strategy of influencing the regulator. The closer the focus on cost-minimisation, which the shareholder value norm achieves, the more intense we may expect this undermining of regulatory pricing of social cost to become.

11.2.5 Summary

The financial crisis reveals disturbing weaknesses in the mechanisms by which corporate externalities are ordinarily thought to be controlled, when confronted by losses having a systemic character. Harm that is imposed on many people is not well-contained by contract; harm that is purely economic (indirect) is not well-contained by tort. And regulatory controls are actively undermined by the shareholder value norm. The combination of activities liable to generate systemic losses with a governance model embracing the shareholder value norm is therefore particularly problematic, because none of the ordinary internalisation mechanisms can be relied upon to protect society.

11.3 A Proposed Solution: Liability for Directors and Managers

11.3.1 The Case for Liability Standards

We believe that the limitations of ordinary internalisation mechanisms in relation to economic or indirect losses support a case for modification of the internal governance arrangements of financial institutions. Two such modifications have already been widely canvassed. The first is concerned with executive pay, seeking to extend the performance criterion for variable pay over a longer time horizon. The second is concerned with board structure, and in particular the implementation of 'risk committees', independent directors tasked with monitoring and overseeing the riskiness of the firm's activities.

We do not doubt there is *potential* for improved control of systemic externalities through such measures. We are therefore generally supportive of the thrust of such reforms. However, we are sceptical about the way in which they are being implemented, through regulatory prescriptions. This approach suffers from three weaknesses. The first is its reliance on rules, the scope and content of which must be specified in advance by regulators. Given the blurriness of the boundaries of systemic externality problems, this approach looks likely to be incomplete and thereby invite regulatory arbitrage. The second weakness is a tendency to impose the same requirements on all applicable firms. This is problematic if—as is widely thought to be the case—different governance structures are appropriate for different firms. Third, as discussed in section 11.2.4, we may expect the application of regulatory measures to be systematically weakened over time through concerted lobbying by the regulated firms (Culpepper 2011: 1–24; Coffee 2012).

In contrast, we propose a solution based on personal liability for those controlling banks, which consequently places court-developed *standards* at the centre of the impetus for change in corporate governance. Such standards—in the form of fiduciary duties—are at the core of the corporate laws of common-law jurisdictions. Because compliance with these standards will be fleshed out *ex post* by courts, problems about arbitraging scope and one-size-fits-all straitjackets of content will be mitigated.

11.3.2 Potential Defendants

It is helpful to distinguish between two classes of controllers. *Executive* officers are tasked with making decisions about the running of the company. They also face very high-powered incentives derived from variable compensation packages. A large proportion of this variable compensation has come in recent years to be determined in accordance with the performance of the share price. This is an important and problematic instantiation of the shareholder value norm.

Directors, in contrast, are tasked with acting as monitors, serving to promote the interests of shareholders by overseeing the performance of the executives. Their control generally takes the form of veto rights—through board decision making on proposals initiated by executives (Fama and Jensen 1983: 303–4). Directors do not typically receive compensation linked to stock price performance; their incentives are consequently much more low-powered, driven by personal integrity and reputational concerns (Kraakman et al. 2009: 42–4). However, they face more genteel pressures of camaraderie and community between themselves and executives, which may have a subtly corrosive effect on their ability to monitor and exert oversight. Moreover, where controlling shareholders are in place, or where executives have de facto control of the directorial nomination process, then the directors will be preselected as individuals willing to toe the line in accordance with the wishes of the firm's real controller.

In contrast with some earlier proposals, we do not suggest imposing personal liability on bank shareholders per se. The drawback with this approach is that abandonment of shareholder limited liability requires the bank to actually fail in order for liability to be imposed. Yet it was precisely the systemic impact of bank failure that governments sought to avoid through bailouts. The virtue of our proposal, by contrast, is that liability can be imposed on executives and directors even if the bank does not fail, but simply suffers a significant loss.

11.3.3 Risk Taking and Fiduciary Duties

Directors and executives are *fiduciaries* for their firms (see Chapter 9 in this volume). It is trite law that a fiduciary is obliged to put his principal's welfare above his own. Yet the modern application of fiduciary doctrine has come a long way from this. In corporations, conflicts of interest are acceptable on the part of those running the company provided that appropriate procedural and substantive safeguards are met. A key procedural safeguard is the approval of an independent board, or committee of the board, whose role is to scrutinise a particular transaction in the interests of the unaffiliated shareholders.[4] The greater the conflict, the more onerous the 'job of work' the independents must perform, and the more carefully the court will scrutinise the genuineness of their independence from management. Notable examples are the role of independent committees in parent–subsidiary merger transactions,[5] or of special litigation committees in relation to derivative actions.[6]

In the case of activities liable to give rise to systemic externalities, the conflict deserves analogous treatment. This should involve subjecting the decision making regarding risk taking to *genuine* review by an independent risk committee of the board. The court should check the genuineness and efficacy of the risk committee's oversight function, in much the same way as is

---

[4] See, e.g., Companies Act 2006 (UK), ss 172, 173, 177; Delaware General Corporations Law §144.

[5] *Weinberger v UOP, Inc.* 457 A. 2d 701 (Del. 1983); *Kahn v Lynch* 638 A. 2d 1110 (Del. 1994).

[6] *Zapata Corporation v Maldonado* 430 A.2d 779 (Del. 1981); Re Oracle Corp. Derivative Litigation 824 A.2d 917 (Del. Ch. 2003). Even if the procedural safeguard has been adequately deployed, the courts may in most cases of conflict also engage in a substantive review of the terms of the transaction with a view to safeguarding its 'fairness' to the corporation: see *Weinberger, supra* note 63; *In re Southern Peru Copper Corp. Shareholder Derivative Litigation* 30 A.3d 60 (Del. Ch. 2011).

currently undertaken for special committees deployed in parent–subsidiary mergers. Under an *ex post* standard of this type, the detail of the appropriate risk oversight mechanism is not specified in advance, but rather it is left to courts to determine after the fact whether or not sufficient steps were taken to control conflicts. The lack of certainty over the appropriate steps will likely encourage controllers to err on the side of caution in ensuring the efficacy of risk management procedures. In contrast to *ex ante* regulatory prescriptions, this will reduce the possibilities for arbitrage, and will engender solutions tailored to the circumstances of particular firms.

The consequence of failure to implement such genuine and independent oversight should be a standard fiduciary remedy: disgorgement of gains made by the fiduciary. In this case, it would comprise any equity-based pay the monetary value of which was liable to be affected by conduct during the period of inadequate oversight. Disgorgement of pay only occurs if the risk control is deemed inadequate; the regime thereby creates a powerful counter-vailing incentive for controllers to take risk management seriously. As no loss need be shown, fiduciary liability may be particularly useful in circumstances where harm is probabilistic, and the proscribed conduct serves merely to increase the chances of it occurring. The plaintiff need not wait to be injured, and so the defendant can expect to be liable far more often than under a loss-based rule. This increase in the probability of enforcement will greatly increase the deterrent effect of liability (Cooter and Freedman 1991). What this means is that the probability of enforcement against *unsanitised* conflicts will be very high. The defendant therefore has a powerful incentive to ensure the establishment of an appropriate sanitisation scheme, in the form of an effective risk oversight function, as described above.

11.3.4 Risk Taking and Duties of Care

Directors are not themselves responsible for the operational decisions that trigger excessive levels of risk. Rather, their role is in high-level oversight of the firm's operations—appointing managers and setting incentive arrangements. Consequently, the relevant category of liability would most likely be for what has come to be known as 'oversight'. Here liability is imposed not for having made inappropriate decisions regarding risk taking, but rather for having delegated these decisions to others and failed to oversee their decision making.

The extent of such liability, as it exists in Delaware, the jurisdiction of incorporation for most public companies in the US, is very limited in its scope. It is framed purely in subjective terms: the board is under an obligation simply to make a 'good faith attempt' to ensure that a monitoring system is in place, only facing liability if they have 'utterly failed' to implement oversight, or have 'consciously failed' to monitor activity.[7] Second, any attempt by courts to articulate a more onerous liability standard would be thwarted by DGCL § 102(b)(7), which permits companies to exculpate directors from liability for breach of their duty of care provided they did not act in bad faith.

The obligation should instead be to oversee systems to assess potential downside consequences of the firm's business strategies and to factor these into its decision making appropriately. This would create an oversight obligation the scope of which would be independent of regulatory norms to which the firm might otherwise be subject. It would require directors to set up and oversee risk management systems. These would need to engage in quantification of exposure: that is, stress testing for worst-case scenarios. These results would then need to be made subject to execution mechanisms that factor potential costs to the firm into operational incentive systems for decision-makers capable of affecting the firm's exposure.

Divorcing the oversight obligation from regulatory norms has a powerful advantage in a world in which regulation is imperfect. It tells boards that compliance with regulatory norms is not necessarily enough to ensure freedom from potential liability. Such a duty reserves to the courts the power to assess *ex post* whether or not the risk management systems (both as regards *quantification* and *execution*) were adequate, regardless of the level of regulatory compliance. It would necessarily entail the repeal of section 102(b)(7) for banks and similar provisions for firms subject to this enhanced oversight obligation.

In order to induce appropriate deterrence, the economic analysis of law suggests that expected damages payable should in principle equal the expected social cost of activities imposing externalities (Shavell 2004). Where the defendant is risk-averse, then the effect of the payment of damages on their wealth must also be considered. If the defendant is liable for social costs should harm occur, then the expected damages $\bar{d}$ are a function of the likelihood of harm and its magnitude. A risk-averse defendant would view this expected cost as equal to $\bar{d}(1 + r)$, where r represents the level of risk aversion. This would lead such a defendant to invest $\bar{d}r$ in precaution above the socially optimal level. In other words, it would provoke overdeterrence. This could take the form of excessive precautionary oversight by risk management committees. But an even more effective precaution is simply not to engage in a particular activity at all. This feeds into the central concern of the business judgement rule, that fear of liability may induce directors to take fewer business risks. *In extremis*, the most utterly effective precaution is simply not to become a controller in the first place.

---

[7] *Stone v Ritter* 911 A. 2d 362, 370 (Del. 2006).

The problem of overdeterrence is very real if the expected damages equal the expected social loss, as standard theory directs. However, in the case of systemic externalities, recall that a key part of the problem is that indirect (or 'economic') losses defy quantification. Consequently the actual expected damages payable $\bar{d}$ will be far less than optimal expected damages representing the true social loss, which we will term $\bar{d}*$; that is, $\bar{d} < \bar{d}*$. Under such circumstances, then the risk aversion of defendant morphs from being an independent problem to a component of the solution, because the *effective* deterrent power of damages can be raised to $\bar{d}(1+r)$ (Kraakman 1984).

But if the social loss cannot be quantified, how can damages be calculated at all? As regards risk oversight duties, we are proposing that the board face liability to the company quantified in terms of *the company's* loss under circumstances where systemic risk oversight was inadequate.[8] This would comprise a subset of the true social loss. In the case of banks, it would encompass contractual liabilities. In the case of other firms carrying on hazardous activities, the losses to the firm from hazardous activities will include its tortious liabilities for the harms directly caused by the activities in question. There might also be regulatory penalties. Whilst we can be sure that on this approach the aggregate amount of liability will under-represent the social loss, the unquantifiable nature of indirect (economic) losses means we cannot precisely track the relationship between the marginal loss to the firm and the marginal social loss.

Tying these points together: personal liability for directors who are found to have taken less than reasonable care in the management of risks likely to lead to systemic harms should, we argue, face liability to their companies for the losses caused *to the company* by reason of this lack of oversight. The total liability will, where systemic externalities are involved, significantly under-represent the true social cost. Moreover, the challenges in proving that the lack of oversight *caused* the loss will also reduce the probability of liability being imposed. However, the fact that defendants are risk-averse individuals will mean that the *effective* deterrent power of such liability will be far greater than its dollar value. This will go to make up for the fact that the expected quantum of liability is much less than the true social cost.

---

[8] Liability might be imposed on managers in a variety of ways. They might be made directly liable to injured third parties, jointly and severally with the corporation. Alternatively, the managers' liability could be made indirect: the corporation being solely liable to the injured parties and the controller in turn made liable to the corporation for losses it has suffered through liability to the third parties. There should in principle be little distinction between direct and indirect versions of liability. However, direct liability would be more difficult to implement. It would require a significant restructuring both of the law regarding liability of controllers for corporate torts, and of the law of agency regarding liability of controllers for corporate contracts. Indirect liability would only require a relatively modest amendment to the liability position of those controlling a company.

Given the structure of our proposed liability regime, it would be neces-sary also to prohibit firms from insuring controllers against liability arising in connection with breach of these duties. Insurance reallocates liability risk to a party with lower risk-bearing costs, which is problematic where what is desired is to use personal liability specifically to capture the increased mar-ginal deterrence associated with risk-averse individuals (Kraakman 1984). An obvious problem, however, is that directors could acquire insurance individu-ally, and firms could increase director compensation to cover these premi-ums.[9] A mechanism that undermined the controllers' incentives to take care would defeat the liability scheme. As a condition for taking a controllers' position in the relevant set of financial firms, the parties should agree not to obtain such insurance. It would, however, be necessary to continue to permit companies to insure or indemnify directors against the *costs* of litigation—as opposed to the amount of any damages payment—in order to permit them to defend against nuisance suits.

11.3.5 Enforcement

The liability standard we have articulated has an important advantage over agency rule-making in that it allows for *ex post* determinations to be made by courts on a case-by-case basis. It also, however, has another important potential advantage: enforcement. As a general matter, the incentives of private plaintiffs to bring lawsuits are stronger than those of public enforc-ers, because the former get to keep the rewards from the litigation (Hay and Shleifer 1998). Moreover, as with the strictness of substantive regulation, the intensity of public enforcement may be expected to vary with the success or failure of the financial system, depending on the degree of political pressure exerted on agencies (Gerding 2006).

To be sure, where plaintiffs are corporate shareholders, private enforce-ment faces some particular challenges of its own. Collective action costs as between the shareholders make it difficult to coordinate the bringing of liti-gation. Potential downside costs to unsuccessful litigation—in particular, any liability for legal fees—tend to encourage free-riding behaviour, which in turn makes it less likely that suits will be filed. All of this reduces the probability of enforcement, so much so that in many legal systems, shareholder litigation is practically non-existent. For example, one of us reports in a recent empirical study that the level of shareholder litigation against directors of public com-panies in the UK is indistinguishable from zero (Armour et al. 2009).

---

[9] The US Federal Deposit Insurance Corporation (FDIC) current prohibits banks from providing D&O insurance that covers 'Civil Money Penalties' that can be assessed for violation of banking laws and regulations. See 12 CFR §359.

The US system of class action litigation manages to overcome these limitations, and then some. By permitting the aggregation of a class on an 'opt out' basis, coordination costs are greatly reduced. And offering contingency fees to class action lawyers means that individual plaintiffs have little to worry about as regards costs. The concern with US class action shareholder suits is with too much, rather than too little, litigation. In another empirical study, one of us reports that the rate of class action litigation in relation to large M&A transactions in the US is approaching 100% (Armour et al. 2012). As it is implausible that there is misconduct in relation to every transaction, this implies a lot of nuisance litigation. Clearly, if this were replicated as respects personal liability for risk oversight, it would be enormously problematic. However, the absence of insurance for director defendants will we believe make 'strike suits' far less likely. The presence of insurance means that plaintiffs are assured of being able to receive a payout from a defendant, at least up to the limit of insurance cover. Moreover, it creates a perverse dynamic towards settlement. Plaintiffs allege fraudulent conduct, which would not be covered by insurance; defendants offer to settle provided allegations of fraud are dropped, and the insurer picks up the tab (Baker and Griffith 2010). This incentive is particularly pronounced in the case of a corporate transaction for which the absence of material litigation related to the deal is a condition of closing. What is more, the expectation of this dynamic surely acts as a stimulus to plaintiff attorneys to file suit. The *absence* of insurance for payments of damages would reverse the incentive to settle; the value to the plaintiffs of a lawsuit would depend on the merits of the case.

11.4 Conclusion

For the shareholder value norm to enhance social welfare, the social costs of the firm's activities must be internalised into its profit function. We have argued that the extent to which they fail to do so in relation to 'economic' or indirect harms has been underappreciated. The case of banks is a stark illustration. Their activities can cause economic losses to large numbers of parties through indirect and diffuse causal channels. This is outside the boundaries of what tort law, with its focus on direct physical harm to individual plaintiffs, is about. Turning to regulation, we observe that the shareholder value norm creates incentives for firms systematically to undermine the efficacy of regulatory internalisation mechanisms.

We have proposed an 'internal' or corporate governance solution to this problem; that is, one which affects directly the pay-offs of parties controlling the firm, as opposed to external measures designed to affect the firm's profit function. In particular, we make the case for liability rules for directors and officers of banks. Negligence liability, appropriately structured, is likely to make managers behave in a more risk-averse fashion. This is desirable in the context of firms—such as banks—capable of inflicting significant social losses.

References

Acharya, V. (2009). 'A Theory of Systemic Risk and Design of Prudential Banking Regulation', *Journal of Financial Stability*, 5: 224–55.

Armour, J. et al. (2009). 'Private Enforcement of Corporate Law: An Empirical Comparison of the UK and US', *Journal of Empirical Legal Studies*, 6: 687–722.

Armour, J., Black, B., and Cheffins, B. R. (2012). 'Is Delaware Losing its Cases?', *Journal of Empirical Legal Studies*, 9: 605–56.

Baker, D. and McArthur, T. (2009). 'The Value of the "Too Big to Fail" Big Bank Subsidy', *CEPR Issue Brief*, September 2009.

Baker, T. and Griffith, S. J. (2010). *Ensuring Corporate Misconduct*. Chicago, IL: University of Chicago Press.

Bank of England (2009). *Financial Stability Report Number 26*. London: Bank of England.

Bebchuk, L. and Fried, J. (2004). *Pay Without Performance: The Unfulfilled Promise of Executive Compensation*. Cambridge, MA: Harvard University Press.

Beltratti, A. and Stulz, R. (2012). 'The Credit Crisis Around the Globe: Why Did Some Banks Perform Better?', *Journal of Financial Economics*, 105: 1–17.

Bernanke, B. S. (1983). 'Nonmonetary Effects of the Financial Crisis in the Propagation of the Great Depression', *American Economic Review*, 73: 257–76.

Bernstein, H. (1998). 'Civil Liability for Pure Economic Loss Under American Tort Law', *American Journal of Comparative Law Supplement*, 46: 111–31.

Bishop, W. (1982). 'Economic Loss in Tort', *Oxford Journal of Legal Studies*, 2: 1–29.

Black, B. and Cheffins, B. (2012). 'Is Delaware Losing its Cases?', *Journal of Empirical Legal Studies*, 9(4): 605–56.

Brewer, E. and Jagtiani, J. (2013). 'How Much Did Banks Pay to Become Too-Big-To-Fail and to Become Systemically Important?', *Journal of Financial Services Research*, 43: 1–35.

Calabresi, G. (1971). *The Costs of Accidents*. New Haven, CT: Yale University Press.

Calomiris, C. W. and Herring, R. J. (2011). 'How to Design a Contingent Convertible Debt Requirement', working paper, Columbia Business School, New York.

Chari, V. V. and Jagannathan, R. (1988). 'Banking Panics, Information, and Rational Expectations Equilibrium', *Journal of Finance*, 43: 749–61.

Coase, R. H. (1960). 'The Problem of Social Cost', *Journal of Law and Economics*, 3: 1–44.

Coffee, J. C. (2012). 'The Political Economy of Dodd-Frank: Why Financial Reform Tends to be Frustrated and Systemic Risk Perpetuated', *Cornell Law Review*, 97: 1019–82.

Cooter, R. D. and Freedman, B. J. (1991). 'The Fiduciary Relationship: Its Economic Character and Legal Consequences', *New York University Law Review*, 66: 1045–75.

Culpepper, P. D. (2011). *Quiet Politics and Business Power*. Cambridge: Cambridge University Press.

Erkens, D. H., Hing, M., and Matos, P. (2012). 'Corporate Governance in the 2007–2008 Financial Crisis: Evidence from Financial Institutions Worldwide', *Journal of Corporate Finance*, 18: 389–411.

European Commission (2011). *Executive Summary of the Impact Assessment Accompanying Proposal for a Council Directive on a Common System of Financial Transaction Tax and Amending Directive 2008/7/EC, SEC(2011) 1103 final*. Brussels: European Commission.

Fama, E. F. and Jensen, M. C. (1983). 'Separation of Ownership and Control', *Journal of Law and Economics*, 26: 301–25.

Freixas, X. and Rochet, J.-C. (2008). *Microeconomics of Banking*. Cambridge, MA: MIT Press.

Friedman, M. (1970). 'The Social Responsibility of Business Is to Increase its Profits', *New York Times Magazine*, 13 September.

Friedman, M. and Schwartz, A. J. (1971). *A Monetary History of the United States, 1867–1960*, Princeton: Princeton University Press.

Gerding, E. F. (2006). 'The Next Epidemic: Bubbles and the Growth and Decay of Securities Regulation', *Connecticut Law Review*, 38: 393–453.

Goldberg, V. P. (1994). 'Recovery for Economic Loss Following the *Exxon Valdez* Oil Spill', *Journal of Legal Studies*, 23: 1–39.

Gorton, G. (1988). 'Banking Panics and Business Cycles', *Oxford Economic Papers*, 40: 751–81.

Hay, J. R. and Shleifer, A. (1998). 'Private Enforcement of Public Laws: A Theory of Legal Reform', *American Economic Review*, 88: 398–403.

Independent Commission on Banking (2011). *Final Report*. London: Independent Commission on Banking.

IMF (2011). *World Economic Outlook September 2011*. Washington, DC: International Monetary Fund.

Kraakman, R. (1984). 'Corporate Liability Strategies and the Costs of Legal Controls', *Yale Law Journal*, 93: 857–98.

Kraakman. R., Armour, J., Davies, P., Enriques, L., Hansmann, H., Hertig, G., Hopt, K., Kanda, H., and Rock, E. (2009). *The Anatomy of Corporate Law*, 2nd edition. Oxford: Oxford University Press.

Murphy, K. (1999). 'Executive Compensation', in O. C. Ashenfelter and D. Card (eds), *Handbook of Labor Economics*, Vol 3. New York: North Holland, 2485–563.

Pigou, A. C. (1920). *The Economics of Welfare*. London: Macmillan.

Schildbach, J. (2010). 'Direct Cost of the Financial Crisis', *Deutsche Bank Research*, 14 (May), <http://www.dbresearch.com/PROD/DBR_INTERNET_EN-PROD/PROD0000000000257663.PDF>, accessed 30 March 2014.

Schwartz, A. J. (1971). *The Great Contraction 1929–1933*. Princeton, NJ: Princeton University Press.

Schwarcz, S. L. (2008). 'Systemic Risk', *Georgetown Law Journal*, 97: 193–249.

Shavell, S. (2004). *Foundations of Economic Analysis of Law*. Cambridge, MA: Belknap Press.

Stapleton, J. (2002). 'Comparative Economic Loss: Lessons from Case-Law-Focused "Middle Theory"', *UCLA Law Review*, 50: 531–83.

Stern, G. H. and Feldman, R. J. (2004). *Too Big to Fail: The Hazards of Bank Bailouts*. Washington, DC: Brookings Institute.

Stout, L. (2012). *The Shareholder Value Myth*. San Francisco, CA: Berrett-Koehler.

Turner, A. (2009). *The Turner Review: A Regulatory Response to the Global Banking Crisis*. London: Financial Services Authority.

Walker, D. (2009). *A Review of Corporate Governance in UK Banks and Other Financial Industry Entities*. London: HM Treasury.

Part IV
Crafting the Remedies

12

Ethics Management in Banking and Finance

Boudewijn de Bruin

In the wake of the global financial crisis, the financial services industry has attracted caustic criticism for its lack of ethics. Assets have been mismanaged, customers misled, governments misused, risks miscalculated, and rating agencies misinformed. Do banks and bankers not know what they ought to do, morally speaking? Do finance firms not know the ethical risks of their operations? Do they not see what their clients and society expect from them? The Edelman Trust Barometer seems to provide an answer to this question: finance is the most distrusted industry worldwide (Edelman 2014).

While the public's distrust of bankers is explicable, it is, I believe, based on exaggerated and often ill-informed views. This is not to say, however, that banks should not do their utmost to improve their morals. This chapter surveys a number of practical tools and techniques that banks could use to boost ethics management. The chapter floats a new form of stakeholder engagement based on deliberative democracy, gives an example of a trust-centred ethics training programme developed with a finance firm in the Netherlands, and critically evaluates the idea of a professional code of ethics for bankers.

Concentrating on communication among management and employees (communication inside the firm) and communication with other stakeholders (communication outside the firm), this chapter helps the professionals in the financial services industry to ensure that they know what they ought to do, what the ethical risks of their operations are, and what clients and society expect from them.

I first discuss communication with external stakeholders (clients, governments, NGOs, etc.) and suggest that the financial services industry would benefit from using a tool that is gaining popularity in political decision making: deliberative polls. I then turn to ways in which financial firms can communicate with their employees and give an example of an ethics training programme inspired by O'Neill's views of trust, which were discussed in Chapter 8. Finally, I consider codes of ethics, arguing that while several codes may have relevance in finance and banking, pleas for a professional code for bankers are based on conceptual and empirical misunderstandings, and should not be heeded.

12.1 Theoretical Preliminaries

The theoretical underpinnings of the ethics management techniques dealt with here include a theory of ethical decision making (Rest 1986) and a theory of moral intensity (Jones 1991). Rest (1986) distinguished four stages of ethical decision making. Agents first have to *recognise* the decision situation as one that involves a moral issue; they have to see, that is, that their actions may influence other people positively or negatively. Second, they have to form an ethical *judgement* concerning what ought to be done, which requires them to analyse the situation from a moral viewpoint. Third, they have to establish the moral *intention* to act in conformity with what they judged, in the previous stage, to be the right kind of behaviour. And finally, they have to actually engage in that *behaviour*.

Unethical behaviour may result from failures at any of the four stages. Agents may fail to recognise, judge, intend, or behave. Whether they succeed or fail depends on such things as weakness of will, knowledge or ignorance, feelings of control and responsibility, and many other factors. For the purposes of this chapter, however, the most relevant factor is what Jones (1991) calls the *moral intensity* of the issue at stake. An issue's moral intensity depends on the *magnitude* of the consequences of the actions, the *probability* of the consequences, as well as on whether the consequences are *concentrated* on a group of people or rather dispersed among them. Moral intensity, moreover, depends on whether there is any *social consensus* about the fact that particular actions are good or evil, and on whether the consequences and/or people affected by the actions are socially, culturally, psychologically, physically, and temporally close to the agent (*temporal immediacy* and *proximity*). Roughly speaking, when evil consequences are likely or severe, affect people in close proximity, or involve a large number of people, and when the agent rightly or wrongly perceives this to be the case—then the issue's moral intensity is high.

The moral intensity of an issue determines how agents proceed at each of the four stages (Jones 1991). Issues with high moral intensity are more frequently recognised as moral issues; they will lead to more sophisticated forms of moral judgement; and they will more often trigger agents to form moral intentions, and engage in ethical behaviour. This is relevant to ethics management in banking because—unlike the oil industry, the pharmaceutical industry, the nuclear industry, and several other industries—the banking sector's main ethical issues often involve such high levels of detailed technical understanding that their moral intensity is likely to be perceived as rather low. Empirical studies of moral intensity in banking are, to my knowledge, entirely absent, so we should tread carefully here; but the hypothesis has much to recommend it. The consequences of investment decisions are often remote, and they are dispersed over many people. Probability estimates are typically hard to make. Moreover, the technical character of the issues means that consensus is often absent: witness discussions about food speculation, overdraft fees, or bank account number portability.

If ethical issues in finance have limited moral intensity in comparison to other industries, then more often than employees in other industries, bankers will fail to recognise an ethical issue, form a judgement, adopt a moral intention, or engage in ethical behaviour. The primary task of adequate ethics management in banking is, then, to develop tools that help management and employees to recognise, judge, intend, and behave.

A second topic I should briefly introduce here is the distinction between norms and values. I am indebted to Ogien's (1996) excellent introduction. It is fruitful to start by making a logical or linguistic distinction between various statements (Wiggins 1987). One sort of statement is *descriptive*; it aims at representing the world as it is or as it appears to the speaker. The hackneyed example is: 'There is a cat on the mat'. Second, there are *prescriptive* statements which express obligations, prohibitions, or permissions. 'You are allowed to work overtime', 'You must not stop here', and 'You ought to help your friend' are examples. The third type of statement is *evaluative*, communicating the speaker's appraisal of a particular thing or event. 'The wine is excellent', 'The painting is beautiful', 'The presidential candidate is courageous' are examples.

Descriptive statements feature frequently in business ethics research, but only to the extent that it attempts to contribute to economic, sociological, or psychological theories of human behaviour. Prescriptive and evaluative statements are, by contrast, the core business of ethics. The distinction is perhaps less clear-cut than I suggest here, since evaluating a person as 'courageous' also contains a descriptive element. To accommodate that insight, Williams (1985) introduced the distinction between *thick* evaluative concepts that are partly descriptive, and *thin* evaluative concepts that are purely evaluative. Beautiful, good, right, true, then, are thin evaluative concepts. Courageous, competent, honest, harmonious, synchronous are thick evaluative concepts.

Making these distinctions explicit is not merely of academic interest; it also allows us to see more clearly what tools ethics management uses to accomplish its aims. In some cases, too, the distinctions will even help us better formulate these aims. While the philosophical vocabulary is hardly used on the work floor, employees do use them implicitly when speaking about ethics. They use prescriptive and evaluative statements, and when they evaluate things, they may give thick or thin evaluations.

But the theoretical vocabulary they may use to describe conversations about ethics is rather that of norms and values, or that of rules (standards, laws) and principles. It is plausible to claim that prescriptive statements express norms, and evaluative statements express values. A *norm* or a standard is something to which you have to conform, just as you have to conform to obligations, prohibitions, and permissions. A *value* is something that you can ascribe to something or someone, just as an evaluative statement expresses your appraisal of something or someone.

It is also plausible to claim that rules and laws are a particular kind of norm. The rule or law not to use lead in pencils marketed to children is a norm. The word *principle*, however, refers to norms and values. What some companies call their *business principles* are norms when they contain prescriptions of behaviour. Many business principles, though, are readily seen as expressions of the values the business embraces. Goldman Sachs, for instance, emphasises such values as creativity, imagination, honesty, and integrity in its principles.

But does not advocating the principle of honesty amount to postulating the norm 'to be honest'? The exact relation between norms and values is a topic of vehement academic debate. It is often thought that values are subjective and norms objective; that values refer to ideal worlds only, while norms are valid in real circumstances; that values have to do with creating freedom, and norms with erecting obstacles; or that values may be contradictory, and norms always mutually consistent. These conceptions, though, needlessly confuse employees engaged in business ethics management. A more useful way of looking at norms and values, I believe, sees values as inspiring individual and corporate goals and norms as devices helping us to reach these goals (Parsons 1951). In an insurance company, for instance, the value of creativity may serve to define the goal of developing a new insurance policy, and the value of honesty may define the goal of improving customer relations. The value of honesty, that is, entails a number of different norms laying down what embracing the value of honesty requires within a particular profession.

For a value to be 'transformed' into concrete goals, it had better be a thick concept. It is far more informative to strive for creativity, for instance, than for goodness. Effective ethics management, therefore, exploits thick evaluative concepts. Thick evaluative concepts not only evaluate particular behaviour or particular character traits as morally desirable (or as expected by management); they also describe the behaviour or character trait, at least to some extent.

Conceptually, ethics management should start with values, because values inspire norms; but it is also a practical matter, because taking values as a point of departure for ethics in your business compels you to think at a rather fundamental level about what it is you want to accomplish, for whom you are working, and so on. But ethics management should not cease after a discussion of values. It is one thing to declare honesty one of the core values of your organisation; as long as employees do not know what this means for their day-to-day professional lives, the value of honesty will not inform their decision making. This is where norms come into play. If honesty is a value, does it mean that we have to inform our competitors about what goes on in our R&D department if they ask us? Probably not. Values, then, should be translated into norms that are sensitive to the precise environment in which one works.

Ragatz and Duska's (2010) analysis of financial codes of ethics provides an excellent illustration of how values inspire norms. They examined the codes of ethics of actuaries, chartered accountants, financial analysts, and financial advisors, and found that these codes are built on seven core principles or values: integrity, objectivity, competence, fairness, confidentiality, professionalism, and diligence. These values are translated, then, into concrete norms of practice. The Standards of Professional Conduct for Chartered Financial Analysts, for instance, contains the norm that '[m]embers...must not offer, solicit, or accept any gift, benefit, compensation, or consideration that reasonably could be expected to compromise their own or another's independence and objectivity' (Ragatz and Duska 2010: 316).

What I have said so far could be summarised in the following slogans: values are abstract, norms are concrete; values come first, norms follow from values; values without norms are powerless, norms without values are meaningless.

12.2 Stakeholder Engagement

Passed in 2002 by the US Congress in the wake of the Enron accounting scandal and others, the Sarbanes-Oxley law required all publicly traded companies in the US to adopt ethics management involving codes of ethics, whistle-blower regulations, ethics officers and ethics training programmes, with many other policies. To a lesser degree, similar legal requirements have been put in place in the UK and other European countries. These initiatives largely concern stakeholder communication. Companies have attempted to improve their interaction and communication with stakeholders by means of social, ethical, or sustainability reporting, as well as by stakeholder dialogues, reaching out to their shareholders, customers, suppliers, governments, and NGOs. Numerous firms have set in motion a process of culture and leadership change, all with the explicit aim of improving ethical decision making in the corporate world. They have also used ethics training programmes and codes of ethics to communicate their business principles to stakeholders within the firm, in particular their shareholders, management, and employees. I begin this survey of ethics management techniques with communication inside the firm, involving such things as a company's mission statement, ethics hotlines, ethics risk management, and ethics committees. I then turn to communication outside the firm, centred round the concept of *stakeholder engagement*.

An obvious starting point of ethics management is a firm's *mission statement*, which encapsulates its key objectives and corporate beliefs and values. The Markets and International Banking division of the Royal Bank of Scotland's mission, for instance, is to 'provide world-class financing, risk management, transaction services and liquidity to financial institutions, corporates, sovereigns and public sector clients [and to] help them access markets around the globe and seize the opportunities that the future will bring, so they can build their tomorrows'. A frequently heard complaint about mission statements is that without additional ethics management they remain cheap talk, and toothless. How much 'help' is the Royal Bank of Scotland willing to provide to clients who are attempting to 'seize opportunities'? Unless the duties that a firm imposes on management and employees are translated into concrete recommendations or obligations, mission statements are too vague to guide behaviour. Codes of ethics are often seen as the second step in a firm's communication of values and beliefs to employees and other stakeholders. I deal with them separately below because of their perceived importance, and also to caution against an overly optimistic view of their effectiveness.

Ethics management need not resort to codes only, though. In many countries, it includes *ethics hotlines* and related programmes that enable employees to inform a firm's management about ethical transgressions, most often anonymously. J.P. Morgan Chase, for instance, has a Code Reporting Hotline operated by an independent organisation which is staffed 24/7 to receive anonymous reports of alleged ethics violations. The kind of reporting programme depends on the jurisdiction in which it operates, however, and while Webley and Le Jeune (2005) found that around half of all large UK firms have adopted reporting policies, ethics hotlines suffer from privacy issues in other European countries, making them less common on the Continent.

Another form of ethics management is the *risk management* of *ethical misconduct disasters* (Brewer et al. 2006). Such forms of risk management, Crane and Matten (2010) observe in their excellent review of ethics management techniques, tend to emphasise 'easily identifiable legal risks and more quantifiable ethical risks', and if their diagnosis is correct, O'Neill's observations in Chapter 8 suggest that ethical risk management may encourage management to adopt a 'box-ticking' approach to ethics and accountability. Quantification is likely to require the setting of proxies for genuine ethical performance, which will lead to perverse incentives with undesired and often unforeseen outcomes rather than the desired ethical behaviour.

A final ethics management solution is the appointment of an *ethics manager, ethics officer*, and *ethics committee*, whose task it is to provide recommendations about business ethics and corporate social responsibility. ING Group, the Dutch bank and insurance company, has a sustainability and business ethics department that reports directly to the board. Many firms, however, outsource such activities to *ethics consultants*, who often work for branches of accounting firms such as KPMG Ethics and Integrity Consulting, or specialist players such as AccountAbility and Two Tomorrows.

These are internal forms of communication, directed at the firm's management and employees. Their explicit aim is to spread knowledge about what is morally expected of management and employees, and to gain knowledge about areas where these expectations are not met. In order to do the right thing, however, businesses have to gain knowledge *about* their stakeholders, too—that is, about the harms and benefits of the firm's operations to people affected by them. Banks can use a variety of techniques to engage with stakeholders, including *consultation, dialogue*, and *partnership programmes*. In some cases, stakeholder engagement involves one firm only. For instance, ABN AMRO, a large Dutch bank, organises such events especially to discuss decisions that will inevitably harm the interests of particular stakeholders (Jeucken 2004). But firms also set up and participate in wider dialogues, as when HSBC founded the Malaysian Forest Dialogue with, among others, the World Wildlife Fund. It is difficult, however, to gauge the prominence of stakeholder consultation in banking because data are scarce.

A significant challenge to adequate stakeholder engagement is the threat that a gap may open between those stakeholders that the firm is *normatively* obliged to acknowledge, and stakeholders that are actually approached in dialogue, consultation, or partnership. Not all issues have equal moral intensity. Not all voices are listened to equally. One explanation for this may be found in an influential study by Mitchell et al. (1997), who showed that the likelihood that the interests of a particular stakeholder are incorporated in a firm's decision making depends on the stakeholder's perceived *power, legitimacy*, and *urgency*; that is, managers favour stakeholders with a greater influence on policymaking, whose actions and goals are seen as socially legitimate, and whose concerns are seen as pressing and requiring immediate attention.

As mentioned above, the moral intensity of issues in finance can be expected to be relatively low, and this transfers to the perceived power, legitimacy, and urgency of stakeholders. While, in the wake of the global financial crisis, the financial services industry may have started to pay attention to its stakeholders, banks have so far been operating in an environment that is relatively isolated from their stakeholders; they are hardly ever haunted by pressure groups, consumer boycotts, and other exercises of stakeholder power that the chemical or oil industry, for instance, have encountered in the second half of the twentieth century. The Occupy Wall Street movement is only a very recent invention. The risk is that ethical issues involving weaker stakeholders—small and medium-sized enterprises, financially illiterate consumers, microcredit borrowers, governments in the developing world, employees in the 'softer' divisions of the bank, to name only a few—will be perceived as having lower moral intensity.

The relative novelty of stakeholder engagement in the financial industry may, on the other hand, be a blessing in disguise. A bank that is genuinely willing to communicate with all its stakeholders can benefit from some fifty years of experience in other industries. Studies by Elkington and Fennell (2000), Hartman and Stafford (1997), and Selsky and Parker (2005) document that even though stakeholder engagement started out as relatively antagonistic, many firms and stakeholders have gone beyond mere challenge and opposition: today a great number of more cooperative formats of engagement are available. Firm and stakeholder may see each other as sparring partners. There may be one-way or two-way support in the form of corporate charity or sponsorship. Partners may endorse each other by public approval of particular products or services, which may take the form of labelling and accreditation schemes. A recent example from the financial services industry is the global partnership agreement between Rabobank, the Dutch bank, and the World Wildlife Fund to combat climate change. The Dutch Greentech Fund, which invests in Dutch start-up firms that produce innovative sustainability technology, is a product of this agreement.

Partners may also engage in dialogues about particular products or services. A bank may, for instance, consult mortgage brokers, real estate agents, homeowners, prospective buyers, and other partners during the design of a new type of mortgage, or could set up a task force to that end. Similar dialogues with relevant stakeholders may involve strategies rather than products. An insurance company, for instance, may discuss its role and long-term strategies in countering waste of resources in healthcare with patients, doctors, hospital management, government representatives, investigative journalists, and healthcare experts.

Even though these models of stakeholder engagement have much to recommend them to the financial services industry, care has to be taken to steer clear of a number of obstacles that have been studied by academics in recent decades. To begin with, stakeholder engagement is often very *costly* compared to other forms of decision making, and the process may be rather *uncontrollable*, with no guarantee of success. Stakeholders have to be selected carefully to obtain a representative sample; their expenses have to be covered; dialogues have to be led by trained monitors; and, last but not least, in dialogues about product development or strategy, there is an ever-present danger of competitors gaining intelligence. Added to this is the danger that the outcome of stakeholder engagement is hard to predict, ranging from mutually beneficial product design to outright opposition and reputational damage.

Second, a casual glance at the news media illustrates how a dialogue between a bank's management and their frustrated clients can lead to a clash of cultures, expertise, and expectations (Crane 1998). Banks cannot expect clients to understand even the simplest concepts in finance, such as maturity transformation or risk reduction. An FSA study has shown that a significant group of UK citizens have difficulty understanding financial capability (Atkinson and Messy 2012). The film *It's A Wonderful Life* gives a nice illustration. George Bailey (played by James Stewart), representing a plagued bank, is questioned by depositors of the local building and loan association about why he cannot pay their deposits. He has to explain to them that the money in not in the safe, but is invested 'in their neighbours' houses'. Since the Swedish started perfecting the fractional reserve model secretly trialled at the Amsterdam Bank of Exchange in the seventeenth century, a bank vault contains much less of value than most people think.

A third issue could be called *schizophrenia* (Crane and Livesey 2003; Elkington and Fennell 2000). Stakeholders may cooperate in one project, but act very antagonistically in another. This will be typical in banking more than in many other businesses. Banks serve many very different types of clients, often embodied in one and the same person. A person figuring as a stakeholder representing clients from the investment or consultancy branch of a bank may at the same time be the owner of a small company facing tremendous difficulties in obtaining bank finance.

There is an almost opposite phenomenon, in that stakeholder groups are also sometimes accused of *co-optation*. Nader (2000) famously accused Nike and other companies of misusing the UN Global Compact to 'bluewash' their image (blue for the colour of the UN flag). He noted that this not only obscures the fact that such companies score less on human rights and the environment than they claim; even worse, he claimed, it weakens the ability of the UN as an independent critic of business. Relatedly, stakeholder groups are sometimes said to engage in dubious practices of accountability and decision making, with Greenpeace's apparent inability to deal with dissenting voices in the Brent Spar case being a tragic example (Bendell 2000). A similar risk arises when stakeholder engagement involves a form of one-way or two-way support only (a firm supports a specific stakeholder, or firm and stakeholder provide mutual support), as this can easily be seen as preferring one stakeholder over another.

Moreover, firms tend to engage with *representatives* of stakeholder organisations only, rather than with the individual stakeholders themselves. This is witnessed by many CSR (Corporate Social Responsibility) webpages containing logo after logo of environmental, patient, or worker *groups*.

This is unfortunate because many of the difficulties described above can be mitigated by the firm directing its efforts at randomly selected, individual stakeholders. A more advanced form of stakeholder consultation might indeed be developed by learning from experiences with democratic engagement and civic participation obtained by advocates of deliberative democracy. *Deliberative democracy* is a conception of democracy according to which the legitimacy of political decision making depends in part on whether citizens are able to participate in political deliberation (Dryzek 2000). It does not just aggregate individual views into a collective view (the ordinary conception of voting), but also emphasises the need to pay due attention to the ways in which individuals adopt and revise their values and beliefs in the face of information. Advocates of deliberative democracy promote dynamic decision procedures in which citizens are confronted with the views of other citizens, obtain information from experts and other sources, and thereby gain a deeper understanding of the issues at stake. Authors such as Habermas (2006) claim that it leads to an increase in the amount and quality of the information on which decisions are based, and this is supported by research on small-scale 'minipublic' deliberation (Fung 2003). Moreover, deliberative procedures have gained in popularity in many constituencies and jurisdictions, ranging from assemblies reviewing the local authority's budget to European politics.

In particular, a tool that has much to offer to stakeholder engagement is *Deliberative Polling®*, originated by Fishkin (1988). While deliberative polls have mainly been used in political decision making, they are equally suited to stakeholder engagement (Fishkin and Luskin 2011). A deliberative poll would bring together a random sample of stakeholders set to work on a particular ethical issue on which the bank would like to obtain stakeholder feedback. The opinions of the stakeholders are polled before and after the deliberation, while between the two polling moments they discuss the issue among themselves in a monitored setting, consulting and challenging experts, both representatives of the bank and relevant stakeholder groups.

A crucial advantage of a deliberative poll over traditional polls is that the post-deliberation poll is based on the stakeholders' *informed* opinions. If the issue at stake is, for instance, bank lending to small and medium-sized enterprises, stakeholders may learn about relevant regulatory regimes, about capital requirements making it more difficult for banks to meet demands for credit, or about the frustration felt by start-up companies unable to obtain finance; and their post-deliberation vote will incorporate what they have learned. If the majority view that emerges from the post-deliberation poll is used as a basis for a collective decision, this is an informed decision—or at least more informed than a traditional poll would provide.

Another feature that distinguishes deliberative polls from the formation of aggregated collective views on the basis of ordinary majority voting and opinion polling is that individuals who have participated in deliberative polls frequently describe the experience as very worthwhile. They see the deliberative poll as giving them a greater understanding of the issues and of the reasons that other participants have for their views, and this helps them identify with the ultimate post-deliberation majority view, even if that view does not coincide with their own post-deliberation vote.

Deliberative polls, I believe, have the potential to avoid giving too much weight to stakeholders with great perceived power, legitimacy, or urgency. Deliberative polls involve a random sample of stakeholders rather than a group of stakeholder representatives. They provide ample room for debate about the legitimacy and urgency of the stakeholders' concerns. The fact that they are strictly monitored using a protocol carefully designed by Fishkin, Luskin, and other researchers from the Center for Deliberative Democracy at Stanford University, moreover, ensures that stakeholders participate on an equal footing and that the process remains manageable. The most successful deliberative polls are used by parties who commit themselves to adopt a particular course of action or policy, depending on the outcome of the poll. In Groningen, the Netherlands, where we organised such a poll, the municipal authorities made it clear to the participants that if the majority of the post-deliberation votes were to favour a particular policy, the policy would indeed be implemented. Moreover, during a deliberative poll, perceptions of moral intensity may change as proximity increases and judgements of probability become more precise.

12.3 Ethics Training Programmes

The ethics management strategies discussed so far mainly involve communication with stakeholders outside the bank. In the last two sections we turn our eyes inwards and look at the two most important ways by which banks can communicate to and implement ethics among management and employees: ethics training programmes and codes of ethics. *Ethics training programmes* are gaining prominence in the US and in Europe. Corporations show significant willingness to innovate here. To give a well-known example, Novartis, the healthcare multinational, developed a 3D online ethics training programme to guide employees through the code of ethics in playful ways (Edwards 2009). Such programmes typically aim at helping participants to identify situations of ethical decision making, to learn about the company's values, and to gauge the influence of their decisions on the corporation and its stakeholders (Kirrane 1990).

Ethics training programmes are directed either at the organisation as a whole or its individual members. In common with any programme of communication and training, how one communicates and trains has to depend on the needs of the particular audience. Research on ethics training programmes provides evidence to the effect that they have to be sufficiently narrow in scope. A programme that aims to span the entire banking sector is doomed to fail as it does not distinguish between the different needs of, say, a loan officer, an analyst, or the desk employee of a local bank. One can learn from Dutch experiences here, and recommend the development of bespoke programmes rather than the one-size-fits-all approach that was implemented in the wake of the 2010 Dutch Banking Code, which seems to have been rather unsuccessful. Needs are different because people face different ethical challenges, have different levels of knowledge, work with different stakeholders, and have different degrees of influence within the organisation.

In an influential survey of ethics training programmes, Treviño et al. (1999) draw the following useful distinction between four kinds of ethics training programmes. The first approach is directed at ensuring *compliance* with the relevant legal requirements. Related are programmes with a *protective* orientation, which are adopted to protect the organisation itself against legal repercussions of corporate ethical misconduct on the (often justified) assumption that lower fines will result when courts acknowledge that a firm has gone through some form of ethics training. A more deeply ethical approach centres on the *internal values* that define the organisation, as well as on the idea that its members should be inspired by the moral ideal of self-governance. Furthermore, programmes with an orientation toward *external values* attempt to raise awareness of the values of stakeholders external to the firm.

Which approach should be recommended to finance? At first sight it may appear that an approach directed at legal compliance and protection would be hugely inferior to an approach based on internal and external values. Treviño et al. (1999) do indeed conclude from a survey of over 10,000 employees that ethics training programmes inspired by internal values are the most promising route to ethical improvement. But there is reason for caution here. To the extent that relations in banking are contractual, the importance of legal compliance is perhaps greater than in medicine, say, or accountancy. Many scandals in the financial services industry involve a lack of compliance in the first place, and a lack of morals in the second. Financial crimes such as insider trading are often seen to be wrong, not so much because they are immoral (as murder or deception would be), but mostly because they are illegal. And if it is the case that fiduciary duties become less important—another development which one may rightly lament: witness Getzler's diagnosis in Chapter 9—and where plain contractual and legal terms increasingly define the relationship, the importance of compliance in ethics training programmes should not be underestimated.

But how effective can such training be? A recent meta-analysis cautions us against being too optimistic. This study suggests that such programmes are 'at best minimally effective in enhancing ethics among students and business people' (Waples et al. 2009: 146). This does not mean that ethics training programmes are hopeless, the authors claim, but what they do show is that an important determinant of the instruction's success is the way it is organised.

First, it matters what *educational goals* one adopts. Ethics training programmes may aim at improving one's moral reasoning, the adequacy of one's perception of one's own or other people's ethical behaviour, one's ethical judgement of particular situations, one's ethical behaviour (that is, the actions one chooses to perform), or one's awareness of the ethical dimensions or aspects of particular decision situations. The results of the meta-analysis show that programmes concerned with moral reasoning can have great effects, but putting an emphasis on ethical perception and awareness has relatively small effects. Ethics training programmes, that is, are most effective if they are applied to the second stage of Rest's (1986) sequence of ethical decision making, discussed earlier in the chapter.

Another finding of the meta-analysis is the importance of *course design*. The study concludes that a programme is most promising when it is directed at a diverse audience, stretches over less than one month's time, has a seminar format, uses a case-based method, and engages students in activities.

A third observation concerns the *content* of the course materials. A striking finding was that although a wide variety of topics are possible, particular areas should be included if the programme is to be successful. A general introduction to rules and principles taken from normative ethics, followed by a survey of concrete strategies that individuals can use to cope with ethical dilemmas should form an important element of the programme to serve as a point of reference. The authors also found that paying attention to cognitive rather than social—interactional aspects of decision making improves the chances of success. In sum, programmes have the greatest effect if they 'foster critical thought processes, geared toward understanding of the problem at hand and then dissecting the thought and behavior process leading to the resolution of the problem' (Waples et al. 2009: 147).

The remainder of this section briefly presents an ethics training programme that the present author and his co-workers designed in collaboration with a large financial services firm in the Netherlands, informed by the findings of Waples et al. (2009), and inspired by O'Neill's work on trust and accountability (see Chapter 8 in this book). Because of the specific demands from the company—its goal incidentally was to become the most trusted company in its sector—the programme is also indebted to a growing literature in philosophy, showing the importance of what could be called the *ethics of belief*. Authors such as Buchanan (2009) have argued that ethicists have too long overlooked the relevance of belief formation practices to ethical and unethical behaviour, and that rather than being cast in the traditional terminology taken from virtue ethics, Kantian ethics, and utilitarianism, applied ethics should focus on belief, knowledge, and information. Examples illustrating this claim would be the false beliefs that supported such things as apartheid, and the Zimbabwe-style command economy.

These concerns can also be found in guides to ethical decision making in business (Messick and Bazerman 1996). I have elsewhere defended the thesis that, to the extent that the global financial crisis is a *moral* crisis, it is largely a crisis of *epistemic* morals: that is, morality concerned with belief formation (De Bruin 2013, 2014). Popular accounts such as Michael Lewis's *The Big Short*, Harry Markopolos's *No One Would Listen*, and Fintan O'Toole's *Ship of Fools* relate in shocking detail how clients, banks, credit-rating agencies, accountants, governments, central banks, and numerous overseeing authorities took rumours for truth, failed to ask questions, suffered from gullibility, rushed to unjustified conclusions on the basis of very little evidence, and so on. If Lewis (2010) is right, at most a handful of people could tell one mortgage-backed security (MBS) from another or had read the prospectuses. A great many people traded MBSs without knowing what they did. All the same, they knew that they did not know. This is as if a doctor were to prescribe a drug without knowing the side effects. If it is the aim of an ethics training programme to improve ethical decision making in the financial services industry, then a key element ought to be an ethics of belief.

This intuition was unhesitatingly shared by the financial services firm for which we developed the programme. In line with a recommendation of Waples et al. (2009), we opted for ten three-hour seminars for a diverse group of around ten managers from the firm's top management. In order to provide the participants with a clear theoretical framework, we chose three topics. Motivated by the firm's explicitly stated aim to restore trust, each seminar started with a review of O'Neill's views on trust and accountability. Participants were introduced to the relationship between trust and trustworthiness; it was explained to them that intelligently placed trust requires evidence of trustworthiness; they were also familiarised with the distinction between evidence about a person's or organisation's *motivation* to act, and evidence about a person's or organisation's *competence* to perform what one trusts them to perform. Because the management of the firm that commissioned the programme claimed a strong preference for using the normative framework of virtue theory, in the second step we used virtue theory to consider motivation and competence from a moral point of view.

In close collaboration with the firm, a number of virtues were selected to illustrate both motivation and competence. Courage, for instance, was discussed with reference to recent discussions in the Netherlands about the responsibility the financial services industry has for uncovering fraud in healthcare. We also discussed the courage to admit one's lack of competence to perform certain tasks. We discussed a real case in which a committee member would see their personal values conflict with the likely outcome of the organisation's decision, and we asked what courage would require. We also treated such virtues as open-mindedness, the willingness to confront one's prejudices with opposing ideas, and epistemic sobriety, a disposition not to rush to a conclusion too quickly.

While the first two elements of the training course concerned normative theories, the third element introduced Rest's (1986) earlier discussed descriptive model of ethical decision making, distinguishing between the recognition of a moral issue, the formation of moral judgement, the establishment of moral intentions, and moral behaviour. We connected Rest's model to findings from moral psychology and behavioural economics. Participants were introduced to the psychological factors that interfere at each of the four stages. Given the emphasis on ethics of belief, the emphasis was on the first two stages. In particular, such biases as confirmation bias, overconfidence bias, and groupthink were discussed and illustrated.

12.4 Codes of Ethics

The last topic concerns what is arguably the most frequently implemented form of ethics management: codes of ethics. Following the lapidary review by Crane and Matten (2010), to which this chapter is heavily indebted, four kinds of codes can be distinguished. *Corporate* codes of ethics apply to a particular business organisation, and are often called *business principles*. They specify what behaviour is expected from management and employees, are very common in banking, and relatively easily accessed by the general public via the Internet. A second group of codes applies to a particular *industry*. The Dutch Banking Code is a recent example, which has attracted attention outside the Netherlands for its proposal to introduce a professional or Hippocratic oath for bankers. *Group codes* are initiatives undertaken by parties sharing certain values and normative beliefs. An example in banking is the Global Alliance for Banking on Values principles of sustainable finance and sustainable banking, drawing together a number of socially or environmentally responsible banks committing themselves to developing products and services 'to meet the needs of people and safeguard the environment', and to consider 'generating reasonable profit...as an essential requirement of sustainable banking but not as a stand-alone objective'. *Professional codes*, finally, are codes of ethics specific to particular professions such as law, medicine, accounting, architecture, or engineering. They are important in banking because members of various professions working in the financial services industry are obliged to discharge the obligations of these codes. The professional code of ethics of Dutch accountants in business (accountants in business do not work as auditors but as CFOs, controllers, etc.) obliges its members to promote ethical culture in the company for which they work.

Corporate, industry, and group codes have found their justified place in the financial services industry, and to the extent that lawyers or accountants bring their own codes into finance, this is true of professional codes as well. Yet professional codes merit more attention here because voices can increasingly be heard calling for the development of professional codes for bankers. In order that such a code may make sense, however, banking would have to be a genuine profession. Before continuing to look at codes of ethics in banking, I shall argue that the assumption that banking is a profession is questionable.

A profession has to satisfy a number of conditions that set it apart from other occupational groups (Cowton 2009). Members of a profession have to fulfil a particular, clearly described *function* in society (doctors foster health) which requires high-level *expertise* that is generally only useful within the profession (a surgeon's expertise is useless outside of medicine) and is motivated by *beneficence*. Furthermore, professions are granted by the government a right to determine who is to qualify as a member, and thereby effectively obtain a right to *monopoly* and a right to *self-regulation*.

It is tempting, but also misleading, to think that these conditions apply to banking. The precise function in society that bankers fulfil is much less obvious than for doctors or lawyers. Their expertise is also useful outside of banking, and is not even always formally required to become a banker. The Dutch banker Dirk Scheringa was a policeman rather than a finance expert. Moreover, bankers do not have the self-regulatory and monopolistic power to determine who is and who is not to be a banker. Rather, it is the government—typically the central bank—who licenses banks and bankers. A professional code for bankers would portray a misguided picture of what bankers do, and why they do it.

Let me return to the general discussion and ask what it is that codes of ethics aspire to do. There is a fair amount of agreement in the literature that codes ought to do two things. A code should present a set of *principles* reflecting general values of the corporation, industry, group, or profession; and it should include concrete rules of conduct or *practical guidelines*. Some authors defer the former task to codes of *ethics* and the latter to codes of *conduct*, but many codes do both because, as Hoffman et al. (2001: 40) state, 'rules of conduct without a general values statement lack a framework of meaning and purpose; credos without rules of conduct lack specific content'.

As we saw, Ragatz and Duska (2010) analysed a number of codes of ethics in the financial services industry and showed that they are all centred around the following seven values: integrity, objectivity, competence, fairness, confidentiality, professionalism, and diligence. A casual inspection of a number of codes from the financial services industry in the US supports this view. The American Institute of Certified Public Accountants, for instance, requires its members to perform their professional responsibilities with the highest sense of *integrity*; Chartered Financial Analysts have to apply care and judgement in order to ensure independence and *objectivity* in their activities; and the code of ethics of the Institute of Certified Bankers and the American Bankers Association fosters *competence* by obliging its members to be dedicated to lifelong learning programmes, and by monitoring their capacities and training needs.

If one is concerned with the content of the code, another question is what its function is. Jamal and Bowie (1995) argue that the main function of codes of ethics is to provide a form of insurance against *moral hazard*. In any principal-agent relationship, whether it occurs in law, accountancy, medicine, or the financial services industry, there is a possibility that agents will provide lower-quality service to their clients than they are paid for, while the clients are unable to monitor the work of the agents. Effective codes, Jamal and Bowie (1995) maintain, contain regulations that limit such forms of moral hazard. Rules on conflicts of interest, lifelong learning, objectivity, and due care are obvious provisions to that end. But ideally, effective codes also specify rules by means of which employees of one corporation, or practitioners within one industry, monitor each other's behaviour by means of, for instance, ethics hotlines or ethics committees.

From a slightly different perspective, Frankel (1989) observes that codes aim at increasing morality, identity, and reputation, as well as serving the adjudication of conflicts. Even though he is primarily concerned with professional codes, a number of observations are relevant to other codes. In line with what Jamal and Bowie (1995) claim, codes help people to make good decisions, and deter them from performing badly by means of efficient monitoring, disciplining, and punishment. But they also build a professional identity by making explicit what public function the profession is supposed to fulfil, what kind of activities and obligations this function entails, and what demands from society and/or clients would be justified—and unjustified—given this function. Codes, then, also function as a way to communicate with the public.

271

Codes are by no means uncontroversial instruments of ethics management. Codes may suffer from inadequate or incomprehensible wording. They may be too detailed, too vague, too abstract, too concrete, or they may fail to address the common ethical concerns with which employees wrestle. They may not be communicated adequately. They may be forgotten. And, as Crane and Matten (2010: 196) write, 'perhaps worst of all, a code that is introduced and then seen to be breached with impunity by senior managers or other members of staff is probably never going to achieve anything apart from raising employee cynicism'. Consequently, it is no surprise that codes are no guarantee against scandals, that codes may lack adequate enforcement mechanisms (Ragatz and Duska 2010), that codes often play hardly any role in actual decision making (Lere and Gaumnitz 2003), that they may focus disproportionally on quality assurance rather than public interest (Velayutham 2003), that they are frequently seen as not going far enough in protecting the public interest (Jamal and Bowie 1995), that codes are blamed for zooming in on rules rather than moral character (Melé 2005) or on compliance rather than on the practice of ethics (Painter-Morland 2010), and that codes may even bluntly prescribe unethical rather than ethical behaviour (Adams et al. 1995).

A number of academics have sounded a more positive note, though, and recommendations can be garnered here. Newton (1992) shows that it is important that employees participate in developing a code of ethics so as to increase the chances of *buy-in* to the code. Since the codes of ethics discussed in this chapter are primarily industry, programme, and group codes, this will translate into the recommendation to hear as many parties as feasible. Deliberative polls may be useful here too. Treviño et al. (1999) argue that a necessary condition for a genuinely effective code is adequate *follow-through*—that is, that serious and consistent attempts are made to detect violations, and that breaches are punished. Collins (2012) also gives a number of recommendations. He suggests mentioning the code of ethics in job advertisements, introducing the code to prospective candidates and new employees, and calls on the organisation to distribute the code annually, to display the code in newsletters, at places clearly visible by employees, on stationery and on websites, to mention the code in correspondence with customers and suppliers, and to actively monitor compliance with the code.

Let me end with a cautionary note, though: to monitor follow-through, it may be thought that ethical behaviour has to be audited and that machinery has to be developed to detect ethics violations. Sethi (2002) contends that standardised audit instruments ought to be developed to this end, using quantitative assessments of compliance and performance evaluation. I do not share Crane and Matten's (2010) optimism about the prospects of such instruments, however. As O'Neill's critical remarks in Chapter 8 on accountability suggest, such forms of assessment will at best only detect easily quantifiable violations, and probably create incentives among employees to develop creative strategies to ensure that their violations fall outside the scope of the measure. A more qualitative approach giving ample room to the auditor's personal discretion has more to recommend it.

12.5 Conclusion

When it comes to ethical behaviour, one of the most important challenges faced by the financial sector is to enlarge moral intensity. Unlike such sectors as the oil and apparel industry, moral issues in banking are often opaque, hard to discern, and only visible after careful and sufficiently sensitive scrutiny. The consequences of one trader's decision are typically quite remote. They lack, in Jones's (1991) vocabulary, both temporal immediacy and proximity.

Waples et al. (2009) found that while ethics programmes may have a significant positive influence on one's moral judgements, they have little impact on one's awareness of moral issues. This is not to say, however, that the ethical challenge faced by the financial sector is hopeless. Building on an important literature as well as a useful review (Crane and Matten 2010), the present chapter has introduced a number of concrete and practical techniques and tools that banks and other firms may use in their attempts to manage ethics. Not all of these tools will be equally effective, though, which is why I put forward two rather novel suggestions. The first suggestion was to use a model of decision making that has been applied successfully in political contexts: the deliberative poll. A deliberative poll literally brings together a great many different stakeholders in a deliberate attempt to create mutual understanding. Second, I reported on a training programme that was developed in collaboration with a large finance firm in the Netherlands. It applied recent insights into the effectiveness of ethics teaching in an attempt to engage senior management with trust and trustworthiness.

References

Adams, B. L., Malone, F. L., and James, W. (1995). 'Confidentiality Decisions: The Reasoning Process of CPAs in Resolving Ethical Dilemmas', *Journal of Business Ethics*, 14(12): 1015–20.

Atkinson, A. and Messy, F. (2012). 'Measuring Financial Literacy: Results of the OECD/International Network on Financial Education (INFE) Pilot Study', *OECD Working Papers on Finance, Insurance and Private Pensions*, No. 15, OECD Publishing.

Bendell, J. (2000). *Terms for Endearment: Business, NGOs and Sustainable Development*. Sheffield: Greenleaf Books.

Buchanan, A. (2009). 'Philosophy and Public Policy: A Role for Social Moral Epistemology', *Journal of Applied Philosophy*, 26(3): 276–90.

Brewer, L., Chandler, R., and Ferrell, O. C. (2006). *Managing Risks for Corporate Integrity: How to Survive and Ethical Misconduct Disaster*. Mason, OH: Thomson/ Texere.

Collins, D. (2012). *Business Ethics: How to Design and Manage Ethical Organizations*. Hoboken, NJ: John Wiley.

Cowton, C. J. (2009). 'Accounting and the Ethics Challenge: Re-membering the Professional Body', *Accounting and Business Research*, 39(3): 177–89.

Crane, A. (1998). 'Culture Clash and Mediation: Exploring the Cultural Dynamics of Business NGO Collaboration', *Greener Management International*, 24: 61–76.

Crane, A. and Livesey, S. (2003). 'Are You Talking to Me? Stakeholder Communication and the Risks and Ethics', in J. Andriof, S. Waddock, B. Husted, and S. Rahman (eds), *Unfolding Stakeholder Thinking*, vol. 2: *Relationships, Communication, Reporting and Performance*. Sheffield: Greenleaf Books, 39–52.

Crane, A. and Matten, D. (2010). *Business Ethics: Managing Corporate Citizenship and Sustainability in the Age of Globalization*. New York: Oxford University Press.

De Bruin, B. (2013). 'Epistemic Virtues in Business', *Journal of Business Ethics*, 113: 583–95.

De Bruin, B. (2014). *Ethics in Finance: Epistemic Virtues for Bankers, Clients, Raters and Regulators*. Cambridge: Cambridge University Press, forthcoming.

Dryzek, J. (2000). *Deliberative Democracy and Beyond: Liberals, Critics, Contestations*. Oxford: Oxford University Press.

Edelman (2014). 'Edelman Trust Barometer 2014', <http://www.edelman.com/ insights/intellectual-property/2014-edelman-trust-barometer/about-trust/>, accessed 30 March 2014.

Elkington, J. and Fennell, S. (2000). 'Partners for Sustainability', in J. Bendell (ed.), *Terms for Endearment: Business, NGOs and Sustainable Development*. Sheffield: Greenleaf Books: 150–62.

Edwards, J. (2009). ' "Novartis Land" the Latest Entry in Weird Drug-Based Video Game Trend', CBS Moneywatch, 23 March.

Fishkin, J. (1988). 'Washington: The Case for a National Caucus', *Atlantic Monthly*, 8: 16–17.

Frankel, M. S. (1989). 'Professional Codes: Why, Who and With What Impact?', *Journal of Business Ethics*, 8(2–3): 109–15.

Fung, A. (2003). 'Survey Article: Recipes for Public Spheres: Eight Institutional Design Choices and their Consequences', *Journal of Political Philosophy*, 11(3): 338–67.

Habermas, J. (2006). 'Poltical Communication in Media Society: Does Democracy Still Enjoy an Epistemic Dimension? The Impact of Normative Theory on Empirical Research', *Communication Theory*, 16: 411–26.

Hartman, C. L. and Stafford, E. R. (1997). 'Green Alliances: Building New Business with Environmental Groups', *Long Range Planning*, 30(2): 184–96.

Hoffmann, W. M., Driscoll, D., and Painter-Morland, M. (2001). 'Integrating Ethics', in C. Moon and C. Bonny (eds), *Business Ethics: Facing Up to the Interests*. London: The Economist Books, 38–54.

Jamal, K. and Bowie, N. E. (1995). 'Theoretical Considerations for a Meaningful Code of Professional Ethics', *Journal of Business Ethics*, 14(9): 703–14.

Jeucken, M. (2004). *Sustainability in Finance: Banking on the Planet*. Delft: Eburon.

Jones, T. M. (1991). 'Ethical Decision Making by Individuals in Organizations: An Issue-Contingent Model', *Academy of Management Review*, 16(2): 366–95.

Kirrane, D. E. (1990). 'Managing Values: A Systematic Approach to Business Ethics', *Training and Development Journal*, 44(11): 53–60.

Lere, J. C. and Gaumnitz, B. R. (2003). 'The Impact of Codes of Ethics on Decision Making: Some Insights from Information Economics', *Journal of Business Ethics*, 48(4): 365–79.

Lewis, M. (2010). *The Big Short: Inside the Doomsday Machine*. London: W. W. Norton & Co.

Luskin, R. C. and Fishkin, J. S. (2011). 'The Deliberative Corporation', <http://cdd.stanford.edu/events/2011/deliberative-corporation.pdf>, accessed 6 March 2014.

Melé, D. (2005). 'Ethical Education in Accounting: Integrating Rules, Values and Virtues', *Journal of Business Ethics*, 57: 97–109.

Messick, D. M. and Bazerman M. H. (1996). 'Ethical Leadership and the Psychology of Decision Making', *Sloan Management Review*, 37(2) (Winter): 9–22.

Mitchell, R. K., Agle, B. R. and Wood, D. J. (1997). 'Toward a Theory of Stakeholder Identification and Salience: Defining the Principle of Who and What Really Counts', *Academy of Management Review*, 22(4): 853–86.

Nader, R. (2000). 'Corporations and the UN: Nike and Others "Bluewash" their Images', *San Francisco Bay Guardian*, 18 September.

Newton, L. H. (1992). 'The Many Facets of the Corporate Code', in L. H. Newton and M. M. Ford (eds), *Taking Sides: Clashing Views on Controversial Issues in Business Ethics and Society*. Guildford: Dushkin, 81–8.

Ogien, R. (1996). 'Normes et valeurs', in M. Canto-Sperber (ed.), *Dictionnaire d'éthique et de philosophie morale*. Paris: Presses Universitaires de France, 1052–64.

O'Neill, O. (2002). *Autonomy and Trust in Bioethics*. Cambridge: Cambridge University Press.

Painter-Morland, M. (2010). 'Questioning Corporate Codes of Ethics', *Business Ethics: A European Review*, 19(3): 265–79.

Parsons, T. (1951). *The Social System*. Glencoe: The Free Press.

Ragatz, J. A., and Duska, R. F. (2010) 'Financial Codes of Ethics', in J. Boatright (ed.), *Finance Ethics: Critical Issues in Theory and Practice*. Hoboken: John Wiley, 297–324.

Rest, J. R. (1986). *Moral Development: Advances in Research and Theory*. New York: Praeger.

Selsky, J. W. and Parker, B. (2005). 'Cross-Sector Partnerships to Address Social Issues: Challenges to Theory and Practice', *Journal of Management*, 31(6): 1–25.

Sethi, S. P. (2002). 'Standards for Corporate Conduct in the International Arena: Challenges and Opportunities for Multinational Corporations', *Business and Society Review*, 107(1): 20–40.

Treviño, L. K., Weaver, G. R., Gibson, D. G., and Toffler, B. L. (1999). 'Managing Ethics and Legal Compliance: What Works and What Hurts', *California Management Review* 41(2): 131–51.

Velayutham, S. (2003). 'The Accounting Profession's Code of Ethics: Is it a Code of Ethics or a Code of Quality Assurance?', *Critical Perspectives on Accounting*, 14: 483–503.

Waples, E. P., Antes, A. L., Murphy, S. T., Connelly, S., and Mumford, M. D. (2009). 'A Meta-Analytic Investigation of Business Ethics Instruction', *Journal of Business Ethics*, 87(1): 133–51.

Webley, S. and Le Jeune, M. (2005). *Corporate Use of Codes of Ethics: 2004 Survey*. London: Institute of Business Ethics.

Wiggins, D. (1987). *Needs, Values, Truth: Essays in the Philosophy of Value*. Oxford: Oxford University Press.

Williams, B. (1985). *Ethics and the Limits of Philosophy*. Cambridge, MA: Harvard University Press.

13

Toward a More Ethical Culture in Finance: Regulatory and Governance Strategies

Dan Awrey and David Kershaw *

The financial crisis has demonstrated the limits of markets as mechanisms for constraining socially undesirable behaviour within the financial services industry. Simultaneously, conventional approaches toward the law and regulation are often ineffective mechanisms for containing—let alone preventing—the social costs of market failure. So where do we turn when both law and markets fail to live up to their social promise? Two possible answers are *culture* and *ethics*. In theory, both represent potentially powerful constraints on human and organisational decision making. In practice, however, they are often ineffective—crowded out by other countervailing influences.

To many, this may portend the end of the story. From our perspective, however, it represents a useful point of departure. More specifically, it raises an important question as to whether it might be possible to carve out a space within which culture and ethics—or, combining the two, a more *ethical culture*—can be fostered and come to play a more meaningful role in constraining undesirable behaviour within the financial services industry. This chapter explores how various regulatory and governance strategies might be utilised to tilt the cultural and ethical battleground at both the individual and organisational levels in pursuit of this objective.

* This chapter is based on a longer article by Dan Awrey, William Blair, and David Kershaw, 'Between Law and Markets: Is There a Role for Culture and Ethics in Financial Regulation?' (2013), *Delaware Journal of Corporate Law*, 38(1): 191–245.

This exploration takes place across two dimensions. In the first dimension, we hold constant the core internal governance arrangements—e.g. corporate objectives, directors' duties, board composition, shareholder rights and remuneration—within financial services firms. We then examine how novel forms of regulation might be employed to help engender a more ethical culture in two important areas: (1) bilateral counterparty arrangements and (2) socially excessive risk taking. More specifically, we examine how so-called 'process-oriented' regulation—backed by a credible threat of public enforcement and market-based reputational sanctions—might be used to reframe personal ethical choices and foster a more ethical culture within financial services firms.

Intuitively, however, we would expect the success of such regulatory strategies to be a function of the incentive structures generated by the existing constellation of internal governance arrangements. Put simply, for cultural and ethical frameworks to have traction within organisational decision making, they must be given room to breathe. Yet existing governance arrangements in many jurisdictions directly or indirectly give primacy to the financial interests of shareholders, and thereby create incentive structures which reward opportunistic behaviour and socially excessive risk taking. These incentive structures are likely to crowd out efforts to foster a more ethical culture. In the second dimension, therefore, we examine how we might promote a more ethical culture through reforms of the core governance arrangements of financial services firms.

Ultimately, this chapter does not profess to have all the answers. What it does do, however, is ask some important (and too often neglected) questions about the role of culture and ethics in the financial services industry and offer up a framework for more serious and rigorous discussion.

13.1 Making Sense of Culture and Ethics

As a preliminary matter, we are sympathetic to the view that culture and ethics are inherently slippery concepts. Framing policy debates around such inchoate concepts is thus often, and understandably, viewed as fraught with conceptual challenges. Nevertheless, we also know that culture and ethics are important determinants of human and organisational behaviour. What is required, then, is some definitional precision. Specifically, what do we mean by 'culture' and 'ethics'? And on what basis should we distinguish between these two seemingly intertwined (and yet often muddled) concepts?

Robert Ellickson (1994) provides us with a useful framework for thinking about these questions. Ellickson draws a distinction between first-, second-, and third-party behavioural constraints. First-party constraints are those imposed by an actor on him- or herself. This is the domain of personal *ethics*. Second-party constraints are those which flow from systems of reward and punishment within the context of bilateral relationships between promisors and promisees. This is the domain of *contract*. Third-party constraints, meanwhile, are generated by actors or social forces which, in a strictly technical sense, fall outside the perimeter of such contractual relationships. *Culture*—understood as the non-legal norms, conventions, or expectations shared by actors when operating within social or institutional settings—can thus be viewed as one source of third-party behavioural constraint.[1]

Like the law, culture and ethics can accordingly be viewed as mechanisms—empty vessels—through which various substantive norms are generated, monitored, and enforced. The substantive content of cultural and ethical norms (and, indeed, the law) may be identical. The prohibition against the taking of human life, for example, exists across all three dimensions. But equally, cultural, ethical, and/or legal norms may come into conflict with one another. The key distinction for our purposes is the *source* of the behavioural constraint and ultimately the impact this has on its ability to influence behaviour. In the case of culture (and the law), the constraint is an *external* one. In the case of personal ethics, in contrast, it is *internal*.

This, of course, raises an important set of questions. To what extent can culture (or the law) be understood as simply reflecting 'shared ethics'? Conversely, what impact do external behavioural constraints such as culture (or the law) have on our internal ethical perspective? In the discussion which follows we largely bracket these important questions, preferring instead to utilise the term 'ethical culture' where possible to signify that culture and ethics can be employed as mutually reinforcing constraints. Before we articulate the substantive content of this ethical culture, however, it is useful to first understand the role that ethics and culture can play as drivers of human and organisational behaviour.

13.2 Understanding Ethics as a Driver of Behaviour

Ethical constraints are endogenous to each individual actor: part of that individual's identity. It is this internal orientation—along with the inherent subjectivity and unobservability of first-party enforcement—which renders the behavioural impact of ethics difficult to model in theory or measure in the

---

[1] We deviate from Ellickson's framework slightly in that we include constraints generated by private (i.e. non-state) actors as falling into the category of 'norms', whereas Ellickson categorises them as 'organisational rules'. This change is merely to facilitate exposition and not to deny the importance of broader questions surrounding what institutions should or should not be understood as sources of law.

real world. For some, ethics may be a powerful driver of behaviour. For others, it may be dominated by other competing influences. For others still, it may—like Oliver Wendell Holmes's (1897) 'bad man'—not play the slightest role. Moreover, even within these somewhat artificial categories, there are likely to exist substantial problems of interpersonal and intertemporal comparison. This, in turn, makes it difficult to identify 'shared ethics'. It also raises the prospect that, even at the individual level, ethical perspectives may vary over time and across contexts.

The internal nature of ethics also raises a problem for our own exploration: namely, how can regulation or governance influence internal ethical perspectives and decision making? Here, ongoing work in the fields of cognitive and social psychology offers some valuable insights. First, as Thomas Jones (1991) observes, the moral intensity (or salience) of an ethical problem can be an important determinant of ethical decision making.[2] As Jones explains, the moral intensity of a problem is a function of, inter alia: the magnitude of the potential consequences; the probability that they will occur; their concentration; temporal immediacy; social consensus and, importantly, proximity.[3] Proximity is a measure of the physical, psychological, social, or cultural distance between a decision maker and those whom their decisions affect. Thus, for example, the anonymity within large, complex organisations, technologies enabling 'faceless' communication across great distances, and the commoditisation of business transactions and relationships might all be expected to decrease moral intensity. The potential upshot, however, is that by reconfiguring firms and markets with a view to reducing physical or psychological distance, for example, it may be possible to enhance ethical decision making (Jones 1991).

Importantly, the factors identified by Jones as contributing to moral intensity are characteristics of the ethical problem itself, not of decision makers. This introduces the prospect that we might be able to *reframe* elements of the problem so as to highlight their ethical dimensions. The trolley (or footbridge) problem is a paradigmatic example (Thomson and Parent 1986; Foot 1978). In the classical formulation of this problem, individuals are asked to participate in a thought experiment in which a train is speeding toward five people tied to the tracks. Participants are then told that by pulling a switch, they can redirect the train onto a second track to which a single person is tied. In both cases, the person(s) tied to the tracks in the path of the train are certain to perish. Participants are then asked to consider a second hypothetical

---

[2] Consistent with the relevant cognitive science literature, the terms 'moral' and 'ethical' are used interchangeably in this section.

[3] Linked to moral intensity is the concept of normative focus: the notion that social or personal norms will only influence behaviour if salient *at the time of decision making* (Kallgren et al. 2000).

in which they are told that the train can be stopped by pushing a man from a footbridge onto the tracks. Notably, while the welfare implications are identical in both cases, experimental evidence suggests both that participants experience a stronger emotional response to the second hypothetical and are far less likely to push the man in front of the train than they are to pull the switch (Valdesolo and DeSteno 2006; Greene et al. 2001). The implication, in the view of many, is that by forcing people to directly confront the ethical dimensions of their decisions, it may be possible to make ethics a more powerful driver of behaviour.

The second important insight is that contemplation or reflection can enhance ethical decision making (Gunia et al. 2012; Murnighan et al. 2001).[4] Cognitive scientists distinguish between two types of cognitive processes: *intuitive* processes in which judgements are made rapidly and automatically (System 1) and *controlled* processes in which judgements are slower and more deliberative (System 2) (Frederick 2005; Kahneman 2002; Kahneman and Frederick 2002). Several scholars have proposed that utilitarian or consequentialist moral judgements take place within System 2 (Greene 2007; Greene et al. 2004 and 2001). This was given empirical support in a recent study by Gunia et al. (2012) in which test subjects were given three minutes to consider a right–wrong decision—i.e. whether to tell the truth or lie for personal gain—and instructed to 'think very carefully' before making their decision. The authors found that subjects in this contemplation condition were five times more likely to tell the truth than subjects asked to make an immediate decision. In the view of some scholars, this apparent link between intuitive processes and self-interested decisions reflects deeply ingrained evolutionary motives (Murnighan et al. 2001). Moreover, these motives may dominate in environments—such as finance—where a premium is placed on quick thinking and decisiveness (Gunia et al. 2012). Contemplation, in contrast, allows individuals to consciously weigh ethical considerations against self-interest. As a result, slowing decision-making processes down and reflecting on their ethical dimensions may yield socially desirable behavioural effects.

Finally, morally-oriented conversations can promote more ethical decision making in the context of right–wrong decisions pitting values such as honesty against self-interest. Gunia et al. (2012), for example, found that test subjects having even a brief, anonymous and morally-oriented conversation were four times more likely to tell the truth than subjects having a self-interested conversation. In effect, conversation can be utilised to

---

[4] Others, meanwhile, suggest that reflection and reasoning simply serve to generate *ex post* rationalisations of *ex ante* moral intuitions (Haidt 2001). Ultimately, however, Haidt's model is grounded in right–wrong decisions designed to evoke disgust (e.g. incest). We submit that the vast majority of ethical decisions within the business context do not evoke similar emotions.

highlight the ethical dimensions of problems, enhance moral intensity (or normative focus), and thereby put ethical considerations on firmer footing within group decision-making processes (Etzioni 1988).[5] Simultaneously, however, these conversations must be about more than simply allowing decision makers to construct *ex post* explanations which reinforce their *ex ante* intuitions (Gunia et al. 2012; Haidt 2001).

Ultimately, of course, the insights of cognitive and social psychology must be approached with caution. Many strands of this research are still in their theoretical and experimental infancy. Moreover, most of the relevant empirical work has been confined to the laboratory: the real world may confound these predictions. Organisational and other environmental factors may, similarly, interfere with strategies designed to enhance ethical decision making. Nevertheless, as we explore further below, this research may help us better understand ways in which regulation and governance can counteract the emergence of 'bad apples' and 'bad barrels' within financial services firms.

13.3 Understanding Culture as a Driver of Behaviour

Few would argue that cultural, commercial, and other norms are not capable of exerting a profound influence on human and organisational behaviour. Moreover, such norms theoretically offer a number of advantages vis-à-vis other third-party behavioural constraints—e.g. the law—in terms of their responsiveness, adaptability, and relatively low costs of monitoring and enforcement. These norms can also help overcome the information, agency, and coordination problems which can undermine the development of efficient markets (Greif 1993). Perhaps not surprisingly, therefore, a significant body of scholarship has emerged exploring the circumstances in which these norms arise and when they are likely to lead to socially desirable outcomes.

The majority of this scholarship has centred around homogeneous and geographically proximate groups of actors—e.g. ranchers (Ellickson 1994), diamond merchants (Bernstein 1992), and cotton merchants (Bernstein 2001)—engaged in long-term, repeat-play relationships. Broadly speaking, this scholarship supports the intuition that the norms generating the most powerful behavioural constraints will be those where: (1) violations are easily observable; (2) news of violations is easily disseminated within the relevant group; and (3) the group possesses the capacity and incentives to impose meaningful sanctions on violators. These factors provide a framework for thinking about the formation, monitoring, and enforcement of cultural

---

[5] This, of course, works in both directions: conversations which emphasise self-interest may have the opposite effect (Ratner and Miller 2001).

norms not only within the context of market interactions but also, importantly, within individual firms.

The financial services industry has produced numerous codes of conduct, ethics, and best practice which purport to articulate various norms. Prominent examples include the Chartered Financial Analyst (CFA) Institute *Code of Ethics and Standards of Professional Conduct* (CFA 2012a), the Chartered Institute for Securities and Investment *Code of Conduct*, and the Alternative Investment Management Association *Guides to Sound Practices*. But do these norms generate meaningful behavioural constraints? This is an empirical question which, ultimately, resides beyond the scope of this chapter. Nevertheless, there exist a number of reasons to suggest that—in a great many cases—the real-world impact of these norms may be very limited.

First, the complexity of modern financial markets generates acute asymmetries of information and expertise. This complexity undermines the ability of less informed market participants to detect violations of any applicable norms (Awrey 2012). This is especially problematic given that it is these market participants which are—almost by definition—most at risk. In June 2012, for example, the UK's Financial Services Authority (FSA)[6] completed a review which found evidence of widespread mis-selling of complex interest rate hedging products to relatively unsophisticated small and medium-sized enterprises (FSA 2012). Previous FSA reviews have also uncovered extensive mis-selling of payment protection insurance (UK Competition Commission 2011) and subprime mortgage products (FSA 2007a). The US has similarly experienced a spate of mis-selling claims in the wake of the financial crisis. Importantly, this behaviour emerged and persisted despite the existence of industry codes and other pronouncements stating, in effect, that the customer *always* comes first.[7] It did so, at least in part, because the market participants which this opportunistic behaviour targeted were poorly positioned to detect it.

Second, even where violations are detected, there is often no credible threat of enforcement. The CFA Institute *Code of Ethics* provides an illustrative example. The *Code of Ethics* requires CFA members to act with integrity, diligence, competence, respect, and in an ethical manner. In the context of advisory relationships, it also imposes duties of loyalty, fair dealing, suitability, and disclosure of conflicts of interest. The CFA Institute has established a disciplinary procedure to address violations of the *Code of Ethics*, with its most powerful sanctions being to suspend or revoke a violator's membership. Ultimately,

---

[6] On 1 April 2013 the FSA was broken up into the Financial Conduct Authority (FCA) and Prudential Regulatory Authority (PRA). The term FSA will still be used for matters arising before this date.

[7] Perhaps the most (in)famous being Goldman Sach's fourteen principles, the first of which states: 'Our clients' interests always come first.'

however, as an organisation whose reputation and financial resources are derived from its ability to attract and retain its members, the CFA Institute's incentives to vigorously pursue enforcement action are relatively weak. This is reflected in its own enforcement statistics, which report an average of 2.42 suspensions and 0.92 expulsions per year from 2000–11 from a total membership of over 98,000 (CFA 2012b). This data suggests either that members almost never violate the *Code of Ethics* or, perhaps more likely, that the probability of detection and subsequent enforcement is extremely low.

Theoretically, the violation of norms can also be enforced through market-based reputational sanctions (Armour et al. 2012). Once again, however, asymmetries of information can impede the process by which news of violations is disseminated, and thus undermine the potency of such mechanisms. Indeed, even where information costs are relatively low, the mobility and resulting transience of personnel within the financial services industry can make it difficult to effectively target reputational sanctions. Conversely, market participants often make significant relationship-specific investments in the financial services firms with which they do business. This increases the costs of 'exit' in response to the violation of a norm and, as a corollary, the likelihood of *private* renegotiation or alternative dispute resolution (as opposed to *public* litigation) as a means of compensating the aggrieved party for any loss. These factors are likely to have a dilutive impact on any market-based discipline.

While markets may not ultimately provide the most fertile ground for the formation, monitoring, and enforcement of cultural norms, the structure of the firm arguably holds out considerably more promise. First, the frequency of interactions within a firm will often render violations (relatively) observable.[8] Second, news of violations can be disseminated easily up the firm's hierarchy through formal complaint and compliance procedures, management information systems, or simply word of mouth. Third, firms have at their disposal a wide range of disciplinary mechanisms. These mechanisms include dismissal, demotion, the denial of promotion, quality of work flow, and, of course, remuneration.

The key question for firms is thus not how to generate, monitor, and enforce compliance with cultural norms per se, but rather, how to ensure that the 'right' culture—a more ethical culture—shapes individual and organisational decision making. While codes of conduct, ethics, and best practice can be drafted and held up as identifying desirable behaviours, the norms these codes purport to reflect may be overpowered by other countervailing influences. Indeed, there is significant anecdotal evidence which suggests that such

---

[8] Although, as evidenced by various 'rogue trader' scandals, financial services firms provide ample scope for agents to hide their violations.

countervailing norms may exist within many financial services firms. These norms resemble what Rebecca Ratner and Dale Miller (2001) have characterised as 'the norm of self-interest'. Notably, self-interest in this context may encompass the interests of individual employees, teams, or even the entire firm. In fact, a prominent diagnosis of recent events—including the Libor, mis-selling, and money-laundering scandals—is that dysfunctional firm cultures were amongst the primary drivers (UK Parliamentary Commission on Banking Standards 2013).

13.4 Toward a More Ethical Culture in Finance

So what is the substantive content of the ethical culture this chapter seeks to promote? As stated at the outset, our objective is to explore ways in which regulatory and governance strategies might be utilised to engender cultural and ethical constraints on both counterparty opportunism and socially excessive risk taking. Underpinning this objective is the desire to promote what can best be characterised as a norm of 'other-regarding' behaviour within financial services firms—one which persuades firms to take into account the full private and social costs of their decisions. This objective should not, in our view, be controversial given the enormous social impact of the financial crisis and the undesirable conduct and practices which it has brought to light. Moreover, as described above, 'other-regarding' norms are already reflected in many of the codes of conduct, principles of best practice, and other guidance produced by various professional bodies, industry associations, and other organisations. Put simply, our objective in the remainder of this chapter is to see whether we might be able to put this norm on more equal footing within financial services firms and, ultimately, give it some real teeth.

13.5 Regulatory Strategies

Policymakers are well aware of the important role which culture can play within financial services firms (Basel Committee on Banking Supervision 2010). Many senior figures within the financial services industry have, similarly, signalled that they are receptive to the idea that culture is important. To many, however, the objective of fostering meaningful cultural and/or ethical constraints on socially undesirable behaviour is, at best, aspirational. As a result, whilst we have seen the obligatory post-crisis calls for firms to take culture and ethics more seriously, we have not seen substantive policy proposals which would seek to actively promote a more ethical culture in finance.

13.5.1 The Treating Customers Fairly (TCF) Initiative

Nevertheless, there are precedents. One such precedent is a modest scheme implemented by the FSA in 2001, known as the 'Treating Customers Fairly' (or TCF) Initiative. As its name implies, the objective of the TCF Initiative is to compel financial services firms to treat their retail clients fairly. The TCF Initiative was introduced in response to a raft of mis-selling claims involving various financial products (Gilad 2010). Notably, however, the legal obligation on UK financial services firms to treat customers fairly pre-dates the TCF Initiative. The EU Markets in Financial Instruments Directive (MiFID), for example, mandates that financial services firms act honestly, fairly, and professionally in accordance with the best interests of their clients (MiFID Art. 19(1)). These requirements are reflected in the FSA's Principles for Business, which include the requirement to act honestly and with integrity, to treat customers fairly, and to communicate with clients in a way that is fair and not misleading. What distinguishes the TCF Initiative from these broader regulatory pronouncements, however, is that firm processes and culture are the *target* of regulation.

The TCF Initiative identifies six outcomes which financial services firms are expected to achieve on behalf of their retail clients. These outcomes aim to ensure that: (1) fair treatment of consumers is embedded in corporate culture; (2) products and services meet the needs of identified consumer groups and are targeted accordingly; (3) sufficient information is provided to consumers before, during, and after the point of sale; (4) advice is suitable; (5) products and services meet the expectations of consumers; and (6) consumers do not face unreasonable post-sale barriers imposed by firms to change product, switch provider, submit a claim, or make a complaint (FSA 2006). The FSA has also produced extensive guidance about how firms should approach their obligations under the TCF Initiative (Gilad 2010). Compliance with the TCF Initiative is then measured against the extent to which the processes designed and implemented by firms are able to deliver against these outcomes.

The TCF Initiative falls under the umbrella of a diverse collection of regulatory strategies often described as 'process-oriented' regulation (Gilad 2012). Process-oriented regulation proceeds from the acknowledgement that top-down, prescriptive regulation is often ill-suited to heterogeneous and fast-paced industries such as finance, where entrenched asymmetries of information and expertise pervade the relationships between regulators and regulated actors (Black 1997). The hallmark of process-oriented regulation, then, is that it seeks to leverage the information and expertise of regulated actors by granting them the flexibility to design bespoke organisational processes, systems, and controls with a view to achieving a set of broad regulatory objectives or outcomes articulated by the regulator (Parker 2007).

Simultaneously, however, process-oriented regulation is about more than leveraging firm-specific information to produce tailored systems and controls: it is about incorporating the regulatory objectives or outcomes into firm culture (Black 2008; Parker 2007; FSA 2006).

In its *ideal form*, process-oriented regulation promotes dialogue, processes, systems, and controls through which firm-level norms are articulated, disseminated, monitored, and enforced. However, as Parker and Gilad (2011) observe, it is unlikely that firm culture can be instrumentally created in this way. Any attempt to foster specified normative positions takes place through agents—including senior management—who may have countervailing normative commitments and incentives and who may therefore deploy strategies to resist cultural change. A more realistic way to view process-oriented regulation is thus as one of several complimentary strategies designed to increase the probability that certain normative positions can be voiced and gain traction within the firm. Put differently, it seeks to bias the internal battleground of firm culture in favour of regulatory objectives.

Consistent with this process-oriented approach, the TCF Initiative compels firms to design and evaluate their own organisational processes against desired regulatory outcomes. In giving firms this flexibility, the TCF Initiative also shifts at least some of the *responsibility* for meaningfully engaging with—and ultimately achieving—regulatory objectives from regulators to regulated firms. The TCF Initiative places the onus on firms, and specifically on senior management, to promote an organisational culture which encourages meaningful internal dialogue about firm practices, their impact on retail clients, and whether or not they meet the required regulatory outcomes. Indeed, the FSA has described the TCF Initiative as a 'cultural issue', observing: 'it is only through establishing the right culture that senior management can convert their good intentions into actual fair outcomes for consumers' (FSA 2007b: s. 2.4).

At present, there is limited empirical evidence against which to judge the success of the TCF Initiative. Recent qualitative research conducted by Gilad (2010), however, has examined the TCF Initiative and the preconditions to its effective implementation. There are two central findings of Gilad's work. First, external enforcement matters. Her findings suggest that many financial services firms were initially reluctant to engage with the TCF Initiative as, in their view, they already treated their customers fairly.[9] Indeed, for many firms, engagement involved little more than the collection of data to demonstrate that fairness was taken into consideration by their employees. However, as Gilad notes, this view changed—and more meaningful

---

[9] Even when these firms were implicated in various mis-selling claims.

engagement ensued—following an increase in the number of enforcement actions brought by the FSA stemming from the failure of individual firms to treat customers fairly. Importantly, the FSA also signalled that a firm's failure to meaningfully *engage* with desired regulatory outcomes—as well as the failure to *achieve* them—would trigger enforcement action (FSA 2006).

The second important finding relates to the role of senior management in spearheading implementation and ongoing engagement. As described above, the TCF Initiative does not seek to compel compliance per se. Rather, it proceeds on the basis that compliance benefits will flow from dialogue, process design and implementation, and ultimately, cultural formation. All of this requires clear signals from senior management that they support—indeed, *demand*—engagement with the TCF Initiative from all employees. To engage with the TCF Initiative purely through a compliance lens, and thereby to give a firm's compliance personnel primary responsibility for its implementation, would thus undermine its potential efficacy. Gilad's empirical work confirms this view: when firms viewed the TCF Initiative as the responsibility of compliance professionals, implementation was measurably slower and less effective. Notably, then, Gilad's two findings interact: with the threat of external enforcement spurring management buy-in, and management buy-in spurring internal enforcement and, ultimately, cultural change.

While data on the impact of the TCF Initiative may be sparse, there are several reasons for (cautious) optimism. First, the TCF Initiative articulates a relatively intelligible and non-arbitragable standard of 'other-regarding' behaviour. Second, unlike the various codes of conduct and other guidance produced by the financial services industry, the credible threat of formal regulatory sanctions in response to failures—not just of *compliance* but, crucially, of *engagement*—provides powerful motivation for firms to take the TCF Initiative seriously. Simultaneously, the public disclosure of sanctions imposed for violations of the TCF Initiative reveals valuable information to the retail marketplace. This could theoretically provide the basis for enhanced market discipline. If credible threats of internal and external enforcement are together able to send a clear signal that engagement will be rewarded—and non-engagement sanctioned—then the TCF Initiative will have made a meaningful contribution to the promotion of a more ethical culture.

The process-oriented focus of the TCF Initiative thus provides a platform for financial services firms to promote an organisational culture of other-regarding behaviour. To realise this potential, however, regulators would do well to draw on the insights of cognitive and social psychology described above. More specifically, while the TCF Initiative is designed to facilitate dialogue, the content and framing of these conversations can be important determinants of organisational decision making and behaviour. Reframing these conversations to highlight their ethical dimensions could therefore yield significant benefits. Thus, for example, regulators could make it clear that meaningful engagement with the TCF Initiative includes reviewing the results of previous enforcement actions—thereby highlighting the *probability* and *magnitude* of potential consequences and providing the foundations of a 'lessons learned' review of a firm's own practices. It could similarly mandate that, as part of the vetting process for new products and services, decision makers confirm that they would recommend the product or service to their friends or relatives (thus enhancing *proximity*).

Regulators could also mandate that new financial products and services be vetted by an internal (sub-board-level) 'ethics' committee—analogous to existing credit committees—headed by senior management. The introduction of an ethics committee would offer at least four potential benefits in this context. First, it would signal to the lower rungs of the organisation that treating customers fairly was not just a compliance issue, but also an important business issue (Gilad 2010). Second, it would provide an opportunity for *reflection*—for sober second thought about the impact of business decisions on client welfare. Third, it would establish a clear channel of accountability for compliance with the TCF Initiative, thus eliminating any organisational anonymity which might otherwise decrease moral intensity. Finally, it would provide a direct means of monitoring compliance with ethical norms. As examined in greater detail below, many of these same benefits could also flow from the introduction of a *board-level* ethics committee.

Together, these and other mechanisms could enhance moral intensity and put ethical and business considerations on a more equal footing. In the process, they would enable personal ethical commitments that are consistent with the TCF Initiative to be legitimated and play a more prominent role in the formation, monitoring and enforcement of cultural norms within financial services firms.

13.5.2 The Extended TCF Initiative

While further evidence regarding the impact of the TCF Initiative is clearly needed, it is worthwhile exploring the merits (and drawbacks) of extending this process-oriented regulatory strategy beyond its current narrow focus on retail customers to encompass transactions involving ostensibly more sophisticated counterparties. An 'Extended' Treating *Counterparties* Fairly (Extended TCF) Initiative could apply to transactions involving, for example, swaps, structured investment products, and other more exotic financial instruments. Like its retail counterpart, the Extended TCF Initiative could help foster a more ethical culture within a segment of the financial services industry in which it is widely perceived as lacking. Perhaps most importantly, it could serve to deter the design and marketing of financial products and services intended, either in whole or in part, to extract rents from less sophisticated 'sophisticated' counterparties.

As with the TCF Initiative, an Extended TCF Initiative would need to identify the regulatory objectives or outcomes it was designed to achieve. These objectives, which would necessarily be somewhat different from those identified in the retail context, might include: (1) that the fair treatment of counterparties be embedded in corporate culture; (2) that an intermediary disclose to counterparties all relevant information about a product which it is marketing; (3) that an intermediary not attempt to take any steps that could distort the interpretation or weighting of this information; and (4) that an intermediary not market products that a reasonably sophisticated market participant would be unable to understand and/or accurately price. Led by senior management, firms would then be expected to take responsibility for designing systems, processes, and controls to give effect to these objectives.

The success of the Extended TCF Initiative, like the TCF Initiative, would ultimately hinge on the extent to which financial services firms meaningfully engaged with regulatory outcomes. Once again, a credible external enforcement threat—in relation to engagement as well as outcomes—is key. So too is commitment on the part of senior management. The introduction of an ethics committee to scrutinise transactions and oversee engagement with the Extended TCF Initiative would, for the reasons discussed above, also pay potential dividends. Taking another page from cognitive and social psychology, meanwhile, regulators could require counterparties to transact 'face-to-face' (i.e. either physically or via teleconference) or otherwise attempt to increase their physical, psychological, or social proximity. While such proposals might seem too costly, or unrealistic, or remnants of a bygone era, there is no denying the fact—as evidenced by the heightened emotional response to the footbridge problem—that it is often more difficult to rip off your counterparty once you have shaken their hand.

Ultimately, however, there are a number of reasons to suggest that the Extended TCF Initiative might not be as effective as its retail counterpart. Perhaps most importantly, unlike the retail marketplace, there is arguably no underlying norm that sophisticated market counterparties should be treated fairly. Indeed, there is a strong countervailing norm of *caveat emptor* within many wholesale markets. While sophisticated parties may fail to fully understand the risks they contract to assume, the general view is thus that they have no one to blame but themselves, and should accordingly bear the full consequences of their decisions. This, in turn, is likely to dilute the impact of any reputational sanctions for firms which are deemed to have treated their counterparties unfairly. Ultimately, however, these counterarguments arguably miss the point. As Milton Friedman (1962) observed, efficiency demands that contractual exchange is both voluntary and, importantly, *informed*. The

Extended TCF Initiative must therefore be judged on the basis of whether it engenders the formation of cultural norms which would promote more informed contracting.

13.5.3 The TES Initiative

The financial crisis has driven home the reality that financial services firms frequently do not possess the incentives to take systemic risk seriously. While these firms, their shareholders, and employees capture the benefits of their socially excessive risk taking, they bear only a portion of the costs. Indeed, of all the issues to emerge from the crisis, the fact that public resources had to be diverted to private firms to prevent systemic collapse remains the most controversial. The salient question thus becomes: can process-oriented regulation help constrain socially excessive risk taking? Put differently: does the TCF Initiative's process-oriented approach provide a template for what we might for argument's sake call a 'Taking Externalities Seriously' (or TES) Initiative?[10]

The objectives of a TES Initiative might include ensuring that: (1) the identification and avoidance of socially excessive risk taking is embedded in firm culture; (2) any risks generated by the firm's activities which may create or exacerbate systemic risk are promptly identified and continually monitored; (3) firms understand their own exposure to systemic risks; and (4) firms take action to minimise these risks on an ongoing basis. Importantly, these objectives would engage firms in the important and difficult task of developing better metrics of systemic risk—something which represents an ongoing challenge for regulators (Bisias et al. 2012).

Like the TCF Initiative, the TES Initiative would seek to make socially excessive risk taking a business and cultural issue for firms, with compliance measured against both the delivery of desired regulatory outcomes and ongoing engagement. Through internal engagement and dialogue, the TES Initiative would aim to foster the generation of a cultural norm that foregrounds awareness amongst employees that their conduct has social consequences. Awareness, of course, is not the same thing as understanding. Individual employees, no matter how intelligent, are incapable of processing the full systemic implications of their activities. Yet awareness that their actions *may* have systemic implications may generate some individual restraint, as well as encourage engagement with the processes, systems and controls designed to manage these risks.

---

[10] For the present purposes, we bracket questions about the types of financial institutions to which the TES Initiative should apply.

On paper, therefore, the potential benefits of the TES Initiative are compelling. But are they achievable? As a preliminary matter, the conceptual problems associated with the design and implementation of the TES Initiative would be significantly greater than either the TCF or Extended TCF Initiatives. While 'fairness' is in many respects an amorphous concept, it can readily be given more precise content in the context of the bilateral customer/counterparty relationships. Socially excessive risk taking, in contrast, is extremely difficult to *define*—let alone *identify* before it crystallises as a negative externality. These conceptual problems would render it more difficult for regulators to provide meaningful firm-specific and industry guidance. They would also make enforcement action inherently more problematic.[11] These enforcement problems would be compounded by the likely impotence of market-based sanctions in response to socially excessive risk taking (see Armour et al. 2013).

Perhaps the most compelling response to these concerns is that, as described above, process-oriented regulation is designed to promote engagement with desired regulatory outcomes and, through engagement, to promote cultural norms that deter socially undesirable behaviour. In the aftermath of the crisis, it cannot be denied that there is such a thing as socially excessive risk taking. Nevertheless, it is inevitable that when dealing with something this complex, different firms (or regulators) will adopt divergent perspectives respecting, inter alia, whether and to what extent various activities generate systemic risk and how best to address it. What process-oriented regulatory strategies such as the proposed TES Initiative attempt to do is stimulate meaningful and ongoing dialogue within firms about these important questions. It then provides firms with the flexibility to design and implement firm-specific processes which reflect the results of this dialogic process. Put simply, in a domain where there are few right answers, the objective of the TES Initiative would be to engender a culture in which firms continually questioned the impact of their activities on others.

13.6 Governance Strategies

The objective underlying each of the regulatory strategies described above is to foster a more ethical culture within financial services firms. Yet, as the crisis clearly illustrates, private incentives will at times conflict with both pre-existing ethical commitments and public regulatory objectives. It

---

[11] Uncertainty regarding the applicable regulatory standard could of course lead to legal challenges. Moreover, where the materialisation of a risk would wipe out the firm, we would expect the threat of *ex post* enforcement to have little impact on *ex ante* incentives to take the risk (especially where there was no recourse to the assets of the decision makers). This is because in states of the world where the risk materialises, the marginal costs of enforcement action would be zero.

follows that, in order for a more ethical culture to form and flourish through process-oriented regulation, we must first address these countervailing incentives.

The FSA's experience with the TCF Initiative underscores the importance of leadership and commitment on the part of senior management as a necessary precondition to any shift toward a more ethical culture. If the stated commitment on the part of senior managers is not backed up by observable action, it is highly unlikely that the desired cultural shift will take place. However, whereas employees will observe and easily interpret mixed managerial signals, regulators may struggle to differentiate between (unequivocal) managerial word and (equivocal) action. Managers may, therefore, be able to creatively comply through ostensible engagement that ultimately has limited impact on the ground. Clearly, then, managerial incentives are of central importance.

There are two key drivers of managerial incentives. The first is personal compensation arrangements, where those arrangements are linked directly or indirectly to firm performance. The second is managers' relationships with shareholders and, ultimately, shareholder value. Shareholders in financial institutions, as in other firms, possess powerful incentives to encourage managers—through their remuneration arrangements and other means—to focus on value creation. Within systemically important firms, however, these same incentives also drive shareholders to encourage managers to take socially excessive risks. Accordingly, to increase the probability that the regulatory strategies described above will succeed, managers need to be given room to resist shareholder pressure to focus on shareholder value.

What, then, are the governance tools available to create this decision-making space? Below we canvass a range of possible strategies. Some of these strategies—e.g. remuneration and corporate objective rules—may be viewed as prerequisites. Others, meanwhile, may be viewed as facilitative but, ultimately, optional. What is more, certain of these optional strategies may be viewed as, at least in part, substitutes. Accordingly, whether any particular jurisdiction employs governance strategies that provide fertile soil for our proposals must be assessed holistically. Such comparative jurisdictional assessments are beyond the scope of this chapter.

13.6.1 Remuneration

The view is now widespread that one of the primary drivers of socially excessive risk taking within financial services firms prior to the crisis was the structure of remuneration arrangements. These arrangements incentivised decision making that focused on short-term financial gains, often unrealised in cash terms. Indeed, in many instances, financial institutions appear to have remunerated managers and other employees on the basis of the short-term upside of transactions, but not the potential long-term downside (Bebchuk and Spamann 2010). In the wake of the crisis, domestic and transnational regulatory responses have thus focused on ensuring that: (1) pay more accurately reflects both short-term and longer-term risks; (2) there are limits on performance-based pay; (3) any performance-based pay has a limited cash component, and (4) a substantial portion of performance-based pay is deferred over a significant period of time (e.g. three to five years).

However, even where remuneration arrangements are linked to the long-term value of the firm, these arrangements may still generate undesirable incentives. Insofar as firms profit from the exploitation of asymmetries of information and expertise in relation to highly complex products, for example, this imposes costs on their less informed counterparties. In relation to socially excessive risk taking, meanwhile, the long-term outlook of the firm may support an approach to risk that, from society's perspective, is clearly undesirable. Specifically, if the primary objective of firms is to generate shareholder value then rational managers acting in the interests of their shareholders will exploit any implicit and uncosted state guarantee. If the risks pay off, shareholders win; if they do not, society loses. Requiring employees to maximise a firm's value within a three- to five-year time frame (as the new remuneration rules and guidelines contemplate) will thus not necessarily place a break on socially excessive risk taking.

In theory, clawback provisions hold out greater potential to alter managerial incentives. Properly drafted, clawbacks can ensure that the costs generated by socially excessive risks are borne not just by society, but also by the individuals who actually took them. The devil of such clawbacks, however, is in the details. Do they apply to *paid* or merely *deferred* remuneration? If the former, how far is the look-back period? And what is the extent of prior earnings which must be repaid? Clawbacks of the variety set forth in the PRA/FCA's Remuneration Code—which apply only to unvested deferred remuneration—incentivise managers to discount only the deferred benefit of the socially excessive risk taking by the probability that the risks will materialise within the vesting time frame. In these behavioural calculations, we would expect managers to also take into account the benefits of any increase in fixed (and non-recoverable) salary—as well as job security—arising from risk taking aligned with broader institutional incentives. Compounding matters, financial institutions may attempt to realign incentives by simply increasing fixed pay.

The US Dodd–Frank Act, in contrast, authorises the Federal Deposit Insurance Corporation (FDIC) to impose clawbacks on senior executives who are 'substantially responsible' for bank failure. On one level, FDIC clawbacks are broader than those under PRA/FCA rules insofar as they apply to *all* compensation. On another level, however, they are narrower in that they (1) focus on personal rather than collective (e.g. business unit) responsibility and (2) only apply when a bank is in FDIC receivership. Furthermore, the FDIC rules will only apply to compensation earned within one to two years of the appointment of the FDIC as receiver. A rational manager would therefore discount the benefit of risky behaviour against the probability that such risks will result in receivership in a one- to two-year period (as well as the probability that the FDIC will be able to establish 'substantial responsibility'). As the crisis has demonstrated, however, holding individual managers to account is very difficult. It follows that the probability of clawback under these rules is also low.

The personal and institutional incentives of managers and other employees subject to the reformed remuneration rules manifest the potential to crowd out a process-oriented approach toward the promotion of a more ethical culture. Within such an environment, there is a risk that measures such as the TCF, Extended TCF, and TES Initiatives would be reduced to ethical window dressing. At the same time, it has now become relatively commonplace for companies to include non-financial targets such as employee satisfaction, health and safety, and environmental measures alongside financial measures in executive remuneration arrangements (PricewaterhouseCoopers 2010). Indeed, the PRA/FCA Remuneration Code requires that non-financial performance metrics comprise a significant part of the performance assessment process. These metrics include risk management and compliance with the regulatory system. Indeed, some financial institutions have voluntarily gone further than this. Morgan Stanley, for example, has recently altered the provisions in its remuneration arrangements with senior managers to enable clawbacks where, inter alia, there are violations of articulated ethical standards. Such non-financial targets could be extended to explicitly incorporate the level of engagement, implementation, and compliance with the TCF, Extended TCF, and TES Initiatives. Building on the role of ethics committees noted above, and the existing role of risk committees vis-à-vis remuneration, the ethics committee could take responsibility for setting such non-financial remuneration targets. Furthermore, by connecting remuneration to the performance of particular groups—e.g. a product group, business unit, or division —remuneration could drive peer group monitoring.

13.6.2 Composition Reforms: Board-Level Ethics Committees

An important question raised by the crisis is how weaknesses in the structure and composition of boards of directors of financial services firms might have contributed to their failure. The focus to date has been on the competence of independent directors and the role of the board in effectively managing risk (*Walker Review* 2009). The primary regulatory response, then, has been to require that some firms—i.e. banks and other 'credit institutions'—form board-level risk committees under the control of independent directors (Basel Committee on Banking Supervision 2010).

To date, ethics and culture have not featured in this board composition debate. In the UK, for example, the *Walker Review of Corporate Governance in UK Banks and Other Financial Industry Entities* (2009) did not envision a specific role for boards with regard to firm culture. Nevertheless, many UK companies—including financial services firms—do have, and had prior to the crisis, board committees whose remit it is to address firm ethics (*Walker Review* 2009). It is important to keep in mind, however, the limits of board composition reforms. It is unlikely, for example, that such reforms would have prevented any of the major bank failures during the crisis, or indeed have altered the board composition of many of those failing banks.

Nevertheless, the role of a board-level ethics committee is worth canvassing in the post-crisis board composition debate. Indeed, an ethics committee, on which executive and non-executive directors sit and to which senior management reports,[12] could be an important piece of the puzzle in terms of promoting a more ethical culture. First, working together with senior management, an ethics committee could take the lead in establishing and revising a firm's processes, systems, and controls consistent with applicable regulatory objectives. More specifically, an ethics committee could be responsible for setting the firm-specific ethical outcomes and then monitoring the processes developed by management, and benchmarking their effects in practice and over time. An ethics committee could also be responsible for establishing and monitoring the effectiveness of disciplinary procedures and for overseeing the management information systems that gather information about engagement and compliance with the processes and procedures designed to engender a more ethical culture. Second, a board-level ethics committee would send a signal to management and other employees that the firm is serious about promoting a more ethical culture.

13.7 Corporate Law: The Objective of Bank Activity

There is a longstanding debate about in whose interests a company should be run: whose interests directors should consider when they make decisions. Many argue that directors should be required to take into account the interests of *all* corporate stakeholders when they act, without any legal direction to prioritise one constituency over another. This approach is referred to as a

---

[12] As its key function would be to hold management to account for their leadership and engagement, the ethics committee would be majority-controlled by the non-executive directors.

'pluralistic' or 'multiple-interest' model of the corporation (Kershaw 2012). Several justifications have been given for this approach. Some commentators, observing that the corporate form is a 'gift' from the state and that corporations exert enormous influence over all our lives, have argued that this gives rise to a quasi-public responsibility to consider the interests of all stakeholders (Dodd 1932). Economic justifications, meanwhile, focus on the incentives for firm-specific human capital investments by employees which are generated by knowing that their interests count as much as anyone else's (Blair and Stout 1999). Whether or not one is persuaded by such arguments more generally, given the stark consequences of the crisis and the necessity for publicly funded bailouts, the case for a multiple-interest model in relation to financial services firms is compelling. At the very least, there is a powerful justification in relation to systemically important firms for a model that gives more priority to the interests of broader society.

Indeed, a form of the multiple-interest model can be viewed as essential for creating the conditions necessary for the promotion of a more ethical culture through strategies such as the TCF, Extend TCF, and TES Initiatives. All actors, from the board down to the individual trader, need to know that when there is a conflict between regulatory objectives and the pursuit of shareholder value, it is lawful, legitimate, and *expected* that they will prioritise fair treatment or the avoidance of potential externalities. Managerial leadership and commitment will manifestly be undermined if the law's core statement of directors' obligations fails to take account of the 'other-regarding' obligations that are foundational to achieving this objective. Furthermore, the imposition of a legal obligation to make decisions on the basis of an 'other-regarding' standard may assist managers in managing, and at times resisting, shareholder pressure to take excessive risks.

In most jurisdictions, this prerequisite is unproblematic insofar as all corporations are subject to a multiple-interest model. This is the case, for example, for firms incorporated in New York, Germany, or Austria. One jurisdiction where this is not the case, however, is the UK. Indeed, it is worthwhile noting in this regard that the *Walker Review* rejected the suggestion that the existing duty to promote the interests of shareholders should be amended to reflect the fact that banks are different. Encouragingly, however, recent remarks by a former CEO of the FSA on the subject of banking culture suggest that UK regulators may be open to the idea of revisiting this issue (Sants 2010).

13.8 Corporate Law: Shareholder Rights

One needs to be wary of overstating the importance of the corporate purpose debate. Through an instrumental lens, even if given discretion to act in the interests of multiple constituencies, it seems likely that the constituency to whom directors and managers will be compelled to answer will be the one whose interests they prioritise in the case of conflict between shareholder value and other stakeholder interests. That is, the background structure of shareholder rights will continue to influence their decision making. However, whilst in all jurisdictions shareholders have the power to appoint and remove directors, they are not equal when it comes to the nature and extent of shareholder rights. As a result, the impact those rights have on senior management and firm decision making and behaviour may differ.

In the UK, for example, shareholders have very powerful rights. They have the non-waivable right to remove directors without cause by a simple majority, along with the right to call a meeting when 5% of the shareholder body instructs the board to do so (*Companies Act 2006*: ss. 168 and 303). In the US, in contrast, although the rules vary from state to state, it is open to most firms to select jurisdictions which permit weaker removal rights. A firm incorporated in Delaware, for example, can elect to have a classified board where the directors have three-year terms and can only be removed with cause (Delaware General Incorporation Law, s.141(k)). Furthermore, shareholders of a Delaware company only have the right to call an interim shareholder meeting where the charter or bylaws authorise them to do so. In Germany, meanwhile, the supervisory board directors may be removed at any time without cause, but the removal threshold is a supermajority (75%)—making removal difficult in practice.

Recent empirical work suggests that this predicted relationship between shareholder rights and the behaviour of financial services firms is very real. Ferreira et al. (2012) construct a 'management insulation index' (MII) and apply this index to all US banks to measure the extent and variation in shareholder rights. They then regress MII index scores against, inter alia, data on which banks were bailed out through the US Troubled Asset Relief Program (TARP). TARP is viewed by the authors as a proxy for a bank's pre-crisis susceptibility to failure and an arguable proxy for excessive risk taking. They find the banks which were less insulated were more likely to be bailed out. For Ferriera et al., the most compelling explanation for the relationship between managerial insulation and bank failure is that banks which are subject to stronger shareholder rights are more susceptible to shareholder pressure to take excessive risks, and therefore more likely to fail. This generates what would be for many commentators and policymakers a counter-intuitive result: *for banks*, stronger and not weaker shareholder rights are a problem.

For our purposes, this suggests that where directors of financial services firms are subject to powerful shareholder rights, then the objective of fostering a more ethical culture is likely to be subordinated. This effect will be more powerful when strong shareholder rights and pressure are combined with a corporate objective that prioritises shareholder interests. However, even when a bank is subject to a multiple-interest rule, as Ferriera et al.'s (2012) US study shows, such rights may drive behaviour that disregards non-shareholder concerns. It follows that where there are more powerful shareholder rights, managers' commitment to the implementation of the TCF, Extended TCF, and TES Initiatives is likely to more muted, thus undermining their potential effectiveness. This suggests that, to create space for the formation of a more ethical culture, regulators will need to tack against the prevailing consensus that banks should be subject to stronger, not weaker, shareholder rights. It also suggests that, *ceteris paribus*, the US and Germany provide more fertile soil for these regulatory strategies than, for example, the UK.

13.9 Corporate Law: The Duty of Care

We have considered the ways in which a more ethical culture could be connected to remuneration and other governance arrangements which incentivise senior managers to commit to regulatory strategies such as the TCF, Extended TCF, and TES Initiatives. But as managerial leadership is central to the success of these strategies, we also need to consider the role that the threat of potential liability might play.

Imposing liability upon directors for failing to take due care in their treatment of counterparties or in their approach toward risk taking would be one approach to incentivising managerial leadership. At the same time, regulators need to be wary of imposing care expectations on directors. Where the standards are too high, directors will be fearful that carefully taken but unsuccessful decisions will be judged unfavourably with the benefit of hindsight. As a result, directors may either refuse to serve or take an excessively risk-averse approach toward the generation, monitoring, and enforcement of the relevant processes, systems, and controls.

It is this policy concern that explicitly informs Delaware corporate law's gross negligence standard. This standard is violated only where it can be shown that directors were recklessly indifferent to the interests of the corporation (*In re Walt Disney Co.* 2005) or, in relation to internal controls, that there was 'a sustained or systematic failure of the board to exercise oversight—such as an utter failure to attempt to assure a reasonable information and reporting system exists' (*In re Caremark Int'l Inc.* 1996; *In re Citigroup Inc.* 2009; *Stone v Ritter* 2006). Perhaps, as John Armour and Jeffrey Gordon argue in Chapter 11, the policy concerns that underpin Delaware's duty of care jurisprudence are less weighty in economic contexts, such as banking, where risk taking is necessary and socially desirable but where, simultaneously, such risk taking threatens to generate significant negative externalities. In such contexts, dampening directors' incentives to take risks may represent a more defensible policy objective. For our purposes, if regulators make this election in favour of a more demanding standard of care, this could play a role in incentivising managers to meaningfully engage with the TCF, Extend TCF, and TES Initiatives, and thereby help foster a more ethical culture.

In the UK, higher care standards are already in place, although the probability of their enforcement is generally thought to be very low (Armour 2008). The UK standard is that of a hypothetical reasonable average director where—if the *actual* director in question has above-average skills and experience—the hypothetical director is imbued with those qualities. It is worth briefly examining how our proposed regulatory strategies could interact with this general standard. In order to understand the expectations generated by the care standard, recent Australian case law—applying a reasonable average director standard—has begun to draw on best-practice guidance contained in corporate governance codes and trade association guidelines. These sources are used to identify the functions and context-specific expectations of directors when determining whether they have taken reasonable care. In *Australian Securities and Investments Commission v Rich* (2003), for example, the court took into account, inter alia, observations on the roles of directors in UK reports on board composition regulation (Higgs 2003). More recently, the court in *Australian Securities and Investments Commission v Healey* (2011) drew on materials produced by the Australian Institute for Directors about a director's role vis-à-vis financial statements in order to understand the role and function of non-executive directors.

Following the lead of these Australian cases, guidelines and rules about a director's function and role can be used by courts to flesh out the substantive content of the duty of care. It can be argued, therefore, that where the TCF, Extended TCF, and TES Initiatives place explicit obligations on directors to spearhead implementation, a failure to take such duties seriously could expose directors to personal liability. Similarly, non-executive directors on our proposed ethics committee may be subject to liability if they fail to perform their oversight role with due care.

Of course, in any jurisdiction where a high standard of care is adopted, the extent to which it will incentivise directors to take their obligations under the TCF, Extended TCF, and TES Initiatives seriously will be a function not only of the standard itself, but also the probability of enforcement by the firm, a shareholder, or (as is possible in Australia) the regulator. However, here is not the place to address these broader corporate law issues. Furthermore, even in jurisdictions where the standard of care is demanding and the probability of enforcement high, one would not expect to see many cases where directors are found personally liable.[13] Indeed, the imposition of liability on directors is very rare in all jurisdictions (Black et al. 2006). Of course, this does not mean that the threat of liability would not influence behaviour.[14]

13.10 Conclusion

There is little doubt that, for better or worse, culture and ethics play an important role in driving human and organisational behaviour. There is less consensus, however, surrounding the question of how we might go about generating meaningful cultural and/or ethical constraints in pursuit of broader social objectives. This chapter has canvassed some of the ways which we might seek to engender a more ethical culture within the financial services industry. More specifically, it has illustrated how process-oriented regulation, combined with more radical restructuring of the internal governance arrangements of financial services firms, might be leveraged to achieve this objective. Ultimately, however, there are no easy answers. Nevertheless, public support from across the political spectrum—along with the stated commitment of financial leaders themselves—has created the opportunity for reform, and it should be taken.

References

Armour, J. (2008). 'Enforcement Strategies in UK Corporate Governance: A Roadmap and Empirical Assessment', ECGI Working Paper No. 106/2008.

Armour, J., Mayer, C., and Polo, A. (2012). 'Regulatory Sanctions and Reputational Damage in Financial Markets', Oxford Legal Studies Research Paper No. 62/2010.

Australian Securities and Investments Commission v Rich (2003). 44 ACSR 431.

Australian Securities and Investments Commission v Healey (2011). 278 ALR 618.

Australian Securities and Investments Commission v Healey (No 2) [2012]. FCA 1003.

Awrey, D. (2012). 'Complexity, Innovation and the Regulation of Modern Financial Markets', *Harvard Business Law Review*, 2(2): 235–94.

Basel Committee on Banking Supervision. (2010). 'Basel III: A Global Regulatory Framework for More Resilient Banks and Banking Systems' (revised 2011).

Bebchuk, L. and Spamann, H. (2010). 'Regulating Bankers Pay', *Georgetown Law Journal*, 98: 247–87.

[13] Even in Australia, where ASIC has the power to enforce breaches of duty, we still do not see higher levels of director liability. In *ASIC v Healey*, for example, although the directors were found in breach, no financial penalty was imposed upon them; *ASIC v Healey (No.2)* (2012).

[14] Both *positively* in ensuring that regulatory obligations are taken seriously and *negatively* insofar as skilled executive and non-executive directors refuse to serve.

Bernstein, L. (1992). 'Opting Out of the Legal System: Extralegal Contractual Relations in the Diamond Industry', *The Journal of Legal Studies*, 21(1): 115–57.

Bernstein, L. (2001). 'Private Commercial Law in the Cotton Industry: Creating Cooperation through Rules, Norms and Institutions', *Michigan Law Review*, 99: 1724–90.

Bisias, D. et al. (2012). 'A Survey of Systemic Risk Analytics', OFR Working Paper No. 0001.

Black, B., Cheffins, B., and Klausner, M. (2006). 'Outside Director Liability', *Stanford Law Review*, 58: 1055–1159.

Black, J. (1997). *Rules and Regulators*. Oxford: Clarendon Press.

Black, J. (2008). 'Forms and Paradoxes of Principles-Based Regulation', *Capital Markets Law Journal*, 3: 425–58.

Blair, M. and Stout, L. (1999). 'A Team Production Theory of Corporate Law', *Virginia Law Review*, 85: 247–328.

Campbell v Loews, Inc. 36 Del. Ch. 563, 134 A.2d 852 (1957).

Chartered Financial Analyst Institute (CFA) (2012a). *Code of Ethics and Standards of Professional Conduct*.

Chartered Financial Analyst Institute (2000–2012b). Disciplinary Statistics.

Dodd, M. (1932). 'For Whom Are Corporate Managers Trustees?', *Harvard Law Review*, 45: 1145–63.

Ellickson, R. (1994). *Order Without Law: How Neighbors Settle Disputes*. Cambridge, MA: Harvard University Press.

Etzioni, A. (1988). *The Moral Dimension: Toward A New Economics*. New York: Free Press.

European Commission (2004). Markets in Financial Instruments Directive 2004/39/EC.

Ferreira, D. et al. (2012). 'Shareholder Empowerment and Bank Bailouts', working paper.

Financial Services Authority (2006). 'Treating Customers Fairly—Towards Fair Outcomes for Consumers'.

Financial Services Authority (2007a). 'Treating Customers Fairly—Culture'.

Financial Services Authority (2007b). 'FSA Finds Poor Practices by Intermediaries and Lenders within Sub-Prime Market'.

Financial Services Authority (2012). TCF Library.

Foot, P. (1978). 'The Problem of Abortion and the Doctrine of the Double Effect', in P. Foot (ed.), *Virtues and Vices: And Other Essays in Moral Philosophy*, Berkeley: University of California Press, 19–32.

Frederick, S. (2005). 'Cognitive Reflection and Decision Making', *Journal of Economic Perspectives*, 19: 25–42.

Friedman, M. (1962). *Capitalism and Freedom*. Chicago: University of Chicago Press.

Gilad, S. (2010). 'Overcoming Resistance to Regulation via Reframing and Delegation', LSE Centre for Analysis of Risk and Regulation, Discussion Paper 64, June.

Gilad, S. (2012). 'It Runs in the Family: Meta-Regulation and Its Siblings', *Regulation & Governance*, 4: 485–506.

Greene, J. (2007). 'Why are VMPFC Patients more Utilitarian? A Dual-Process Theory of Moral Judgment Explains', *Trends in Cognitive Science*, 11: 322–3.

Greene, J. et al. (2001). 'An fMRI Investigation of Emotional Engagement in Moral Judgment', *Science*, 293: 2105–8.

Greene, J. et al. (2004). 'The Neural Bases of Cognitive Conflict and Control in Moral Judgment', *Neuron*, 44: 389–400.

Greif, A. (1993). 'Contract Enforceability and Economic Institutions in Early Trade: The Maghribi Traders' Coalition', *American Economic Review*, 83: 525–48.

Gunia, B. et al. (2012). 'Contemplation and Conversation: Subtle Influences on Moral Decision Making', *Academy of Management Journal*, 55(1): 13–33.

Haidt, J. (2001). 'The Emotional Dog and Its Rational Tail: A Social Intuitionist Approach to Moral Judgment', *Psychological Review*, 108: 814–34.

Higgs, D. (2003). 'Review of the Role and Effectiveness of Non-Executive Directors'. London: Department of Trade and Industry.

Holmes, O. W. (1897). 'The Path of the Law', *Harvard Law Review*, 10: 457.

In re Caremark Int'l Inc. Derivative Litig., 698 A.2d 959 (Del. Ch. 1996).

In re Citigroup Inc. Shareholder Derivative Litig., 964 A.2d 106 (Del. Ch. 2009).

In re Walt Disney Co. Derivative Litig., 907 A.2d 693 (Del. Ch. 2005).

Jones, T. (1991). 'Ethical Decision-Making by Individuals in Organizations: An Issue-Contingent Model', *Academic Management Review*, 16: 366–95.

Kahneman, D. (2002). 'Maps of Bounded Rationality: A Perspective on Intuitive Judgment and Choice', Nobel Prize Lecture.

Kahneman, D. and Frederick, S. (2002). 'Representativeness Revisited: Attribute Substitution in Intuitive Judgment', in T. Gilovich, D. Griffin, and D. Kahneman (eds), *Heuristics and Biases: The Psychology of Intuitive Judgment*. Cambridge: Cambridge University Press, 49–81.

Kallgren, C., Reno, R., and Cialdini, R. (2000). 'A Focus Theory of Normative Conduct: When Norms Do and Do Not Affect Behavior', *Personality & Social Psychological Bulletin*, 26: 1002–12.

Kershaw, D. (2012). *Company Law in Context: Text and Materials*. Oxford: Oxford University Press.

Murnighan, K., Cantelon, D., and Elyashic, T. (2001). 'Bounded Personal Ethics and the Tap Dance of the Real Estate Agency', in J. Wagner, J. Bartunek, and K. Elsbach (eds), *Advances in Qualitative Organizational Research*. Elsevier/JAI Press, 1–40.

Parker, C. (2007). 'Meta-Regulation: Legal Accountability for Corporate Social Responsibility', in D. McBarnet, A. Voiculescu, and T. Campbell (eds), *The New Corporate Accountability: Corporate Social Responsibility and the Law*. Cambridge: Cambridge University Press, 207–40.

Parker, C. and Gilad, S. (2011). 'Internal Compliance Management Systems: Structure, Culture and Agency', in C. Parker and V. Nielson (eds), *Explaining Compliance: Business Responses to Regulation*. Cheltenham: Edward Elgar, 170–98.

PricewaterhouseCoopers (2010). 'Executive Compensation: Review of the Year 2009'.

Ratner, R. and Miller, D. (2001). 'The Norm of Self-Interest and Its Effects on Social Action', *Journal of Personality & Social Psychology*, 81: 5–16.

Sants, H. (2010). 'Do Regulators Have a Role to Play in Judging Culture and Ethics?', speech to the Chartered Institute of Securities and Investments Conference.

Stone v Ritter, 911 A.2d 362 (Del. Supr. 2006).

Thomson, J. and Parent, W. (eds) (1986). *Rights, Restitution, and Risk: Essays in Moral Theory*. Cambridge, MA: Harvard University Press.

UK *Companies Act 2006*, c. 46.

UK Competition Commission (2011). Payment Protection Insurance Market Investigation Order 2011.

UK Parliamentary Commission on Banking Standards (2013). 'Final Report— Changing Banking for Good'.

US *Dodd–Frank Wall Street Reform and Consumer Protection Act*, Pub. L. No. 111–203 (2010).

Valdesolo, P. and DeSteno, D. (2006). 'Manipulations of Emotional Context Shape Moral Judgment', *Psychological Science*, 17: 476–7.

Walker Review (2009). *A Review of Corporate Governance in UK Banks and Other Financial Industry Entities: Final Recommendations*.

14

Trust, Conflicts of Interest, and Fiduciary Duties: Ethical Issues in the Financial Planning Industry in Australia

Seumas Miller

In the Australian financial planning industry, as elsewhere in the finance sector, ethical issues have come to the fore in recent times. On the one hand, Australia has not entirely escaped the ethical problems underlying, or at least associated with, the Global Financial Crisis and the consequent European Union Sovereign Debt Crisis. Consider in this connection the collapse of Westpoint, Storm Financial, and of Opes Prime (Ripoll 2009: Chapters 3 and 4), and the buying of 'exotic' financial products, such as CDOs (collateralised debt obligations) by local councils in New South Wales (O'Brien, Chapter 10 in this book). Westpoint Corporation was essentially a Ponzi scheme, but one in which financial advisors played a crucial role in recruiting investor-victims. Losses from CDOs have had a significant negative financial impact on various local councils in NSW.

On the other hand, the Australian Government has recently introduced legislation to deal with some of these problems in the professional ethics of financial advisors, in particular. In doing so, it has apparently moved beyond where its counterparts in the US, for example, have been prepared to go.[1] The so-called Future of Financial Advice (FoFA) legislation, for example, bans various forms of conflicted remuneration for financial advisors (Future of

---

[1] The Retail Distribution Review (RDR) in the UK apparently has a number of the key provisions of Future of Financial Advice (FoFA) and was implemented at the end of 2012.

Financial Advice 2011b), and attaches fiduciary duties to their roles (Future of Financial Advice 2011a).[2]

This approach resonates with some of the recent academic literature on these subjects. For example, David Vines and Nick Morris put forward a number of interrelated notions—including those of trust, reputation, professionalisation, and 'integrity systems'—in the service of addressing manifest problems in the financial services industry in the context of the GFC (Vines 2011). Importantly, they identify the problems in question as being largely moral or ethical in character, exemplified through legal and moral offences and a lack of trust. Accordingly, they propose ethics-focused solutions, such as the identification and promotion of professional obligations in the financial services industry (in the context of professionalisation) and, more broadly, the design and implementation of an appropriate integrity system.[3]

Interestingly, the Australian Securities and Investments Commission (ASIC) appears to be offering a not unrelated diagnosis and treatment in relation to the financial products and services industry in Australia. According to Peter Kell, an ASIC Commissioner:

> Holding the gatekeepers of the financial service system to account is an important aspect of ASIC's work and is fundamental to consumer trust. Gatekeepers, in the widest definition of the term, include accountants, directors, custodians, product manufacturers, market operators and participants, and of course financial advisers. ASIC has signalled it will take action where gatekeepers do not meet their responsibilities. (Kell 2012)

I have set myself two principal tasks in this paper. First, I provide a conceptual analysis of the key ethical or moral—I use these terms interchangeably—notions of trust, fiduciary duties, and conflicts of interest as they pertain to the financial planning industry in general. Second, I apply this ethico-conceptual framework to the financial planning industry in Australia in the context of FoFA and the envisaged professionalisation process more broadly, and do so with a view to identifying areas of ethical promise, but also of continued ethical concern.

14.1 Introduction: Financial Advisors in Australia

The term 'financial advisors in Australia' can be understood as an aggregate of individual advisors each going about his or her various advisory and other

---

[2] See Government of Australia (2011, 2012). Hereafter I will refer to these bills as the FoFA legislation. See O'Brien (2010) for a commentary.

[3] For a detailed study of integrity systems for occupations see Alexandra and Miller (2010).

tasks (the set of financial advisors), or it can be understood as an institution-alised occupational group functioning in a particular institutional setting or perhaps a set of interconnected institutional settings (the financial products and services industry). Let us refer to the first mode as a micro-occupational perspective and the latter as a macro-institutional perspective. For my purposes here, understanding of both the micro and macro dimensions is relevant, and especially the relationship between them.

The financial products and services industry in Australia includes manufacturing and selling financial products (e.g. investment and insurance products) and providing custodial or depository services (e.g. basic banking services), as well as providing financial advice. Importantly, the financial services industry in Australia includes the superannuation industry, Australia's system of compulsory retirement savings.[4]

Superannuation differs from some other social institutions, including some of those in the financial services sector, in that it has been intentionally designed by Australian policymakers to serve a particular purpose (provide for the financial needs of retirees) and do so by a specific means (compulsory savings for the workforce).

Employers are required to make tax-deductible contributions on behalf of their employees, equivalent to 9% of their employees' wages or salary. The majority of Australians are members of institutional superannuation funds that are required to be set up as trusts to offer the protection of trust law to members. These institutional funds are regulated mainly by the Australian Prudential Regulation Authority (APRA), although issues related to market conduct, consumer protection, and disclosure fall within the ambit of ASIC. However, the trustees of most funds outsource the investment management and administration to third parties in the private sector.

According to research conducted by ASIC (2010: 17), the biggest areas in which Australians seek professional financial advice are in relation to superannuation, financial investment (e.g. shares and managed funds), and the financing of property investment. Retirement is the main trigger for seeking financial advice. Here it is important to stress the centrality in Australia of financial advice in relation to the provision of funds for retirement, whether by way of superannuation, investment in shares, or other means. Accordingly, the financial advice in question very often has great moral significance by virtue of its influence on the capacity (or not, as the case may be) for ordinary Australians to provide for themselves in retirement.

ASIC's research also found that there are significant gaps in the financial literacy of Australians, and there is significant mistrust among Australians

---

[4] The system recently had an extensive review: see Cooper (2011).

of financial planners with respect to the provision to unbiased professional advice (ASIC 2010: 5). A distinction is typically made between sophisticated investors and unsophisticated or retail investors. However, it is not entirely clear what this distinction is, or where the line is to be drawn, supposing the distinction is clarified. The manufacture of complex, 'exotic' financial products, which almost no one seems to understand adequately, has compounded problems in this area (O'Brien: Chapter 10 in this book). At any rate, my principal concern in this paper is with the unsophisticated end of the scale.

Financial service providers are required to hold an Australian Financial Service Licence (AFSL). AFSLs impose various conduct and disclosure obligations on financial service providers, and licensees are regulated by the Australian Securities and Investment Council (ASIC). Authorised representatives (e.g. many financial advisors) and employees of AFSL holders are not required to hold licences themselves.

There are some 18,000 financial advisors in Australia most of whom operate through one of the 1,600 or so dealer groups. Approximately twenty of these dealer groups have 50% market share (Ripoll 2009: 16). According to ASIC (quoted in Ripoll 2009: 16), there are three main business models: (1) Medium to large dealer groups that operate like a franchise with the licensee providing back-office support. Advisors are authorised representatives of a licensee and provide a percentage of their remuneration to the licensee, e.g. AMP Financial Planning. (2) Institutional-owned financial advisor firms with employed advisors. Advisors are paid a salary and/or a proportion of the commission earned, e.g. Westpac Financial Planning. (3) Smaller firms that have their own licence.

According to ASIC:

> Today financial advisers usually play a dual role of providing advice to clients and acting as a sales force for financial product manufacturers. Approximately 85% of advisers are associated with a product manufacturer, so that many advisers act as a product pipeline. Of the remainder the vast majority receive commissions from product manufacturers and so have incentives to sell products...This structure creates potential conflicts of interest that may be inconsistent with providing quality service and these conflicts may not be evident to consumers. (Quoted in Ripoll 2009: 70 section 5.8)

The Ripoll Report stated: 'the other conflict of interest for advisers stems from the relationship between product manufacturers and the adviser's licensee. Specifically, advisers who are authorised representatives of licensed advisory groups owned by product manufacturers in a vertically integrated business model are conflicted' (Ripoll 2009: 79).

In its submission to the Ripoll Report, the Industry Super Network noted the dominance of large, vertically financial institutions and stated:

These large conglomerate institutions typically own all aspects of the financial services value chain from banking, wholesale funds management, product manufacture, administration and retail distribution including financial planning. The bulk of the financial planning industry is concentrated in the hands of relatively few institutions. Rainmaker Information reports that 73% of adviser groups are institutionally owned, if taken by adviser numbers, or 78% if taken from funds under advice. Many financial institutions operate a number of different sub-brands within their groups...The institutional ownership of the bulk of financial planning dealerships is significant because it reinforces the concern that financial advisers are compromised by the commercial imperative of selling and distributing the products manufactured by their parent or related party organizations. (Ripoll 2009: 79)

The key recommendations of the Ripoll Report in relation to such conflicts of interest are Recommendation 1 regarding the introduction of a fiduciary duty for financial advisors (Ripoll 2009: 150), and Recommendation 4 regarding the cessation of payments from financial product manufacturers to financial advisors (Ripoll 2009: 151).

These two recommendations have found their way into the FoFA legislation, in the case of Recommendation 4 by way of banning certain forms of conflicted remuneration to financial advisors, such as commissions based on selling particular financial products in favour of a fee-for-services model.[5] I return to these issues in the final section of this chapter.

14.2 Financial Advisors: Occupations, Professions, and Social Institutions

I have suggested that financial advisors can be viewed both as an aggregate of individuals who are members of an occupational group (the set of financial advisors) but also as a component of an institutional structure (the financial products and services industry). Let us begin with a description of occupations before turning to institutions.

An occupation is defined by its occupational role (Alexandra and Miller 2010: Chapter 1). Roles are teleological (from the Greek word *telos* meaning point or purpose) in nature; they are distinguished from one another according to the ends or goals which they serve. While necessary to differentiate roles, the telos or end of a role is not sufficient to distinguish one role from another. Perhaps the end of lawyers, like that of police, is to ensure that the law is complied with and, in doing so, that the principles of justice that underpin the law (or which ought to) are not breached. Accordingly, we also

---

[5] See Government of Australia (2011, 2012).

need to attend to the means or type of action or activity by which the end of some occupational role is realised. Police, but not lawyers, uphold the law by means of the use, or threat of the use, of coercive force.

So occupational roles are defined in part by the end or ends that they serve, and in part by the types of action or activities that they perform, which are the means to that end(s). Thus all financial advisors provide financial advice (the means) but what is the end? Is it to sell a product or to serve the financial interests of their client?

In addition, some roles are evidently in part defined by the moral beliefs, commitments, and associated attitudes that practitioners ought to have or adopt. For example, a commitment to the physical and mental well-being of 'clients' is a feature of the so-called caring occupations, e.g. nurses, social workers, psychologists. Likewise, accountants and auditors ought to have moral commitments to accuracy, truthfulness, and so on. Such moral attitudes, if widespread and interdependently held, are constitutive in part of the culture of an organisation or occupational group. So what is the culture of financial advisors? What are their prevailing commitments? Evidently, members of a financial planning business or other group typically have the culture of a sales team, e.g. success is measured in terms of the financial value of commissions earned.

Historically, a further distinction has been made between occupations and professions. All professional roles are occupational roles, but not all occupational roles are professional roles. This distinction is important here because, as mentioned above, the process of professionalisation is a key feature of the strategy, at least in Australia, to deal with ethical issues among members of the occupation of financial advisor.

Notwithstanding attempts to collapse the distinction, there is a large degree of consensus in the sociological and philosophical literature as to the characteristic features of professional occupations—features which serve to distinguish them from other occupations.[6] Three such marks are especially salient. An occupational group counts as a profession by virtue of its following features: the work of its members is oriented to the provision of some good (as opposed to mere desire or preference), e.g. health (doctors), justice (lawyers); members of the group possess and exercise creative expertise in the provision of this good; they possess a high degree of autonomy in the exercise of their expertise. The good or goods in question are typically goods in part constitutive of the interests of the clients of the professional, e.g. the doctor has as his end the good health of the patient and the good health of the patient is in the patient's interest. However, the good served by the profession

---

[6] Other marks, such as self-regulation, are more controversial. See for example Bayles (1986: 27).

and the client's interest can diverge in particular cases. Thus the lawyer serves the interest of her client and that interest, if served, will often coincide with the requirements of justice. However, the requirements of justice might not coincide with the interests of the client, e.g. if the client is rightly found to be guilty and sentenced to a term in jail.

The basic conception of professions is necessarily different from other more market-based occupations.[7] As already noted, on one view, the salient features of professions can be understood and assessed by seeing the role of the professional as the provider of ethical goods, including catering for fundamental needs, as opposed to mere desires and preferences, e.g. desire for an ice cream, a fashionable address, or a Porsche motor car. Unlike desires, needs are objective, limited, and typically—given the harm caused by unmet needs—generate moral obligations (Wiggins 1991). Accordingly, professionals have a duty to provide these goods, satisfy these needs, and the standards of professional practice are often themselves moral standards.

Given this, the relationship between professionals and their client group should not be assimilated to that which holds between buyers and sellers in a market. In the idealised (and by no means uncontested) picture of the market with which we are familiar from the writings of contemporary economists, market actors—buyers and sellers alike—are driven by selfish motivations, the desire to satisfy their own desires. A transaction is rational when, and only when, each of the parties to the transaction believes, with good reason, that their desires will be more satisfied after the transaction than they were before. In my view, as will become clear below, this picture overstates the motive of self-interest and, as a consequence, oversimplifies the motives in play in markets. Nevertheless, the motives and obligations of market actors (qua market actors) stand in some contrast with those of professionals (qua professionals).[8] For example, there is no obligation on the owner of a product to sell it if he prefers to use it, or if he judges that he will not be better off after the transaction than before. Matters are somewhat different for professionals, since they do have an obligation to provide certain kinds of goods to those in need of them. This general obligation helps explain restrictions on the contractual freedom in dealings between clients and professionals. A professional is obliged to do what is necessary for the satisfaction of a client's needs, so they are not free to enter into agreements which would prevent them from so acting. More generally, unlike market actors, when the interests of professionals and their clients conflict, professionals are obliged to act in their clients' interests.

---

[7] See Miller (2010b: chapters 6 and 10) for discussions of some of these issues.

[8] Many professionals are, of course, also market actors. However, historically, as mentioned, professionals' role in the market was constrained. This is much less so now.

We have dealt extensively with occupations and professions; what of institutions? Social institutions need to be distinguished from less complex social forms such as conventions, social norms, roles, and rituals. The latter are among the constitutive elements of institutions.

Social institutions are often organisations. Moreover, many institutions are *systems* of organisations. For example, capitalism is a particular kind of economic institution, and, in modern times, capitalism consists in large part in specific organisational forms—including multinational corporations—organised into a system. Further, some institutions are *meta-institutions*, which are institutions (organisations) that organise other institutions (including systems of organisations). For example, governments and regulatory bodies, such as ASIC, are meta-institutions. The institutional end or function of a government and its regulatory agencies largely consists of organising other institutions (both individually and collectively); thus regulatory agencies, such as ASIC and APRA, regulate and coordinate financial systems largely by way of (enforceable) legislation. Note that in the modern world many global social institutions (e.g. the global financial system) transcend, in various respects, the boundaries and jurisdictional and/or enforcement reach of the meta-institutions (e.g. national governments) that regulate and coordinate their activities.

On this teleological account of social institutions, collective ends are collective goods by virtue of their possession of the following three properties:[9] (1) they are produced, maintained, or renewed by means of the *joint activity* of members of organisations, e.g. schools, hospitals, welfare organisations, agribusinesses, electricity providers, police services, banks, superannuation trusts, i.e. by institutional role occupants; (2) they are *available to the whole community*, e.g. clean drinking water, clean environment, basic foodstuffs, electricity, banking services, legal services, education, health, safety, and security; and (3) they *ought* to be produced (or maintained or renewed) and made available to the whole community since they are desirable (as opposed to merely desired) and such that the members of the community have an *(institutional) joint moral right* to them. (See below for more on the notion of a joint right.)

Note that our notion of a collective good, as defined, is different from standard notions of so-called public goods deployed by economists and others. Economists typically define public goods as being non-rival and non-excludable. However, our notion of a collective good is defined not in terms of non-rivalness or non-excludability but in terms of its being *jointly produced* and having an explicitly normative character as the object of a *joint*

---

[9] I outline this account and the arguments for it in detail in Miller (2010b: chapter 2).

moral right, a right that each of the contributors to the joint product possesses jointly with the other contributors.[10] As such, it is available for use in relation to market-based institutions which produce goods which are rival and/or excludable, as well as in relation to non-market-based institutions.

Note also that on this teleological account the distinction, and the relationship, between the institutional (occupational) activity and its ends, on the one hand, and the rewards which may flow from that activity on the other (salaries, commission payments, profits, dividends, etc.) come into sharp focus. The rewards, e.g. so-called shareholder value, should not be confused with institutional purpose; the rewards are at best a proximate rather than an ultimate purpose and, as such, are in general overridden by the ultimate purpose, should there be a conflict. In short, the rewards exist (or ought to exist) to ensure the institutional purpose rather than the other way around. Accordingly, if financial planners are to become professionals then they ought to be aiming to have the provisions of a financial service as their ultimate and overriding aim, rather than the gaining of financial rewards for themselves.

Thus the teleological account is at variance with the shareholder view of corporate purpose. Simply put, the purpose of corporations cannot be to reward certain stakeholders, be they shareholders, managers, or workers. Rather the rewards to shareholders, managers, and workers should be determined by their contribution to the realisation of the pre-existing corporate purpose.[11]

On this teleological account of institutions (and the related teleological account of occupations described above), the collective good(s) which is the collective end of the institutions generates an array of institutional rights and duties that attach to the constitutive roles of the institution (occupations). The rights and duties in question are both institutional and moral. For example, a trustee has a legal and moral duty to avoid conflicts of interest. These rights and duties are above and beyond universal rights and obligations, e.g. the obligation not to kill or steal.

An important underlying assumption here is that contrary to much economic theory, human beings, including market actors, are not always and everywhere motivated by individual, rational self-interest, although self-interest is a powerful and pervasive driver and can be privileged in certain institutional settings, including markets. Moral beliefs and, specifically, fulfilling one's moral duty for its own sake—as the famous German philosopher, Immanuel Kant, stressed—are an important additional motivation for action. This moral sense of duty is not reducible to self-interest (no matter how self-interest is conceived, e.g. self-centredness, pursuit of one's own goals

---

[10] But a right which is not possessed by non-contributors to the joint product.

[11] For a different, but important, critique of the shareholder value theory see Stout (2012).

(whatever they might be) at the expense of the goals of others (Sen 2002)). Moreover, human beings are often irrational, both in terms of their individual and their collective self-interest. Consider the phenomena of herding and cognitive bias evidenced in booms and busts on the share market. In addition, consider the lack of knowledge and the unwillingness or inability to acquire it, on the part of so-called unsophisticated investors. Therefore, institutional design needs to proceed on the following two assumptions. First, rational self-interest, irrationality, and morality are all important drivers of, and motivations for, human action. Second, none of them necessarily dominates the others when they come into conflict, as they often do.

A further issue that arises here concerns the relationship between markets and social institutions. Markets often cater to desires and preferences, rather than collective goods in the above sense. This is as it should be. However, markets also facilitate the provision of collective goods, e.g. farming markets, banks, insurance companies, superannuation funds. The point to be made here is that the provision of collective goods ought to take priority over the satisfaction of mere aggregate desires; basic foodstuffs ought to take priority over ice cream, affordable housing for all over speculative real estate gains for some, and the availability of a pool of low-cost capital for long-term investment in bona fide businesses over profits made from trading on short-term fluctuations in share prices.[12]

14.3 Trust and Integrity Systems: Markets, Regulation, and Reputation

Having offered normative theoretical accounts of the general framework in play, namely, that of occupations, professions, and institutions, it is now time to turn to some key moral notions and, in particular, the notion of trust. I suggest that trust has a pivotal role to play in relation to compliance with, and commitment to, moral principles, on the one hand. On the other hand, trust is the principal institutional vehicle for maintaining such compliance and commitment, namely, integrity systems.

Note that by the lights of the teleological account of institutions and occupations, integrity systems presuppose that institutional and occupational normative purposes, and the institutional (moral) rights and duties that derive from them, exist and are well understood. To the extent that this is

---

[12] See the *Kay Review of UK Equity Markets and Long-Term Decision-Making: Final Report* (Kay 2012), which found that short termism is a problem in UK equity markets and largely consists of asset managers focusing on short-term movement of shares (trading) rather than long-term economic fundamentals of companies.

not so, the integrity system will lack direction. This is because its designers will not have a clear picture of the obligations and ethical purposes which the integrity system they are constructing is supposed to ensure compliance with or otherwise promote.

It goes without saying that trust is a key relationship in markets and elsewhere (O'Neill 2002): consumers trust that the products they are sold are safe, not counterfeit etc.; depositors trust banks to keep their funds safe and secure; employees trust their employers to pay the wages they owe; clients trust their lawyers; investors trust auditors; taxpayers trust their accountants; retirees trust their financial planners; and so on and so forth. Indeed, it is a truism that, without trust, human institutions, including markets and financial institutions, would collapse. Nevertheless, trust presupposes the prior notion of ethical or moral obligations and, in particular, ethical or moral virtue in a manner I try to make clear below.

As a preliminary it might be useful to distinguish trust from confidence. One speaks of having confidence in oneself or others and, in economic parlance, of confidence in the market; alternatively, there can be a loss of confidence. The notion of confidence is essentially tied to performance and, in particular, to future performance. One has confidence to the extent that one 'believes' or, more likely, acts as if one believes that oneself, others, or the market etc. will perform well. Since current decisions with respect to the future necessarily have to be made on imperfect and partial knowledge, confidence necessarily to some extent outruns evidence. Importantly, confidence is itself a determining factor in relation to future outcomes; other things being equal, a confident person is more likely to succeed than someone who lacks confidence. On the other hand, overconfidence can lead to disaster, if it ceases to bear any relationship to underlying ability.

In many collective action contexts, including markets, there is a degree of self-sustaining interdependence with respect to confidence; one person's confidence is dependent on that of others and vice versa. Moreover, as in the individual case, only multiply so, there is the possibility of confidence ceasing to bear any relation to the underlying, for example, economic fundamentals. Accordingly, confidence in collective action contexts can come to profoundly influence future outcomes, for better or worse. Hence confidence can promote investment, and hence long-term, broad-based, economic well-being; on the other hand, a collapse in confidence can restrict investment, and retard economic activity, notwithstanding the soundness of underlying economic fundamentals.

Confidence is related to, but should not be confused with, trust. Like confidence, trust pertains to future actions and outruns the evidence for those future actions. However, unlike confidence, trust involves a moral obligation on the part of the person trusted to the one doing the trusting.[13] Let me explain.

If person A trusts person B then A is dependent on B in some respect—and, therefore, to some extent vulnerable to B—and dependent on B to perform some action x. Moreover, B is under a moral obligation to perform x, or at least A believes that B is under this obligation, and believes also that B believes this. So it is not just that A is dependent on B to perform x, or even that A has brought it about that he is dependent on B to perform x; rather this dependence is such that B has a moral obligation to perform x.

In the case of confidence, matters are somewhat different. Perhaps person A forms the belief that company B will perform well and buys shares in B in order to make a good return; A has confidence in B. Indeed, A may well be, albeit perhaps unwisely, depending on B to perform well. However, it does not follow that B is under a moral obligation to A,[14] such that B will have failed to discharge that obligation if in fact B does not do well; the relationship is one of confidence, but not necessarily of trust.

Naturally, it is consistent with the above relationship of confidence that there is *in addition* a relationship of trust. For example, A trusts that B is a bona fide company that is competing in a given market, as opposed to a sham company set up to fail after an asset-stripping exercise. In the latter case, B has failed to discharge its moral obligations to A; A has breached the relationship of trust (among other moral infractions).

We should further distinguish between breaches of trust between A and B, and other breaches of moral principles on the part of B that may negatively impact on A. In particular, there are various universal, or at least very general, moral principles that each of us is obliged to comply with and each of us relies on others to comply with. Thus there is a moral principle not to kill, assault, steal from, and so on. However, the failure to comply with these principles is not necessarily a breach of trust. If B is unknown to A and B steals A's car, then B has committed a moral and legal offence. However, B has not necessarily breached A's trust in B; for there might not be any relationship of trust between A and B to breach.

Trust is a relationship between specific individuals or between groups of individuals,[15] e.g. the citizenry and government (the public trust), and one from which other individuals (or groups) are excluded. To say that A trusts B

---

[13] I am here concerned with trust relationships between institutional actors; I am not concerned with trust in personal relationships, e.g. between friends.

[14] Or at least that A believes B is under such an obligation and believes, also, that B believes this.

[15] Typically, such individuals are individual human beings. Perhaps trusting collective entities, such as corporations, is (or should be) in the last analysis trusting individual human beings. See Miller (2006: 176–93).

is not to say that A trusts C, even if in fact A *also* trusts C. Moreover, trust is a contingent relationship which is created and can cease to exist, notwithstanding the continued existence of the trustee and the person trusting.

The paradigmatic relationships of trust are between promisors and promisees (and, relatedly, parties to agreement, contracts etc.). Without trust, promises are unlikely to be believed or even made; and trust is often destroyed by broken promises. Here one needs to keep in mind that promises can be implicit as well as explicit.

Trust relationships do not necessarily involve promises. Take assertions for example. Hearers trust speakers to speak the truth (as opposed to performing some future action, as in the case of promises). However, the social practice of promising presupposes that of assertion; so presumably assertions do not necessarily involve promises.

A further category of trust relationships in institutional settings, in particular, is between professionals and clients, e.g. lawyers and clients, doctors, and patients. As mentioned above, professionals have moral obligations to their clients and clients are typically in a relation of dependence vis-à-vis professionals. This gives rise to the need for trust.

I suggested above that trust relationships in institutional settings exist at the interface between compliance with moral principles and integrity systems. Thus far I have indicated the relationship between moral principles and trust. What of the relationship between trust and integrity systems? Here there is a prior question: What are integrity systems?

So-called integrity systems[16] are arguably the primary institutional vehicle available to ensure ethico-professional obligations are discharged and to combat crime and corruption (both being very serious forms of moral offence).

Arguably, integrity systems have four principal aspects, at least potentially. First, they comprise enforceable laws and regulations, e.g. criminal codes. Second, they rely to some extent on markets. Markets serve multiple purposes, one of which is, I suggest, to incentivise ethical behaviour, e.g. customers who are cheated by a supplier are unlikely to return, other things being equal. Third, there are reputational systems, of which more is discussed below. Finally, there are socio-moral norms, the moral principles which have been internalised by members of a social group and which motivate (in part) their behaviour. Ultimately compliance with laws, and ethical incentives provided by markets and reputational devices, depend on a bedrock of widely accepted moral beliefs and other motivating moral attitudes. Integrity systems seek to maintain and reinforce these motivating attitudes by, for example, training and education programmes.

---

[16] See Miller (2010b: Chapter 6), and Alexandra and Miller (2010).

In relation to markets, integrity systems focus on removing or adjusting incentive structures which perversely promote unethical behaviour (e.g. systems of remuneration in which liability does not track responsibility), and developing or reinforcing incentive structures which reduce unethical behaviour (e.g. disclosure requirements) (Miller 2011b and Miller 2007: 297–327).

What of reputation and its relation to integrity systems? Reputation is importantly related to the discharging of moral obligations (virtue) (Miller 2011a and Miller 2010a: 387–400). Deserved or warranted reputation can provide a nexus between self-interest (including the desire to be approved of) and virtue, and between (say) the financial self-interest of financial advisors and lenders, on the one hand, and due diligence, truthfulness, etc. in their dealings with investors, and borrowers. Here there are three elements in play: (i) reputation; (ii) financial self-interest; and (iii) virtue (e.g. ongoing compliance with ethico-professional obligations). These three elements need to interlock in the following way. First, reputation is linked to financial self-interest; this is obviously already the case—individuals, groups, and organisations desire high reputation and benefit materially and in other ways (e.g. their desire for approval of others is satisfied) from it. Second, reputation needs to be linked to ethics in that reputation ought to be deserved; the integrity systems are the means to achieve this. Third, and as a consequence of the two already-mentioned links, financial self-interest is linked to ethics; given robust integrity systems that mobilise reputational concerns, it is in the self-interest of individuals, groups, and firms to comply with ethico-professional obligations. Naturally, the key virtues of the professions in question need to be identified and a reputational index which determines the presence/absence/extent of these virtues in given firms needs to be devised. The index can then be used to evaluate firms and the results promulgated, thereby promoting the spread of deserved or warranted reputation.

Given this account of integrity systems, and our description of trust (above), what is the relationship between moral principles, trust, and integrity systems? I have suggested that trust has a pivotal role to play in relation to compliance with moral principles, on the one hand, and integrity systems on the other.

With respect to such trust-dependent institutional obligations, integrity systems can only do so much. In particular, integrity systems cannot eliminate the vulnerability of promisees to promisors or of clients to professionals, and therefore cannot obviate the need for trust. An integrity system can be designed and implemented to provide for sanctions against failure to discharge contractual obligations, to incentivise market actors not to cheat, and (by way of reputational devices) to incentivise members of occupational groups to aim for high ethical standards. However, it can neither eliminate the vulnerability of promisees, clients, and the like, nor guarantee moral rectitude on the part of promisors, professionals, and so on. This explains the irreplaceability of trust.[17]

One feature of contemporary integrity systems is the increase in enforceable regulations and in ever more complex enforceable contracts in an attempt, at least in part, to do the job trust is (apparently) failing to do. However, as phenomena such as the legal 'industry' of finding and exploiting regulatory loopholes (MacBarnet 2010) and the practice of passing on the costs of corruption and fraud to consumers illustrate, the trust gap, supposing it exists—as it evidently does in the Australian financial services industry—can never be successfully bridged in this manner. If finance companies cannot be trusted by their consumers to sell 'safe' financial products, or financial advisors to give independent professional advice, then recourse to regulations is unlikely by itself to deal adequately with the problem and may, instead, simply create additional costs. If employees cannot be trusted by their employers, or vice versa, then compliance and accountability mechanisms are not going to guarantee their honesty, and instead may simply result in greater costs, albeit not necessarily only to the employers and/or employees themselves.

So integrity systems cannot replace trust. Moreover, integrity systems cannot guarantee moral compliance more generally. Here I am speaking of the general reliance on others to comply with moral principles, e.g. not to murder, assault, rape, thieve, etc., albeit such reliance takes us beyond the reach of trust in the sense of interest to us here.

In addition to the distinction between trust and general reliance on others to comply with moral principles, there is a genus/species distinction between the moral obligations involved in trust relationships (in the sense elaborated above) and fiduciary duties; fiduciary duties are a species of trust obligations. Here I am speaking of fiduciary duties qua *moral*, as opposed to legal, duties.

14.4 Fiduciary Obligations in the Financial Services Industry

The legal notion of a fiduciary duty is evidently variable from one legal system to another, and even within a given legal system it has been the source of much legal debate.[18] For our purposes here we need a serviceable *moral* notion of a fiduciary obligation, albeit inevitably any such notion will be to some extent a term of art and one derived, in part at least, from legal contexts.

---

[17] See Onora O'Neill's work for a closely related point regarding accountability (O'Neill 2002).

[18] For example, there has been a debate as to whether or not a fiduciary duty is owed by virtue of a status, e.g. lawyer, or is necessarily the product of a voluntary undertaking. See, for example, Edelman (2010: 302–27). On more general issues see Finn (1977).

Fiduciary obligations arise in the context of a trust relationship, and therefore are such that one party, A, is dependent on another party, B, to perform some action (or set of actions) x, and B is under a moral obligation to perform x. Such trust-based obligations have a variety of sources, including promises, assertions, and professional relationships. However, from the mere fact that a promisee trusts a promissor or a hearer trusts a speaker it does not follow that there is a fiduciary relationship or fiduciary obligation.

Nor are the moral commitments of professionals necessarily fiduciary obligations per se. For example, the highest duty of lawyers is to the courts and to the law more generally, but this is not a fiduciary obligation.

Fiduciary obligations are related to, but need to be distinguished from, duties of care. Drivers of automobiles have a duty of care in relation to pedestrians, but not necessarily any fiduciary obligations.

Perhaps the best way to think of fiduciary obligations, at least in institutional settings, is as a species of specific, trust-based obligations that attach to an institutional role, such as a lawyer, trustee, or financial advisor (the fiduciary), but only come into existence as a result of the voluntary agreement (explicit or implicit) of the institutional actor and the person to whom the obligation is to be owed (the beneficiary).[19] Moreover, the agreement is to the effect that the fiduciary will pursue the beneficiary's interest in some area in which the beneficiary is in competition with others, at least potentially (e.g. asset security, legal defence, financial investments), and in which the fiduciary has competence or expertise which the beneficiary lacks.

Interest in this sense is an objective or quasi-objective notion, e.g. it is not equivalent to desires or preferences. However, interest in such contexts is also typically underspecified and a matter for discretionary judgement, e.g. What are the best legal arguments in favour of the defendant's actions? What are the best investments for retiree Jones in terms of level of risk as well as rate of return?

Furthermore, these obligations are weighty, stringent, and *partialist* in character, i.e. they are owed to the beneficiary but not necessarily to others, and especially not others whose interests—in the context of some overall competitive framework, e.g. the market, a courtroom setting—are in potential conflict with those of the beneficiary. In this respect, fiduciaries are different from members of those occupations, including some professions, who cater to the needs of the community and/or their clients but do so in an essentially *impartial* manner, e.g. police officers, doctors in an emergency ward operating under a triage system.

---

[19] In the case of children, the guardian would need to consent to the arrangement. The guardian might be, for example, the child's parents or the state.

These weighty, stringent, and partialist fiduciary obligations override the interests of the fiduciary and the obligations the fiduciary might have to others (should there be a conflict). Indeed, being partialist, these obligations are ones that the fiduciary should not even owe to other persons if this could lead to conflict. In particular, the fiduciary relationship should not be entered into if it would lead to a conflict with existing fiduciary obligations.

Given this description of fiduciary obligations, and our (above-described) normative account of occupations and social institutions, the question that arises for financial advisors is whether or not the occupational role of financial planner ought to have fiduciary obligations attached to it and, if so, what they ought to be.

The answer to this question may well vary from one context to another. In this chapter, we are considering the Australian financial industry, of which more is discussed in the final section. Let us now turn to conflicts of interest; the last key moral notion that we need to elaborate.

14.5 Conflicts of Interest

What is generally wrong with conflicts of interest is that they render one's judgement less reliable than it should be, and result in a failure to properly discharge one's duty. This is so whether they are conflicts between one's personal interest and one's duty or conflicting duties.

The most obvious way to deal with conflicts of interest that might result in corruption or other unethical behaviour is to avoid them. In cases where there is a potential conflict between an institutional actor's self-interest and the duties of his institutional role, regulations requiring avoidance of these conflicts need to be introduced and some form of accountability mechanism established.

It is not always possible to avoid conflicts of interest. The next best solution is to disclose them. However, disclosure is only acceptable in the case of otherwise ethically acceptable practices. It would not be ethically acceptable for a regulator to be among those regulated. Accordingly, disclosure would not be a solution to that conflict of interest.

As already stated, in the Australian financial services sector, conflicts of interest have been rife. Specifically, financial advisors have undertaken both an advisory role in relation to financial products and a sales role in relation to those same products; so there has been role conflict. Financial advisors have also, and relatedly, typically been in receipt of conflicted remuneration, e.g. received commissions for their advice to clients from financial product manufactures. I note that the Ripoll Report and FoFA concentrate their attention on conflicted remuneration, rather than role conflicts.

The conflicts of interest in question, both role conflicts and conflicted remuneration, are structural in character, given the vertically integrated nature of the sector. This vertical integration embraces the manufacturing of financial products, the selling of those products, the advisory role in relation to the same products and (crucially) the modes of compensation to advisors (e.g. commissions based on sales by these advisors of the very same products or salaries paid by organisations with a financial stake in those products).

Such conflicts of interest are especially acute if one considers the financial advisory role to be fiduciary in character (in the moral, if not legal sense), i.e. if a client considers that the client's financial advisor has a weighty, stringent, and partialist obligation to the client, and therefore ought not even allow him/herself to have, let alone be prioritising, a competing self-interest (e.g. commission payment), or competing commitment to the interest of others (e.g. employer or owner of the financial advisor's business). The existence of such a fiduciary duty is highly plausible in the area of financial planning in Australia at this time, given the preponderance of people needing to provide for their own retirement and their vulnerability (given, in particular, relatively low rates of financial literacy).

14.6 Professional Ethics and Financial Advisors in Australia

In the light of (i) our description of the financial planning industry in Australia and the role of the occupation of financial advisor within it, and (ii) our account of the key moral notions in play, let us now turn to a consideration of the likely moral impact (so to speak) of the recent FoFA legislation and related developments in the financial planning industry in Australia, bearing in mind the essentially speculative nature of any such consideration.

The key informing notion in play here seems to be professionalisation, understood as including and in part being driven by the FoFA legislation. Professionalisation is evidently a large part of the proposed solution to identified problems in the financial planning industry. Here we need to make some general points about professionalisation and integrity systems.

Professionalisation is perhaps best thought of as a set of closely related processes rather than a single, unitary process; the process of professionalisation cannot be a 'one-size-fits-all' affair. The professionalisation of journalists, for example, cannot mean the same thing as it does for lawyers, given the potential problems posed for freedom of the press by the establishment of a regulatory authority. More specifically, it is not self-evident that the members of all occupations that are professions, or should professionalise, have or should have a fiduciary duty, e.g. journalists arguably should not.

Professionalisation in the sense in use here is simply the process, or processes, by means of which an occupation lacking the features characteristic of a profession—the features listed above—is transformed into an occupation which has those features; or, at least, the process by means of which such an occupation comes to have most of those features. Professionalisation in this sense is decidedly not the process by means of which an occupation acquires various trappings of the professions for the purposes of achieving a higher status, more institutional power, and greater financial and other rewards than otherwise might be forthcoming.

Professionalisation in our favoured sense can be an important component of an integrity system for an occupation, assuming that the occupation is one that ought to be a profession. Here we need to bear in mind that many occupations are not, and ought not ever to become, a profession. Let us assume, then, that in the evolving financial sector there is a need for a profession of financial advisors, i.e. a professionally accredited occupational group possessed of expert knowledge, professional independence, and with a fiduciary duty grounded in the vulnerability of the needy, e.g. retirees, and so on. If so, and given the problems identified in the financial planning sector—e.g. conflation of sales and advisory roles—there is good reason to think that professionalisation can function as an important component in building an overall integrity system for financial advisors.

That said, it should also be emphasised at the outset that professionalisation is only one component in the construction of such an integrity system. It would be illusory, I suggest, to think that it could provide the complete solution to all the problems. Specifically, what I referred to earlier as the macro-institutional context, e.g. of the financial products and services industry, needs to be attended to when focusing on micro-occupational reform, e.g. of the occupation of financial advisor.

Further—and, again, notwithstanding the general contribution that professionalisation might make to occupational 'integrity'—it is important to maintain a distinction between those occupations that have a distinctive role as key elements of an integrity system (e.g. auditors), and those who have obligations the discharging of which it is a function of the integrity system to ensure (e.g. the corporations whose financial records are audited). This point is germane to ASIC's invocation of a wide array of occupations in the financial services as so-called 'gatekeepers'. Different occupations have different roles in relation to integrity systems: auditors are 'gatekeepers' in the sense of independent scrutineers of financial health, lawyers have an important role in relation to ensuring understanding and compliance with the law (e.g. on the part of their corporate clients/employers), and so on (this is 'gatekeeping' in a different sense).

Naturally, in one sense, the members of an occupation, profession, or institution are themselves both part of the integrity system and simultaneously actors with obligations the discharging of which it is a function of the integrity system to ensure. However, the truth of this general point does not obviate the need to identify the precise role each relevant occupation ought to play in an integrity system for (say) financial services and, therefore, what professionalisation ought to consist of for each of these occupations. Here, as elsewhere, the devil is to some extent in the detail. For example, a financial advisor who was a member of a fully professionalised occupational group of financial advisors would be entirely independent of financial product manufacturers. Moreover, such a professional would presumably not only have a detailed understanding of any relevant financial product and of the desirable economic purposes served by that product, but would also take him or herself to have a professional and moral obligation to provide advice to clients, licensees, financial product manufacturers, regulators such as ASIC and, for that matter, the public at large with respect to the risks attached to specific financial products. Indeed, such a professional advisor would, if he or she deemed it to be appropriate, strongly recommend—perhaps via the professional association—that certain financial products be banned as serving no useful economic purpose and as likely to do serious harm. Such a professional financial advisor would indeed be part of the overall integrity system for the financial products and services industry, and would be providing that 'ethics' service as part and parcel of their professional role as a financial advisor and not, this should be stressed, as a 'knight on a white horse' engaged in supererogatory good works. If members of the medical profession keep quiet about the deficiencies of certain drugs and, indeed, continue to prescribe them, should this not be regarded as a breach of their professional moral obligations? Likewise, if lawyers are principally engaged in finding and exploiting loopholes for their well-healed clients, and without regard to the larger purposes of the law in their particular legal sphere—as has evidently recently been the case in various sectors of the corporate and financial sectors—are they not breaching their professional moral obligations in relation to the larger purpose of the administration of justice (and irrespective of whether or not they have breached any particular law)? Moreover, should not their fellow lawyers—again perhaps via the relevant professional association—be doing something about this?

The legislation changes under FoFA—notably, the establishment of a legally based fiduciary duty (of sorts) and banning certain forms of conflicted remuneration—are intended to contribute to building occupational 'integrity' among financial advisors, both directly and indirectly (via professionalisation). The likelihood of these intentions at the micro-occupational level being successful depends in part, I suggest, on some larger issues concerning the macro-institutional framework—an institution, and therefore an institutional framework, itself being comprised of function(s), structure, and culture(s).[20] What is the macro-institutional framework in which the envis-aged process of professionalisation is to take place? What impact, if any, are the legislative changes going to have on that institutional framework?

More specifically, is the above-described vertically integrated structure of financial product manufacturers, financial advisory licensees, and financial advisors likely to undergo any functional (i.e. in terms of their de facto insti-tutional goals or purposes), structural, and/or associated cultural changes; and if not, what are the implications for the success or otherwise of the FoFA legislation and the envisaged process of professionalisation of financial advi-sors (of which the FoFA legislation can be regarded as a key component)?

I have suggested that integrity systems are the principal institutional vehi-cle for promoting ethical conduct and combating crime and corruption. If this is right, then it ought to be instructive to view the FoFA legislation and the proposed process of professionalisation of financial advisors through the lens of an appropriate integrity system for this occupation. How do the FoFA legislation and this professionalisation process complement and complete an appropriate integrity system?

The FoFA legislation and the envisaged professionalisation process more generally straddle the four dimensions of an integrity system identified above: namely, regulation, market incentives, reputational incentives, and underlying, widely accepted moral beliefs and attitudes. Moreover, as well as functioning as a part of the (so to speak) external integrity system for finan-cial advisors it provides for a new set of (so to speak) internal obligations constitutive of the role of the financial planner. So, in a sense, it seeks to build integrity both from without and from within.

In relation to the regulatory dimension of the integrity system for financial advisors, what is most salient is, of course, the FoFA legislation itself which provides a regulatory framework conducive to professionalisation. Naturally this legislation is enforceable, and ASIC, in particular, has been provided with enhanced powers to revoke the licences of those who fail to comply with the new requirements and to ban individual advisors who fail to meet their pro-fessional obligations.[21]

Crucially, the FoFA legislation provides for a number of specific measures expressly designed to contribute to the process of transformation of an occu-pation formerly comprised essentially of sales personnel into a profession comprised of purveyors of high-quality, independent financial advice. To reiterate: these measures include the creation of a (legal) fiduciary obligation,

---

[20] See Miller (2010b: Introduction).
[21] Government of Australia (2011) Items 2–4. ss. 913B(1)(b), 913B(4)(a), and 915C(1)(aa) (licence cancellation). Items 5–7. ss. 920A(1)(ba), 920A(1)(d), 920(1)(da) and 920A(1)(f) (banning of individuals).

and a ban on various forms of conflicted remuneration in favour of a bona fide fee-for-services model.[22] The list of conflicted remunerations is lengthy, but it includes such ones as commissions to financial advisors emanating (ultimately) from the financial product manufacturers with respect to whose products the advisors are giving their advice.

In relation to underlying, widely accepted moral standards and values, a process of understanding and internalisation of ethico-professional standards and values by individual financial advisors is envisaged. Hence, there is a focus on codes of ethics and relatedly on professional ethics awareness raising, training, and education, including through professional bodies such as the Financial Planner's Association. To this extent, there is an attempt to specify and communicate professional obligations and values and, in doing so, to tap into the underlying, widely accepted, and pre-existing general moral standards and values of the institutional actors in question.

As far as reputational incentives are concerned, there does not seem to be any plan to utilise reputational devices as an additional and complementary layer of the overall integrity system for the occupation. For example, a reputational index (comprised of objective indicators of ethical 'health') could be constructed, an ethics audit conducted (by an independent body)—the results of which would give a comparative picture of the various firms in the industry—and these results promulgated.[23] Given the sensitivity of many actors in the financial services industry to reputational risks, notably lack of trust on the part of customers/clients in the independence of financial advisors, this is arguably a significant omission.

However, it is the area of (so to speak) market-induced 'integrity', at what I have referred to as the macro-institutional level, that is the greatest source of concern. This is not to deny that there are the standard market incentives and disincentives in place which (respectively) encourage ethical behaviour and discourage unethical behaviour especially, but not exclusively, among independent financial advice providers. These incentives do exist and they are strengthened by the proposed greater emphasis on appropriately communicated disclosure, enhanced financial literacy of consumers/clients, and the like.

Nevertheless, market incentives and disincentives are heavily influenced by the particular (as it were) macro-institutional structure of the market in question, and in the case of the financial service industry in Australia, that structure is, as we have seen, characterised by a small number of large, vertically

---

[22] By bona fide I mean one that excludes all conflicted remuneration including links between advice given and transactions made, as in so-called asset-based fees. See below in the text of this final section.

[23] For further details on this and other reputational devices see Alexandra and Miller (2010: Chapter 5). See also Miller (2011b) and Miller (2010a).

integrated, organisations. Moreover, functionally, these organisations are market actors driven by the profit motive. It follows that the pervasive culture in these organisations will be reflective of this function and structure.

Naturally, this macro-institutional framework and its constitutive function(s), structure, and culture(s) are not themselves immutable. Indeed, it is part of ASIC's strategy, as I understand it, to introduce reform across the whole spectrum of the financial products and services sector; hence its focus (quoted in the introduction to this paper) on 'gatekeeping' for product manufactures, bankers, etc., and, of course, financial advisors alike. I return to this point below.

At any rate, the question that arises at this point in the discussion is whether or not the process of professionalisation of financial advisors, at least in the form in which it is being proposed, is likely to be substantially diluted and/or diverted in important respects in the *current* institutional setting. In short, is the macro-institutional environment likely to derail the micro-occupational agenda?

14.7 Conclusions

I conclude this paper by making some specific points which give some substance to these worries.

(i) If a financial advisor's business is owned by, or otherwise associated with a financial product manufacturer, such as a bank, insurance company, or fund manager—as is frequently the case in Australia—then there is the potential for a conflict between the financial advisor's commitment to that product manufacturer and the requirement to act in the 'best interest' of their client. This is a conflict of roles.

Likewise, if the financial planner's fee for services is linked in some way to a product transaction (e.g. if the investment recommended by the advisor increases by x%, then the fee increases by x%), then there is a potential conflict between the advisor's interest and the client's interest.[24] This is conflicted remuneration.

The FoFA regulation focuses on various forms of conflicted remuneration, but arguably neglects role conflicts. This is understandable, given that the elimination of such role conflicts would require structural institutional change in the financial services industry. On the other hand, the 'best interests' provision requires that when such conflict arises in practice, i.e. on any

---

[24] FoFA bans such fees on borrowed amounts only (Government of Australia (2012), ss. 964B–G). Various commentators have suggested multiple conflicts of interest remain post FoFA.

specific occasion of financial advising, that they be resolved in favour of the client's interest.

However, fiduciary obligations are not simply ones which in fact 'trump' (so to speak) the interests of the fiduciary or trump other interests to which the fiduciary may have obligations; rather such conflicts are not supposed to arise in the first place. So if there are such conflicts of interests, then irrespective of whether they are disclosed or otherwise managed, fiduciary duty has been compromised, at least to some extent.

Moreover, where there is a conflict of interest in relation to the provision of some piece of financial advice, it is not self-evident that the regulation will ensure that it is resolved in the client's favour, especially if the advisor has a conflict of roles. For 'best interest' financial advice is inherently *discretionary*, notwithstanding that under FoFA, advisors are required to comply with a somewhat objective procedure of taking 'reasonable steps' to demonstrate that an advisor acted in their client's best interest.[25] Here the notion of 'discretionary space' is salient. For how this space is filled is inevitably to some degree a matter of contestable judgement and, as such, beyond the reach of regulation. Importantly, that the content of this discretionary judgement of the advisor is in the client's interest is ultimately a matter of trust on the part of the client. If the content of this discretionary judgement is determined not by the client's best interest but by some other interest, like the commercial interest of the product manufacturer which owns the financial advisor's business, then the client will likely not be in a position to know that the advice is in fact driven by this other interest and not by the client's own. This remains true even if the potential role conflict is disclosed to the client. On the other hand, if the client suspects that there are other interests in play than his or her own, then there may well be a breakdown in trust.

I note that insofar as the above-mentioned conflicts of interest (both role conflicts and conflicted remuneration) are a function of the macro-institutional framework, they constitute structural conflicts of interest and are, to that extent, inherent, if not endemic, in the financial planning industry.

(ii) There is a question mark in relation to the *ability* of financial advisors to discharge their newly acquired professional obligations, as opposed to any direct ethical concerns in relation to conflicts of interest and/or fiduciary obligations. As stated above, professionals are distinguished in part from other occupations by virtue of the possession of a body of expert knowledge; and financial planners in Australia are required to have tertiary training. However, in the absence of any requirement that financial advisors have an understanding of the *full* array of competing financial products available in

---

[25] Government of Australia (2012), s961B.

the market (or perhaps even of the ones they are familiar with, should they be complex 'exotic' products), are individual financial advisors likely to be in a position to adequately satisfy the financial needs of their clients, i.e. to provide unbiased advice based on a complete, or near-complete, detailed understanding of the available products?

(iii) Given the current institutional structure of the financial planning industry in Australia and, specifically, the fact that most financial planning businesses in Australia are owned by, or otherwise associated with, financial product manufacturers, there is a question as to whether the culture of members of the occupation of financial advisor will shift from, so to speak, a sales-based culture to the culture of a profession. Will the substantial impetus that has been provided by FoFA and the associated professionalisation process be decisive? Of particular importance here will be the growth in the relative numbers of genuinely independent financial planning businesses.

In the light of these specific points, (i), (ii) and (iii), what are the prospects for the professionalisation process currently underway in relation to the financial advisor's occupation in Australia? Is the occupation of financial advisor on its way to becoming a profession serving the financial needs of clients and thereby the economy more generally (e.g. in relation to a well-functioning system of retirement savings)?—in which case it will surely also become a key element of the integrity system for the financial products and services industry. Or is the occupation of financial advisor to continue to serve its master, the financial products and services sector, albeit under some additional constraints? Notwithstanding the considerable progress that has been made with the introduction of FoFA and the professionalisation process more generally, evidently the jury is still out on this. However, the answer is likely to depend on whether or not the macro-institutional framework itself is going to undergo changes conducive to this outcome. This will, no doubt, in turn depend in part on the success of various other parts of ASIC's strategy, elements of which I have mentioned. Of crucial importance here, I suggest, is the identification and realisation of the various interconnected institutional purposes that ought to be served by banks, insurance companies, capital markets, the superannuation industry, and so on, i.e. the *collective goods*, such as the provision of sufficient retirement savings for Australian workers, and an adequate supply of low-cost capital for bona fide businesses, that are their *raison d'etre*.

References

Alexandra, A. and Miller, S. (2010). *Integrity Systems for Occupations*. Padstow: Ashgate.
Australian Securities & Investments Commission (December 2010). 'Report 224
    Access to Financial Advice in Australia', Canberra: Australian Government, <http://

www.asic.gov.au/asic/pdflib.nsf/LookupByFileName/rep224.pdf/$file/rep224.pdf>, accessed 23 July 2013.

Bayles, M. D. (1986). 'Professional Power and Self-Regulation', *Business and Professional Ethics Journal*, 5(2): 26–46.

Cooper, J. (2011). 'Super System Review: Final Report. Review into the Governance, Efficiency, Structure and Operation of Australia's Superannuation System', Canberra: Australian Government, <http://www.supersystemreview.gov.au/content/content.aspx?doc=html/final_report.htm>, accessed 23 July 2013.

Edelman, J. (2010). 'When do Fiduciary Duties Arise?', *Law Quarterly Review*, 126: 302–27.

Finn, P. (1977). *Fiduciary Obligations*. Sydney: Law Book Co. for New South Wales Bar Association.

Future of Financial Advice (2011a). 'Bill No. 2 s.961B (on 'Best Interest' Requirement)', Canberra: Australian Government.

Future of Financial Advice (2011b). 'Bill No. 3 ss.963E-963L (on Conflicted Remuneration)', Canberra: Australian Government.

Government of Australia (2011). 'Corporations Amendment (Future of Financial Advice) Bill 2011', Canberra: Australian Government, <http://www.comlaw.gov.au/Details/C2011B00208>, accessed 23 July 2013.

Government of Australia (2012). 'Corporations Amendment (Further Future of Financial Advice Measures) Bill 2012', Canberra: Australian Government, <http://www.aph.gov.au/Parliamentary_Business/Bills_Legislation/Bills_Search_Results/Result?bId=r4689>, accessed 23 July 2013.

Kay, J. (July 2012). 'Kay Review of UK Equity Markets and Long Term Decision-Making: Final Report', *ECGI*, <http://www.ecgi.org/conferences/eu_actionplan2013/documents/kay_review_final_report.pdf>, accessed 23 July 2013.

Kell, P. (May 2012). 'The Future of Advice Post FoFA', *Australian Securities and Investments Commission*, <https://www.asic.gov.au/asic/asic.nsf/byheadline/Future-of-advice-post-FoFA?openDocument>, accessed 23 July 2013.

MacBarnet, D. (2010). 'Financial Engineering or Legal Engineering? Legal Work, Legal Integrity and the Banking Crisis', in I. MacNeil and J. O'Brien (eds), *The Future of Financial Regulation*. Portland: Hart Publishing, 67–82.

Miller, S. (2006). 'Collective Moral Responsibility: An Individualist Account', in P. A. French and Howard K. Wettstein (eds), *Shared Intentions and Collective Responsibility* (Midwest Studies in Philosophy, 30). Malden, MA: Blackwell, 176–93.

Miller, S. (2007). 'Institutions, Integrity Systems and Market Actors', in J. O'Brien (ed.), *Private Equity, Corporate Governance and the Dynamics of Capital Market Regulation*. London: Imperial College of London Press, 297–327.

Miller, S. (2010a). 'Financial Service Providers, Reputation and the Virtuous Triangle', in I. MacNeil and J. O'Brien (eds), *The Future of Financial Regulation*. Portland: Hart Publishing, 381–94.

Miller, S. (2010b). *The Moral Foundations of Social Institutions: A Philosophical Study*. New York: Cambridge University Press.

Miller, S. (2011a). 'Financial Service Providers: Integrity Systems, Reputation and the Triangle of Virtue', in N. Dobos, C. Barry, and T. Pogge (eds), *The Global Financial Crisis: Ethical Issues*. Basingstoke: Palgrave, 132–57.

Miller, S. (2011b). 'Global Financial Institutions, Ethics and Market Fundamentalism', in N. Dobos, C. Barry, and T. Pogge (eds), *The Global Financial Crisis: Ethical Issues*. Basingstoke: Palgrave, 24–51.

O'Brien, J. (2010). 'After the Deluge: Rebuilding Trust and Integrity in the Financial Planning Industry', *CLMR*, <http://www.clmr.unsw.edu.au/sites/default/files/attached_files/after_the_deluge.pdf>, accessed 23 July 2013.

O'Brien, J. (2011). 'Lehman Brothers: Wholesale Investor Protection in the Aftermath of the Financial Crisis', *CLMR*, <http://www.clmr.unsw.edu.au/article/compliance/market-conduct-regulation/lehman-brothers-wholesale-investor-protection-afterma-2>, accessed 23 July 2013.

O'Neill, O. (2002). 'Reith Lectures 2002: A Question of Trust', *BBC*, <http://www.bbc.co.uk/print/radio4/reith2002>, accessed 23 July 2013.

Ripoll, B. (2009). *Parliamentary Joint Committee on Corporations and Financial Services: Inquiry into Financial Services and Products in Australia*. Canberra: Parliament of Australia.

Sen, A. (2002). *Rationality and Freedom*. Cambridge, MA: Harvard University Press.

Stout, L. A. (2012). *The Shareholder Value Myth: How Putting Shareholders First Harms Investors, Corporations and the Public*. San Francisco: Berrett Keohler Publications.

Vines, D. (2011). 'The Oxford Project: The Exclusivity and Exclusionary Power of Reputation', *CLMR*, <http://www.clmr.unsw.edu.au/article/ethics/codes-of-conduct/oxford-project-exclusivity-and-exclusionary-power-reputation>, accessed 23 July 2013.

Wiggins. D. (1991). *Needs, Values, Truth: Essays in the Philosophy of Value*. Oxford: Blackwell.

15

A Warrant for Pain: *Caveat Emptor* vs the Duty of Care in American Medicine, c.1970–2010*

Avner Offer

The doctrines of economics are indifferent to ethics. This may be disturbing, but it is not easy to specify what might be wrong about it, and to show that it is harmful. The unfolding financial crisis has left a sense of moral unease, a concern that ethical transgression might be undermining the orderly working of markets. The drift of the American healthcare system towards market norms, described below, shows more clearly how bad ethics can lead to inferior economic outcomes.

I

Ethics aspires to the Good, but the Good is not easy to identify. Plausible arguments are made for principles which are incompatible with each other. Both Freedom and Justice are compelling, for example, but the two principles are not easy to reconcile. A concept from social psychology may help: it is 'Just-World Theory' (Rubin and Pelau 1975; Lerner and Miller 1978; Lerner 1980). In social psychology the 'theory' is informal and attributed to individuals. Here it is applied to social and political doctrines. The basic idea is simple: a 'Just-World Theory' says that everyone gets what they deserve. If the Inquisition burned heretics, that was only what they deserved. If Kulaks were starved and exiled in Soviet Russia, they only got what they deserved.

* An earlier version published in *Real-World Economics*, 61 (2012), 85–99.

Likewise the Nazis and the Jews. Just-World Theories are ubiquitous. The criteria are political, religious, ethnic, gendered, and cultural. They justify the infliction of pain. Classical liberalism is also a 'Just-World Theory' of this kind. Milton Friedman wrote: 'The ethical principle that would directly justify the distribution of income in a free market society is, "To each according to what he and the instruments he owns produces"' (Friedman and Friedman 1962: 161–2). In other words, everyone gets what they deserve. The norm of individual freedom justifies the inequalities of market society. As we shall see, it also justifies the infliction of pain.

If there cannot be agreement about the Good, can we agree about the Bad? To achieve broad consent, the Bad needs to be defined tightly. One such approach would be a narrowly hedonic one that focused exclusively on the harms of pain and death. Physical pain is not good. It provides a warning signal, but otherwise there is little to be said for it. Likewise death is sometimes sought out by individuals for themselves as being the lesser Bad, but has few other attractions.

I propose an ethical criterion of 'Warranted Pain'. The criterion is: 'No infliction of unwarranted pain or death'. Who would wish to argue the opposite? The infliction of pain or even death is not forbidden, but it requires a satisfactory warrant. Pain or death need to be justified. That narrows the issue to the quality of the warrant. What benefits can justify the infliction of pain or death? How much good can it deliver, and to whom? The principle is not absolute: but it narrows the scope for disagreement. And once the warrant is on the table, we can reach for ethical intuitions.

For example, for the purpose of cost–benefit analysis of regulation, a life is evaluated at about $6 million. This figure is normally arrived at by capitalising the wage premium required for risky occupations, where the risks are known. If the cost of a protective measure is more than $6 million per life saved, then it will not be implemented. This may be a warrant for somebody's death. But is it a good warrant? To begin with, it assumes identical risk preferences, but the vast majority of workers actually turn down the wage deals on which this figure is based. Those who accept them are likely to be atypical, both in their appetite for risk and in their economic circumstances. So their lives may be undervalued. The second point is that this figure is not the value of a particular life, but a costing of the risk. It would be the aggregate of six million people paying a dollar each to avoid a one-sixth of a millionth chance of death. People are paid a premium to take on a risk, not to die. A single, particular life is unpriceable. You cannot pay somebody $6 million dollars for permission to kill them. Third, in a market economy, those who take on the risk, rarely get the benefits. If the repeal of a costly regulation benefits 'the economy', those exposed to the risk are worse off, and those who were previously regulated are better off. Not society 'as a whole'.

The corporate demand for relief from regulation increases death and injury for workers (Tombs and Whyte 2010). How much pain and death does laissez-faire warrant? And who gains? Instead of the supposed value of market and individual freedoms, we can focus on more precise metrics: does privatisation (for example) actually raise productivity, who stands to benefit, and can the gain for shareholders and managers justify disease and death for consumers and workers? If the price of competition is inequality, are the benefits worth an expanding gap in life expectation, even if on average, all classes benefit? Or if more gain at the bottom could be had for less at the top? And what if only a few benefit? And if productivity does not actually increase?

There is no simple algorithm for such questions, so this is the point where ethical intuitions can enter. Agreement may still be elusive, but the issues and metrics provide a sharper focus, and show how to make and defend an ethical judgement. In policy, the criterion of warranted pain implies that a bad ethical call has a cost in the currencies of pain and death. And even if economic output is all you care for, then pain and death, even of others (as we shall see), can diminish productivity and economic welfare. The criterion appears to be narrow, but it can do a lot with a little, not only in ethics, but also in policy.

In science, the test of a theory is what grounds it gives for belief ('justification'). A rough and ready test is how well the model fits with experienced reality. When used to derive policy, an economic model not only describes the world, but aspires to change it. For example, the market-liberal model of 'rational expectations' implies that benign government interventions will be anticipated and thwarted, and are therefore futile. If the model is wrong however, then a policy of non-intervention can well be harmful. In policy, if the model is bad, then reality has to be forcibly aligned with it by means of coercion. How much coercion is actually used provides a rough measure of a model's validity.

Coercion is a feature of societies that rest on strong 'Just-World' doctrines. Such societies have resorted to witch-hunts, secret police, concentration camps, and worse. Classical liberalism and its offspring, neoclassical economics, are also such Just-World Theories. They accept as legitimate all existing endowments and property rights, and they endorse the market distribution of final rewards. Market-liberal societies make Just-World claims, and also inflict a great deal of coercion, pain, and death. The United States is the most market-oriented of affluent societies, and also leads the developed world, and much of the rest, in the size and severity of its penal system. It continues to inflict the death penalty. Until very recently, it denied secure healthcare to one-sixth of its population, and it tolerates hundreds of millions of firearms in private possession. It has troops all over the globe, and uses them readily. It leads the developed world in the proportion of supervisory and coercive 'guard labour' (Bowles and Jayadev 2008). More than a million people have been killed by guns in the United States since 1968, and more than two million were in prison at any one time during the last decade. How much pain is warranted has been discussed literally with regard to the torture of terrorist suspects, in both the USA and apparently in the UK, and some of it has been found to be acceptable (Cole 2010). All this without considering pervasive incidence of poverty, hunger, illness, and early death arising at the lower end of society as a consequence of labour market inequalities and social neglect. Lower-income people even suffer pain more frequently than those of higher income (Krueger and Stone 2008; Stone et al. 2010). These costs can be measured against the tangible and intangible benefits of 'economic freedom', such as they are, and such as it is.

II

The abstractions of ethics come to life in the recent record of healthcare in the United States. Some ill-health is unavoidable. It exposes everyone to suffering and ultimately to death. Ill-health is a state of dependence on the knowledge and goodwill of others. The entitlements of patients are affected by an enduring tension, between two principles which are as old as economics: on the one side, the selfish principle of 'me-first', and on the other the social norm of looking after those who cannot fend for themselves (Force 2003; Offer, Chapter 7 in this book). If the baker serves up stale bread, we may be able to go elsewhere. But the patient cannot be sure how well he is being treated. His suffering is an urgent matter, while for the doctor, however compassionate, it is all in a day's work. The nurse and the doctor have vital knowledge which is too extensive to convey to the patient. When it comes to payment, the patient's predicament means that doctors can drive a hard bargain. Even a patient who is robustly self-centred himself, does not like to think that those who treat him are in it only for themselves. Nor would any healer wish to convey that impression. But the patient cannot rely entirely on compassion. He hopes that the doctor is also mentally disciplined and morally robust, that she has a sense of duty to the patient and to scientific truth, that she was licensed by impartial assessors, and that the knowledge she uses has been validated by disinterested experts.[1]

In his *Theory of Moral Sentiments* Adam Smith describes the mechanism of ethical validation. The 'impartial spectator' (an inner voice of conscience) is driven by the desire for social approbation, to 'do the right thing' (Offer, Chapter 7 in this book). Even if the doctor cares but little for any particular patient, we trust that she is kept in line by the judgement of her peers. The

---

[1] The doctor is female and the patient male for clarity of exposition.

norm of impartial sympathy is codified as a fiduciary duty, a duty of care, whose first principle is 'do no harm'. Obligations are spelled out in professional codes of practice, backed by the sanction of exclusion, and enforced by the state. These codes can be taken to formalise the norms that the impartial spectator would have us internalise. They restrict the room for discretion, and commit practitioners to the client's interest (Rayner 1999).

The ethical code of practice binds the profession to refrain from abusing power. The commitment to do no harm has made it easier for society to grant a monopoly of medical practice to certified doctors (Arrow 1963). Another token of this deal is tax-exempt status for medical schools and teaching hospitals. In return for this power, the healing professions used to promise, implicitly, not to abuse it: 'The organisational culture of medicine used to be dominated by the ideal of professionalism and voluntarism, which softened the underlying acquisitive activity' (Starr 1982: 448). The deal with the state assumes that both sides are acting in good faith. The provider takes responsibility for the treatment and for its consequences.

Market liberals do not believe in the good faith of either doctors or the state. Their solution to the problem of unequal power is to 'let the buyer beware' (*caveat emptor*). The duty of care is laid on the patient, with little regard for his ignorance of the relevant information. The standard assumption in market liberalism is that people are well-informed, and they are at fault if they are not (in the extreme Chicago version, they know everything at no cost). The vendor has a duty only to himself. It is the credo of the strong. As for the others, let the buyer beware.

American anti-trust legislation began in the late nineteenth century in order to bring more fairness into market competition, as an aspect of the broader Progressive movement. But market advocates after the Second World War (a different group, and hostile to the historical Progressives) cared little about monopoly (Bork 1978; Van Horn 2009). Chicago economists are averse to anti-trust (Pitofsky 2008; White 2008).[2] As a rule, however, their partiality to market power does not extend to workers (Friedman and Friedman 1962: ch. 8). The Chicago argument is that corporate monopolies, unlike unions, can be challenged by new entrants. The licensing monopoly of the medical profession has also attracted the ire of Chicago. Milton Friedman advocated free entry into medical practice, with the onus of diligence transferred to the patients (Friedman and Friedman 1962: ch. 9). These views gained currency with the rise of market liberal influence during the 1970s. In *Goldfarb v Virginia State Bar* (1975), the United States Supreme Court handed down a judgement that the ethical codes of professional associations were

---

[2] Henry Simons was the last major Chicago economist to advocate anti-trust.

not immune to anti-trust legislation. The case concerned the legal profession, but doctors embraced it too, and their associations accordingly relaxed the anti-competitive elements in their codes (Relman 1992; Relman 2007: ch. 1). Fees were quick to follow: American doctors are the best-paid in the world by far (Laugesen and Glied 2011). Competition was not enhanced: the medical profession continued to control education, certification, standards, and numbers. But the duty of care was relaxed. Pricing power was given to impersonal commercial entities, insurance companies that only acted, as Friedman has advocated, in their own interest. In a market where prices are set by corporations, there is little room for obligation or a duty of care. At the point of contact with the patient, however, the unpriceability of human life kicks in, but provides an incentive for indulgent and sometimes futile overtreatment (Gawande 2009). Doctors and hospitals had financial incentives to treat expansively with little regard for cost. The insurance companies' incentive was to maximise net revenue. Unlike the doctors, however, insurance providers retained their immunity from anti-trust legislation, and many of them came to dominate their territories (American Medical Association and Center for Health Policy Research 2009). In consequence, healthcare providers increasingly charged as much as the patient could bear, and often a great deal more than that. The poorest patients and the uninsured were grotesquely overcharged, with large differences in charges for the same procedures among different providers (Brill 2013).

III

Increasingly, knowledge in healthcare is embodied in drugs and other medical technology. Doctors have to take drug value on trust, but the vendors have no other duty than to maximise their profits. Drug making is among the most profitable industries in the United States. By the end of the 1990s the ten Fortune 500 drug companies had profits about four times as high as the median corporation, and between 2006 and 2009 the industry was typically the second or third most profitable one in the USA, with profits at between 16% and 19% of revenues (Public Citizen Congress Watch 2003: 9, fig. 5; CNN Money 2009). This was not the work of the invisible hand, but of monopoly patents. Drug prices are much higher in the United States, with its policy norm of 'free markets', than in the variously socialised medical systems of other countries. When the United States Senate created a Medicare drug benefit for seniors, it specified that the government would not use its buying power to negotiate prices. Such was the political heft of Big Pharma. In the recent congressional debates on healthcare in the United States, the statements of more than a dozen lawmakers were ghostwritten, in whole or in part, by lobbyists working for Genentech, a large biotechnology company. One statement was prepared for Democrats and another for Republicans. The company, a subsidiary of the Swiss company Roche, estimated that forty-two house members used some of its talking points. Several different statements in the *Congressional Record* matched each other word for word. The boiler-plate that appears in the *Congressional Record* even included some conversational touches, as if actually delivered on the congressional floor. A lobbyist close to the company said 'this happens all the time. There's nothing nefarious about it' (Pear 2009). One senator, who has acted successfully to protect health-additive companies from scrutiny of general health claims (of the sort made by patent medicines), has been richly rewarded with financial contributions (Lipton 2011).

In the United States, drug companies deploy consumer advertising to nudge patients into asking for particular drugs, and also perhaps to reassure the doctors (Hightower 2012). But this reassurance is often misplaced. A top medical journal editor has written: '"Caveat emptor" may be a reasonable approach for many consumer products, but not for prescription drugs' (Angell 2006: 7). Expensive prescription drugs are often little or no better than generic ones, or than over-the-counter remedies. The rheumatism painkiller Vioxx had few clear advantages over aspirin, but made profits for its producer Merck. Evidence began to emerge that it raised the risk of stroke and heart disease. When the company became aware of those risks, it did not rush to disclose them, and fought to prevent the drug from being banned (Angell 2006).

The approval procedure administered by the Federal Drug Administration (FDA) in the United States is no longer slow and thorough, and provides only a flimsy defence for patients. Since the early 1990s, the FDA has been half-funded by drug company 'user fees' (Angell 2005: 208–11). It evaluates drugs partly on the basis of tests submitted to it by the producers. Experts with financial ties to the companies sit on drug approval boards, where it is not uncommon for them to be in the majority. They can look forward to consultancy and speaking fees. The trials are often poorly designed, and investigators frequently fail to report their links with the industry (Angell 2005). The figures are dressed up to favour the drugs, and trials are often carried out by investigators with a financial interest in the outcome. Some of the tests are even fraudulent. The standard of efficacy required is low: merely better than placebo. Negative findings tend to be suppressed, and approval not always retracted. The majority of new drugs are variations on old ones, and the industry produces a regular flow of products that are unsafe and ineffective (Light 2011; Rosenberg 2012). The drug companies have teams of ghostwriters who write up the research for publication under the names of academic investigators. A study found that 10.9% of articles in the *New England Journal of Medicine* were ghostwritten in this way, 7.9% of articles in the *Journal of the American Medical Association*, and 7.6% in *The Lancet* (Wilson and Singer 2009; Singer 2009; US Senate Committee on Finance 2010). In psychiatry, enterprising doctors seek to define new disorders which are treatable by drugs. Ordinary social attributes, like shyness or sadness, increasingly become medicalised (Healy 1997; Lane 2007). Richard Horton, editor of *The Lancet*, has defended non-disclosure of conflict of interest, on grounds that it has become impossible to prevent. He preferred the term 'dual commitment'. This position was contested by the editor of the *British Medical Journal* (Horton 1997; Smith 1997). Marcia Angell, for two decades the editor-in-chief of the top medical journal in the United States, *The New England Journal of Medicine*, has written that 'It is simply no longer possible to believe much of the clinical research that is published, or to rely on the judgement of trusted physicians or authoritative medical guidelines. I take no pleasure in this conclusion, which I reached slowly and reluctantly over my two decades as an editor' (Angell 2009; Healy 2012). In response to public criticism, journals and medical schools are beginning to respond, but slowly: few universities impose a cap on how much a faculty member can be paid by those who make a product they are investigating (Wilson 2010).

Top doctors get large kickbacks. Ordinary ones benefit too (Kassirer 2005; Nguyen et al. 2011; Healy 2012). The companies lay out hospitality at symposia and conferences, often at distant and attractive locations (Nguyen et al. 2011; Pear 2012). 'Marketing and administration' is by far the largest cost of drug production. Salesmen press drugs and procedures aggressively, and push them for off-label prescription, i.e. for purposes for which they are not tested. There is large divergence in levels of medical costs across the United States, with areas in the South tending to prescribe, test, and treat more heavily than in other parts of the country, often at the expense of Medicare. Doctors prescribe tests from labs which they own. In the medical economy where every service is provided as a commodity, fraud is rife, and antifraud control is also outsourced to private contractors (Gawande 2009; Forden 2011; Leap 2011). Drug companies heavily overcharge public health systems (Pope and Selten 2012). A home care company submits false claims to the Federal government (Lefcourt 2011). Media and journal sources (which pick up these abuses) depict the medical market as a war of all against all (which is what a competitive market is meant to be, although cheating is left out of the model). Every relationship offers opportunities for deceit: insurance companies and doctors discriminate against different classes of patients, patients resell Medicare drugs, doctors overcharge insurance companies, and insurance companies undercompensate doctors (Rashbaum 2012; Smith 2012; Terhune 2012; Pear 2012). Fraudulent billings alone are estimated by the FBI to cost between 3% and 10% of total health expenditures, or approximately 0.5–1.7% of national income. Healthcare is a 'criminogenic' industry (Leap 2011: ix, 3, 11).

Adam Smith's norms of sympathy, approbation, reciprocity, and virtue might have protected the integrity of medical treatment and of medical research, if they were not challenged so forcibly by the policy norm of *caveat emptor* (Offer, Chapter 7 in this book). At the point of delivery, healthcare is not a commodity trading impersonally, but is mediated by personal interaction. However, what matters is not compassion, but integrity—the impartial spectator's injunction to do the right thing. Medicine is a vast enterprise, in which everyone has to trust that knowledge is created, validated, and used impartially, and in the interests of the patient. If the authority of scientists and doctors can be purchased by interested parties, its quality is no longer secure. *Caveat emptor* applies. Opportunistic professionals are tempted to cash in the reputation for probity of which they are the transient custodians. The word liquidation has two meanings: destruction and converting an asset into money. Opportunistic doctors have been doing both: appropriating for their private gain the authority built up by generations of scientists and doctors, and leaving it diminished after they are gone. This ethic of opportunism is pervasive (Washington 2011). More medical doctors think like entrepreneurs, and seek to qualify as MBAs (Freudenheim 2011). In return for immediate gain, they sacrifice present and future patients, and undermine the work of more selfless colleagues. They are able to exploit a position of authority and knowledge to dismantle the safeguards of knowledge and authority, for what they see as their own immediate advantage.

IV

It was not only individuals who were placed at risk. The cost of healthcare in the United States has risen to a level which threatens macroeconomic stability. Healthcare costs (at around 17% of GDP) are almost twice as high per head as in comparable countries (Figure 15.1).

These expenditures are creating havoc in public expenditures, and dragging down employers, who provide most health insurance. And yet healthcare outcomes (on average) are the worst among the top seven countries (Table 15.1).

A study of mortality reduction in seventeen countries over twenty-five years to 2005 found the United States to have the highest health expenditure per head and also the highest mortality rate. The USA ranked seventeenth in the ratio of expenditure to lives saved, and eleventh in the rate of reduced deaths (Pritchard and Wallace 2011). Another study indicated that the USA ranking for various measures of mortality declined between five and nine ranks among thirty-four OECD countries between 1990 and 2010, depending on the measure used. Its average ranking of Years of Life Lost due to Premature

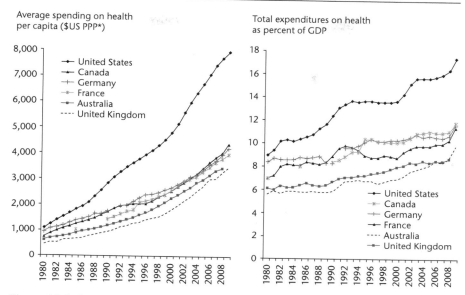

Figure 15.1. International comparisons of spending on health, 1980–2009

Source: Commonwealth Fund, *Why Not the Best? Results from the National Scorecard on U.S. Health System Performance, 2011* (New York: Commonwealth Fund, 2011), Exhibit 3, 20. Based on OECD Health database.

Mortality (YLL) in twenty-five causes of death among OECD countries is twenty-sixth (calculated from Murray 2013: E14, figure 4).

Standards of treatment are good, but many people cannot access them. The proportion of uninsured during the last three decades has been typically higher than 15% of the population. It currently stands at almost 17%, or more than fifty million people (US Census Bureau 2010). Many more are underinsured. In 2010, more than eighty-one million working-age adults, 44% of those between the ages of 19 to 64, were uninsured or underinsured during the year. In the economic downturn, nine million working-age adults lost their health coverage together with their jobs (Commonwealth Fund 2011: 9). Medical insurers deny cover for millions with pre-existing conditions (Potter 2009). Forty-five thousand excess deaths a year were recently attributed to the absence of medical insurance, comparable to around 33,000 deaths on the roads (Wilper et al. 2009). As many as 91,000 fewer people would die prematurely if the US could achieve the leading country's rate in terms of healthcare. The US ranks last among sixteen industrialised countries for preventable death (Commonwealth Fund 2011: 9, 43). For those without insurance or with insufficient coverage, a major illness was an economic calamity. Personal bankruptcy in the United States has risen sharply in the last three decades. In 2001, about 1.5 million experienced bankruptcy—more,

Table 15.1. Overall ranking of healthcare performance

	AUS	CAN	GER	NETH	NZ	UK	US
OVERALL RANKING (2010)	3	6	4	1	5	2	7
Quality Care	4	7	5	2	1	3	6
Effective Care	2	7	6	3	5	1	4
Safe Care	6	5	3	1	4	2	7
Coordinated Care	4	5	7	2	1	3	6
Patient-Centred Care	2	5	3	6	1	7	4
Access	6.5	5	3	1	4	2	6.5
Cost-Related Problem	6	3.5	3.5	2	5	1	7
Timeliness	6	7	2	1	3	4	5
Efficiency	2	6	5	3	4	1	7
Equity	4	5	3	1	6	2	7
Long, Healthy, Productive Live	1	2	3	4	5	6	7
Health Expenditures/Capita, 2007	$3357	$3895	$3588	$3837	$2454	$2992	$7290
Rankings 1–2.33							
Rankings 2.34–4.66							
Rankings 4.67–7							

Source: K. Davis et al., *Mirror, Mirror on the Wall: How the Performance of US Health Care System Compares Internationally, 2010 Update* (New York: Commonwealth Fund, 2010), Exhibit ES-1, v

for example, than heart disease or divorce (Warren and Tyagi 2003: 80–5; Offer 2006: 293–4). Medical costs were implicated in half to two-thirds of all cases of personal bankruptcy (Himmelstein 2009). Some couples who would otherwise divorce chose to stay together to benefit from medical coverage, while others separated to protect a partner from medical costs. But assets of divorced spouses can still be seized for medical expenses five years after the break (Kristof 2009). To keep their health coverage, people stayed in jobs they disliked.

The conflict between the care ethic and the market ethic is exposed in the efforts to make the underinsured pay for their treatment. An entitlement to hospital emergency room attention is the US medical system's ultimate safety net; it is a statutory expression of the duty of care. In law, however, it is restricted to the relief of symptoms. But emergency room hospitals still demand payment for treatment, and sign up patients on high-interest credit cards in order to collect their fees. These obligations are pursued, and are ultimately sold at a discount to financial companies. 'If you go to a veterinarian, you have to pay, one health-care executive notes. Why should a hospital be different?' (Grow and Berner 2007). Patients with assets can have them seized; those without can lose their credit ratings, and their ability to borrow for a car or a house (Harney 2011). This is consistent with the norms of profit-making hospitals, but has caused some heart-searching among non-profits. 'In a lucrative new form of fiscal alchemy... a growing number of hospitals, working with a range of financial companies, are squeezing revenue from patients with little or no health insurance' (Grow and Berner 2007). Some non-profits were relaxed about charging patients a high rate of interest, but others were uneasy. One medical administrator in Memphis said: 'If we heal somebody medically, but we break them financially, have we really done what is in the best interest of the patient?' (Grow and Berner 2007). Debt collection companies have stationed agents in emergency rooms and hospital departments to get patients to pay before treatment, and have gained illegal access to personal health records (Silver-Greenberg 2012).[3] With no burden of corporate taxation, non-profits often had larger surpluses than for-profit hospitals, and paid their managers and doctors disproportionately well (Brill 2013).

A software programme widely used in hospitals ('Conifer') works out how to maximise cost extraction from indigent patients. 'One of our main values is to take care of the poor and vulnerable', says Mary Jo Gregory, Chief Operating Officer of the Sisters of Charity of Leavenworth Health System, which operates eleven hospitals west of the Mississippi and is using Conifer software. 'How do you fulfil that role and still have a sustainable ministry? Our bad debt is high, and we're facing the same issues as everyone else in terms of collections' (Olmos 2010: 22–3). The cases described are heart-breaking: pain and death galore. Profits are not as high in health insurance as they are in drug manufacturing. Instead, as in other industries, the surplus is appropriated by the managers (Strauss 2011). Managers of non-profits also rake it in (Buettner 2011; Brill 2013). Physician-managed hospitals had higher outcome quality scores than those run by managers (Goodall 2011).

The Obama healthcare reform has given priority to the ethical issue, the denial of medical care, while setting aside the economic one of unsustainably rising costs. The actual form of the Health Care Act is an unwieldy compromise. It has left intact the commercial profit-seeking framework of healthcare provision, protecting insurance company profits and medical overtreatment. In order to achieve its ethical objective of extending healthcare to all, it has resorted to a moderate form of compulsion, and has extended eligibility for subsidised programmes. The Act only went through because it did nothing to threaten the revenues of insurance companies and health providers. It became the focus of political unrest, most notably by the so-called Tea Party

---

[3] There is rich further testimony in 1159 readers' comments, with the majority indignant and a minority supporting the practices.

movement. Inconsistently, these protesters oppose the reduction in Medicare benefits for the old, while objecting to the fiscal cost of extending coverage to other people. In its continued support for Medicare, the Tea Party movement embodies the tension between the 'me-first' ideology that is pervasive in United States, and the contrary intuition that care for the ill is an obligation and entitlement.

It is revealing to discuss market efficiency in terms of these external costs of pain and death. In the UK, there is more than a decade's difference in life expectation between people at the two ends of the socio-economic scale, a gap wider than at any time since 1921 (Thomas et al. 2010). The prevalence of obesity is much higher in the cluster of English-speaking market liberal economies. Statistically, the most important driver appears to be the extent of economic insecurity, and that is affected by the risk of incurring high private medical costs (Offer et al. 2010). Obesity is an important risk factor for disease and early death. Economic insecurity has risen sharply in United States during the last three decades (Hacker et al. 2010). There is a trade-off, then, between opportunity for some and pain and death for others. A market in healthcare is consistent with higher cost and worse outcomes. Even in theory, markets only work if participants are well-informed. That is not the case for health, and indeed, not the case for a great many other purchases, either because information is not readily available, or because it will only be revealed in the future. It is certainly not the case in the purchase of financial products.

We began with the financial crisis. For doctors, write bankers. Do bankers have a duty of care for anything except their private gain? Pain or death are not so directly at stake here, so the issue may not be so clear-cut. But when bankers are bailed out by taxpayers, the pursuit of self-interest affects the access of others to necessities like housing, education, job security, pensions, and healthcare. From the point of view of high finance, its transactions are impersonal. But the marketing departments of retail banking strive to convey the impression of a caring relationship, and the purchase of financial products typically involves a face-to-face interview. The existence of face-to-face interaction, suggests that it would be appropriate to apply the reciprocal norms of the impartial spectator to this type of interaction. Consequently, this aspect of retail banking makes it tempting for reformers to impose a duty of care on bankers, on pain of expulsion. Ed Miliband, current leader of the Labour Party has proposed a duty on bankers of this kind, explicitly modelled on the medical one (BBC 2011). But what the medical analogy really shows is that neither an interpersonal relationship, nor a strict code of professional practice is sufficient. Even in medicine, where the norm of care is so powerful, it is inadequate to counteract the ravages of market forces. What is needed in this area of personal service, for the duty of care to be effective, is an explicit rejection of the norm of *caveat emptor*, of the licence to exploit counterparty ignorance. Even Milton Friedman stressed that an economic exchange is advantageous to both sides, only 'provided the transaction is bi-laterally voluntary and informed' (Friedman and Friedman 1962: 13). If we want to follow Adam Smith, his teaching requires a modicum of virtue on the part of bankers, both individually and in their corporate capacity. The less-demanding 'economy of regard' requires that whatever their real motives, bankers should be able to send an authentic signal, and not a fake one, that they respect their clients' interests, and do not feel entitled to cheat them (Offer, Chapter 7 in this book). For the signal to be authentic, they must genuinely place their clients' interests on a parity with their own.

References

American Medical Association and Center for Health Policy Research (2009). 'Competition in Health Insurance: A Comprehensive Study of US Markets, 2009 Update'. Chicago, IL: American Medical Association.

Angell, M. (2005). *The Truth About the Drug Companies: How They Deceive Us and What to Do About It.* New York: Random House.

Angell, M. (2006). 'Your Dangerous Drugstore', *New York Review of Books*, 53(10): 38–40.

Angell, M. (2009). 'Drug Companies and Doctors: A Story of Corruption', *New York Review of Books*, 56(1): 8–12.

Arrow, K. J. (1963). 'Uncertainty and the Welfare Economics of Medical Care', *American Economic Review*, 53: 941–73.

BBC (2011). 'Ed Miliband Seeks Banker Disciplinary Code', *BBC News* [online news website], September <http://www.bbc.co.uk/news/uk-politics-14869650>, accessed 25 August 2013.

Bork, R. H. (1978). *The Antitrust Paradox: A Policy at War with Itself.* New York: Basic Books.

Bowles, S. and Jayadev, A. (2008). 'The Enforcement-Equality Trade-Off', in L. Constabile (ed.), *Institutions for Social Well Being: Alternatives for Europe.* New York: Palgrave Macmillan, 74–94.

Brill, S. (2013). 'Bitter Pill: Why Medical Bills Are Killing Us', *Time*, Special Issue, 20 February.

Buettner, R. (2011). 'Reaping Millions from Medicaid in Nonprofit Care for Disabled', *The New York Times*, 2 August.

CNN Money (2009). 'Fortune 500, Top Industries, Most Profitable', *CNN Money and Fortune Magazine* [online news website], <http://money.cnn.com/magazines/fortune/fortune500/2009/performers/industries/profits/>, accessed 9 March 2014.

Cole, D. (2010). 'They Did Authorize Torture, But...', *New York Review of Books*, 57(6).

Commonwealth Fund (2011). *Why Not the Best? Results from the National Scorecard on U.S. Health System Performance.* New York: Commonwealth Fund.

Davis, K., Schoen, C., and Stremikis, K. (2010). *Mirror, Mirror on the Wall: How the Performance of the U.S. Health Care System Compares Internationally.* New York: Commonwealth Fund.

Force, P. (2003). *Self-Interest before Adam Smith: A Genealogy of Economic Science*. Cambridge: Cambridge University Press.

Forden, S. (2011). 'Why Medicare Can't Catch the Fraudsters', *Bloomberg Business Week*, 10–16 January, 23–6.

Freudenheim, M. (2011). 'Adjusting, More M.D.'s Add M.B.A', *The New York Times*, 5 September.

Friedman, M. and Friedman, R. D. (1962). *Capitalism and Freedom*. Chicago: University of Chicago Press.

Gawande, A. (2009). 'The Cost Conundrum: What a Texas Town Can Teach Us About Health Care', *The New Yorker*, 1 June, 36–44.

Gawande, A. (2010). 'Letting Go: What Should Medicine Do When It Can't Save Your Life?', *The New Yorker*, 2 August, 36–49.

Goodall, A. (July 2011). 'Physician-Leaders and Hospital Performance: Is There an Association?', *Vox, Research-Based Policy Analysis and Commentary from Leading Economists* [online commentary], <http://www.voxeu.org/index.php?q=node/6779>, accessed 25 August 2013.

Grow, B. and Berner, B. (2007). 'Fresh Pain for the Uninsured', *Business Week*, 9 December, 35–41.

Hacker, J. S. et al. (2010). *Economic Security at Risk: Findings from Economic Security Index*. New York: Rockefeller Foundation.

Harney, K. R. (2011). 'Debts that Unsettle the Score', *Washington Post*, 17 June.

Healy, D. (1997). *The Antidepressant Era*. Cambridge, MA: Harvard University Press.

Healy, D. (2012). *Pharmageddon*. Berkeley, CA: University of California Press.

Hightower, J. (2012). 'The Great American Medicine Show, a Spectacle of Deceit, Manipulation, and Flimflammery', *OpEd News* [online commentary], April, <http://www.opednews.com/articles/The-great-American-medicin-by-Jim-Hightower-120427-544.html>, accessed 25 August 2013.

Himmelstein, D. U. et al. (2009). 'Medical Bankruptcy in the United States, 2007: Results of a National Study', *American Journal of Medicine*, 122(8): 741–6.

Horton, R. (1997). 'Conflicts of Interest in Clinical Research: Opprobrium or Obsession?', *The Lancet*, 349(9059): 1112–13.

Kassirer, J. P. (2005). *On the Take: How Medicine's Complicity with Big Business Can Endanger Your Health*. New York: Oxford University Press.

Kristof, N. D. (2009). 'Until Medical Bills Do Us Part', *The New York Times*, 30 August.

Krueger, A. B. and Stone, A. A. (2008). 'Assessment of Pain: A Community-Based Diary Survey in the USA', *The Lancet*, 371(9623): 1519–25.

Lane, C. (2007). *Shyness: How Normal Behavior Became a Sickness*. New Haven, CT: Yale University Press.

Laugesen, M. J. and Glied, S. A. (2011). 'Higher Fees Paid to US Physicians Drive Higher Spending for Physician Services Compared to Other Countries', *Health Affairs*, 30(9): 1647–56.

Leap, T. L. (2011). *Phantom Billing, Fake Prescriptions, and the High Cost of Medicine: Health Care Fraud and What to Do About It*. Ithaca, NY: ILR Press.

Lefcourt, D. (2011). 'A Corporate "Culture of Fraud" ', *OpEd News* [online commentary], September, <http://www.opednews.com/articles/A-Corporate-Culture-of-Fr-by-Dave-Lefcourt-110913-182.html>, accessed 25 August 2013.

Lerner, M. J. (1980). *The Belief in a Just World: A Fundamental Delusion.* New York: Plenum Press.

Lerner, M. J. and Miller, D. T. (1978). 'Just World Research and Attribution Process: Looking Back and Ahead', *Psychological Bulletin*, 85(5): 1030–51.

Light, D. (ed.) (2011). *The Risks of Prescription Drugs.* New York: Columbia University Press.

Lipton, E. (2011). 'Support Is Mutual for Senator and Makers of Supplements', *The New York Times*, 20 June.

Murray, C. J. L. (2013). 'The State of US Health, 1990–2010: Burden of Diseases, Injuries, and Risk Factors', *Journal of the American Medical Association*, 310(6): 591–606.

Nguyen, D., Ornstein, C., et al. (2011). 'Dollars for Docs: How Industry Dollars Reach Your Doctors', *Propublica: Journalism in the Public Interest*, <http://www.propublica.org/>, accessed 18 July 2012.

Offer, A. (2006). *The Challenge of Affluence, Self-Control and Well-Being in the United States and Britain since 1950.* Oxford: Oxford University Press.

Offer, A., Pechey, R., and Ulijaszek, S. (2010). 'Obesity under Affluence Varies by Welfare Regimes: The Effect of Fast Food, Insecurity, and Inequality', *Economics and Human Biology*, 8(3): 297–308.

Olmos, D. (2010). 'Getting Patients to Pay before They Go Home', *Bloomberg Business Week*, 16 May.

Pear, R. (2009). 'In House, Many Spoke with One Voice, Lobbyists', *The New York Times*, 15 November.

Pear, R. (2011). 'Report on Medicare Cites Prescription Drug Abuse', *The New York Times*, 3 October.

Pear, R. (2012). 'U.S. To Force Drug Firms to Report Money Paid to Doctors', *The New York Times*, 16 January.

Pitofsky, R. (2008). *How the Chicago School Overshot the Mark: The Effect of Conservative Economic Analysis on U.S. Antitrust.* New York: Oxford University Press.

Pope, R. and Selten, R. (2012). 'Public Debt Tipping Point Studies Ignore How Exchange Rate Changes May Create a Financial Meltdown', *Real-World Economics*, 59: 2–38.

Potter, W. (2009). 'Health Insurance Exec Speaks: Testimony of Wendell Potter before the U.S. Senate Committee on Commerce, Science and Transportation', *The New Republic*, 24 June.

Pritchard, C. and Wallace, M. S. (2011). 'Comparing the USA, UK and 17 Western Countries' Efficiency and Effectiveness in Reducing Mortality', *Journal of the Royal Society of Medicine Short Reports*, 2(7): 60.

Public Citizen Congress Watch (2003). *2002 Drug Industry Profits: Hefty Pharmaceutical Company Margins Dwarf Other Industries.* Washington, DC: Public Citizen.

Rashbaum, W. K. (2012). 'A $250 Million Fraud Scheme Finds a Path to Brighton Beach', *The New York Times*, 29 February.

Rayner, C. (1999). 'Integrity in Surgical Life, What Happens If It Is Missing?', in A. Montefiore and D. Vines (eds), *Integrity in the Public and Private Domains*. London: Routledge, 62–71.

Relman, A. S. (1992). 'What Market Values Are Doing to Medicine', *Atlantic Monthly*, 269(3): 99–106.

Relman, A. S. (2007). *A Second Opinion: Rescuing America's Healthcare: A Plan for Universal Coverage Serving Patients over Profit*. New York: Public Affairs.

Rosenberg, M. (2012). 'Why Have Medical Journals Not Retracted these Fraudulent Articles', *OpEd News* [online commentary], April, <http://www.opednews.com/articles/Why-Have-Medical-Journals-by-Martha-Rosenberg-120426-320.html>, accessed 25 August 2013.

Rubin, Z. and Peplau, L. A. (1975). 'Who Believes in a Just World?', *Journal of Social Issues*, 31(3): 65–89.

Silver-Greenberg, J. (2012). 'Debt Collector Is Faulted for Tough Tactics in Hospitals', *The New York Times*, 24 April.

Singer, N. (2009). 'Senator Moves to Stop Scientific Ghostwriting', *The New York Times*, 19 August.

Smith, G. B. (2012). 'Are Cheating Doctors Running Bill Scams to Insurance Companies? Charging Huge "Out of Network" Fees', *New York Daily News*, 18 February.

Smith, R. (1997). 'Conflict of Interest in Clinical Research, Opprobium or Obsession?', *The Lancet*, 349(9066): 1703.

Starr, P. (1982). *The Social Transformation of American Medicine*. New York: Basic Books.

Stone, A. A. et al. (2010). 'The Socioeconomic Gradient in Daily Colds and Influenza, Headaches, and Pain', *Archives of Internal Medicine*, 170(6): 570–1.

Strauss, G. (2011). 'Outgoing Aetna Chairman Gets a $68.7 Million Goodbye', *USA Today*, 11 March.

Terhune, C. (2012). 'Many Hospitals, Doctors Offer Cash Discount for Medical Bills', *Los Angeles Times*, 27 May.

Thomas, B., Dorling, D., and Davey Smith, G. (2010). 'Inequalities in Premature Mortality in Britain: Observational Study from 1921 to 2007', *British Medical Journal*, 341: c3639.

Tombs, S. and Whyte, W. (2010). *Regulatory Surrender, Death, Injury and the Non-Enforcement of Law*. Liverpool: Institute of Employment Rights.

United States Census Bureau (2010). 'Income, Poverty, and Health Insurance Coverage in the United States 2009', Washington, DC: Bureau of the Census.

United States FDA (2011). 'Notification to Pharmaceutical Companies: Acceptance of Third-Party Data Integrity Audit for Cetero Studies Conducted from March 1, 2008 to August 31, 2009', FDA, Washington, DC [online government website], <http://www.fda.gov/Drugs/DrugSafety/ucm265559.htm>, accessed 25 August 2013.

United States Senate Committee on Finance (2010). 'Ghostwriting in Medical Literature', Washington, DC: US Senate, 1–31, <http://www.grassley.senate.gov/about/upload/Senator-Grassley-Report.pdf>, accessed 25 August 2013.

Van Horn, R. (2009). 'Reinventing Monopoly and the Role of Corporations: The Roots of Chicago Law and Economics', in P. Mirowski and D. Plehwe (eds), *The Road from Mont Pelerin: The Making of the Neoliberal Thought Collective*. Cambridge, MA: Harvard University Press, 238–79.

Warren, E. and Tyagi, A. W. (2003). *The Two-Income Trap: Why Families Went Broke When Mothers Went to Work*. New York: Basic Books.

Washington, H. (2011). 'Flacking for Big Pharma', *The American Scholar Summer 2012* [online journal], <http://theamericanscholar.org/flacking-for-big-pharma/>, accessed 25 August 2013.

White, L. J. (2008). 'The Growing Influence of Economics and Economists on Antitrust: An Extended Discussion', Working Paper 08-05, Washington, DC: Reg-Markets Center.

Wilper, A. P. et al. (2009). 'Health Insurance and Mortality in US Adults', *American Journal of Public Health*, 99(12): 2289–95.

Wilson, D. (2010). 'A Tougher Conflict Policy at Harvard Medical School', *The New York Times*, 21 July.

Wilson, D. and Singer, N. (2009). 'Ghostwriting Is Called Rife in Medical Journals', *The New York Times*, 11 September.

16

Restoring Trust

Sue Jaffer, Nicholas Morris, and David Vines

16.1 Trust and the Financial Services Industry

The chapters of this book have argued that trust and trustworthiness are both important in the financial services industry. Trust matters in market transactions when one person's decision depends on the actions of other parties, and those actions cannot be readily controlled or monitored. This is particularly true if the decision depends on information held by other people who may not reveal or tell the truth about that information (Hay 1999). In financial services, such information asymmetries are particularly strong, so it is important to be able to rely on other parties being trustworthy.

Financial products are complex and not well understood by ordinary people, making customers reliant on advice. Often a chain of intermediaries is involved, reducing the extent of face-to-face relationships and introducing principal-agent problems. In addition, time frames for judgements are long, so that the holders of assets often do not find out the real value of their purchases for many years, by which time it may be too late to rectify mistakes.

Moreover, trust in and the trustworthiness of the financial sector matters in a wider economic sense, because their absence results in poor outcomes for the whole economy. We have reviewed a number of ways in which these outcomes can occur. Without trust in the sellers of financial products, people are inclined to reduce their level of saving, resulting in lower incomes in retirement and greater reliance on the state (Springford 2011). For some, a lack of trust could result in (continued) exclusion from the financial system altogether, imposing higher costs and greater risk on the most disadvantaged. Without a bank account, utility bills are higher and services such as insurance and credit are difficult or impossible to obtain (Pomeroy 2011). The risk of withdrawal from financial services is greater than for other services because people by and large do not naturally seek out financial products (Lipsey 2011). They have to be persuaded to purchase them, and to trust those who sell the services or products.

As Chapter 2 describes, the decline in the trustworthiness of individuals and firms in the financial sector created a raft of adverse effects. Many institutional investors bought what turned out to be toxic products on the strength of misplaced trust in those selling and rating the products (O'Brien 2010). The consequences included a significant loss of wealth for the ultimate customers and reduced retirement incomes. Misplaced trust in the ability of the financial institutions to identify, manage, and price risk appropriately imposed heavy costs on taxpayers and the wider community, through the need for bailouts, recession, and the other consequences of the financial crisis.

Numerous enquiries and recommendations for regulatory reform have been made in the five years since the Global Financial Crisis (GFC). Useful reforms are underway, and the courts are establishing precedents which will assist the policing of conflicts of interest. However, although these regulatory developments are useful, we do not believe that they will solve the problem by themselves. This has led to our search for additional ways of rebuilding trust.

Thus our aim in this chapter is thus to identify the requirements for trustworthiness. Drawing on the lessons from previous chapters and case studies of how these matters are dealt with in other industries, we recommend where and how it might be possible to improve the trustworthiness of the finance industry. In doing this, we draw particularly on the lessons from framing elaborated by Gold in Chapter 6, on O'Neill's ideas about intelligent accountability from Chapter 8, and on experience in developing ethical frameworks and integrity systems as discussed by de Bruin and Miller in Chapters 12 and 14. We also recognise the potential contribution of the law in holding to account those responsible for delivering their obligations, as explored by Getzler, by Armour and Gordon, and by Awrey and Kershaw in Chapters 9, 11, and 13.

In what follows, we first reiterate what is required for trustworthiness to flourish. Then we set out four steps as to how trustworthiness may be developed and enforced: by defining obligations, identifying those with responsibility for delivering obligations, identifying mechanisms for encouragement of trustworthiness, and holding those responsible to account. How these mechanisms have been applied in other industries is explored to provide useful lessons for financial services. We then focus on five obstacles to trustworthiness, examining what reforms have been proposed, whether these reforms are likely to further develop strong trustworthiness in financial services, and what more should be done. The final section summarises our conclusions on what further needs to be done to achieve each of the four steps for improved trustworthiness.

16.2 Requirements for Trustworthiness

The trustworthiness of a person depends on three necessary elements: competence, willingness, and reliability. Competence concerns the extent to which the person who is trusted has the necessary skills, knowledge, and abilities. Willingness concerns their intention to keep commitments. Reliability is concerned with whether the person performs as expected. We seek trustworthiness of this kind in the financial services industry.

These requirements for trustworthiness apply equally to individuals and institutions. However, the trustworthiness of individuals within an institution will not be translated into trustworthiness on the part of the institution unless there are mechanisms in place to ensure consistency of these attributes within the institution, and their transmission over time through institutional values and memory (Montefiore 1999).

Motivations are important, as discussed by Gold in Chapter 6. Gold distinguishes strong from weak trustworthiness. Weak trustworthiness can emerge even if the person being trusted is self-interested. Strong trust emerges only when there are other-regarding motivations, such as altruism or other pro-social motivations, procedural motivations including professionalism, or the desire for approbation or esteem. Given the obstacles to trustworthiness that exist in the financial sector, it is our belief that only the cultivation of strong trustworthiness will lead to better outcomes.

We can define four necessary steps which assist in achieving strong trustworthiness:

1. a description of the obligations to be delivered;
2. identification of the responsibility of different players;
3. establishment of mechanisms to encourage and enforce trustworthiness;
4. rendition of an account of performance and methods of holding the individual or institution to account for that performance.

The first step is to describe the duties or obligations to be delivered. Without a clear understanding of the ultimate ends of a person's activity, or that of an institution, any method of enhancing trustworthiness is without direction. The purposes of an activity lead to the obligations which are assumed by the person or institution being trusted (Miller 2011b). As argued by O'Neill in Chapter 8, this involves focusing on the tasks to be done, rather than on second-order targets which can misrepresent overall objectives.

Next, those responsible for delivering the obligations need to be identified and they need to accept their obligations. Part of the public's anger over the role of the banks in precipitating the GFC rests on the failure of those concerned to take responsibility for their actions. For example, under questioning by the Financial Crisis Inquiry Commission, Lloyd Blankfein, Chairman and CEO of Goldman Sachs claimed that 'The standards at the time were different' (Harrington 2011). He did not admit to a lack of personal responsibility, or to a failure in fiduciary duty, or to any public obligation on the part of either himself or his banking colleagues. Similarly, Barclays suffered greater reputational damage because it sought to present its Libor transgressions as a failure of internal systems rather than as a failure of leadership (O'Brien 2012).

The third step is to establish the mechanisms intended to secure and support the delivery of obligations. A wide range of such mechanisms has been used by professions and organisations, including codes of conduct, reputational indices, membership and powers of exclusion, and fraud investigation units. Different mechanisms work to support different types of strong trustworthiness: for example, membership of a professional association and codes of conduct seek to encourage procedural motivations. Reputational indices and fraud investigations support motivations based on esteem and approbation. Ethics committees and ethics training are designed to support pro-social motivations directly. Such mechanisms have been discussed by de Bruin, by Awrey and Kershaw, and by Miller in Chapters 12, 13, and 14. These mechanisms can be reactive (such as exclusion upon wrongdoing) or preventative (e.g. education, elimination of conflicts of interest). Mechanisms to redress transgressions need to be proportionate, but at the same time provide serious remedies for failure.

The final step is to require those with responsibility to render an account of the adequacy of their performance in delivering their obligations, and to hold them to account for that performance. This is an essential part of the 'willingness' component of trustworthiness.

Of course, the implementation of these steps relies on self-interest as well as supporting other-regarding motivations. Self-interest is important both through the provision of positive incentives and through methods which promote compliance through the threat of punishment. The threat of punishment in itself only promotes weak trustworthiness. But at the same time it can support strong trustworthiness by reinforcing the desire for a good reputation and by reinforcing shared values.

16.3 Mechanisms to Promote Trustworthiness

A range of mechanisms can be used to ensure compliance with minimum ethical standards. These may include external regulatory mechanisms, which ought to complement and reinforce internal mechanisms within institutions

(Miller 2011b). They encompass compliance and enforcement mechanisms, as well as rules and principles for dealing with issues such as conflicts of interest. They need to be able to identify the causes of ethical failure, assign responsibility for their remedy, and ensure accountability.

The range of mechanisms that could potentially be used include codes of conduct, ethical risk management systems, effective complaints and discipline systems, internal anti-fraud and anti-corruption systems, an external independent ethics audit, and (building on the latter) reputational indices. In addition, products and markets can be designed and regulated so that it is easy for purchasers to understand what is being charged and to check whether it is offered at a competitive price. The nature of the different mechanisms that can be employed, the way in which they support strong trustworthiness, and the issues which arise in their use, are discussed below.

16.3.1 Professional Associations

Membership of a professional association implies that members are qualified and agree to act professionally, in a way that directly supports procedural motivations for strong trustworthiness (Phillips 2011). In effect, the association seeks to ensure that its members carry out their activities in a trustworthy manner, and to differentiate members from those who might carry out the activities of that profession in a less trustworthy way.

Professional associations protect the reputation of their members through requirements for qualification (often by formal examination), disciplinary procedures when the performance of members is below the standard required, and the ultimate sanction of exclusion. In the UK, professional lawyers, doctors, and architects, for example, can have their licences to practise withdrawn. The London Stock Exchange and Lloyds of London occasionally exclude those who fail to obey their rules from participating in the market.

By preventing the participation of unqualified individuals, professional associations attempt to raise the standard of service provided and to make it harder for the general public to be exploited by untrained or unscrupulous suppliers. They are designed to take responsibility for standards, and for this responsibility to be assumed by the association's members.

Such professional associations attempt to ensure that ethical values are not undermined by market forces, and to avoid an outcome in which competition brings down the quality of service. Sometimes they enable members to charge higher fees for their services, in a way which is intended to support a higher quality of service. In this manner professional associations such as the General Medical Council and the former Law Society attempt to align the self-interest of members with the interests of their patients or clients.

The issue of whether professional associations are able to create systems which operate to the public benefit has been much debated (Alexandra and Miller 2010). The perception that prices are higher than necessary has led to the criticism that professional associations mainly seek to protect the market position of their members (Loughrey 2012). Similarly, the 'club culture' created by professional associations has been derided as self-serving (O'Neill 2005). The nexus of self-interest, collective interest of the profession, and the interests of clients, customers, or wider society is subtle. Whether a professional association will focus on the latter depends both on how important reputation is to the members, and on the underlying values of those in the profession. In Chapter 8, O'Neill argues that genuine professional integrity grows out of 'tough institutional structures' which include robust systems for dealing with conflicts of interest and which contain serious remedies for failure. In our view, this is one of the major challenges facing the establishment of a professional association for banking if it is to be effective in promoting trustworthiness in the industry.

16.3.2 Self-Regulation

Self-regulatory organisations (SROs) perform a similar function to professional associations. The major difference between the two is that SROs focus on the behaviour of the firm, while professional associations focus on the behaviour of the individual. Properly applied, self-regulation can improve the competence, willingness, and reliability of firms within an industry.

Self-regulation occurs when industry members jointly pursue regulatory or standard-setting activities in the absence of explicit legal requirements. They might do this in relation to the disclosure of product information, the policing of deceptive practices, the establishment of minimum standards of safety and quality, the grading of products, and the creation of industry codes of conduct. An obvious extension of self-regulation is co-regulation, where regulatory responsibility is shared between industry bodies and regulatory authorities.

Proponents of self-regulation argue that it enables the expertise and practical experience of the industry to contribute to the development of regulatory policy, that administrative and compliance costs are lower, and that voluntary compliance is more likely if industry players are also stakeholders in the rule-making body. Opponents argue that self-regulatory bodies are often subject to conflicts of interest between their regulatory responsibilities and their business objectives, encourage anti-competitive practices, and lack transparency. Garvin (1983) summarises the issues:

> Self-regulation is no panacea. Like most public policies, it must be tailored to circumstances and employed with restraint. Applied wisely, it offers the opportunity for efficient, cooperative decision making with a degree of flexibility unlikely

from a more centralized federal agency. Applied improperly, it enables firms to cartelize their industries, with a few large companies dictating terms to other industry participants.

It is clear that there is a need for effective enforcement of self-regulatory rules (De Jong et al. 2004). Self-regulation can support strong trustworthiness through the promotion of procedural motivations. Explicit penalties and sanctions to prevent firms from free-riding off others' efforts do not support strong trustworthiness, except insofar as it affects their reputation. However, the need for such sanctions can be reduced by the transfer of norms, and the diffusion of best practice (Greif 1997; Nash and Ehrenfeld 1997).

16.3.3 Codes of Conduct

Codes of conduct are frequently used to set ethical standards for professional behaviour. They typically form the basis of self-regulation by covering the basic requirements for establishing trust in a professional relationship. If adhered to, codes of conduct can improve the strong trustworthiness of individuals and firms within an industry by supporting procedural motivations. Such codes typically require that:

- professional activities are conducted with integrity and honesty;
- advice should be given objectively and impartially;
- all client information should be strictly confidential;
- standards of practice should be adhered to and conflicts of interest disclosed; and that
- business is conducted in a way that is considerate of the public interest (Daykin 2004).

Codes of conduct can be self-regulatory or enforced by an external regulator. Many of the codes which characterise self-regulatory activity in the US were written in the 1970s, following the Watergate scandal and the departure of President Richard Nixon (Cressey and Moore 1983). At the time, large public companies were keen to emphasise their social responsibility.[1] Business leaders feared that unless they took steps to put their own house in order, the public might demand more restrictive regulation. At the time, the Cohen Commission emphasised the need for corporate executives to recognise the ethical standards, traditions, and concerns of society as well as company

---

[1] F. T. Allen was quoted in the Wall Street Journal (19 October 1975) as saying that 'corporate officials were beginning to be perceived as "little more than manicured hoodlums".'

profits in order to reduce the 'substantial gap...between some corporate behaviour and society's view of appropriate corporate conduct' (Cohen 1977).

The influence of codes of conduct clearly comes under pressure when there is moral hazard involved, for example, where the disclosure of a competitor's better offering would erode profits or reduce an individual's remuneration. As discussed by Awrey and Kershaw in Chapter 13, the success of mechanisms such as codes of practice will depend on the strength of the countervailing incentives. Thus ethical codes will only work in some circumstances (Armstrong 2012). It must be possible to observe whether the code is being met for the desire for approbation to support the code. The ability to exclude those who fail to meet the required standards is also necessary to support strong trustworthiness.

16.3.4 Ethical Risk Management Systems, Ethical Audits, and Reputational Indices

Miller (2011b) suggests that an ethics risk assessment process is a useful mechanism for ensuring trustworthiness. Identifying ethical risks, such as conflicts of interest, is likely to support both procedural motivations and pro-social motivations (in the case of the latter by highlighting the consequences of ethical breaches). However, ethics risk assessments require data gathering and analysis. Thus Miller is in agreement with O'Neill that good evidence is essential in designing what he calls integrity systems and in improving professional standards. He recommends evidence-based institutional design and, in particular, the practice of what has been referred to as evidence-based designing-in of ethical standards.

Miller also recommends the use of ethical audits to ensure that appropriate processes are in place and that they are operating appropriately. An ethics audit seeks to measure the ethical performance of individuals or firms. It requires objective measures of performance, such as numbers of warranted complaints, but would also involve review of institutional processes such as codes of conduct, ethical risk assessments, ethics committees, and professional development programmes.

Miller suggests that a reputational index could be used to harness the desire for reputation, to create a self-reinforcing 'triangle' between reputation, self-interest, and ethical standards. Individuals and organisations benefit from a good reputation: it is in their self-interest to earn a reputation for complying with ethical and professional standards, and it supports strong trustworthiness through the desire for approbation. The purpose of a reputational index is to ensure that such a reputation actually aligns with ethical practice.

16.3.5 Intelligent Accountability

Encouraging trustworthiness depends crucially in all cases on rendering an appropriate account of performance. As O'Neill argues in Chapter 8, intelligent accountability requires that agents be held to account for meeting their primary obligations. Performance needs to be judged competently and fairly, which means that those judging must be both informed and independent. Their judgements also need to be communicated intelligently if accountability to wider audiences is to be secured.

O'Neill argues also that the intelligent placing of trust requires evidence, albeit necessarily incomplete. Thus, one aim must be to improve the information available to customers and regulators to allow the placing of trust that is warranted. Intelligent systems of accountability should provide evidence to allow those affected to judge whether others' claims are true and their commitments reliable.

There are also issues surrounding the accountability of individuals who work within large complex organisations. One person within a system may act in a trustworthy manner, whilst others may not. It may also be the case that although individuals within a system act in a trustworthy manner, the system is itself designed to exploit customers. Several submissions to the Parliamentary Commission on Banking Standards quoted examples of employees being bullied to meet sales targets regardless of whether the products were appropriate for customers, with unachievable targets often being set (see, for example, Unite the Union 2012). It is necessary therefore, that senior management is held to account over the design of systems, as well as individuals for their performance working within them.

16.4 Improving Trustworthiness: Lessons from Other Industries

Other industries provide useful examples of self-regulatory and professional systems which have improved trustworthiness. Such systems have been introduced in a wide range of different circumstances. It is useful to consider, in each of these cases, the way in which the systems have carried out each of the four necessary steps which we identified as assisting in the achievement of trustworthiness: a description of the obligations to be delivered; an identification of the responsibility of different players; an establishment of mechanisms to encourage and enforce trustworthiness; and a rendition of an account of performance and the adoption of methods of holding the individual or institution to account for that performance. In particular, it is useful to see that a variety of mechanisms have been used to achieve the required outcomes, including self-regulatory organisations, the setting of professional standards, the cultivation of reputation, and the encouragement and sustaining of mutually beneficial cooperative outcomes. Furthermore, the examples illustrate the range of procedures that have been used for holding individuals and institutions to account for their performance.

16.4.1 Response to Crisis

In some industries the emergence of new procedures and institutions emerged as a response to a major crisis which threatened the industry. The Three Mile Island nuclear accident in 1979 exposed severe failings of risk management and lax safety procedures in the US nuclear industry and led to a damning Presidential Inquiry (Kemeny 1979). The gas leaks from a Union Carbide plant in Bhopal, India (which killed thousands of people) in 1984 damaged the credibility of the chemical industry worldwide. Both events led to a realisation by industry leaders that a proactive approach to repairing reputation was necessary, and in particular that the perceived and actual trustworthiness of the industry needed to be re-established. In both cases an improved self-regulatory system was subsequently created which has remained in place, and been strengthened, for thirty years. The initiatives were also motivated by a desire to head off potentially damaging government intervention. These examples show that such actions can be made to succeed, even in complex and global industries, and that this is a workable alternative to formal regulatory intervention.

The US nuclear industry did not wait for a Presidential Inquiry, but took action within two weeks of the accident. A committee of nuclear utility Chief Executive Officers set up a private regulatory organisation, the Institute of Nuclear Power Operations (INPO). The system was aimed at increasing both the perceived and actual competence and reliability of the industry. Today, the INPO is a thriving non-profit organisation, and is credited with improving nuclear safety in the US. 'Excellence in operating nuclear plants' is INPO's mission, seeking to 'resist the natural business tendency to reduce the resources dedicated to fostering safe and excellent practices' (Rees 1994). INPO carries out independent evaluation of the knowledge of plant personnel, the condition of systems and equipment, the quality of programmes and procedures, and the effectiveness of plant management. Nuclear plants are given a score, which is circulated to all CEOs of nuclear plants at an annual gathering, and which has become an important benchmark in the industry. Trustworthiness is expected from all companies in the industry, and systems are in place to monitor whether trust is warranted. Occasionally, adverse INPO comments can lead to the dismissal of management. INPO has also developed training and accreditation processes now used throughout the industry, coordinates information exchange, and has become an effective professional association for the industry.

Industry response to the difficulties faced by the Japanese nuclear industry following the seismic shocks and tsunami of 2011 has also been rapid. The American Society of Mechanical Engineers (ASME) has worked with Japanese counterparts since spring 2011 to explore the impact of the events on nuclear codes and standards. A Presidential Task Force was set up shortly after the disaster and reported in June 2012 (ASME 2012). The report found that the Fukushima Dai-ichi accident revealed no fatal flaw in nuclear technology, and the reasons why the plants suffered core meltdowns were clear and correctible. Relevant safety improvements are now being implemented in the global nuclear fleet.

Taylor and Wolak (2011) compare the regulation of risk in the nuclear power industry today with that of financial services. They note that the safety record of the nuclear industry is considerably better than that of the financial industry, attributing this difference to the effectiveness of INPO in encouraging trustworthiness and enforcing self-regulation, to the legal framework under which nuclear regulatory agencies operate,[2] and to the lack of regulatory capture (despite considerable potential for the use of informal mechanisms). For example, communication between parties prior to nuclear hearings (managed by an Administrative Law Judge) is strictly prohibited. Taylor and Wolak conclude by recommending that a financial industry analogue of INPO be given serious consideration.

The leakage of methyl isocyanate gas and other chemicals from a Union Carbide plant in Bhopal, India on 2 December 1984 led to a substantial reduction in public trust in the chemical industry (Rees 1997). Polls at the time, for example those carried out by Dow Chemical, showed that restoration of trust was not possible by the actions of a single company, as public attitudes did not adequately distinguish between ethical and non-ethical companies. Leaders of the industry decided that they needed to be proactive, partly to improve public image and partly to pre-empt government intervention. They recognised that unless attitudes in the industry changed, they would not be able to restore public trust. The Chemical Industry's Responsible Care Programme ('Responsible Care') was initially launched by the Canadian Chemical Producers Association (CCPA) in 1985 (Moffet, Bregha, and Middelkoop 2004). Today it is run in fifty-two countries and covers chemical industries which account for nearly 90% of global production.

Responsible Care is a code of conduct which includes guiding principles, codes covering over one hundred management practices, and a Global

---

[2] The Nuclear Regulatory Commission (NRC) and the Federal Energy Regulatory Commission (FERC).

Charter. The codes cover interaction with the community (the community awareness and emergency response code), facilities management (the pollution prevention, process safety, and employee health and safety codes), and treatment of suppliers and customers (the distribution and product stewardship codes) (King and Lenox 2000). Compliance with the programme is achieved through peer pressure between companies, and through dissemination of best practices.

The experience of the chemical industry demonstrates the importance of coordinated action where industry-wide reputation can be damaged by the actions of one or few actors, and the ability of a global, complex, industry to establish such a system. The initiatives that were taken after the Bhopal disaster, and since, have made a substantial difference to the trustworthiness of the industry.

16.4.2 Self-Regulation of Output

The advertising industry provides an example of how an effective self-regulatory system can be developed by agreement between stakeholders. The development of sophisticated, internationally agreed controls over advertising content followed concern from major retailers about adverse customer reactions which were perceived to damage both the specific advertiser and the wider industry (Boddewyn 1989). Major issues covered by the self-regulation of advertising are deception and controls over advertising to vulnerable groups such as children. As with the examples discussed above, the objective was to re-establish public trust in the industry, in this case in order to prevent wide-scale consumer defection. The system has been successful in encouraging trustworthiness with regard to these issues using an industry-funded self-regulatory agency. Self-regulation is underpinned by cooperation with and reinforcement by government agencies such as the UK Office of Fair Trading, also providing a good example of co-regulation.

In the UK, the Committee on Advertising Practice (CAP) publishes codes of practice for both broadcast and non-broadcast media. CAP also runs extensive training and advice on how to comply with the codes. CAP set up an independent adjudicator, the Advertising Standards Authority (ASA), in 1962, and since 1988 the Office of Fair Trading (OFT) has provided a legal backstop through enforcement of various regulations on referral from ASA. Both CAP and ASA are funded by a levy on the industry. The European Advertising Standards Alliance (EASA) and the International Chamber of Commerce (ICC) also promote business ethics through codes and guidelines on commercial communications. All these bodies believe that commercial communications are best managed by self-regulation within a legal framework that protects consumers from false and misleading claims.

A high degree of compliance is achieved by this system, partly because advertisements are easy to monitor and breaches are challenged by competitors or through customer complaints. Here self-regulation seems to be more effective than government intervention, because it allows the industry to deal with 'soft' issues such as taste, decency, and sexism. Subtle nuances which are misleading, unfair, or use 'hidden persuasion' are more likely to be uncovered by industry experts than by outsiders (Boddewyn 1989). Thus advertising provides a helpful example of mechanisms that have been established to encourage trust, because advertisers desire the esteem of their customers.

16.4.3 Professional Standards

A prime example of the promulgation of professional standards is provided by the medical profession. It has developed an integrity infrastructure which seeks to ensure competence, accuracy, and reliability of medical practitioners, and as a result the medical profession is mostly held in high regard in the UK, and medical practitioners are regarded as trustworthy in surveys (Goold 2002). The main elements of this system are qualifications for all types of medical practitioner, registration of doctors, pharmacists, and other key experts, ethical and performance standards, codified as Good Medical Practice, and fitness to practise panels which have the power to remove doctors' registration. Doctors take oaths which emphasise that they will, at all times, act in the best interests of their patients. Because of the nature of the profession, and arguably of the type of people who undertake it, their actions exhibit and encourage a stronger form of trust than in many other industries.

The General Medical Council (GMC) has origins as far back as 1421, when physicians sought to prevent those who did not have the requisite expertise from practising medicine (Raach 1944). Today, the Healthcare Commission seeks to ensure quality of performance in institutions such as NHS trusts and health authorities. However, the system has not always prevented major breaches of trust (as for example the case of Harold Shipman who murdered 215 patients over a period of 24 years before being apprehended). The Shipman Inquiry led to the introduction of new public agencies, such as the National Patient Safety Agency, thus moving the system away from self-regulation by the profession and towards formal statutory intervention (Shipman Inquiry 2003). As Offer explores in Chapter 15, US experience shows that the introduction of market pressures in the supply of health can cause major conflicts of interest for doctors and consultants, with adverse effects for the trustworthiness of doctors and for the system as a whole.

The legal profession also has a well-established enforcement system, which until 2007 was administered by the Law Society (for Solicitors) and by the Bar

Council (for Barristers). Trustworthiness in the provision of legal advice has long been recognised as a key element of a successful society (Leland 1979). This system worked well from the nineteenth century for over one hundred years, until the 1990s. Then changes to the size and structure of the industry, and the introduction of Limited Liability Partnerships in 2000, put increasing strain on the effectiveness of this self-regulatory system. The Law Society was also criticised for combining representative with regulatory functions and there was a political concern to introduce greater competition to the profession. This led to the Legal Services Act 2007, which transferred regulatory responsibility to a new government agency, the Legal Services Board. The Act also opened up the possibility of alternative business structures in which non-lawyers can buy law firms or invest in them, and which give law firms the opportunity to seek out external investment to grow their businesses. The outcome is now much harder to self-regulate. The larger international firms have recently taken action to reinforce self-regulation through Authorised Internal Regulation (AIR), in an attempt to re-establish the trust mechanisms that they see as having been eroded.

Medicine and law provide useful guidance for financial services as to how professional standards can be established and maintained, and how such systems evolve from the self-interest of members. Both have succeeded in providing a framework that encourages professionalism on the part of members. These frameworks have made a significant contribution to maintaining trust in the professions, and have encouraged the trustworthiness of members. The formal processes for licensing, training, and enforcement of codes of practice provide valuable guidance for the establishment of such systems to create a more professionalised financial services industry. The medical profession provides particular guidance on how to reduce problems with asymmetric information, while the legal profession has been particularly concerned with conflicts of interest. However, recent changes to business structures for lawyers have arguably eroded their ability to self-regulate, emphasising the need to adapt trust mechanisms to evolving industry structures.

16.4.4 The Importance of Membership and Reputation

Financial exchanges have historically been active promoters of self-regulation, wishing to convince investors that they will be protected in order to prevent them going to another exchange with a better regime. Stock and futures exchanges have developed extensive sets of rules with which members are expected to comply. Failure to comply with the rules set by an exchange can lead to material penalties including exclusion from the market.

Self-regulation, based on a reputation for trustworthiness, is in the interest of participants, as they share a common interest in attracting investors to the market of which they are a member. However, government support for self-regulation is also important, to give legal underpinning to the solution of contractual disputes and to reinforce investor protection (as for example through the Financial Services Compensation Scheme in the UK).

Futures markets provide an example where social control has proved to be more effective than formal regulation. Futures contracts have considerable social benefits, enabling hedging of risks which might otherwise be intolerable. However, because they are complex they provide considerable opportunities for deception, fraud, and criminal behaviour. These are difficult to counter through government-imposed regulation, so that rules and surveillance mechanisms imposed by the exchanges themselves provide the front line. These are backed up by systems based on peer group pressure, the leverage of large institutional clients, transparency in market dealings, and encouraging repeat business (Gunningham and Sinclair 1998).

The fact that self-regulation has developed and persisted in some complex financial markets is encouraging for potential improvements to trustworthiness in other parts of the industry. Recognition that the reputation of the market is important has led to agreement by self-interested participants on codes of practice and enforcement mechanisms. In some circumstances, the existence of an effective self-regulatory apparatus has removed the need for formal intervention (Carson 2011). Canada, for example, has several national self-regulatory bodies for the securities market but does not have a national government securities regulator.[3]

The success of self-regulation in financial exchanges has depended on the ability of the relevant exchange to detect and exclude those who do not abide by the rules of the exchange. As a result, the rules are mostly obeyed because exclusion has a large cost to those who transgress. In other words, they encourage only weak trust.

The New York Diamond Exchange provides a further example of how self-regulation in other markets can be made to work. In this case, exclusion has an extremely high penalty—inability to continue trading. The enforcement mechanisms used rely both on the threat of exclusion and the impact of publicity on reputation (Richman 2002).

In principle, regulating the diamond industry should be very difficult. Diamonds are small and easy to conceal yet valuable. Provenance is important to avoid trading in 'blood diamonds', but hard to establish. Yet the New York Diamond Exchange runs a remarkably successful system of self-regulation which rarely has to deal with cases of fraud (Shainberg 1982). The system also facilitates credit sales and ensures merchants fulfil their payment obligations,

---

[3] The Investment Dealers Association, Mutual Fund Dealers Association, Market Regulation Services, and the Montreal Exchange.

despite the need to hold diamonds they would not have the liquidity to possess outright. The governance of the Exchange relies on a system of private arbitration, which spreads information regarding merchants' past dealings and hence provides a reputation monitoring mechanism (Bernstein 1992). Entry is restricted to those who can inherit good reputations from family members. The outcome appears to be one which resolves an 'endgame problem' and induces merchants to deal honestly through to their very last transaction. The sustainability of trust mechanisms in this case provides useful guidance on how peer group pressure can be used to encourage trustworthiness.

16.4.5 Encouragement of Cooperative Outcomes

Several industries have responded when untrustworthy behaviour by some players has damaged the wider interests of the industry. The common problem they shared was that uncontrolled self-interested behaviour created externalities for other players, and cooperation in enhancing trustworthiness was beneficial in remedying such externalities. Similar initiatives to encourage and enforce trustworthiness may be possible for financial services on an industry-wide basis, or for specific product groups or locations.

Clothing retailers such as Gap and Nike introduced mechanisms to prevent the exploitation of child labour by their suppliers, in response to adverse public opinion (Kolk and van Tulder 2002). This initiative relied on the development of codes of practice, enforced by sanctions imposed by the main international purchasers of the goods (Gunningham and Rees 1997). The system succeeds because of the interest of major players in protecting their reputation, and hence brand value. As with previous examples, codes of practice encourage and enforce trustworthiness. They have proved to be an effective method of improving working conditions in South America and worldwide. This in turn benefited the industry as it countered pressure by non-governmental organisations which could have led to intrusive and costly external regulation. The system thus both improved brand value and reduced pressures for external regulation.

The Brazilian Extractive Reserve System provides another example of how peer pressure has improved cooperation and trust relationships. This system provided a method of using forest resources sustainably—something that was crucial for the longer-term sustainability of the industry (Assier 1998; Cardoso 2002). The principal method used was the creation of a locally run integrity infrastructure, including mechanisms both for assessment and compliance, in partnership with public authorities. Community associations were given exclusive use of particular land, but were required to produce utilisation plans, which had to be approved by a government agency. Each association was responsible for enforcement of the plan, including the prevention of migration by unauthorised settlers. Peer pressure was used to deter non-compliers, and the association could also impose formal sanctions (for example, by withdrawing use of communal storage or processing facilities). This improved the competence of those involved (in ensuring a sustainable system for themselves and others in the longer run) and also their reliability.

The US Sustainable Forestry Initiative (SFI) has acted in a similar manner by bringing together a number of stakeholders in the forest product industry to develop principles, guidelines, and goals which guide sustainable forestry (Gunningham and Rees 1997). This is backed by certification processes, and implemented by some 200 member companies in the US Forest Product industry. To verify that the industry is following its SFI guidelines, a panel of independent experts, including conservationists and university scientists review self-reported data and observe operations. A comparable system was also established by the Canadian Standards Association, motivated by the threat of a European consumer boycott.

Taken together, these examples provide guidance for how cooperative outcomes may be established to address adverse external effects on others in the industry or more widely. Possible application within the financial services industry might include coordinated action to counter the poor selling standards which have damaged the reputations of banks and reduced trust in the financial products being offered to customers.

16.5 Obstacles to Trustworthiness

Earlier chapters have identified a number of obstacles to trustworthiness in the financial services industry. To what extent do the myriad of recent reform proposals address these obstacles, and in what areas does more need to be done to engender strong trustworthiness? Here we briefly summarise the key obstacles to trustworthiness which have been identified in these chapters, coming from the primacy of shareholder value in UK equity markets, from leverage and moral hazard, and from personal incentives. In what follows we concentrate on three key areas of the financial services industry: retail banking, investment banking, and pension funds.

16.5.1 The Primacy of Shareholder Value

Chapter 2 identified the primacy of shareholder value thinking as one of the factors contributing to the lack of trustworthiness of the financial sector in the run-up to the GFC. As explained by Stout (2012) and Mayer (2013), the emphasis given to shareholder value has encouraged managers of firms to behave in an untrustworthy manner. Kay (2012) describes how this has led to managerial behaviour which is focused on short-term profit maximisation, so as to achieve a short-term influence on movements in share prices. Such behaviour has led managers to take risks which were excessive from a social point of view, by seeking short-term gains at the expense of longer-term outcomes for the business. Managers were rewarded for maximising short-term gains, both in terms of cash bonuses and also in shares, and were enthusiastic about taking on risks and passing them on to others.

16.5.2 Leverage and Moral Hazard

High leverage reinforced the incentive for financial institutions to behave in this way, and hence take excessive risks, since shareholders gained all of the upside but their downside was limited by the small portion of the balance sheet represented by equity. At the same time, the discipline normally provided by creditors was lacking due to the implicit guarantee provided by government for too-big-to-fail institutions. Furthermore, the loss absorbency of debt was compromised by fears of contagion, so that the burden of rescuing the financial system fell to governments and taxpayers. The mechanisms used to monitor leverage and risk taking were also found to be wanting. As described in Chapter 5, the risk weights specified by Basel II were arbitraged to gain the greatest returns achievable within regulatory requirements, and became unreliable measures of risk.

The imperative of removing these incentives for untrustworthy behaviour lies at the root of many of the recent reform proposals. Otherwise the task of reforming standards remains one of pushing against a headwind.

The Vickers ring fence (ICB 2011) seeks to limit the government guarantee to the parts of the financial system that provide essential banking services and support the payments systems. Keeping investment banking services outside the ring fence lessens the incentive to take on high leverage and excessive risk because the implicit guarantee (which subsidises too-big-to-fail institutions) is no longer available. Making institutions easier to resolve adds credibility to the ring fencing of retail banking as it makes it easier to avoid contagion.

Reforms have also targeted leverage directly, in order to increase the ability of institutions to absorb losses and in so doing ensure that the consequences of risk taking are borne by shareholders. Basel III continues to rely on risk weightings, imposes an equity requirement of 7% on risk-weighted assets, and has also introduced a minimum leverage ratio of 3%. However, the ICB was concerned that this level of equity buffer was too low, and recommended capital requirements of at least 10% of risk-weighted assets and primary loss-absorbing capital, which includes bail-in bonds and contingent capital, of at least 17% to 20% (ICB 2011).

Some argue that still greater loss absorbency is needed if incentives for excessive risk taking are to be curbed. Thus the Parliamentary Commission into Banking Standards recommends that the Financial Policy Committee should have the discretion to set a minimum leverage ratio above 3%. Other authors recommend capital requirements of 20% to 50% of total assets (Admati and Hellwig 2013).

Together these reforms will provide an additional equity cushion and reduce the incentives for excessive risk taking. However, the requirements are regulatory rules and hence are open to arbitrage and lobbying. For example, the ring fence relies on a distinction between proprietary trading (which is outside the fence) and normal hedging activity (which is inside) and this distinction is difficult to make in practice.

At first sight, therefore, none of the reforms appear to strengthen the trustworthiness of the financial industry by bringing other-regarding motivations into play, or by limiting risk-taking behaviour. This is a point which was recognised by the Parliamentary Commission into Banking Standards (2013). However, as discussed by Mayer (2013), corporations are devices for making commitments: financial capital in the case of shareholders and human capital in the case of employees. Increasing the equity of the firm involves a greater commitment by shareholders and managers to the values of the corporation. Other-regarding motivations can help to sustain these commitments and so make it possible for a stronger form of trustworthiness to emerge. This might lead to a reduction in risk-taking investments, reflecting a greater commitment by shareholders and managers to the values of the corporation which themselves would involve acting in a less risky manner.

The ICB (2011) considered the arguments for and against complete separation of retail from investment banks, rather than the imposition of a ring fence. One argument in favour of full separation is that the type of people required to maintain a safe and secure retail banking system are different from those who seek high rewards through taking risks, and it is important that, even with ring fencing, the outlook of management in the risk-taking part of a universal bank is likely to influence the behaviour of management in the retail banking part. We consider below the extent to which the recent proposals of the Parliamentary Commission into Banking Standards (2013) are likely to assist in defining the obligations and responsibilities of these different parts of the financial system.

16.5.3 Personal Incentives

As we have seen in Chapters 2 and 3, the incentives provided by remuneration levels and structures work directly against trustworthiness. They encourage the kind of risk taking described above, rewarding the wrong things, and measuring the performance to be rewarded in the wrong ways. In the run-up to the GFC, investment banks rewarded the design and sale of products which had a high likelihood of failure, using time frames that were too short to enable the true performance of products to be revealed. Pension funds rewarded asset managers on short-term performance relative to benchmarks, encouraging herding and the management of expectations rather than true stewardship of assets (Kay 2012). In retail banks remuneration rewarded revenue generation regardless of the riskiness to consumers of the products sold, or of their suitability.

Behavioural experiments suggest that people are more likely to act in a way which is of benefit to others if it does not cost them too much (Stout 2010). Conversely, the experience of the GFC shows that when the rewards are very large, the incentives towards selfish behaviour can easily overwhelm other, more other-regarding, cultural norms within an organisation. Indeed the Parliamentary Commission into Banking Standards (2013) argued that such incentives led directly to the dysfunctional cultures which allowed the Libor and other scandals. If other-regarding motivations are to gain traction, therefore, it is essential that the incentives be reconfigured, so that they do not incentivise selfish behaviour. This is what Stout (2010) meant when she said 'conscience needs room to breathe'.

Many proposals for the reform of remuneration have been made, most recently by the Parliamentary Commission into Banking Standards (2013). Proposals focus on the need to align incentives with the long-term interests of banks and their shareholders. Approaches include changing the period of deferral of bonus payments, imposing clawback and fines in cases of blatant wrongdoing, restricting the form of payment in terms of equity and bailable-in bonds, and requiring increased disclosure of remuneration criteria and greater regulatory involvement in ensuring that risks and rewards are aligned.

These initiatives will help by reducing the countervailing incentives for untrustworthy behaviour. However, as discussed by Gold in Chapter 6, remuneration arrangements are often concerned with aligning self-interest with the interest of the organisation. These arrangements can only encourage strong trustworthiness if financial institutions articulate the standards which are expected from those who work for them, and if remuneration arrangements then reflect these standards. Doing this will then encourage what Gold, in Chapter 6, describes as 'procedurally motivated strong trustworthiness'.

The difficulty of aligning incentives with the interests of others, without adverse unintended consequences, should not be underestimated. The Parliamentary Commission into Banking Standards warns of the potential for gaming remuneration criteria and rules, that sales-based remuneration rewards can continue informally, and the complications that ensue as staff move between employers (PCBS 2013).

In addition, the complexity of products and the asymmetric expertise enjoyed by investment banks and their employees may make it difficult to judge whether any given product was appropriate for the needs of the client at the time or was simply taking advantage of fat-tailed risks as described by Noe and Young in Chapter 3. These asymmetries have enabled the industry to profit from selling products that customers did not understand and did not serve their interests.

A number of proposals have sought to improve the ability of customers to understand what they are buying in the retail market, only some of which have been successful. These sought to increase the ability of customers to compare between products by making simple and straightforward products available for comparison with other product offerings. Thus the Sandler Review (Sandler 2002) recommended that a suite of simple 'stakeholder' products be offered. The products were to be designed so that they could be purchased safely without the need for regulated advice. Instead, product features and annual charges were to be regulated, with limits on the level of risk attached to the product. In this way, the products were designed to provide embedded protection with a minimum of fixed costs.

However, these stakeholder products did not sell well. Their low profitability (a result of their regulated charges) meant that they were not marketed and the stakeholder pension proved unsustainable. Nonetheless, the stakeholder pension was seen as successful in acting as a 'benchmark product' and stimulating price competition in the wider pension market (Springford 2011).

Recently further proposals have been made to establish simplified products. The Sergeant Review (2012) recommended that simplified products be designed to meet basic needs, and be 'non-advice' products that can be bought directly from providers. This is intended to ensure that the products will be both affordable for customers and commercially viable for providers. Similarly Springford (2011) recommended the establishment of 'trusted products' to drive improvements in competition throughout the product market.

An important aspect of the proposals is the visible branding of products. For example, Springford recommended that a 'trusted products' kitemark be established under which products would have to meet certain criteria such as that they do not take advantage of customer inertia or exploit small print conditions. Likewise the Sergeant Review proposed that there be a 'Simple Products' brand, with accredited products clearly signposted with a badge.

The Parliamentary Commission into Banking Standards argues, along similar lines, that a 'relentless drive towards the simplification of products' is needed and may be more effective than detailed conduct regulation (PCBS 2013). This is because such proposals support strong trustworthiness. By enabling customers to better judge the usefulness and value of products on offer, they encourage other-regarding behaviour, in that retail institutions will be encouraged by customers to pay more attention to the quality of products and the outcomes which they are likely to deliver.

16.6 How Can We Move Towards Strong Trustworthiness in Financial Services?

The discussion above suggests that the reforms proposed to date may make only limited progress in promoting strong trustworthiness. The reforms are nonetheless important because they lessen the obstacles to trustworthiness that we have identified. In a number of cases the reforms encourage weak trustworthiness and in a few cases they directly support strong trustworthiness. Some reforms have the potential to encourage strong trustworthiness, provided attention is paid to the way in which the reforms are implemented and their effect on other-regarding motivations.

We turn now to what further changes are needed to encourage strong trustworthiness more directly. We do this by returning to the four steps which help to achieve strong trustworthiness: a description of obligations, identification of where responsibility lies for the delivery of obligations, mechanisms to ensure appropriate delivery, and methods for holding individuals or institutions to account for their performance. In the discussion that follows we examine to what extent current practice and recent proposals make adequate provision for these four steps, again focusing on three key components of the financial services industry: retail banking, investment banking, and pension funds. In this discussion we make use of suggestions which come from our review, earlier in this chapter, of other industries.

16.6.1 Description of Obligations

As de Bruin emphasises in Chapter 12, the values of a firm encapsulate its other-regarding obligations. Mayer (2013) suggests that all corporations should elaborate a set of values, and give expression to these values, and that such values will enable the corporation to make commitments as an institution, as well as encouraging commitment from shareholders, employees, and other stakeholders. This is something which we support.

Recent proposals, for example by the Parliamentary Commission into Banking Standards (2013), have focused on the imposition of specific obligations on directors to ensure the safety and soundness of banks and on the duties owed by these banks to their customers. But there has been little discussion of the broader need for financial institutions to specify their purpose and values. This is despite the fact that the GFC and subsequent conduct scandals have called into question the purpose and structure of financial institutions, and that neither regulation nor integrity systems can resolve the resulting problems until these questions on purpose and values have been understood (Miller 2011a).

Mayer's proposal for the articulation of firm values would achieve a change in the objectives of financial services firms away from the maximisation of shareholder value. The commitments given by firms would—in principle—enable them to constrain managerial behaviour focused on short-term profit maximisation, to constrain excessive risk taking, and to move towards satisfying the needs of customers, over a longer-term time horizon. The aim would be to strengthen the trustworthiness of the financial industry by encouraging other-regarding motivations, and so enable what we have called a 'stronger' form of trustworthiness to emerge.

The formation of a board-level ethics committee would form part of the process by which this articulation of values would be carried out. This committee would be the place in which the obligations to be placed on individuals would be set out. Moves towards the implementation of an industry-wide professional body for financial services would help with the articulation of standards expected both from firms and from the individuals who work within these firms.

There is of course a wide range of activities undertaken by the financial services industry, and these activities vary in the extent to which they involve a relationship of trust, and so in the obligations which are necessary. In each of the different activities which we discuss below we seek to identify the nature of the trustworthiness which is required and hence the obligations which are appropriate. These are obligations which would be in addition to the normal relationships between contracting parties, and in addition to regulatory requirements.[4]

Activities which necessarily involve a relationship of trust are those of financial advisors to their clients and those of pension fund managers to their investors. Each of these activities gives rise to a necessary obligation. Financial advisors owe their clients a duty of care to take into account their particular circumstances and requirements, and to recommend products that are appropriate to these circumstances. Following the various mis-selling scandals, the need to avoid any conflict of interest in the provision of advice

---

[4] Our aim here is different from that of Morrison and Wilhelm (2013). Morrison discusses how legalised contracting and regulatory requirement have become more necessary when relationships of trust break down, and argues that this becomes increasingly important as the scale of financial systems increases, and personal contact between parties is replaced by large impersonal markets. Here we seek to argue the reverse—that trustworthiness remains necessary in impersonal markets, that it is important to foster strong trustworthiness in such markets, and that means must be found to make this possible.

has been highlighted by Miller in Chapter 14. Where such advice is provided by retail banks, fiduciary duty could be strengthened and a clear separation made between advice and sales activities, in order to avoid the conflicts of interest which drove mis-selling in the past.

The obligations of asset managers and trustees—not only pension fund trustees—are also of this kind; these too cannot only be managed by contractual means. The Kay Review (Kay 2012) made this clear. That Review articulated a set of obligations which need to be accepted by asset managers and trustees. These obligations have two parts.

First, the Kay Review recommended that a fiduciary relationship be recognised between asset managers and investors, and that this duty be incapable of being overridden by contractual terms. This view is reinforced by the arguments made by Getzler in Chapter 9. Other commentators have made similar calls for the application of fiduciary duties; for example, Johnson (2012) calls for all pension funds, including contract-based defined-benefit schemes, to be subject to fiduciary-like obligations to pensioners. Such fiduciary duties would be designed to prevent the kinds of risk taking described by Noe and Young in Chapter 3, in which fund managers engage in risky activities which are not in the interests of those who provide them with funds to invest, by, for example, making investments with tail risks which allow the possible loss of all of their assets.

Second, the Kay Review recommends a form of stewardship between fund managers and the firms in which they invest. Such stewardship would involve a commitment to engage in longer-term investment, in such a way as to avoid pressure to deliver short-term investment returns. Companies can attempt to build their core competencies over the longer term, or they can aim for shorter term rewards. An unwillingness by financial institutions to invest for the longer term leads to a focus by firms on delivering short-term rewards and the pursuit of short-term financial deals, as distinct from long-term productive skills, pushes further in this direction. Instead there should be a willingness to invest for the long term. This willingness must be based on analysis by the financial intermediaries. The ability to carry out analysis requires a specialisation of a few companies in which money is invested, and the investment of resources in analysis. Such stewardship will be costly.

Banks also need to have obligations which go beyond contractual requirements. Banks owe a duty of care to customers, in terms of the provision of information, dealing with complaints, and in the design and sale of products. The Parliamentary Commission into Banking Standards proposes that these obligations be specified in the Corporate Governance Code and the Senior Persons regime.

Obligations for a duty of care in product design are relatively uncontroversial on the retail side of banking. However such obligations run against notions of *caveat emptor* under contracting arrangements for the so-called sophisticated customers of investment banks. In Chapter 10 O'Brien argues that the past bifurcation between sophisticated and unsophisticated customers is untenable, citing a recent Australian court decision regarding the duty of care owed by Grange Securities to a local council in NSW.

There also need to be obligations concerning disclosure and product testing. The approach of the Parliamentary Commission into Banking Standards to this question appears to be surprisingly conventional, suggesting that sophisticated customers can understand the transactions entered into, so that obligations are not needed, at least for these customers. However, the discussion provided by Noe and Young in Chapter 3 suggests that this may not be enough. Asymmetries of information and expertise are too pervasive and it appears possible for investment banks to design products which are not in the interests of even sophisticated customers. In our view there should be an obligation on investment banks to owe a duty of care in relation to the products/services created, one which is applied irrespective of level of sophistication of customer. Where products are created which are known to have toxic effects or include tail risk, there should be a duty to make this sufficiently clear to the consumer. There would be a breach of trustworthiness if consumers were not made aware of these risks. The sale of such products should thus be permitted only if these facts are sufficiently identified. The failure to take sufficient care in the design of such products, so that products of this kind are unknowingly supplied, should also prevented. That is, the obligation should not only extend to disclosure, but to a requirement that there be a thorough investigation of the risks involved.

Many recent proposals about obligations focus on preserving the safety of the overall financial system, on the protection of the payments system from failure, and on the need to avoid excessive risk taking to ensure these requirements are not jeopardised. Thus the Parliamentary Commission into Banking Standards proposed that directors of banks outside the ring fence should be required to have regard to the safety and soundness of the firm (PCBS 2013) and that such a requirement should apply to other institutions as well. This requirement is to be implemented through changes to the UK Corporate Governance Code, the PRA Principles for Business, the Senior Persons responsibilities, and changes to the Companies Act.[5] Similarly, the Treasury's report on sanctions for the directors of failed banks recommended a regulatory duty for directors to ensure that banks run their affairs in a prudent manner (HM

---

[5] The Chancellor's response to the Parliamentary Commission into Banking Standards recommendations rejects the need for any change to director's duties under the Act. The Walker Report into governance also rejected changing the promotion of shareholder interests under the Act (Walker 2009).

Treasury 2012a). The desire to avoid punishment (whether legal or regulatory) leads to only weak trustworthiness, with its effectiveness dependent on the realistic threat of being caught. Strong trustworthiness requires that such obligations be recognised and accepted by directors and others, rather than merely being imposed. For this reason, the way in which this obligation is formalised by each bank will be important, and in particular the extent to which internal processes are designed to manage risk. This is discussed further below.

16.6.2 Identification of Responsibility

Assignment of responsibility for the delivery of obligations is our second step towards securing trustworthiness. The Parliamentary Commission into Banking Standards considered that insufficient personal responsibility was a key problem, and a centrepiece of the report is its recommendations concerning the Senior Persons Regime, the Licensing Regime, and board governance (PCBS 2013). Together these proposals attempt to assign responsibility for all key activities and risks to nominated individuals within the banks. The reforms respond to perceived evasion of responsibility by senior bankers following the GFC, which was a source of much public anger. We see these as useful reforms, which should contribute towards improved trustworthiness in the industry.

The Senior Persons Regime is intended to assign responsibilities for all prudential and conduct activities, including product design. The Licensing Regime covers a wider group of staff and seeks to ensure that staff understand and demonstrate the behaviour expected of them. Under the governance proposals, greater protection is to be given to the independence of the heads of risk, compliance, and internal audit, alongside increased accountability to the board (PCBS 2013).

A particular area of tension is the supervisory relationship between regulators and banks. Thus the PCBS expressed concern that regulators not become shadow directors. Similarly the PCBS suggested that banks retain responsibility for the design of products, with the FCA's new tools not being used to intervene too early and distort the market. This reflects concern that the asymmetric information and skills involved in the development of products enable banks to develop innovative products to the benefit of clients. These same advantages put the regulator at a disadvantage in terms of detecting products that are abusive. Strong trustworthiness requires that the responsibility for preventing the design of abusive products lie within and be accepted by the industry.

Defining responsibility for the appropriate design of products is complicated by the fact that the appropriateness of products depends on the circumstances of the customer, and that those selling the product may be different to those designing the product. The product engineer has a clear responsibility to the product seller to ensure that information about the product is accurate and not misleading. The product seller has a responsibility to his customer or client to ensure that he investigates the product sufficiently. Neither should sell to third parties products they would not be happy to invest in themselves. In submissions to the Banking Standards Inquiry, retail banks have recognised that the products they sell need to serve customers' interests, with some seeking 'more certainty up front that product attributes and sales processes are acceptable' (HSBC 2012).

Within pension funds the management of assets is typically carried out by a wide range of different entities, with trustees coordinating the activities of others such as custodians and investment managers. The responsibility of those managing pension assets involves ensuring that investment is directed to profitable ends, so as to ensure low costs of intermediation and moderate levels of risk. This responsibility rests primarily with asset managers and with trustees, but, as we discussed above, there is scope for clarifying the responsibility of other parts in the chain of intermediaries. The PCBS recommended that fiduciary duties apply to all elements of the investment chain.

Where a business is very complex, as in much of financial services, there is also a role for gatekeepers. Gatekeepers include accountants, lawyers, and credit-rating agencies, and their responsibility is to certify to the quality of a firm's activities and the truthfulness of its promises. Yet the gatekeepers are widely seen as having failed in that role in the run-up to the GFC. Credit ratings were undermined by a combination of conflicts of interest and excessive regulatory reliance which undermined market processes (Morrison and Wilhelm 2013). Accountants signed off on accounts that were subsequently found to have been highly misleading—with many now facing litigation over their failures. This has led the PCBS to conclude that it is essential for regulators to reduce their dependence on credit-rating agency ratings when assessing capital adequacy (PCBS 2013). In Chapter 10 O'Brien describes responses in Australia to the perceived decline in trustworthiness of accountants.

16.7 Mechanisms

There are a variety of mechanisms that can be used to try to encourage strong trustworthiness, several of which are discussed in detail in earlier chapters of this book. In the present chapter, we have described how these mechanisms have been used in other industries. Here we focus on the mechanisms which have received most attention in the context of financial services, and examine their potential to support strong trustworthiness.

Professional bodies and codes of conduct have been used in a variety of industries to ensure the maintenance of standards, in ways which we have described above. However, the Parliamentary Commission on Banking Standards considered that neither could be relied upon for the banking industry, arguing that 'robust regulatory underpinning' was required to bring about a change in standards and culture (PCBS 2013). The Commission's concern was that banking consists of a broad range of activities which lack a common core of learning, that a professional body does not necessarily guarantee high standards, and that its development could divert attention away from the regulatory changes needed. The Commission accepted that a professional body has the potential to promote higher standards, but argued that such a body will take time to develop and prove itself.

A professional body provides a mechanism for defining expectations and promoting understanding of what those expectations imply for individuals, and hence we believe that a professional body could contribute towards improved trustworthiness. As discussed by the Commission, however, there would need to be a commitment on the part of the banks to ensure that such a body was effective. Only with such commitment would the body be in a position to engender a positive change in the norms of the industry, and to provide a countervailing influence to the existing culture of self-interest. In doing so, a professional body would assist Senior Persons to fulfil the responsibilities given to them under the regulatory framework.

The existing code of conduct under the Approved Persons Regime has low credibility and was widely disregarded. The principles for behaviour were simply overwhelmed by the incentives for self-interested behaviour provided by remuneration systems and by the general culture which these incentives created. Lack of enforcement and the inability of customers to detect abusive products were also contributory factors. It is not surprising that the Parliamentary Commission on Banking Standards considered that it was not a sufficiently robust foundation for improving standards.

However, as de Bruin discusses in Chapter 12, there is a role for codes to articulate both general values and specific norms in order to provide guidance for the reinforcement of trustworthiness. Thus a well-designed code should present a set of principles reflecting the general values of an institution, as well as concrete rules of conduct and practical guidelines. This could include guidance, for example, on sales of inappropriate products, on misrepresentation of the characteristics of products, and on how to identify and deal with conflicts of interest. Methods of implementing codes of conduct, and the forms which these may take, are discussed in detail by de Bruin in Chapter 12.

A large part of the value of codes of conduct lies in the framing they provide to individuals to encourage other-regarding motivations. Important in this is the morally-orientated discussion which codes engender—for example, in discussions of how to manage a specific conflict of interest or how to balance the interests of different customers. By reinforcing procedural motivations, they make staff less tolerant of breaches and encourage strong trustworthiness both directly and through motivations based on esteem.

Awrey and Kershaw discuss in some detail in Chapter 13 how firms might go beyond codes of conduct in the promotion of norms which might encourage other-regarding behaviour. Their chapter has canvassed some of the ways in which we might seek to engender a more ethical culture within the financial services industry. It discusses how process-oriented regulation, combined with restructuring of the internal governance arrangements of financial services firms, might be used to achieve this objective.

The 'tone at the top' will be important in bringing this about, something which is identified by the Parliamentary Commission on Banking Standards (PCBS 2013). This 'tone' includes the implementation of appropriate disciplinary measures for violation of codes of conduct. The advantage of internal discipline mechanisms is that violations are likely to be more visible within the firm than to the regulator, and more capable of nuanced response. In turn this encourages stronger procedural other-regarding motivations and strong trustworthiness.

Particular emphasis was placed by the Kay Review on the value of a stewardship code for the pension fund industry. The Review argued that short termism and a lack of engagement by shareholders are having a damaging effect on the performance of UK businesses, and that this should be recognised through the development of a stewardship code for asset managers, supported by good practice statements (Kay 2012).

The 'tone at the top' is likely to be both enhanced and more effective in terms of filtering down with the introduction of an ethics committee. It would signal real engagement by senior management in improving standards and culture and indicate that the Senior Persons Regime will not be treated as just an exercise in compliance. An ethics committee could be responsible for identifying ethical risks and implementing processes for managing problem areas. To this end it would need to collect evidence, identify transgressions, design systems, and conduct audits to ensure that these systems are working (Miller 2011b). An ethics committee could then play an important role in ensuring that Senior Persons are able to deliver the responsibilities given to them by the regulatory framework. 'Trustee' firms, of the kind advocated by Mayer (2013), would adopt a set of obligations broader than the obligations to their shareholders, and this would clearly influence the 'tone' of a firm. The board of trustees would act as the guardian of the firm's values. As noted above, the ethics committee could then be responsible for ensuring that these values are adhered to, as proposed by Awrey and Kershaw in Chapter 13.

An ethics committee of the board of trustees would also address the difficulty of identifying objective measures of ethical performance. This difficulty (raised by O'Neill in Chapter 8) includes the risk of diverting attention onto secondary targets which capture the underlying obligations only imperfectly. For example, how should socially excessive risk taking be defined? Being integral to the firm, such bodies would also assist in countering the problem that measures of performance tend to be subject to gaming, particularly when they are imposed by regulation.

Another proposal with merit is the establishment of an independent authority for the industry which would certify products which are kite-marked or branded as being safe and having well-understood characteristics. The advertising industry provides an example of how mechanisms to enhance trustworthiness in sales processes through the creation of an enforcement agency (the Advertising Standards Authority) can be implemented. In the finance industry such an authority would reflect a commitment to market easily benchmarked products. Such products would enable customers to compare value for money in a transparent manner and would improve competition between banks (including competition across non-simple products as customers would have a better point of reference). The authority would publish prices and information, and could also develop and publish reputation indices. This would enable retail banks to compete on reputation to improve the trust of customers (Armstrong 2012). It could also be given powers to punish those who do not comply with the ethical standards agreed by the industry.

A particular concern is that neither internal risk management systems nor regulatory rules have proved effective in managing the risks generated on the investment banking side of the industry. Incentives to 'bet the bank' overrode the concern of risk assessment officers. Regulatory rules were comprehensively arbitraged. To counter these problems, a cooperative agreement to an industry-sponsored risk control mechanism could be established if managers of (important) firms regard the dangers of another major crisis as sufficiently great, as was the case with the nuclear and chemical industries. To some extent, the opportunity and motivation for a voluntary arrangement is being overtaken by regulatory reform. Nonetheless, a voluntary arrangement could bring benefits, including reduced risk of arbitrage, greater flexibility, and potentially greater expertise being brought to bear on the process of scrutinising performance.

In the nuclear industry an industry-wide risk control apparatus emerged after Three Mile Island because key players in the industry wanted to prevent a subsequent crisis which could result in the public turning against the industry. The Institute of Nuclear Power Operations (INPO) now provides effective risk management for the industry, with which all companies involved in the industry comply (although what happened in Japan shows that further improvements in risk management processes are still needed). Similarly, the process which followed the Bhopal disaster led to the creation of the chemical industry's responsible care programme.

16.7.1 Holding to Account

Strong trustworthiness, willingness and competence in keeping commitments, requires that the person/institution responsible for delivering an obligation both render an account of their performance, and be held to account for that performance. This requires an informed and independent judgement about what has been done (in comparison with what ought to have been done), and this assessment needs to be communicated in an accessible manner.

Accountability is not just about sanctions and enforcement. As Gold emphasises in Chapter 6, strong trustworthiness does not follow from the desire to avoid punishment. Rather, it is about intelligent processes for judging the performance of obligations. A major failure of accountability in the period prior to the GFC was the resort which was made to 'tick box' regulation and compliance testing. Northern Rock's celebration of compliance with Basel II was short-lived, and demonstrated a lack of judgement of the underlying risks to the company's financial stability.

In the pension fund industry the Kay Review has sought more intelligent accountability by changing the criteria and time horizon by which asset managers are assessed (Kay 2012). Instead of short-term assessment of relative performance, the Review advocates that performance be judged and rewarded on the basis of the long-term value of investments. Consistent with this, the Kay Review is critical of the current disclosure regime, which produces a 'cascade' of data that focuses attention on short outcomes (which are often the result of little more than noise) rather than long-term, underlying value.

Any assessment of performance requires clarity on the standards of performance to be met. The absence of agreed standards to which key roles should be performed was identified by the Treasury as a major barrier to holding directors of a failed bank to account (Treasury 2012a). Similarly, Awrey and Kershaw provide some discussion in Chapter 13 of the difficulties of defining socially excessive risk taking, let alone identifying it in advance. They suggest that process-orientated regulation can help, stimulating dialogue and promoting firm engagement. On this basis, the assessment of performance, and enforcement, could be based on the effectiveness or otherwise of the engagement.

Part of the process of holding to account involves the provision of information to allow customers and stakeholders to assess trustworthiness.

Reputation can assist in this way, but reputation needs to be warranted. Reputational indices could be helpful, provided they capture internal processes honestly, and measure the features of concern to people placing trust (rather than comprising a set of second-order targets which then become the subject of manipulation). The creation and publication of reputational indices could be undertaken by the independent authority established to certify products.

But while recent proposals address obligations, responsibilities, and enforcement, there is little consideration of how performance can or should be judged intelligently. The Parliamentary Commission on Banking Standards suggests that regulators provide guidance on standards in the form of a new set of Banking Rules, and that the regulators will need to make judgements, but there is no discussion of the difficulties of assessing how well or otherwise obligations are performed. The discussion of Special Measures perhaps comes the closest in this regard, sketching out the approaches used by the PRA and FCA to identify conduct risks and the increased reporting requirements that accompany the identification of 'red flags' (PCBS 2013). Much more detailed work on this is necessary.

16.8 Conclusion

We have argued throughout this book that reform of the financial sector needs to rely upon motivations which go beyond the selfish-motivation assumption on which economic analysis is normally based. The authors of the chapters have suggested that other-regarding motivations might lead those in the financial sector to act in a more trustworthy manner, and that they might help to underpin a public policy which is directed towards such an end. We have described how other professions, including medicine and the law, are built upon a sense of professional responsibility for patients and clients. The task is to ensure that those who work within the financial sector become more strongly bound by professional standards of behaviour, as in these other professional sectors, and as once happened in finance. We have discussed how changes might help to bring this about, at the personal level, at the institutional level, and through legal and regulatory intervention. These changes need to include a description of the obligations to be honoured by players in the financial sector, clear identification of who is responsible for honouring these obligations, well-specified mechanisms designed to ensure that these obligations are in fact honoured, and a well-informed process through which those involved can be held to account. Only with such changes is reform of the financial sector likely to succeed.

References

Admati, A. and Hellwig, M. (2013). *The Bankers' New Clothes*. Princeton: Princeton University Press.

Alexandra, A. and Miller, S. (2010). *Integrity Systems for Occupations*. Aldershot: Ashgate Publishing.

Armstrong, A. (2012). 'Restoring Trust in Banking', *National Institute Economic Review*, 221 (July), [online journal], <http://niesr.ac.uk/sites/default/files/publications/Trust%20in%20banking.pdf>, accessed 17 March 2014.

ASME (2012). 'Forging a New Nuclear Safety Construct', Technical Report of the ASME Presidential Task Force on Response to Japan Nuclear Power Events, June.

Assier, W. (1998). *Going Nuts for the Rainforest: Non-Timber Forest Products, Forest Conservation and Sustainability in Amazonia*. West Lafayette: Purdue University Press.

Bernstein, L. (1992). 'Opting Out of the Legal System: Extralegal Contractual Relations in the Diamond Industry', *Journal of Legal Studies*, 21(1): 115–57.

Boddewyn, J. J. (1989). 'Advertising Self-Regulation: True Purpose and Limits', *Journal of Advertising*, 18(2): 19–27.

Cardoso, C. A. S. (2002). *Extractive Reserves in Brazilian Amazonia: Local Resource Management and the Global Political Economy*. Aldershot: Ashgate Publishing.

Carson, J. (2011). 'Self-Regulation in Securities Markets', World Bank Policy Research Working Paper 5542, January.

Cohen, M. F. (1977). 'The Work of the Commission on Auditors' Responsibilities', <http://newman.baruch.cuny.edu/digital/saxe/saxe_1976/cohen_77.htm>, accessed on 15 June 2013.

Cressey, D. R. and Moore, C. A. (1983). 'Managerial Values and Corporate Codes of Ethics', *California Management Review*, 25(4), 53–77.

Daykin, C. (2004). 'Trust and Professional Responsibility in a Liberal Market', *Journal of Economic Affairs*, 24(2): 11–18.

De Jong, A. et al. (2004). 'The Role of Self-Regulation in Corporate Governance: Evidence and Implications from the Netherlands', *Journal of Corporate Finance*, 11(3): 473–503.

Garvin, D. A. (1983). 'Can Industry Self-Regulation Work?', *California Management Review*, 25(4): 37–52.

Greif, A. (1997). 'Microtheory and Recent Developments in the Study of Economic Institutions through Economic History', in D. Kreps and K. Wallis (eds), *Advances in Economics and Econometrics: Theory and Applications*, vol. II. Cambridge: Cambridge University Press, 79–113.

Goold, S. (2002). 'Trust, Distrust and Trustworthiness: Lessons from the Field', *Journal of General Internal Medicine*, 17(1): 79–81.

Gunningham N. and Rees J. (1997). 'Industry Self-Regulation: An Institutional Perspective', *Law and Policy*, 19(4): 363–414.

Gunningham, N. and Sinclair, D. (1998). 'Designing Environmental Policy', in N. Gunningham and P. Grabosky (eds), *Smart Regulation: Designing Integrated Environmental Policy*. Oxford: Oxford University Press, 375–454.

Harrington, J. C. (2011). 'Ethical Investing in an Age of Excessive Materialistic Self-Interest', in N. Dobos, C. Barry, and T. Pogge (eds), *Global Financial Crisis: The Ethical Issues*. Basingstoke: Palgrave Macmillan, 82–119.

Hay, D. (1999). 'Do Markets Need a Moral Framework?', in A. Montefiore and D. Vines (eds), *Integrity in the Public and Private Domains*. London: Routledge, 258–68.

HM Treasury (2012a). *Sanctions for the Directors of Failed Banks*, London.

HM Treasury (2012b). *Sergeant Review of Simple Financial Products: Interim Report*, <https://www.gov.uk/government/uploads/system/uploads/attachment_data/file/191730/sergeant_review_simple_financial_products_interim_report.pdf>, accessed 17 August 2012.

HSBC Holdings Plc (2012). 'Submission from HSBC (SO19)', in Parliamentary Commission on Banking Standards, *Banking Standards: Written Evidence*. London: The Stationery Office Ltd, 166–78.

ICB (2011). *Independent Commission on Banking: Final Report*, London.

Johnson, M. (2012). *Put the Saver First: Catalysing a Savings Culture*. London: Centre for Policy Studies.

Kay, J. A. (2012). *The Kay Review of UK Equity Markets and Long-Term Decision Making: Final Report, BIS*, <www.bis.gov.uk/kayreview>, accessed 30 July 2012.

Kemeny, J. G. (1979). *The President's Commission Report on the Accident at Three Mile Island: The Need for Change: The Legacy of TMI*. Washington, DC: US Government Printing Office.

King, A. A. and Lenox, M. J. (2000). 'Industry Regulation without Sanctions: The Chemical Industry's Responsible Care Program', *Academy of Management Journal*, 43(4): 698–716.

Kolk, A. and van Tulder, R. (2002). 'Child Labor and Multinational Conduct: A Comparison of International Business and Stakeholder Codes', *Journal of Business Ethics*, 36: 291–301.

Leland, H. E. (1979). 'Quacks, Lemons, and Licensing: A Theory of Minimum Quality Standards', *Journal of Political Economy*, 87: 1325–46.

Lipsey, D. (2011). 'Trust, Advice and Financial Services', in J. Springford (ed.), *A Confidence Crisis? Restoring Trust in Financial Services*. London: The Social Market Foundation, 98–105.

Loughrey, J. (2012). 'The Oxford Project: A Corporate Law Ethicist Responds', CLMR, <http://www.clmr.unsw.edu.au/article/ethics/the-oxford-project/oxford-project-organisers-respond-0>, accessed 28 August 2012.

Mayer, C. (2013). *Firm Commitment*. Oxford: Oxford University Press.

Miller, S. (2011a). 'Global Financial Institutions, Ethics and Market Fundamentalism', in N. Dobos, C. Barry, and T. Pogge (eds), *Global Financial Crisis: The Ethical Issues*. Basingstoke: Palgrave Macmillan, 24–51.

Miller, S. (2011b). 'Financial Services Providers: Integrity Systems, Reputation and the Triangle of Virtue', in N. Dobos, C. Barry, and T. Pogge. (eds), *Global Financial Crisis: The Ethical Issues*. Basingstoke: Palgrave Macmillan, 132–57.

Moffet, J., Bregha, F., and Middelkoop, M. J. (2004). 'Responsible Care: A Case Study of a Voluntary Environmental Initiative', in Kernaghan Webb (ed.), *Voluntary*

Codes: Private Governance, the Public Interest and Innovation. Ottawa: Carleton Research Unit for Innovation, Science and Environment, 177–207.

Montefiore, A. (1999). 'A Philosopher's Introduction', in A. Montefiore, and D. Vines (eds), *Integrity in the Public and Private Domains*. London and New York: Routledge, 3–18.

Morrison, A. D. and Wilhelm, J. (2013). 'Trust Reputation and Law: The Evolution of Commitment in Investment Banking', unpublished mimeograph.

Nash, J. and Ehrenfeld, J. (1997). 'Codes of Environmental Management Practice: Assessing Their Potential as a Tool for Change', *Annual Review of Energy and Environment*, 22: 487–535.

O'Brien, J. (2010). 'The Future of Financial Regulation: Enhancing Integrity through Design', *The Sydney Law Review*, 32: 63–85.

O'Brien, J. (2012). 'Banking Scandals: Where the Buck Stops: Updated 27 July 2012', *Financial Review*, August [online newspaper], <http://www.afr.com/p/lifestyle/review/enforcement_facade_P9ktF6hpSWWgRZ4vmx7UtJ>, accessed 27 August 2012.

O'Neill, O. (2005). 'Accountability, Trust and Professional Practice', in N. Ray (ed.), *Architecture and its Ethical Dilemmas*. London: Taylor & Francis, 77–88.

Parliamentary Commission on Banking Standards (PCBS) (2013). *Changing Banking for Good: First Report of Session 2013–14*. London: The Stationery Office Ltd.

Phillips, A. (2011). 'The Role of Professionalism', in J. Springford (ed.), *A Confidence Crisis? Restoring Trust in Financial Services*. London: The Social Market Foundation, 106–14.

Pomeroy, B. (2011). 'Trust and Financial Exclusion', in J. Springford (ed.), *A Confidence Crisis? Restoring Trust in Financial Services*. London: The Social Market Foundation, 90–7.

Raach, J. (1944). 'English Medical Licensing in the Early Seventeenth Century', *Yale Journal of Biology and Medicine*, 16(4): 267–88.

Rees, J. V. (1994). Hostages of Each Other: The Transformation of Nuclear Safety Since Three Mile Island. Chicago: Chicago University Press.

Rees, J. V. (1997). 'Development of Communitarian Regulation in the Chemical Industry', *Law and Policy*, 19: 477–52.

Richman, B. D. (2002). 'Community Enforcement of Informal Contracts: Jewish Diamond Merchants in New York', Harvard Business School, Discussion Paper 384, September.

Sandler, R. (2002). *Medium and Long-Term Retail Savings in the UK: A Review*. London: HM Treasury.

Shainberg, A. M. (1982). 'Jews and the Diamond Trade', in Ivan L. Tillem (ed.), *The Jewish Directory and Almanac*, vol. 1. New York: Pacific Press, 301–11.

Shipman Inquiry (2003). *Third Report 'Death Certification and the Investigation of Deaths by Coroners'*, CM 5854, July.

Springford, J. (2011). 'Trust and Financial Market Failure', in J. Springford (ed.), *A Confidence Crisis? Restoring Trust in Financial Services*. London: The Social Market Foundation, 19–72.

Stout, L. (2010). *Cultivating Conscience: How Good Laws Make Good People.* Princeton: Princeton University Press.

Stout, L. (2012). *The Shareholder Value Myth.* San Fransisco: Berrett-Koehler Publishers.

Taylor, J. B. and Wolak, F. A. (2011). 'A Comparison of Government Regulation of Risk in the Financial Services and Nuclear Power Industries', paper presented at the Nuclear Enterprise Conference, Hoover Institution, Stanford University, 3–4 October 2011.

Unite the Union (2012). 'Submission from Unite the Union (SO27)', in Parliamentary Commission on Banking Standards, *Banking Standards: Written Evidence.* London: The Stationery Office Ltd, 228–34.

Walker, D. (2009). *A Review of Corporate Governance in UK Banks and Other Financial Industry Entities: Final Recommendations.* London: HM Treasury.

Index

Printed and bound by CPI Group (UK) Ltd, Croydon, CR0 4YY